GENESIS

OLD TESTAMENT STUDIES

Volume 6

Genesis

A Commentary for Students, Teachers, and Preachers

John J. Scullion, S.J.

A Michael Glazier Book
THE LITURGICAL PRESS
Collegeville, Minnesota

A Michael Glazier Book published by The Liturgical Press

Cover design by David Manahan, O.S.B.

1   2   3   4   5   6   7   8   9

Library of Congress Cataloging-in-Publication Data

Scullion, John.
    Genesis : a commentary for students, teachers, and preachers / John J. Scullion.
        p.   cm. — (Old Testament studies ; v. 6)
    "A Michael Glazier book."
    Includes bibliographical references.
    ISBN 0-8146-5659-5
    1. Bible. O.T. Genesis—Commentaries. I. Title. II. Series: Old Testament studies (Wilmington, Del.) ; v. 6.
BS1235.3.S37   1992
222'11077—dc 20   92-12322
                                                CIP

In Memoriam

John Arnold Phillips, S.J. (1904–1987)
A priest of the Book and the Word

Contents

Genesis

Then Eve picked the apple
and taking a good bite
learned the first lesson of humanity
which is knowledge, pain and loss,
so that Adam following after
but out of the seeds of love
took an apple to eat,
becoming in this our first father
to labour, sweat and face
darkness welling like a spring tide
in narrow straits.

Darkness, darkness in sunblaze,
then a whole garden transfigured
to the serpent's glittering delight.
Look, look at the fruits,
prolific, dangling in mass and tone,
blush on the peach-soft cheek,
cherries like gems, oranges burning,
sex of the pomegranate cracked wide open,
swelling in fig and pear—
that whole estate was suddenly filled
with new discriminations,
with choices to be plucked.
Why was Adam bitterly weak,
reproaching God and woman
like a spoilt child with broken toys
snivelling and whingeing?
Why were his guts weak

when he was called on to make a stand
in this brash new medium,
fast-flowing time?

It only took courage.
Be a man, said Eve;
Be a man, said ambiguous God;
yet Adam snuck away and moped
like a poor put-upon creep
in the shrubbery, in the evening,
scared of the too much light.
Know yourself, Adam.
Why was Adam bitterly weak
with her love, their sweep of knowledge,
work to be done
all over the face of the earth?
Everything was possible
that you could hurl in death's teeth:
the agricultural revolution
slept in ungathered grain.

The serpent was finished, mere reptile;
you break the back of a tiger snake
as soon as look at him,
farmers hang them on fences.
But there was a question for Adam to ask;
why on earth had Eden's God
chosen to make the serpent subtle,
crammed its jaws with language of men,
a trick to cap all creation?
who was kidding whom?

I hate the story and love it,
detesting death, a vast stupidity,
but glorying that Eden
could be smeared with, flashing with, energized
by the first colours of love.
Everything came alive.
The dull stuffy paradise park,
that silly supermarket
frozen away

under Claude Lorrain's stiff glazes
became part of the world;
here a fresh wind tossed the branches,
rotten fruit fell, green fruit waited,
ripeness was all, all transient
as man's quick breath. Things mattered
and love, anxious love
rose and put forth its flags.

Chris Wallace-Crabbe
The Emotions are not Skilled Workers.

The poem is printed with permission of the publishers, Angus & Robertson, Unit 4, "Eden Park," 31 Waterlook Road, North Ryde, N.S.W., 2113, Australia, and of the author.
Chris Wallace-Crabbe is Professor of English at the University of Melbourne and Director of the Australian Centre. In 1987–1988 he was Professor of Australian Studies at Harvard University, U.S.A.

Foreword

Two great commentaries on the Book of Genesis appeared at the
beginning and in the last quarter of this century, the earlier by Hermann Gunkel (1901; 1910³, unaltered ninth edition 1977) and the
later by Claus Westermann (3 vols., 1974, 1981, 1982, English 1984,
1985, 1986). In between came the commentaries of John Skinner
(1910; 1930²), Otto Procksch (1924), Gerhard von Rad (1936; English 1972 from ninth German ed.), Bruce Vawter (1956; 1977), to
select but a few. I am indebted to all these scholars, and to many
others. Their prints appear throughout this commentary, even though
I go my own way.

When a commentary is directed to students, teachers, and
preachers, one may ask, why such a detailed and diffuse bibliography? The reasons are: (1) to draw attention to the basic work done
by major scholars in the past without whom there could have been
no progress in biblical studies, even though we disagree with them
today; (2) to insist that biblical exegesis requires detailed study of
the Hebrew and Greek texts as well as the broad overview; (3) to
indicate places where readers may pursue a point or theme further
and draw their own conclusions.

I have made my own translation of the Hebrew text and have erred
on the side of literalness in an attempt to allow something of the
original to be heard, however faintly.

During my years of lecturing on Genesis I have received much
stimulus from the students and staff of the United Faculty of Theology, the Jesuit Theological College, the Regional Seminary (all in
Melbourne and its environs), as well as from members of the Catholic
Biblical Association of Australia and the Fellowship for Biblical
Studies (Melbourne). I thank my religious superiors and the facul-
ties in which I teach for allowing me a period (January–June 1989)
at the University of Heidelberg where the commentary on the Joseph

story was written. I added the final touches to the manuscript while teaching a course on Genesis at the Pontifical Gregorian University, Rome (October–February, 1989–1990), at the invitation of the Dean of the theological faculty, Gerald O'Collins, S.J. My Jesuit brethren, Robert North, Luis Alonso Schökel, and Emilio Rasco took of their time to share the reading of the manuscript between them and to offer suggestions. Of course, I alone am responsible for the final draft.

The dedication of the commentary is to a fellow Jesuit who encouraged me in my youth to study the Scriptures seriously.

Once again I am indebted to Mrs. Leonie Hudson, secretary of Jesuit Theological College. As always, she produced a well nigh perfect manuscript and had installments waiting for me on schedule in various European cities during my sabbatical year in 1989.

P.S.

I read Thomas L. Thompson's *The Origin Tradition of Ancient Israel* (1987) only after I had completed the commentary. We agree in substance that (1) the documentary hypothesis has run aground, and (2) the narratives of Genesis 1–11 and 12–36 as they lie before the reader are chains or collections of disparate stories which have been linked together. We do not agree in our ideas of theology in general and of theology as "applied" to the Old Testament if I understand correctly Thompson's epilogue (pp. 199–212) and much of what he writes about theology in chapters 1–6. Certainly, the history and archaeology of Syria and Palestine are disciplines to be studied in their own right. And story is to be read as story. But the very great amount of God-talk (theology) in the narratives of Genesis as they lie before us constitute these narratives. That "Israel's own tradition is radically irrelevant to writing such a history" (p. 41), i.e., a history of its own origins, may be contested. But this can be a matter for scholarly discussion. I am more at home with James Barr when he writes: "It would be more accurate to say that for modern scholarship the centre of understanding is the theology, and that history plays an important role in enabling us to know what that theological sense was" ("The Literal, the Allegorical, and Modern Biblical Scholarship," *JSOT* 44 [1989] 3–19 [p. 16]). In any case, Thompson has confirmed me in my general approach to Genesis as a "traditional complex-chain narrative." My earlier forays into this area may be found in: "Some Reflections on the Present State of the Patriarchal Narratives," *Abr-Nahrain* 21 (1982-83) 50-65; " 'Die

Genesis is eine Sammlung von Sagen' (Hermann Gunkel). Independent Stories and Redactional Unity in Genesis 12–26'', in *"Wünscht Jerusalem Frieden,"* Collected Communications to the XIIth Congress of the IOSOT, Jerusalem 1986, editors Matthias Augustin, Hans-Dietrich Schunck (Frankfurt am Main-Bern-New York-Paris: Peter Lang, 1988, 243–47).

John J. Scullion, S.J.
February 1990

United Faculty of Theology
Parkville, Vic.
Australia

Newman College
(University of Melbourne)
887 Swanston St.
Parkville, Vic. 3052
Australia

Editorial Note

Fr. John Scullion, S.J., held out against myeloma for almost a decade. Shortly after the completion of this manuscript, he suffered a near-fatal relapse while in Rome. Flown back to Australia early in 1990, he recovered a considerable degree of health for much of the year, until he went into a rapid decline. Father Scullion died on November 24, 1990. May his memory be in benediction.

The Liturgical Press is grateful to Father Scullion's colleagues for their help in seeing the manuscript through the press.

Abbreviations

AB	Anchor Bible
Akk.	Akkadian
ANEP	Ancient Near East in Pictures relating to the Old Testament
ANET	Ancient Near Eastern Texts relating to the Old Testament
Bab.	Babylonian
B.C.E.	Before the Common Era
BDB	Brown, Driver, Briggs, Hebrew and English Lexicon
BHS	Biblia Hebraica Stuttgartensia
CAH	Cambridge Ancient History
C.E.	Common Era
dtn/dtr	deuteronomic/deuteronomistic
dtr	deuteronomistic
EBB	Elenchus Bibliographicus Biblicus
Eng	English
Ges-K	Gesenius-Kautzsch, Hebrew Grammar
Hebr.	Hebrew
IOSOT	International Organization for the Study of the Old Testament
JB	Jerusalem Bible
JPSA	Jewish Publication Society of America
JSOT	Journal for the Study of the Old Testament
LXX	Septuagint
MT	Massoretic Text
NAB	New American Bible
NEB	New English Bible
NIV	New International Version
OL	Old Latin
pl.	plural
RSV	Revised Standard Version
Sum.	Sumerian
ThHAT	Theologisches Handwörterbuch zum Alten Testament
ThWAT	Theologisches Wörterbuch zum Alten Testament

Introduction

The standard introductions to the Old Testament by Otto Eiss-feldt (English 1965) and Georg Fohrer (English 1968) give adequate accounts of the history of the study of the Pentateuch and of the Book of Genesis in particular. Eissfeldt's analysis of Genesis appeared in the *Interpreter's Dictionary of the Bible,* vol. 2, cols. 366–80, in 1962. It was a translation of the second edition of his monograph, *Die Genesis der Genesis* (1958, 1961). R. N. Whybray (1987) has written a comprehensive, clear, critical, and up-to-date account of the problems of pentateuchal studies. Hence, I will give here but (1) a brief statement of the position of Wellhausen, (2) a thumbnail sketch of the two centuries of pentateuchal study leading up to Wellhausen, (3) an outline of an alternative approach which still retains the essential Wellhausian hypothesis, (4) a more modern approach which dispenses with essential Wellhausianism, and (5) the approach adopted in this commentary.

(1) When Julius Wellhausen (1844–1918) published his hypothesis on the formation of the text of the first five books of the Hebrew Bible in his *Prolegomena to the History of Israel* (1878; 1883; 1889; English translation in 1885 of second German edition of 1883) he was the heir of two hundred years of scholarly study. Wellhausen studied the Pentateuch as a professional historian. He had a document before him which he analyzed. He noted, as had many of his predecessors, the different names for the divinity, God (Elohim), the Lord (YHWH), used with apparent consistency in definite blocks of text, the differences in style and language between the blocks of text, the contradictions and discrepancies, the doublets and repetitions, the variety of theological points of view. He came to the conclusion that the document known as the Pentateuch was the final product of the juxtaposition of three documents running parallel to each other and covering virtually the same material, plus a fourth document, Deuteronomy. The first document, J, named from the

1

divine name YHWH (German, Jahweh), the Lord, was the oldest and had its origin in the early period of the Judean monarchy; the second document, E, named from the general Hebrew name for God, Elohim, had its origin in the period of the northern, Israelite, monarchy some time in the ninth century. The period after about 700 B.C.E. was the period of the origin of the Book of Deuteronomy. Some time during the exile (587–538) or after it, the fourth document, P, so named because of its alleged origin from priestly circles, was composed. These four documents, J E D P, were then, in the post-exilic period, combined into that text now known as the five books of Moses, the Torah, or the Pentateuch. A contribution unique to Wellhausen was his late dating of the priestly document. Wellhausen was aware that each of these documents had its own history. But that was not his interest. He was concerned, as a historian, with the document before him, the Hebrew text of the first five books of the Bible. His point of departure was the Hebrew text and its analysis. Wellhausen's documentary hypothesis, that the Pentateuch was composed of four separate and independent documents, J E D P, which were written in that order over a period of four to five centuries, has, in its essentials, ruled pentateuchal studies for a century. In many circles it became dogma.

(2) The following are the more important scholars who preceded Wellhausen, with the briefest note on the substance of the contribution of each:

Richard Simon (1638–1712): Moses was the source of the laws, but not the author of the Pentateuch in its present form; his "public scribes" wrote the historical parts; other "public scribes" later adapted, abbreviated, and edited the Pentateuch in the course of history. Disorder is due to the accidental transposition of leaves or "small scrolls."

Henning Bernhard Witter (1683–1715): noted the different names used for God in Genesis 1:1–2:4 and 2:5–3:24 and the different content of these passages.

Jean Astruc (1684–1766): noted the different names for God throughout Genesis; there were two documents, one using YHWH, the other Elohim, which, with ten fragments, Moses joined together.

Johann Gottfried Eichhorn (1782–1827): applied Astruc's source division of Genesis to the whole Pentateuch.

Karl David Ilgen (1763–1834): the Pentateuch comprised two sources which used the name Elohim, E^1 and E^2, a Yahwistic source, J, and a Deuteronomic source, D.

Alexander Geddes (1737–1802): not impressed with the division of the Pentateuch into two continuous documents using the names YHWH and Elohim. The Pentateuch is a collection of fragments, larger or smaller, from different circles and different dates, completely independent of each other.

Johann Severin Vater (1771–1826): took up Geddes' "fragment" proposal, found some forty of them in Genesis alone, and set out to analyze the fragments in the whole Pentateuch.

Wilhelm Martin Leberecht de Wette (1780–1839): accepted the "fragment" hypothesis; Deuteronomy, D, was the book of the law discovered in the temple during the reign of Josiah (640–609).

Hermann Hupfeld (1796–1866): the Pentateuch comprised an early Elohistic source, P, and a later Elohistic source, E, and a further source which made use of the name YHWH. A fourth party united them; hence a documentary hypothesis in which the order was P E J D.

Heinrich Ewald (1803–1875): one of Wellhausen's teachers; the Pentateuch was basically a continuous, simple narrative that used the name Elohim and which was supplemented later by a YHWH document covering the same subject, and by other material.

Karl Heinrich Graf (1815–1869) and *Abraham Kuenen* (1828–1892): these two scholars, each in his own way, refined the work of their predecessors and contemporaries so that Wellhausen was able to formulate in a definitive form what has become the classical documentary hypothesis, which should really be known as the Graf-Kuenen-Wellhausen hypothesis.

(3) For all these scholars the point of departure was the Hebrew text and its analysis. It was Hermann Gunkel (1862–1932) who took a different point of departure. Gunkel accepted the classic documentary hypothesis, but wanted to go behind the documents, particularly behind the Yahwistic document, to the "original" stories. Gunkel was stimulated by the Grimm brothers, Jakob (1785–1863) and Wilhelm (1786–1859), and their work on folktales; he was also much in debt to Johann Wolfgang Goethe (1749–1832) and to Johann Gottfried Herder (1744–1803), especially to Herder's *Vom Geist der Ebräischen Poesie* (1782–1783). Under their influence he worked out his own theory of the history of literature, literary forms, and story as applied to the Bible.

Gunkel's commentary on Genesis appeared in 1901 with an introduction of seventy-one pages. The third edition, completely revised, and with an introduction expanded to ninety-four pages, appeared in 1910. This edition has been reprinted unaltered up to a ninth edition (1977). Due regard being had to the limitations of the period in which the third edition was printed, on which light from the ancient Near East had just begun to dawn, it is probably the finest commentary ever written on this great book.

Gunkel gave his introduction to Genesis the title "Die Sagen von Genesis," and he headed the first section "Die Genesis ist eine Sammlung von Sagen," "Genesis is a collection of stories." The German word *Sage* means folkstory or simple story; it has nothing to do with "saga" from which it should be distinguished carefully (Scullion 1984:324–31). Gunkel understood story as "the way of transmission of those groups which are not familiar with writing; history belongs to the scholarly occupations and presupposes the skill of writing." In distinguishing story from history, Gunkel wrote that story (*Sage*) belongs to oral tradition, deals with personal and family affairs, derives from tradition worked over by imagination, moves in the area of the incredible, and is poetic prose by nature. History is the opposite of this. Gunkel put great emphasis on the word "Sammlung," "collection." The editors were collectors of stories rather than redactors of them; they were more subject to the stories than the stories to them. The Yahwistic document, J, is a collection of collections. The collectors supplied link passages between some of the stories, left others hanging loosely together, and found other groups of stories already woven together into some unity.

Gunkel distinguished two types of stories in Genesis: (1) those about the origins of the world and the human race; (2) those about the fathers of Israel and their sons. The divinity is the main actor in the primeval stories. But anything mythical, that is, "stories about the gods," has come down in very faded colors. The writer or poet was expected to subordinate the mythical to the one God of all. Many a story in Genesis is etiological, that is, it asked the cause of something. Such stories were (1) geological: where did this strange and desolate land formation come from? Genesis 19; (2) etymological: how did this place get its name? Genesis 11:9; 16:14; 22:14; (3) ethnological: whence the Ishmaelites? Genesis 16:12; 21:13; (4) cultic: why is this a holy place? Genesis 22:10-22.

Gunkel was very sensitive to the aesthetic side of the stories and considered an aesthetic appreciation of biblical narratives an essential element of exegesis. He wrote in the foreword to the first edition of Genesis that "a treatment of the Old Testament in which philology, archaeology, or 'criticism' alone predominate is inadequate," and complained in the foreword to the third edition that exegetes continued to neglect the truly literary side of the narratives. Story *(Sage)* does not, Gunkel insisted, raise the question of belief or unbelief. It has no bias either way as to whether it narrates what really happened or not. It is simply what it is, a narration. The story of its very nature moves into the short story or *Novelle* (Joseph story). It was Gunkel who gained acceptance in biblical circles for the now accepted thesis that religion and religious truth can be conveyed as adequately through story as through history.

Gunkel always remained faithful to the classical documentary hypothesis and never seemed to be fully aware of the tensions between it and his own pre-literary and aesthetic approach.

Two giants of twentieth century biblical scholarship, Gerhard von Rad (1901–1971) and Martin Noth (1902–1968), both adherents to the documentary hypothesis and both inspired by the work of Gunkel, applied, each in his own way, his genius to the problem of the Pentateuch. For von Rad (1966; German 1938), the Yahwist, J, was the great theologian who made a unified, coherent, theological work out of a vast array of disparate material that lay before him. The Yahwist contemplated the sin and revolt of the human race (Gen 2–11), showed how God chose, preserved, and guided the fathers of Israel (Gen 12–50), brought them to and delivered them from Egypt (Exod 1–15), bound them to himself (Exod 19–24), guided them through the desert (Exod 15:22–18:27 and Num 10:11–20:13), and brought them to the land of Canaan (Joshua). The whole story is basically an elaboration of the "little Credo" of Deuteronomy 26:5-9. The other writers, E and P, follow J's pattern with variations on his theme. J wrote his synthesis in the second half of the tenth century in the time of Solomon. The other two contributions followed and were united with J's work much in the manner of the classical documentary hypothesis. Martin Noth (1972; German 1948) proposed that in the pre-literary period there were five basic traditions, independent of each other and independent of the figure of Moses: (1) the leading out of Egypt; (2) the guidance in the desert; (3) the revelation on Sinai; (4) the possession of Palestine; (5) the promise to the fathers. These were the traditions that lay behind the written Pentateuch. Like Gunkel, Noth assumed that the narratives that contained these traditions were brief and that they underwent a process of growth in the course of their history. The basic traditions were later linked with Moses. Noth put great confidence in the reliability of traditions connected with places, like Bethel and

Shechem. These were reliable. He also insisted that the ancient traditions were recited in places of cult and that the narratives gradually grew out of the cultic tradition. The traditions of Israel, according to Noth, were gathered together into a basic document G (*Grundschrift,* basic text) which both J and E used. In Genesis, the basic Jacob story was in essence the combination of traditions from east and west of the Jordan linked with places and centers of cult. Noth maintained further that figures in oral tradition, like Abraham and Isaac, readily changed their roles in the stories, and that what was said of one in this story could be said of the other in another story. Hence, figures were often changing their position and significance.

Gunkel, von Rad, and Noth share two basic tenets in common: (1) they adhered to the essence of the classical documentary hypothesis; (2) they went behind the written text to speculate on the process of growth that lay behind the written text. None of the three brought a real assent to the difficulties that underlay the combination of the two approaches.

A word must be said here about what is known as the "newer" or "more recent" form of the documentary hypothesis. Allowing for considerable variations at times, it proceeds more or less as follows. One must adhere to the three classical narrative sources in the Pentateuch as self-contained documents as well as to the usual dating of them. There was material available to the "Yahwist" (J) in the earlier monarchy and he made use of it and impressed his own theological outlook on it. The "Elohist" (E) either used J as his basis or wrote or was redacted with a knowledge of J. The parallelism between J and E is not due to a common source (G, *Grundlage,* basic source) which J and E each used independently. A writer known in some circles as the "Jehowist" (R^{JE}) put J and E together. He was not just an assembler but a real composer who as a creative re-worker produced by his genius something new and hence is a real author. This amalgam was there in its entirety when P made his contribution. Some exegetes do not consider P to be a continuous, coherent source. Rather P contributed chronologies, dates, frameworks, lists, annotations. One can subtract easily (especially in the Joseph story) what "everyone" (?) agrees to be from P, and one is left with the synthesis of the "Jehowist" (R^{JE}) the material of which one then assigns to J or E. There would also be some complementary material to JE.

(4) Rolf Rendtorff (1977a, b) dispensed with the documentary

hypothesis as tried in the fire, found wanting, and leading to an impasse. Rendtorff attended first to the larger units of the text: the primeval story; each of the patriarchal stories of Abraham, Isaac, and Jacob, as well as units within them, such as the Jacob-Laban story; the story of Moses and the exodus; the Sinai passage; the story of the wandering in the desert. One must first of all analyze these larger units, see how they hang together, and note the cross references within each unit. Rendtorff concluded that these larger pentateuchal units are self-contained pieces independent of each other. The patriarchal story, for example, that is, the combined cycles about Abraham, Isaac, and Jacob, form a large independent unit which has been reworked at different stages in the course of transmission and has been subject to ongoing theological interpretation. These three cycles have been forged together into a unity by means of the promise texts, carefully distributed throughout, each of which has its own history in the process of transmission, and which look both forwards and backwards across the combined cycles. Each of the three ancestors is to be a blessing for the whole of the human race: Abraham (12:3; 18:18; 22:19); Isaac (26:4); Jacob (28:14). This blessing stands at the beginning of each cycle. It stands as a heading over the Abraham cycle (12:1-3) and dominates the whole patriarchal story.

Looking at the Pentateuch as a whole, Rendtorff finds there a deliberate and planned composition and interpretation both in the larger and smaller units that it comprises. For the composition as a whole, Genesis 50:24 and Exodus 33:1-3a are important. Both passages take up the oath sworn to Abraham, Isaac, and Jacob that the descendants of the three patriarchs, the people of Israel, will possess the land of promise. The passages clamp all pentateuchal traditions together into one comprehensive, all-embracing theme: YHWH has given the land to the people of Israel. The whole reworking of the traditions is couched in the language and reflects ideas of Deuteronomy. The traditions, intact, are framed in Deuteronomic thinking.

(5) In the exposition that follows, attention will be given first to the general structure and theological thrust of the larger units, namely the primeval story (1:1-11:26), the Abraham cycle (11:27-25:18), the Jacob cycle (25:19-36:43), and the Joseph story (37-50). Attention will then turn to the individual passages that make up the unit, the main concern in each being the literary structure and the theological thrust. Brief notes, historical, archaeological, and philological

will follow the comments on each passage. There will be a general theological survey at the end of the primeval story, and excursuses on the patriarchs in history, the religion of the patriarchs, and the promises to the patriarchs at the conclusion of the patriarchal story.

1

The Primeval Story
(1:1–11:9 + 11:10-26)

The events of Genesis 1:1–11:9 (the genealogy in 11:10-26 leads from the very general "a plain in the land of Shinar" [11:2] into the framework of history [11:27-32]) are set in primeval time or mythological time or in the era "before history." Their purpose is not to describe "how it actually happened," as Leopold von Ranke (1795–1886), one of the fathers of modern documented history, programmed his massive work, but to reflect on the state of the human race in and from its beginnings. At the conclusion of the story of the Tower (11:1-9), one can almost hear the sigh of the writer, "such is the race of humans from the beginning, such will it always be."

It is generally agreed that one finds in Genesis 1–11 the standard example of the amalgamation of sources, the Priestly and the Yahwistic, and the sources can be separated easily. There is much in this. The usual division is given in the table (*Fig. 1*). Some modifications and discussion of details will be found in the exegesis. The writer responsible for the stories and the "additional comments" (e.g., 4:20b, 21b; 5:29, etc.) I prefer to call the storyteller. He is usually known as the Yahwist. The traditional priestly writer may be designated such, though I sometimes call him the systematic theologian, the systematic editor, or simply the systematizer. The main stories (2:4b–3:24; 4:1-16; the flood, 6:5–8:22, a complex combination of sources; 11:1-9) follow a common pattern and theological outlook that argue strongly for a common author. I think that the (or "a") priestly writer has edited the sources at hand to him into the present text of 1:1–11:9. The introduction, of capital importance inasmuch as it is the introduction to the Pentateuch and to the Bible itself, may well be the work of the priestly writer (or of one of the "priestly school," if such existed). I think that the opening unit consists of 1:1–2:1. The same writer has added the two verses on the divine rest and the sabbath (2:2-3), tying them firmly into 2:1. He has constructed 2:4a as a link verse pointing both backwards and forwards.

Throughout chapters 1–11 I have transliterated the word for "man" as *hā'ādām,* and the word for the ground as *hā'ădāmâ.* The reason is that I want to emphasize, as the Hebrew writers emphasized, that the chapters are about the human race, not just about the male of the species. It happens that in English the words for the male and the race, "man," are the same (not so, for example, in German where the word for the human person, *der Mensch,* is neutral). The storyteller continually links *hā'ādām* with its origin, *hā'ădāmâ,* the ground, and the transliterations underscore both the link between the two and the word play.

The usual word for God, *'ĕlohîm,* is rendered simply by God. The proper name for the God of Israel, the tetragrammaton (i.e., the four letters), is always turned as YHWH. There are two reasons for this: (1) to stress that it is a proper name; (2) to respect Jewish tradition. The holy name is not pronounced in the synagogue nor in the Hebrew text. The reader bows the head at the tetragram, YHWH, and says *'ădonāy,* my Lord, a form of the word *'ādôn,* lord, master. The particular form, *'ădonāy,* is reserved for the divinity.

All else that I want to say about Genesis 1–11 will be found in the translation, comments, and notes.

1. God's Creation: The Word of God Creates Cosmos (1:1–2:1)

1:1 In the beginning God created the heavens and the earth.
²The earth was a formless waste and there was darkness over the surface of the deep and a mighty wind was moving to and fro over the surface of the waters.

³And God said: let there be light.
And there was light.
⁴And God saw how right the light was.
And God separated the light from the darkness;
⁵and God called the light day and the darkness he called night;
and it was evening and it was morning
a first day.

The Primeval Story
Genesis 1:1–11:26

Creation of universe and inhabitants	1:1–2:3, 2:4a (link verse)	
Creation of mankind and transgression		2:4b–3:24
Transgression		4:1-16
Genealogy with notes		4:17-22
Song of defiance		4:23-24
Genealogy with notes		4:25-26
Genealogy: God's blessing in act	5:1-28, 30-32	
Genealogical note		5:29
Transgression: Preface to flood		6:1-4
Introduction to flood	6:9-22	6:5-8; 7:1-5
The flood	7:6-24 (mingling of sources)	7:6-24
End of flood	8:1-2a, 3b-5, 13a, 14-19	8:2b-3a, 6-12, 13b
Conclusion of flood story	9:1-17	8:20-22
Transgression		9:20-27
Conclusion of genealogy (from ch. 5)	9:28-29	
Table of nations	10:1a, 2-7, 20, 22-23, 31, 32	10:1b, 8-19, 21, 24-30
Transgression		11:1-9
Genealogy	11:10-26	

Figure 1

⁶And God said: let there be a vault amidst the waters,
so that it may stand separating
the waters from the waters.
⁷And God made the vault and it separated
the waters that were below from those
that were above it.
                              And it was so.
⁸And God called the vault the sky.
            And it was evening and it was morning
                  a second day.

⁹And God said: let the waters under the sky gather
into one so that dry land may appear.
                              And it was so.
¹⁰And God called the dry land earth and the
gathering of the waters he called seas.
            And God saw how right it was.

¹¹And God said: let the earth sprout fresh green,
plants bringing forth plants,
fruit trees bringing forth fruit according to their kind on earth
in which their seed is.
                              And it was so.
¹²And the earth sent forth fresh green,
plants bringing forth plants according to their kind,
trees bringing forth fruit according to their kind,
in which their seed is.
            And God saw how right it was.
            ¹³And it was evening and it was morning
                  a third day.

¹⁴And God said: let there be lights in the vault of the sky
to separate the day from the night and to be signs
for the seasons, the days, and the years,
¹⁵and let them be lights to cast light on the earth.
                              And it was so.

¹⁶And God made the two great lights,
the great light to rule the day
and the small light to rule the night and the stars.
¹⁷And God put them in the vault of the sky
to cast light on the earth
¹⁸and to rule the day and the night
and to separate the light from the darkness.
            And God saw how right it was.
            ¹⁹And it was evening and it was morning
                  a fourth day.

²⁰And God said: let the waters swarm with swarms of living beings
and let flying things fly across the earth
and across the surface of the vault of the sky.
²¹And God created the great monsters
and every creeping being with which the waters swarm
according to its kind and every winged being
according to its kind.
And God saw how right it was.
²²And God blessed them saying: increase and multiply
and fill the waters of the sea
and let the winged beings multiply on earth.
²³And it was evening and it was morning
a fifth day.

²⁴And God said: let the earth send forth living beings
according to their kind, cattle, reptiles and wild animals,
each according to its kind.
And it was so.
²⁵And God made the wild animals, each according to its kind,
the cattle, each according to its kind,
and everything that creeps upon the ground according to its kind.
And God saw how right it was.

²⁶And God said: let us make *'ādām* in our image and likeness
and let them rule
over the fish in the sea
and over the flying things in the sky
and over the cattle and all wild animals
and over all reptiles that creep over the earth.
²⁷And God created *hā'ādām* in his image,
in the image of God he created it,
male and female he created them.
²⁸And God blessed them and said to them:
increase and multiply and fill the earth,
subdue it and rule
over the fish in the sea
and over the flying things in the sky
and over all wild animals
(and over) all that creeps over the earth.

²⁹And God said: see, I give you all green things,
each bearing its seed, over the surface of the earth,
and all trees each bearing in its seed its own fruit,
to serve you as food;
³⁰and to every animal on earth and to everything
that flies in the sky and to everything

that creeps over the earth,
all that has the breath of life in it, (I give)
every sort of green and plant for food.
And it was so.

[31]And God saw how very right all that he had made was.
And it was evening and it was morning
a sixth day.

2:1 And the heavens and the earth and all their adornment were completed.

Comment

This unit (1:1–2:1) from a priestly writer (or systematic theologian) of the priestly circle, defines itself by its formulas in the introductory and concluding verses: "In the beginning God created (*bārā'*) the heavens and the earth (*haššāmayîm wĕ hā 'āreṣ*)" (1:1), and "the heavens and the earth and their adornment (*ṣĕbā'ām*) were completed" (2:1).

What is the literary form of this passage? To what category of literature does it belong? Scholars have called it a confession of faith, a hymn of praise to the creator, a narrative, an account, a recitative. But it is really none of these and should not be forced into any literary category. It is unique, not only in its form, but also in that it is the only creation account from the ancient Near East that follows the sequence of the seven day week, six days of work followed by a day of rest. It is best to note its links with Psalms 104 and 136. Psalm 104 is a hymn of descriptive praise. God who is—the Hebrew of verses 1-6 contains a series of active participles—brings order into the universe by his rebuke of the unruly waters (vv. 7-8); he is the one who waters the ground (vv. 10-13), provides food for animals and humans (vv. 14-18), marks off the seasons and the night and the day (vv. 19-23), causes the seas to swarm with living things and makes the great sea monsters (vv. 24-26), and whose Spirit sustains them all (v. 30). The response of the creature is praise, acknowledgment that God has done this (vv. 24, 33). Psalm 136 is the great Hallel, a litany of praise to God for his action of creation and redemption; verses 4-9 recall Genesis 1. Genesis 1:1–2:1 is an acknowledgment in a rhythmic, repetitive, prose pattern that God is, and that the universe and all that is in it comes from him. The passage should be read aloud and slowly to achieve its full effect. On

July 20, 1969, as American astronaut Neil Armstrong soared towards the first landing on the moon with the eyes of the whole world fixed on him and his companions, so bringing to a climax a stupendous work of scientific and technological cooperation, he read: "In the beginning God created the heavens and the earth." Taking up the words of the great religious thinkers of ancient Israel he proclaimed to hundreds of millions, to believers and non-believers, to agnostic and doubter, God, standing over against the universe as the unique transcendent one. At this moment of supreme scientific achievement, the scientist and technologist in the spaceship could say nothing more appropriate than, "In the beginning God created the heavens and the earth." It was a response of praise and awe like the response of the writer of Psalm 104. Some think that Genesis 1 is dependent on the psalm (Day 1985:51–55).

This account of the creation of the universe and its trappings fits eight works into six days. There is a day for the creation of light (vv. 3-5), and a day for the creation of the vault and the division of the waters (vv. 6-7). On the third day the waters gather into one and the dry land appears (vv. 9-10); and on the same day the earth sprouts its fruits (vv. 11-12); twice on this day "God saw how right it was" (vv. 10,12). The fourth day is given to the creation of the "hosts" in the heavens (vv. 14-19), and the fifth to the animals of the waters and the air (vv. 20-23). On the sixth day the land animals and the human race are created and food is provided for them (vv. 24-25 and vv. 26-30). Now there is nothing mysterious about "eight into six." Six days were all that the writer had for work. And he fitted his eight works of creation into them very smoothly.

The writer distinguishes at once between God and "not-God." "In the beginning God created the heavens and the earth" (v. 1) has become as it were the superscription under which the Bible stands (see the notes below for a discussion of the individual words and the sentence structure of the first three verses). It is an affirmation that God is supreme and alone to be worshipped. But the story of the human race and of the people of Israel has been the story of the worship of "not-God." Verse 2 describes "before creation." Creation is order; "before creation" is the opposite of order; it is *tôhû wā bôhû,* a formless waste or chaos. The priestly writer is not concerned with the origin of the formless waste or chaos; he does not ask about the formless pre-existing matter. Creation for him is order and so it is NON-sense to speak of God as the creator of chaos or non-order. The writer thinks with Second Isaiah: "he (God) did not create (*bārā*) a chaos (*tôhû*); he formed it to be inhabited" (Isa 45:18). Before creation there is nothing that stands in opposition to God; there is only the opposite to order and light, the conditions necessary for all life, human, animal and vegetable. The question of *creatio ex nihilo,* creation out of nothing, was not part of the writer's thought pattern. It was not a problem. It became one later when Hebrew and Hellenistic cultures came together in the fourth century B.C.E. The second book of the Maccabees records that about 167 B.C.E. the mother of the seven boys who faced the tyrant Antiochus Epiphanes encouraged the youngest: "I beseech you, my child, to look at the heaven and the earth and see everything that is in them, and recognize that God did not make them out of things that existed (OR that God made them out of things that did not exist)" (2 Macc 7:28). The author of the Wisdom of Solomon, writing about 50 B.C.E., spoke of " . . . thy all-powerful hand which created the world out of formless matter" (Wis 11:17), using the words well known from Aristotle, *hylē* (matter) and *morphē* (form), whence the philosophical term hylomorphism, a theory to describe the nature of being. But the account of creation " . . . does not speculate about the origin of matter; it rather attempts to account for the emergence of an ordered livable universe" (Vawter 1977:38).

There was darkness over the face of the deep (*tĕhôm*). *Tĕhôm* always means a mass of water in the Old Testament. "Thou didst cover it (the earth) with the deep (*tĕhôm*) as with a garment" (Ps 104:6); (creation context also in Ps 33:7; Job 38:16; Prov 8:24-27). Darkness is characteristic of other creation stories. Primeval darkness is opposed to creation, to an understanding of the world, to the human race (" . . . the light is shining in the darkness, but the darkness has not confined it;" John 1:5).

"And the Spirit (or wind) of God was moving to and fro over the face of the waters" (RSV). There are many renderings of *rûaḥ 'ĕlohîm:* a mighty wind (NEB and NAB), God's spirit (JB), an awesome wind (AB), the Spirit of God (NIV), a wind from God (JPSA). Given the context, namely the disorder that preceded God's creative word which issues at once into order, "a mighty wind" is the correct version; it moved to and fro across the surface of the waters (Luyster 1981). The writer speaks out of the ordered universe of his experience in which with unerring regularity day follows night, season follows season, plants sprout and animals breed at their proper times, and water and land have their proper place. Verse 2 describes the opposite of this. It is chaos as opposed to "cosmos" (the Greek word for order). There is confusion, darkness, wetness, and wind. The language and imagery reflect faintly rather than strongly the traditional language and imagery of the ancient Near East. But there is no sign of a primeval struggle in this biblical text.

Verses 3-31 spell out the opposite of verse 2, namely cosmos or order as opposed to chaos, effected by the creative word of God. 2:1, by way of inclusion and conclusion, resumes the point of departure, 1:1. The pattern is tight and, despite a few dislocations and omissions, constant. God speaks the word of command which takes effect immediately (vv. 3, 6, 9, 11, 14, 20, 24, 26, 29); "and God saw how right it (in v. 4, 'the light') was" (vv. 4, [8]), 10, 12, 18, 21, 25, 31). That is, the effect of his command was just as it should be (vv. 3, 7, 9, 11, 15, 24, 30). The pattern is very tight in the Greek text of verses 3-25 (the Greek text, known as the Septuagint and abbreviated as LXX, is a translation of the Hebrew Bible into Greek made by Jewish scholars in Alexandria in Egypt in the third and second centuries B.C.E.; the name Septuagint derives from the Latin word for seventy, *septuaginta,* the number of translators who took part in the work according to the second century B.C.E. letter of Aristeas). The pattern is WORD-FORMULA-EVENT. God's word is fulfilled in an event immediately following his word and in exact accordance with what is said. There is an inner connection between God's word and event. God's word *is* event. The Hebrew text differs from the Greek in the following ways: verse 7: "and it was so" occurs at the end of verse 7 in the Hebrew text, but at the end of verse 6 in LXX; verse 8: "and God saw how right it was" is not in verse 8 of the Hebrew, but is there in the LXX; verse 9: after "and it was so" in verse 9, the LXX adds "and the waters under the sky gathered together and dry land appeared," words which are not in the Hebrew; verse 20: the LXX adds "and it was so" at the end of verse 20. Whether the Hebrew text before the translators was as precise and systematic as the Greek and later suffered a slight disarrangement, or whether the translators imposed this strict pattern, we do not know. In any case God's word dominates the whole. God speaks again when he creates the race of humans (vv. 26-27), and when he provides food for them and the animal kingdom (vv. 29-30). The pattern WORD-FORMULA-EVENT embraces also the second part of the work of the sixth day, though in an expanded form. "And God said" (v. 26) is followed by God's creative action (v. 27); then there is the blessing and the function that God assigns to the human race in the universe. "And God said" occurs again when God provides food for humans and land animals. God has produced order by his word (vv. 29-30); "and it was so" (v. 30). The whole of creation was very right, just as it should be as it came from the word of God (v. 31).

Elsewhere, the Old Testament describes the word of God in graphic terms: "by the word of YHWH the heavens were made, and all their host by the breath of his mouth" (Ps 33:6). God's word that brings order governs Psalm 104:5-7; the creative and the redeeming word are together in Psalm 147:12-20. The most penetrating description of the word and its effect is at the end of Second Isaiah:

> For as the rain and the snow come down from heaven,
> and return not thither but water the earth,
> making it bring forth and sprout,
> giving seed to the sower and bread to the eater,
> so shall my word be that goes forth from my mouth;
> it shall not return to me empty,
> but shall accomplish that which I purpose,
> and prosper in the thing for which I sent it (Isa 55:10-11).

God not only speaks, he also separates (v. 4b, 7); he makes (vv. 7, 16, 25, 26); he causes the earth to sprout green (v. 11); he makes the waters swarm (v. 20); he makes the earth produce living beings (v. 27). There were many traditions of creation in the ancient Near East: creation by the word, by making, by separation with or without a struggle with the primeval elements, by education or drawing things forth from the earth or water, by spontaneous generation by Mother Earth or the waters. The traditions of creation with which the writer was familiar were stamped with this imaginative thinking, hence their traces, faint or firm, in the biblical text. The writer, putting all creation under the creative word of God, has not eliminated these traces nor smoothed out all incongruities.

FIRST DAY, VERSES 3-5: God creates light which is necessary for all life to exist. Light comes directly from God's word. There is something of a polemic here. Light is not divine like the Egyptian Re (or Ra) who shines over chaos. Light is not the uncreated and eternal sphere of Persian cosmogony in which Mazda dwells. The writer does not say that God created darkness, which belongs to the elements of chaos. God simply creates and separates, effecting the succession of night and day. Second Isaiah, using the extremes of light and darkness, good and bad, to compass totality, speaks of God as "forming light and creating (*bārā'*) darkness, making prosperity and creating (*bārā'*) ill" (Isa 45:7). He is saying that God is the source of "the whole." The writer of Genesis is not concerned that the creation of light precedes the creation of the sun and the moon. His only concern is to identify nothing but God with God. God "calls" or "names." To name is to exercise dominion. So God exercises his mastery and assigns these elements their function in his ordered creation (for other traditions and reflections on light, cf. Pss 27:1; 104:2; 1 Tim 6:16; Jas 1:17; 1 John 1:5, "God is light and in him there is no darkness").

SECOND DAY, VERSES 6-8: the world view behind these verses is that the universe consists of a solid vault, the sky, holding up the waters above, and that the earth is a disc floating on the waters below (the abyss) with the shadowy Sheol down under somewhere, and that the primeval river encircles the earth; the heavenly bodies are set in the vault. Pillars reaching down into the abyss support the vault (Job 26:11; 38:4; Ps 104:5). The function of the vault is to hold the waters apart permanently. There are openings or sluice gates in it through which the rain falls (Gen 7:11; 8:2; 2 Kgs 7:2, 19). There is no word about the origin of the waters; they are just there.

THIRD DAY, VERSES 9-12: God continues his work of ordering and gives the earth and the waters their function. God is the power who brings forth grass, plants, and trees (Pss 104:14, 16; 148:9), not Canaanite Baal. Two works of creation are fitted into one day.

FOURTH DAY, VERSES 14-19: the heavenly bodies, the sun, moon and the stars, are not divine; they are God's creatures, a part of his created order, to which he assigns functions, namely to determine the calendar, the seasons, and the feasts (Ps 104:14). The writer mentions two lights, a large and a small. He does not give them their proper names, *šemeš*, sun, and *yarēaḥ*, moon, but merely calls them "lights," lest there be the remotest equation between them and the divine.

FIFTH DAY, VERSES 20-23: God creates the creatures of the water and the sky; literally, "let the waters swarm with a swarm, living being (singular) and let flying things fly. . . . " The living being is, literally, a living soul (*nepeš*); it is the vital, breathing animal or human. A new element is introduced here, namely the blessing of living beings. To bless in the context of creation is to endow with a dynamism to increase (Koehler 1967:152-53; Westermann 1978;

1984:139–40). The combination "increase and multiply" occurs again in 1:28; 9:1, 7, and in the patriarchal stories in 28:3; 35:11; 47:27; 48:4. Blessing becomes a paternal and liturgical act later in the Pentateuch. God created the great monsters, the *tannînîm*. This is the first use of *bārā'*, create, since verse 1. The struggle with a primeval monster was well known from Mesopotamian mythology. But neither here in verse 21 nor in verse 2 is there any sign of a struggle. All is subject to the serene creative word of God.

SIXTH DAY, VERSES 24-31: the creator brings the land animals into being and divides them according to their genus and species. The work of creation reaches its climax on the sixth day with the creation of the human race. The word of God continues as the effective force (v. 26). With a deliberative plural, "let us make . . .," God's word issues into action and he creates *'adam,* mankind, the human race. *hā'ādām* means one of the human race; the various meaning groups in which it is used relate to the human's state as a creature. *'ādām* is made or created in the image (*ṣelem*) and likeness (*dĕmût*) of God; the former word is very concrete, indicating an image, a plastic work, a piece of sculpture; the latter is an abstract formation. The words are governed by the prepositions *bĕ* and *kĕ* respectively, *bĕṣelem, kidmût*. In the continuation of the priestly writing in chapter 5, Adam (the word *'ādām* is used as a proper name for the first time in 5:1a and 3a), when 130 years old, became the father of a son "in his own likeness (*bidmût*), after his image (*kĕṣelem*)"; the same two nouns are used with the prepositions reversed. This indicates that we have a composite phrase known as a hendiadys, i.e., the expression of a complex idea by two words connected with "and." There is something of the father, *'ādām,* in the son, Seth; there is a relationship between the father and the son; something can happen between them. So too, there is something of the creator, God, in the creature, *'ādām;* there is a relationship between God and *'ādām;* something can happen between God and *'ādām* (v. 26). The focus is not on a quality of *'ādām,* but on the relationship between God and *'ādām.* God creates a being with whom he can communicate. An event can happen between God and *'ādām.* "Every human being of every religion and in every place, even where religions are no longer recognized, has been created in the image of God. . . . The relationship to God is not something which is added to human existence; humans are created in such a way that their very existence is intended to be their relationship to God" (Westermann 1984:158).

God creates *'ādām* (singular) and says: "and let them (plural) rule"; that is, the human race, male and female, is to control and rule the animal world. The important verse 27 may be set out thus:

> and God *bārā hā'ādām* in his *ṣelem,*
> in the *ṣelem* of God he *bārā'* it (lit., him),
> male and female he *bārā'* them.

Three times God is the subject of *bārā';* three times the object of *bārā'* is the human race, *ha'ādām,* it (lit., him), male and female with them in apposition. Hence *ha'ādām* = it = male and female = them. The human race is only the human race when constituted as male and female. With the act of creation God gives his blessing, i.e., he bestows the dynamism to increase: "God blessed them" (v. 28a), and gives them their destiny in the world: "subdue it and rule. . . . " (v. 28b). The word *rādāh,* to rule, to dominate, is resumed from verse 26, and is used with *kābash,* to subdue. They form a hendiadys. "But it is not a domination of exploitation, not an arbitrary rule however absolutely it may be phrased" (Vawter 1977:58). God has entrusted his world to men and women; they are to exercise their rule facing that immense order, but with God as their point of reference. There is no rule dissociated from God. The language has echoes of the technical language of royal rule (Pss 72:8; 110:2; 1 Kgs 5:4 [English 4:24]; Jer 14:6; Ezek 34:4).

The text says something, at least implicitly, about the modern problem of ecology. The human race, collectively and individually, has a responsibility for the environment. The scientist, the technologist, and the industrialist cannot prescind from the consequences of their work. Because they do prescind, or are restricted by their own tunnel vision, we have the science of ecology which may be described negatively and roughly as the science of getting us out of the mess into which we have been and are being plunged by the avarice of man and the indiscriminate and thoughtless distribution of the products, by-products, and waste products of modern science, industry, and technology.

The human being is created to rule and control the universe. It belongs to its nature to work. Work is not a consequence of sin, which has not yet been mentioned. The human person cannot get to God but through creation.

God provides humans and animals with food (v. 29). It seems that we have here traces of a reasonably widespread golden age tradition, in which flesh was not eaten, that preceded the historical one (Isa 11:6-9). God's work is now finished and the final word of praise is spoken; everything is just as it should be coming from God's creative word (v. 31). In 2:1, the writer resumes from 1:1 the words "the heavens and the earth" and says that all has been completed. His own statement on creation is finished.

These thirty-two verses are priestly teaching, the fruit of long theological reflection (von Rad 1972:63).

Notes

1. IN THE BEGINNING. The great Jewish scholar of the middle ages, Rashi, Rabbi Solomon, Son of Isaac (d. 1105), read verse 1 as a temporal, subordinate clause (protasis), in construct with verse 3 (apodosis), and verse 2 as a parenthesis: "When God began to create the heaven and the earth—the earth being unformed and void, with darkness over the surface of the deep and a wind from God sweeping over the water—God said, 'Let there be light'; and there was light." (This is the version adopted by The Jewish Publication Society of America in *The Torah,* 1963; Orlinsky 1983:207–09; Speiser 1964:12–13.) The NEB joins verses 1 and 2 as protasis and apodosis, and reads verse 3 as an independent principal sentence: "In the beginning of creation, when God made heaven and earth, the earth was without form and void, with darkness over the face of the abyss, and a mighty wind that swept over the surface of the waters. God said . . . " The NAB is virtually the same. The NIV and JB (2nd edition, 1985) retain the more familiar RSV translation reading verse 1, 2, and 3 as three successive main sentences. In yet another view, the action begins with the third part of verse 2: "When God began to create . . . , the earth was . . . and the spirit of God was moving over the surface of the waters, and God said . . . " The writer, it is claimed, goes as it were a step behind creation; the creative breath of God had not yet become the creative word; verse 2c is a circumstantial sentence referring to God before he begins the work of creation (Steck 1981:236–37). The question cannot be settled on grounds of philology and syntax alone. The structure of the remainder of the chapter, especially the phrase "And God said," *wayyo'mer,* must be drawn into the discussion. The position adopted here is that "and God said," the creative word of God, introduces, according to a pattern, each work of creation after the stark presentation of chaos.

GOD. The form of the common word for God, *'ĕlohîm,* is plural. When used of the God of Israel as the subject of a sentence, the verb is virtually always in the singular. *'ĕlohîm* is used in the Old Testament canon with the following meanings: God, the God of . . . , a god, gods, the gods. The priestly writer understands the word only as a singular noun. *'ĕl* is the common semitic word for god; Assyrian *'ilu.;* Ugaritic *'il;* in the Ugaritic pantheon, El is a god of special rank and El is a proper name; he is "father of the gods" and "creator"; *'ĕl* occurs 286 times in the Old Testament.

CREATED. *bārā'* (forty-nine times in the Old Testament). The word is used only with the God of Israel (YHWH) as subject, never with another god or a human; it is never used with a preposition nor has it ever as its object the material out of which God created. It occurs ten times in the priestly writing in Genesis 1–11, seven of which are in the creation account (1:1, 21, 27 [three times]; 2:3, 4), and seventeen times in Second Isaiah (40:26, 28; 41:20; 42:5; 43:1, 7, 15; 45:7 [two times], 8, 18 [two times]; 48:7; 54:16 [two times]). There is a very common Hebrew word *'āśāh,* that means to do or to make. God made the firmament (v. 7), the heavenly bodies (v. 16), the beasts of the earth (v. 25), and says "let us make mankind" (v. 26). But he created, *bārā',* the universe (v. 1), the sea monsters (v. 21), and mankind (v. 27), where the verb is used three times. We can say no more than that the writer shows a preference for *bārā'* in certain places, while in others he uses *bārā'* and *'āśāh* without distinction. "Theologically, the statement that God is the Maker and that God is the Creator are not different at all" (Anderson 1977:154).

Wellhausen considered both the word *bārā'* and the concept of creation to be late: "Such abstraction is unheard of in an undeveloped people; it is only after the exile that such words and ideas came more and more into common use among the Hebrews. . . . (1957 [1878]:305). The majority of scholars have maintained the same view in substance. However, the great pioneer of the study of biblical literary forms, Hermann Gunkel (1862–1932), reckoned *bārā'* to be a very old narrative term (1910:102). The recent discoveries (since 1977) at Elba (Tell Mardikh in Syria, some sixty kilometers [thirty-eight miles] southwest of Aleppo) from about 2200 B.C.E. reveal the following names: *ba-ra-gu*ki = voice has created; *gu-ba-ri-um*ki= = the voice is the creator; *e-ba-ri-um*ki = the temple of the creator; *ib-ta-ra-gu*ki = the voice has created for itself. In each case *bārā'* is part of the word (this information was supplied to me by the late

Mitchell Dahood in the year before his untimely death in March 1982). There are scholars who think that the language of Elba, despite its great difficulties and complications and the very notable signs of Mesopotamian influence, is a northwest semitic language and related to the Canaanite group to which Hebrew belongs. The idea of creation in some form and the word *bārā'* have a long history in the ancient Near East.

THE HEAVENS AND THE EARTH. Hebrew has no single word for the cosmos or the universe.

2. FORMLESS WASTE. This is *tōhû wā bōhû; tōhû* occurs twenty-five times in the Old Testament, *bōhû* three times (Gen 1:2; Isa 34:11; Jer 4:23), always with *tōhû;* it is an alliterative strengthener.

THE DEEP. The word *tĕhôm* occurs thirty-five times in the Old Testament, twenty-one times in the singular and, apart from Isaiah 63:16 and Psalm 106:9 (plural), always without the article. In all cases *tĕhôm* designates a mass of water. Some scholars (von Rad 1972:50) link *tĕhôm* mythologically with the Babylonian primeval monster Tiamat that Marduk inflated with the Evil Wind, split in two with his arrow, and formed the firmament from one part and the lower waters from the other. But the biblical writer is not demythologizing a mythical idea or name. "When P inherited the word *tĕhôm,* it had long been used to describe a flood of water without any mythical echo" (Westermann 1984:105; Lambert 1965). There is no sign of a struggle in Genesis 1:2. It is likely that Tiamat and *tĕhôm* are linked philologically, each deriving from the same old semitic root.

A MIGHTY WIND. Literally, "the wind (breath) of God (*'ĕlohîm*). The word for God, *'ĕl* or *'ĕlohîm,* is used at times with a noun in the construct or "genitive" state to express a superlative, e.g., Psalm 36:7 (6): the psalmist addresses YHWH: "Your righteousness is like the *hārĕrê 'ĕl* (the mighty mountains, the-mountains-of God), your judgment like *tĕhôm rabbāh* (the great deep)"; the parallelism indicates strongly that *'ĕl* is used with mountains as a superlative adjective; Psalm 80:11 (10): the psalmist speaks of the vine (Joseph v. 2 [1]) that God led out of Egypt: "The mountains were covered with its shade, the *'arzê 'ĕl* (the mighty cedars, the-cedars-of God) with its branches"; again the parallelism shows that *ĕl* is the equivalent of an adjective in the superlative; 1 Samuel 14:15: the narrator tells that after Jonathan's victory at Michmash, *ḥerdat 'ĕlohîm* (lit., the-fear-of God), "a very great panic" (RSV) ensued; Jonah 3:3: Nineveh is *'îr gĕdolāh le'lohîm* (lit., a great city to God), "an exceedingly great city" (RSV). There is, however, an opinion that the words *rû-aḥ 'elohîm* do mean the breath of God (Friedman 1980). The Hebrew particle *waw,* which immediately precedes *rûaḥ,* would be understood as an adversative, "but"; "but the breath of God was hovering over the waters," a non-mythological contrast to the mythological language and imagery of the first two parts of the verse. The creative power of the divine breath is emphasized in Isaiah 40:13; Psalms 33:6; 104:3; Job 26:13. As noted in the first note on verse 1, Steck (1981:236-37) argues that verse 2c is the breath of God that stands in close relationship to speech and that will take the form of creative speech, bringing about order; the "breath" is the "ante-creative" word. Day (1985:52-53) defends the view that *rûaḥ 'elo-hîm* refers to the wind of God (Ps 104:3). " . . . Genesis 1:2 has taken up a tradition concerning Yahweh's driving of the waters off the earth by his wind." Day underscores the dependence of Genesis 1 on Psalm 104. This wind derives ultimately from the wind of Baal employed against the sea monster in the texts of Ugarit.

WAS MOVING TO AND FRO. The Hebrew is an intensive, *pi'el,* participle from the root *rḥp* and means "hovering" in Deuteronomy 32:11; in Jeremiah 23:9 the perfect form occurs in the second part of a colon: "my heart is broken within me, all my bones shake." These are the only two uses of the word outside Genesis 1:2. The LXX renders by *epephereto,* and the Vulgate by *ferebatur;* both words mean "was being borne" or "was bearing itself."

3. AND GOD SAID. One of the leading authorities on Mesopotamian religion, Thorkild Jacobsen, has written: "The creative power of the word underlies all mesopotamian religious literature" (1976:15). It is also effective in the Old Testament. However, there is nothing in the Old Testament of the magic that occurs at times when the word is at work in the literature of Mesopotamia. A section of the Babylonian creation epic, Enuma Elish, reads:

> Lord, truly thy decree is first among the gods.
> Say but to wreck or create; it shall be.
> Open thy mouth: the cloth will vanish!
> Speak again, and the cloth shall be whole!
> At the word of his mouth the cloth vanished.
> He spoke again and the cloth was restored.

> When the gods, his fathers, saw the fruit of his word,
> Joyfully they did homage: "Marduk is king!"
> (ANET 1955:66, Tablet iv, 21–28).

The word is presented often as a natural cosmic power through which the voice of God comes, and this has left its mark, for example, in Psalm 29 where the voice of YHWH sounds in nature seven times. Creation through the word is also the end of a long process of development in the Egyptian theology of Memphis, one of the most ancient and famous cities of Egypt, about thirty kilometers (eighteen miles) south of Cairo on the west bank of the Nile. Memphis, the capital of the Old Kingdom, flourished during the third and fourth Egyptian dynasties in the second and third quarters of the third millennium when the great pyramids were built. So there is ample ancient Near Eastern background for the Old Testament word.

6. VAULT. The Hebrew word *rāqîa'* derives from a verb *rq'* which means to hammer out, to flatten, to tread down, to stamp with the feet. Homer refers to the heavens as *chalkeos* or *sidereos,* bronze or iron made. The Vulgate renders it by *firmamentum.*

7. GOD MADE. Some scholars (Schmidt 1964; Westermann 1984, but with modifications) are of the opinion that two accounts of creation lay before the author of Genesis 1, one an "action account" in which God created by some form of activity such as making or separating, the other a "word account" in which the creative word dominated. These, it is claimed, were gradually blended so as to form the traditional text. This is possible. But whatever the case, the priestly tradition of creation has brought all under the creative word of God which dominates the universe and its adornments.

14. LIGHTS. The Akkadian Shamash (the word is cognate with the Hebrew *šemeš*) was a solar deity (ANET 1955:538, and index for many references). The sun was invoked as a deity in Egypt, for example, in *A Universalist Hymn to the Sun* in the time of Amenhotep III, 1413–1377 B.C.E.

> Hail to the sun disc of the day time,
> Creator of all and maker of their living (ANET 368).

The sun disc is Aton, to whom a long hymn is addressed (ANET 369–71). There was a moon deity whom the Amorites worshipped as Warah or Yarah (the Hebrew for the moon is *yārēaḥ*). A moon deity was revered in Phoenicia. The Israelites came under the influence of these deities and were warned constantly against turning to them: "And beware lest you lift up your eyes to heaven, and when you see the sun and the moon and the stars, all the host of them, you be drawn away and worship them and serve them, things which the Lord your God has allotted to all the peoples under the whole heaven" (Deut 4:19; cf. Deut 17:3; Job 31:26-28). Josiah in his reforms did away with the priests who sacrificed to the heavenly bodies and destroyed the chariots and horses dedicated to the sun at the entrance to the temple of the Lord (2 Kgs 23:5, 11; similar reforms by Asa, 1 Kgs 15:11-15; many of the Jewish women who fled to Egypt at the time of the destruction of Jerusalem worshipped "the queen of heaven," Jer 44:15-19). But the heavenly bodies are mere creatures of God; their "deified" names are not to be mentioned in the accounts of God's creation. They serve but to function in his created order. Their function is underscored again in Psalms 104:14-19; 136:7-9 (cf. ANET 67–68, Tablet v).

20. LIVING BEINGS. *nepeš ḥayyah,* a living soul, means animals in general, animals and humans together, and the breath of life that makes animals and humans living beings. The expression occurs in Genesis 1–11 in 1:20, 21, 24, 30; 2:7; 9:10, 12, 15, 16. In 2:7 *hā'ādām* becomes a living being; in 9:12-14, God makes a covenant with all living beings. *nepeš* carries the concrete meanings of breath, neck, throat, e.g., "Save me, O God! For the waters have come up to my neck" (Ps 69:2 [1]). One's *nepeš* longs, hungers, thirsts, hopes, loves, hates, endures; one prays to God to save, preserve, my *nepeš;* one calls on "my soul (*napšî*)" to bless the Lord (e.g., Pss 103:1; 104:1).

FLYING THINGS. One recalls here Psalm 8:9 (8): "the birds of the air, and the fish of the sea, whatever passed along the path of the sea." The Egyptian Hymn to Amon-Re (Eighteenth Dynasty, 1550-1350 B.C.E.) speaks of him "who made that (on which) the fish in the river may live, and the birds soaring in the sky" (ANET 366, vi).

21. THE GREAT MONSTERS. These are the *tannînîm.* The Supremacy of the God of Israel over the powers of chaos is described in the language and imagery of a triumph over a monster: over Rahab, (Isa 51:9; Ps 89:11 [10]); over Leviathan, (Isa 27:1; Ps 74:14); *tannîn* is included in the description in Isaiah 51:9 and 27:1 (these references to the primeval monsters in the Old Testament are only the

most important). How ready the writers in Israel were to make use of traditional imagery from surrounding cultures may be illustrated by reading Isaiah 27:1 together with the vivid description from a Canaanite text from Ras Shamra (Ugarit, fourteenth century B.C.E.):

> Crushed I not El's beloved Yamm?
> Destroyed I not El's flood Rabbim?
> Did I not, pray, muzzle the Dragon?
> I did crush the crooked serpent,
> Shalyat the seven-headed (ANET 137, lines 35-37).

The proper name of the serpent is Lotan = Leviathan. An illustration of a god confronting a seven-headed monster may be found in the *Biblical Archaeology Review,* 11, 2 (March–April 1985) 30; the incised shell on which it is carved dates from about 2600 B.C.E.

26. LET US MAKE. This plural has caused, I am sure, more confusion, disagreement, and comment than the author of Genesis 1 could ever have imagined. Are the words a myth fragment, an address to creation, an address to a heavenly court, a plural of majesty, a simple self-deliberation, a sign of duality within the Godhead? (Miller 1978:9-20). Some of the Fathers of the Church saw here the beginnings of an expression of the doctrine of the Trinity. Some scholars have invoked the phenomenon of the heavenly court or the assembly of the gods (Mullen 1980) current in Canaan and known in Israel (1 Kgs 22:19-23; Ps 29:1; Job 1:6; demythologization and references to angels or heavenly messengers in Pss 103:20-21; 148:2) and see a vestige of it here (Miller 1978:18). But the strictly monotheistic priestly writer would entertain no thought of this. Schmidt (1964) and Steck (1981) reject the formula of self-deliberation and argue in favor of self-command. There is no royal plural in Hebrew. The plurals of Genesis 1:26; 3:22; 11:3, 7, and Isaiah 6:8 are best understood as plurals of deliberation and rhetorical devices (Westermann 1984:144-45; Vawter 1977:53-54).

'ĀDĀM. The word occurs 562 times (ThWAT) in the Old Testament, forty-six times in Genesis 1-11 which is concerned with *'ādām*. *hā'ādām* means the man, mankind, the human race; in Genesis 5:1a, 3, 4 *'ādām* is used as a proper name.

IMAGE AND LIKENESS. *ṣelem* is the ordinary word for a concrete image, while *dĕmût* is an abstract from the verb *dāmāh,* to resemble; the verb and the noun, *dāmāh-dĕmût,* are used together "something

which is like.'' In February 1979 a statue was discovered in north
central Syria at Tell Fekkeriyeh (ancient Sikan) on the Khabur, south
of Ras el-ÆAyn, about two kilometers (one and two-tenths miles)
from Tell Halaf, close to the Turkish-Syrian border. It is inscribed
in Aramaic and Akkadian and is from the ninth century B.C.E. (Millard 1982; Abou-Assaf 1982). The word *dmwt',* image, introduces
the first part of the Aramaic section, and *ṣlm,* statue, the second.
This, of course, like all archaeological discoveries, proves the Bible
neither right nor wrong. But it is of interest to note that both words
occur together on a royal statue and this may confirm the opinion
of those who see a royal background to Genesis 1:26-28.

28. SUBDUE AND RULE. The destiny of the human race is to civilize
the earth. A number of creation stories from antiquity relate the purpose for which mankind was created. The Sumerian-Babylonian tradition is that the race was created ''to carry the yoke of the god,''
i.e., in mythical language to relieve the gods of their burden of daily
drudgery. In the Atrahasis epic (Lambert and Millard 1969:42, lines
1-4; 57, lines 190-97; 59-61, lines 235-43; ANET 99), a group of
lesser divinities, to whom the difficult daily work had been assigned,
revolts. The assembly of the gods, which had been called to deal
with the matter, decides to create man and impose the work on him.
This act is then celebrated as the freeing of the gods from the yoke
of work.

2. God's Rest and the Sanctification of the Seventh Day (2:2-3)

²And God had completed the work that he had done on the seventh
day, and he rested on the seventh day from all the work that he had
done.
³And God blessed the seventh day and sanctified it, because on it God
rested from all the work that he had done when creating.

Comment

With the work of creation finished, the writer now introduces two
new elements, the repose of God and the Israelite Sabbath. In 2:1
''the heavens and the earth and all their adornment had been completed.'' The word ''completed,'' *kalah,* the first word in 2:1, is resumed as the first word in 2:2. The idea of the repose of the divinity
at the end of the work of creation is widespread in the history of

religions (Pettazzoni 1954:32-34). The activity of the work of creation has ended on the sixth day. But creation in the priestly plan covers the seven day week. Hence, God's creative work includes a day of rest; his work moves from action into rest. Israel's Sabbath has, in the priestly perspective, its origin in the divine rest at the end of the process of creation (Wolff 1972:50). Further, the goal of the human race is not just work and the mastery of the universe. The creature that is made in the image and likeness of God is to share in the repose of God. The writer, by way of a second conclusion and inclusion, refers back to 1:2 and the "making" of chapter 1 with his last words in 2:3: "God rested from all his work that he had created (*bārā'*) and made" (lit., by, in, when, making, *la'ăśôt*).

Notes

2. HE RESTED. The verb is *šābat,* to desist from. The noun, sabbath, is *šabbāt.* The obscure history of the Sabbath is discussed by de Vaux (1961:475-83), Morgenstern (1962:135-41), and Rordorf (1968). The word *šabbāt* has nothing to do with the word for adornment or "hosts," *ṣābā',* as in "Lord God of hosts (*ṣĕbā'ôt*)."

3. SANCTIFIED. The verb *qādaš* means to separate out, to declare holy.

3. Prospect and Retrospect
(2:4a)

⁴ᵃ"This is the story of the heavens and the earth when they were created.

Comment

This half verse is a link verse. It looks forward to the story of the human race, and through it to Israel, which lives out its course in God's created order. The Hebrew word *tôlĕdôt,* story, occurs a further ten times in the book of Genesis, on each occasion introducing a genealogy (see *Notes*). Each time, the ancestor whose descendants are enumerated or whose family story is narrated has already been introduced by name. "The heavens and the earth" of 2:4a have been introduced in 1:1 and 2:1. Their story looks forward; it is the story of the world in which *hā'ādām* lives with God's creation.

Notes

4A. STORY. *tôlĕdôt* derives from *yālad,* to beget. BDB (410) renders it by "generations, especially in genealogies = account of a man and his descendants," and "successive generations (in) of families." *Tôlĕdôt* occurs elsewhere in Genesis in 5:1 (Adam); 6:9 (Noah); 10:1 (Noah's sons); 11:10 (Shem); 11:27 (Terah); 25:12 (Ishmael); 25:19 (Isaac); 36:1, 9 (Esau); 37:2 (Jacob).

WHEN THEY WERE CREATED. *bĕhibbārĕ'ām:* literally, "in their having been created."

4. The Creation of Man and Woman: Their Transgression (2:4b-3:24)

(The Hebrew *hā'ādām* is left untranslated; it occurs twenty-four times; the definite article, *hā,* is missing in 2:5, 20b; 3:17, 21; in the three latter cases BHS proposes that it be added.)

⁴ᵇWhen YHWH-God made earth and heavens,
⁵there was not yet shrub nor plant growing wild on earth,
because YHWH-God had not rained upon earth
   and there was no *'ādām* to work the ground;
⁶but he made a stream rise from the earth
   so as to water the whole surface of the ground;
⁷then YHWH-God formed *hā'ādām* (out of) dust from the ground,
   and breathed into his nostrils the breath of life,
   and *hā'ādām* became a living being.
⁸And YHWH-God planted a garden in Eden away to the east and put *hā'ādām* there whom he had formed. ⁹And YHWH-God made every (kind of) tree spring up, pleasant to look at and good to eat, and the tree of life in the middle of the garden and the tree of the knowledge of good and bad.

¹⁰Now there is a river going out from Eden to water the garden, and from there it divides into branches and becomes four sources. ¹¹The name of the first is Pishon, the one that flows around the whole of the land of Havilah where there is gold; ¹²and the gold of this land is precious; and there is sweet-scented resin there and onyx stone. ¹³The name of the second river is Gihon, the one that flows around the whole of the land of Cush. ¹⁴The name of the third river is Tigris, the one that courses to the east of Ashur. The fourth river is the Euphrates.

¹⁵And YHWH-God took *hā'ādām* and put him in the garden of Eden to work it and care for it. And YHWH-God ordered *hā'ādām:* ¹⁶You may eat from all the trees of the garden: ¹⁷but you may not eat from the tree of the knowledge of good and bad, because if you do eat from it you will die.

¹⁸And YHWH-God said: It is not good for *hā'ādām* to be alone. I will make for him a partner equal to him. ¹⁹So YHWH-God formed from the ground every (kind of) animal of the field and every (kind of) flying thing of the heavens and brought them to *hā'ādām* to see what he would call them, and whatever *hā'ādām* called a living being, that was its name. ²⁰And *hā'ādām* gave names to all cattle, all flying things in the heavens, and every animal of the field; but as for *'ādām,* he found no partner equal to him.

²¹So YHWH-God brought a deep sleep upon *hā'ādām* so that he fell asleep, and he took one of his ribs and filled up its place with flesh. ²²And YHWH-God made the rib that he had taken from *hā'ādām* into a woman and brought her to *hā'ādām.* ²³And *hā'ādām* said:

This one at last is bone from my bone and flesh from my flesh;
this one will be called woman (*'iššâ*) because from a man
(*'îš*) has this one been taken.

²⁴For this reason a husband shall leave his father and his mother and stay fast with his wife and they shall become one flesh.
²⁵And the two of them, *hā'ādām* and his wife, were naked but they felt no shame before each other.

3:1 Now the serpent was the most astute of all the animals of the field that YHWH-God had made and it said to the woman: Did God really say that you may not eat from any of the trees of the garden? ²And the woman said to the serpent: We may eat from the fruit of the trees of the garden, ³but God said: You may not eat from the fruit of the tree that is in the middle of the garden nor may you touch it, lest you die. ⁴But the serpent said to the woman: You will certainly not die! ⁵Indeed, God knows that if you eat from it your eyes will be opened and you will be as God knowing good and bad. ⁶And the woman saw how good the tree was to eat from and how attractive to the eyes and how desirable so as to gain wisdom and she took from it and ate and gave it to her husband with her and he ate. ⁷And the eyes of the two of them were opened and they realized that they were naked and sewed fig leaves together and made aprons for themselves. ⁸Then they heard the voice of YHWH-God moving to and fro in the garden at the time of the day breeze, so *hā'ādām* and his wife hid themselves from the presence of YHWH-God among the trees of the garden. ⁹And YHWH-God called to *hā'ādām* and said to him: Where are you? ¹⁰And he said: I heard your voice in the garden and I saw that I was naked and I hid myself. ¹¹And he said: Who told you that you were naked? Have you eaten from the tree from which I forbade you to eat? ¹²And *hā'ādām* said: The woman whom you gave me to be with me, she is the one who gave me of the tree and I ate. ¹³And YHWH-God said to the woman: What is this that you have done? And the woman said: The serpent deceived me and I ate. ¹⁴And YHWH-God said to the serpent:

> Because you have done this, cursed are you among all cattle and all animals of the field; you shall crawl on your belly and you shall eat dust all the days of your life.

¹⁵Enmity I put between you and the woman,
> between your seed and her seed;
> it will strike at your head and you will strike at its heel.

¹⁶To the woman he said:
> I will multiply your pains in child birth,
> in pain shall you bear children;
> your longing shall be for your husband, but he shall lord it over you.

¹⁷To *'ādām* he said:
> Because you listened to the voice of your wife
> and ate from the tree from which I forbade you to eat,
> cursed is the ground because of you,
> in toil you shall eat from it all the days of your life.

¹⁸Thorns and thistles it shall bear for you,
> and you shall eat the plants of the field.

¹⁹In the sweat of your face you shall eat your bread
> until you return to the ground, because you were taken from it.
> Yes, dust you are and to dust you shall return.

²⁰*hā'ādām* named his wife Eve because she was the mother of all the living.

²²And YHWH-God said: *hā'ādām* has indeed become like one of us in knowing good and bad; so now, lest he stretch out his hand and take also from the tree of life and live for ever!

²³YHWH-God sent him out of the garden of Eden to work the ground from which he was taken. ²⁴So he drove *hā'ādām* out and to the east of the garden of Eden he stationed cherubim and the flickering flaming sword to guard the way to the tree of life.

Comment

Scholars are virtually unanimous that Genesis 2:4b–3:24 comes from a hand other than that which wrote chapter 1. Hitherto we have been listening to the "systematic" theologian; now we hear the storyteller. The story as it lies before us is a well-knit unity, though not cut from whole cloth or, to use a metaphor from the German, not moulded from one pouring (*nicht aus einem Guss*). There was much material at hand to the author. Westermann (1984:191) is of the opinion that 2:4b-24, without verses 9-17, is a self-contained whole into or over which has been fitted a paradise-transgression story. Steck (1981:54) divides the chapters into a story of the creation of and provision for the human race (2:4b-25), the transgression (3:1-6), the consequences (3:7-24); the curse passage (3:14-19) is the work of the Yahwist; 2:4b-5, 7, 18-24 as well as 3:1-13 are dependent on and colored by the curse passage. One can say that the author was familiar with stories of the creation of man from clay or dust, with the theme of Eden and transgression, with the motif of the tree of life, with a snippet of ancient geography; he knew that the serpent had a variety of associations. He has woven what lay before him into a unified whole, though not without sutures and rough edges, in such a way as to make his own real and personal contribution. He is no mere assembler of parts of a jig-saw puzzle. He plays the three-fold role of receiver, transmitter, and contributor. The final product, with its parts neatly fitted together, is his own work and it is from this careful arrangement with its cross references that his theology emerges.

In 2:7, God forms *hā'ādām* (out of) *'āpār* (dust) *min hā'ădāmâ* (from the earth); the verse anticipates 3:19 where *'ādām,* addressed in 3:17, is to return to the dust, " . . . until you return to the *'ădāmâ,* because you were taken from it. Yes, dust (*'āpār*) you are and to dust (*'āpār*) you shall return." The theme recurs in 3:23 where God "sent him (*hā'ādām*) out of the garden of Eden to work the ground (*hā'ădāmâ*) from which he was taken." The theme of the tree of life (2:9) is resumed in 3:22. The theme of knowledge of, or knowing, good and bad is sounded in 2:9, and resumed in 2:17; 3:5, 22. The theme of the divine prohibition runs through the whole; 2:15-17; 3:1-6, 9-13, 17b, must be read together; the theme sounded in 2:15-17 is left echoing in the background while the woman is created. The nakedness of 2:25 is resumed in 3:7. On the other hand, the tree of life is in the middle of the garden in 2:9, while the forbidden tree of 2:17 has become the tree in the middle of the garden in 3:3. The note on the river and the four sources into which it divides (2:10-14) holds up the narrative. The author, conscious of this, resumes 2:8 in 2:15. The individual punishments (3:14-19) seem to come from another source, though 3:19bc echoes 2:7. In brief, the author has deliberately given a unity to disparate parts.

The story is clearly about *hā'ādām* (twenty-four times in 2:4b–3:24, forty-five times in chs. 1–11), everyman, and *hā'ădāmâ* (seven times in passage, twenty-seven times in chs. 1–11) from which *hā'ādām* is taken and to which everyman must return (Miller 1978:37-42).

2:4b-7, 8, 9: The combined name *YHWH-'ĕlohîm* occurs only in Genesis 2–3 in the Old Testament (in Exod 9:30, the text is uncertain). It is very likely a construction of the storyteller. The structure of the passage verses 4b-7 resembles the structure of the opening of the Akkadian epic, Enuma Elish (see note): 4b: "When . . . (5) there was not yet shrub nor God formed. . . . " The four negatives are roughly the equivalent of 1:2. They are not an attempt to describe chaos. Reality as we know it was not yet there. God, the cause of rain, had not yet rained. But God caused water to rise up from the earth. There is an incongruity here between the dry land and the primeval water on its surface (vv. 6b, 7a). Then God formed *hā'ādām* with whom we are familiar from 1:26-27. The first of many word plays in these early chapters occurs here. God takes some dust that lies on the surface of the ground and forms *hā'ādām* (out of) *'apār min hā'ădāmâ*. This creature is to return to the place whence it came, 3:19. The author underscores from the beginning the limitation of *hā'ādām*. His journey through life is from the womb of his natural mother to mother earth. The writers of the Old Testament were not pessimists, just realists. The theme occurs often in the psalms: "Thou turnest man back to dust" (90:3); "for he knows our frame, he remembers that we are dust" (103:14); "when thou takest away their breath, they die and return to their dust" (104:29); "when his breath departs he returns to his earth" (146:4). As the Greek dramatists were fond of saying, man is the creature of a day, *ephēmeros*. And the greatest poet of the English language reflected:

> What a piece of work is man! how noble in reason!
> how infinite in faculty! in form and moving how
> express and admirable! in action, how like an angel!
> in apprehension how like a god! the beauty of the
> world, the paragon of animals; and yet to me, what
> is this quintessence of dust? (Hamlet II, 2)

God breathed into this creature the breath of life (*nišmat ḥayyîm*). We are not in a school of later Greek philosophy where the human person was analyzed as a composition of body and soul. This is nothing wrong with such philosophical analysis, but it was not part of the biblical writer's thought pattern. The breath of life means simply being alive; *hā'ādām* becomes a living unity and is understood as a whole. All living beings have the breath (Gen 7:22) or spirit (Gen 6:17) of life; but " . . . all are from dust and all turn to dust again" (Qoh 3:20).

The garden that God planted is in Eden and Eden is in the east. The garden in Eden becomes the garden (of) Eden in 2:15; 3:23, 24. Eden and the Garden are not symbolic of an elevation to a higher or supernatural state. There is nothing in the text to indicate this. The Eden tradition of Ezekiel 28:11-19 has some elements in common with the Eden of Genesis but is at the same time different. Where was Eden? One might as well try to locate the land of Nod or Utopia or Shangri La. In verse 9 the writer introduces the motifs of the tree of life and the tree of the knowledge of good and bad. The tree of life is mentioned again only in 3:22, 24. The tree of knowledge of good and bad (2:9, 17) is, in the rest of the story, the tree in the middle of the garden or the tree from which I forbade you to eat or simply the tree (3:2, 3, 5, 6, 11, 12, 17).

The author now incorporates into his story an ancient piece of geography that lay before him. He is saying that the four great rivers have their origins from the one river that flows from Eden through the garden. As the river leaves the garden it divides into four (the number expresses fullness). So the great rivers known to the world of the ancient Near East rise from the river of the garden and bring blessing and fertility to the earth. Primeval event and primitive historical geography are joined.

After this brief geographical excursus, the author resumes in verse 15 the interrupted thread of verse 8. *hā'ādām* is to work and care for the earth. Work is not a consequence of sin but belongs to the destiny of the human race. The prohibition in verses 16-17 is essential to the story of chapters 2–3 (cf. 3:1-6, 9-13, 17b). There is plenty for *hā'ādām* to eat in the garden. The prohibition imposes no real deprivation but tells the man that God, the creator, who possesses a will beyond the creature, requires him to live according to the creator's will. The human being is by its very nature limited; the creature cannot be the creator. The prohibition implies the possibility of the opposite; this creature too has a will which it can exercise freely against the creator. The penalty is pronounced in the form of a capital offense: if or when you do so, you are guilty of a capital crime, a traditional formula from the sanctions in the legal books of the Pentateuch. The man and the woman commit the capital offense in chapter 3 and are banished from the presence of God.

God's work of creating the human race is not yet finished. The episode of verses 18-24 is peculiar to the Old Testament. It is not as if God had forgotten to create woman, or that he experimented to see if the man could get on alone or that he took a wrong track in parading the animals before the man to see if he could find a partner among them. There is nothing of this sort in the text. It is NONsense, just as it is NON-sense to think of God creating chaos (disorder) in 1:2. God is supreme in both the priestly theological writing and in the stories of the storyteller. The story—and it is a story (*Sage*)—of the creation of the human race is continued and brought to a conclusion. When the writer presents God as reflecting that it is not good for the man to be alone, he is saying that the human being is meant for community and that all human community is centered ultimately in the community of man and woman. There was "no partner equal to him," verses 18b, 20b. Like *hā'ādām,* the animals are taken from *hā'ādāmâ.* The survey of the animal kingdom is part of the story. It is not a parade of every beast from the dinosaur to the domestic flea. The man has dominion over the animals (cf. 1:28); he names them. Animals as such have no names. As mastadon hooted to mastadon across the primeval deep, I don't know what it called its mate. It is the world of the human being that creates names, and it is speech that makes the world human. It is *hā'ādām* who decides that there is no "partner equal to him" among the animals; there is none in which *hā'ādām* can recognize *hā'ādām.*

When God leads the new creature to the man, it is *hā'ādām* who acknowledges that she is his equal. Three times he repeats the strong demonstrative "this one" (*zō't*). "This one," in contrast to the animals, is "bone from my bone and flesh from my flesh." The writer is not referring to the material rib from which the woman was taken. The formula is a traditional expression of a lasting relationship. Laban says to Jacob: "Surely you are my bone and my flesh" (Gen 29:14); Abimelech says to the people of Shechem: " . . . I am your bone and your flesh" (Judg 9:2b); the tribes of Israel say to David in Hebron: " . . . we are your bone and flesh" (2 Sam 5:2); David sent a message to Zadok and Abiathar to say to the elders of Judah: " . . . you are my bone and my flesh," and to Amasa: "Are you not my bone and my flesh?" (2 Sam 19:13 [12], 14 [13]). The man and the woman belong to each other. The woman is to be called *'iššâ* (woman, wife) because she has been taken from *'îš* (man, husband). The word play is yet another sign of the unity of (the) man and (the) woman (v. 23b).

A brief epilogue follows (v. 24). It is a reflection on that power-ful attraction, namely their love for each other, that unites man and woman in lasting union: " . . . and they shall become one flesh (*bāśār*)"; *bāśār* refers to the whole person under the bodily aspect. The man leaves his father and mother and forms a stable relation-ship (*dābaq*, cleaves to) with the woman based on love. "One flesh" expresses the whole of family union.

Verse 25 is a transition which sets the stage for 3:1, 7. The couple were naked and experienced no shame before each other, the oppo-site of human experience in the concrete. They were naked (*'ărûm-mîm*, pl., *'êrom*, sing.); the serpent was astute (*'ārûm*). The two wanted to be *'ārûm*, but by defying God they became conscious that they were *'ărûmmîm* (3:7, 10).

The serpent was the most astute of the animals that God had made. God had formed the serpent from the ground, *min hā'ădāmâ* (2:19), just as he had formed *hā'ādām* (2:7). Why one creature of God should entice another from the creator remains a mystery that the author leaves unsolved and without comment. There are three ques-tions to ask about the serpent: 1) What is its function in the story? 2) What did it symbolize in the ancient Near East? 3) What associa-tions would it have evoked in the minds of the people of Israel as they listened to the story? The first question will be commented on here, the second and third in the notes. The function of the serpent in the story is to act as a foil to the woman. It appears, entices her successfully, and then, having fulfilled its function, is no longer part of the story. It is cursed in 3:14-15. There is no sign in the text that it represents Satan in serpent form (Wis 2:23-24), or that it is a sym-bol of human curiosity or desire, or a mythological being represent-ing or embodying chaos or a power inimical to God. That the serpent has a vivid ancient Near Eastern background and that Israel was fa-miliar with the serpent form in art and story is another matter (see *Notes*). The serpent talks, as does Balaam's ass (Num 22:28-30). A talking animal is a trait of the fairy-tale or folk-tale (*Märchen*) in modern study of folklore. The tree of the knowledge of good and bad is now in the middle of the garden (3:3); formerly the tree of life was there (2:9). The serpent exaggerates God's prohibition (3:1b); the woman in defense builds a fence around it, "nor may you touch it" (3:3b), something that God did not say. The woman knows of the prohibition of 2:16-17, though she was not present when it was pronounced. This is no problem for a storyteller, though it may be that he has not smoothed out entirely the join in his sources. Her husband is with her (3:6b)—in front of the tree? The temptation to "be as God knowing good and bad" is too much; the fruit was "desirable so as to gain wisdom." The Hebrew "know" (*yāda'*) adds something to our way of thinking; for the Hebrew knowledge was empirical and experiential, whereas we view knowledge intellectually. But we must not exaggerate so as to think that the Hebrew was devoid of reasoning power (Albright 1964:92–100). "Good and bad" is a mode of speech known as merism(-us), in which the two extremes are mentioned so as to cover the whole, e.g., the heavens and the earth mean the universe; God is he who "forms light and creates darkness, who makes prosperity and creates adversity" (Isa 45:7), i.e., God is the creator of all and is responsible for all. The woman will experience, master, all; she will determine all, be autonomous. She will be independent of God; she, not God, will determine what is useful or harmful in life. Her husband eats with her and consents (it scarcely needs saying that there is no sign in the text of the woman seducing the man). They defy God together; they sin as a pair, i.e., socially. There is in the human being a threefold drive; to continue the species, to know, to survive. These drives are good. But man and woman continually strive to transcend themselves by stepping beyond their limits. There is that general human phenomenon of the attraction of what is forbidden. There is nothing wrong in the fruit of the tree being good to eat and attractive to the eyes and desirable to gain wisdom. Desire in itself is not bad. But it leads to badness when it draws one beyond the limits of the creature. The author does not explain the persistent tendency of the human person to reach beyond itself. He simply reflects that it is so; that it is his experience.

It is futile to ask, what was the first sin? Was it a sexual act? The biblical text is very clear—sin is a defiance of God, deliberately perpetrated by man and woman (2:16-17; 3:1-6, 9-13, 17b); " . . . you may not eat from the tree of the knowledge of good and bad" (2:17); the couple ate from the tree, wanting to be "as God knowing good and bad" (3:5); "you have eaten from the tree from which I forbade you to eat" (3:11); "because . . . you ate from the tree from which I forbade you to eat" (3:17). The prophet Nathan puts sin into the clearest relief when he confronts David who has committed adultery and murder: "Why have you despised the word of the Lord, to do what is evil in his sight? . . . because you have despised me . . . " (2 Sam 12:9-10). The couple have sinned together, they have defied God together; they now know by experience that their relationship to each other and to God has changed (3:7-8). They cover themselves before each other; they are *'ărûmmîm* (naked), and not *'ārûm* (astute, wise). The rustling of the leaves in the trees is a sign of God's presence in the garden; the man and the woman are at a loss to come to terms with their changed relationship before God; so they hide themselves.

The judicial interrogation begins: "Where are you?" (The question has become the title of an important essay by Rudolf Bultmann, "Adam, wo bist du?" [1961:105–06], and of a novel by Nobel Prize winner [1972] Heinrich Böll [1917-1985], "Wo warst du, Adam?") The interrogation leaves no doubt that the man and the woman are fully responsible for their action, and that the action is an act of defiance of God (3:11b; cf. Cain, 4:9-11; David, 2 Sam 12). That the man and the woman can defend themselves is a consequence of their freedom, but it does not take away their responsibility.

The punishments (vv. 14-19) inflicted separately on each of the three actors in the drama appear to derive ultimately from a source other than the present account of the transgression. The natural punishment is expulsion from the garden (3:23-24). The author of the biblical text, however, has tied these verses (vv. 14-19) to his story (3:1 and 3:14; 3:19 and 2:7). The punishments are etiological; that is, the author takes as his point of departure the situation with which he is familiar—people's fear (however irrational) of the serpent, the fact of the pains that a woman experiences in childbirth and her position of subjection to the master of the household, the brute experience of the frustration and difficulty of agriculture. He asks the cause (Greek, *aitia,* cause [a]etiology) of this, and finds his answer in the primeval transgression of the first representatives of the human race.

God addresses the serpent first. It was introduced as the most astute (*'ārûm*) of all the animals of the field (3:1); now it is most accursed (*'ārûr*) of all beasts and all animals of the field (3:14). There was an ancient belief that the snake ate dust as it hissed its way along on its belly; in the end period when "I create a new heaven and a new earth . . . dust shall be the serpent's food" (Isa 65:17, 25c); and nations in their humiliation "shall lick the dust like a serpent" (Hos 7:17). The second part of the pronouncement is not linked grammatically with the first. There is to be a long and deep-seated hostility between the posterity (lit., seed) of the serpent and the woman; each will continually strike at the other (for 3:15 as Proto-evangelium, see *Notes*). God addresses the woman under her double aspect of wife and mother. Just where a woman finds her life's fulfillment, her dignity, and her joy, all is not bliss, but pain and subordination as well. God addresses the man as the one who works and cares for the land (2:15). The ground (*hā'ădāmâ*) is cursed, not man ('*ādām*); but precisely because *hā'ādām* has defied God, he is involved in the consequences of the curse on the ground. The man will always be at variance with the ground and his environment until he returns to the ground itself. He was taken from the ground (2:7); he returns to it (3:19). The cycle is closed. That is his natural life cycle. *hā'ādām* is not by nature immortal, nor is there any sign in the biblical text of Genesis 2–3 that he has been granted immortality by God. Verses 19b and c say the same thing twice. The whole arch of the narrative from 2:7 to 3:19 brings *hā'ādām* from the '*adāmâ* and returns him to it.

In none of the three punishments is it a case of "before and after." That is, there was not a time when the serpent moved along otherwise than on its belly, when childbirth was painless and domestic subjection non-existent, when the ground did not produce weeds and the farmer did not sweat at his work; the author is simply asking— why all this?

Some have thought that verse 20 is out of place and belonged once to the Cain story. It would be the husband's response to the first birth. This may be. The Hebrew word to live is *ḥāyāh; ḥay* is a living being; the woman is the mother of "all living" (*kōl ḥay*); hence her name is *ḥaww(yy)āh* or, in Greek, *Zōē*. One recalls the reflection of Sirach:

> A great anxiety has God allotted,
> and a heavy yoke to the sons of men;
> From the day one leaves his mother's womb,
> to the day he returns to the mother of all the living (Sir 40:1).

The journey of *hā'ādām* is from his mother's womb to the womb of Mother Earth.

YHWH-God cares for '*ādām* and his wife (3:21). They had tried to take away their own shame by sewing fig leaves (3:7), but they still hid themselves from God. Now he, and it can be he alone, takes away their shame. R. A. Oden (1987:98–104) has proposed an alternative explanation. He argues well that clothing in general is symbolic of a state and, quoting extensively from the Epic of Gilgamesh and the Tale of Adapa, that clothing in the present context is symbolic of the human state, "a state symbolized by the donning of manufactured garments" (p. 102).

Expulsion from the garden is the original punishment for defiance of God (3:23). It has been argued (Westermann 1984:270–75) that verses 22 and 24 and verse 23 form two separate endings which differ from each other; one, verse 23, simply naming the punishment, the other verses, 22 and 24, concerned with protecting the tree of life and forestalling *hā'ādām's* reach for immortality. The tree of life is mentioned only in 2:9 and 3:22 and 24. But YHWH-God is the subject of both verse 22 and verse 23, and Genesis 2–3 are the only chapters in which this composite appellation is used. If there were two endings (each using YHWH-God?), then the final author has brought them both together in his unified narrative. Both verse 22 and verse 23 are rooted in what has preceded: " . . . like one of us, knowing good and bad" (3:22; cf. 2:9, 15; 3:5). "YHWH-God sent him out of the garden of Eden to work the *'ādāmâ* from which he was taken" (3:23; cf. 2:5, 7, 8, 15; 3:19). Because *hā'ād-ām* may try again to be "as God," which he cannot, and overcome the limitations of death and "live for ever" (3:22b), which is impossible, God puts his cherubim as guardians of the way to the tree of life. These are not the chubby, rosy-cheeked, winged little boys of Renaissance art, but equivalents of huge composite beings of Assyria that were the guardians of temples and palaces. *hā'ādām* and his wife leave the garden alienated from God.

THE STATEMENT OF 2:4b–3:24

The story in these chapters, a tightly-knit unity in the biblical text, is the story of *hā'ādām,* man and woman, in primeval time. It is beyond history. It is the story of Everyman. The author reflects on his experience. What is *hā'ādām?* A creature of God, limited, subject to God, comprising male and female, intelligent, capable of decision, with an in-built drive to know, to continue the species, to live on and to reach beyond, and hence burst its limitations and be independent of the creator. This is *hā'ādām* of the writer's experience; so has *hā'ādām* been from the beginning. The story is not concerned with *hā'ādām* endowed with supernatural powers that were lost. It is not concerned with hereditary sin as such or with death as a punishment for sin. It is making a basic statement about the human being which no religious, philosophical, scientific, technical, or medical advance can alter: the human being has never been anything else but limited and defectible. The story is about the representatives of the human race in the primeval period who, for the writer and his listeners, were people in history, the first man and the first woman. To avoid distortion and misrepresentation, the story must be read with the other stories of the transgression of *hā'ādām* in chapters 1-11; *hā'ādām* is their central concern.

Notes

(H. N. Wallace [1985] discusses extensively the ancient Near Eastern background to these chapters.)

4B. YHWH-GOD. The divine name, most likely pronounced Yahweh, was revealed to Moses when he received his call (Exod 3:13-15; 6:2-3). Yahweh is a proper name. Speiser (1964:15-16) has suggested tentatively that the formation of the combined name, *YHWH-'ĕlohîm,* may be analogous to Akkadian practice, where the proper name of the god, e.g., Ash-shur, is preceded by the cuneiform sign *ilu,* god, indicating that the name following the sign is the name of a god. However, in the Hebrew the proper name precedes the general name. Yahweh may well mean "he causes to be." After the Exile, and in the period of the synagogue, the reader did not pronounce the divine name; *'ādôn,* lord, was substituted in the form *'ădonāy,* my Lord. Later, the consonantal text, Y-H-W-H, received the vowels of *'ădonāy,* ă(e)-o-ā, which gave the form Y(J)ehow(v)ah. The reader in the synagogue today never utters the divine name; *'ădonāy* is always read, accompanied by a bow of the head.

4B-7. The structure of these verses resembles that of the opening of the Akkadian epic, Enuma Elish:

> When on high the heaven had not been named,
> Firm ground below had not been called by name,
> Naught but primordial Apsu, their begetter . . .

> No reed hut had been matted, no marsh land had appeared,
> When no gods whatever had been brought into being,
> Uncalled by name, their destinies undetermined,
> Then it was that the gods were formed within them (ANET 60).

The when . . . then in both biblical and Mesopotamian accounts frame a series of negatives.

5. 'ĀDĀM. See note on 1:26.

6. HE MADE A STREAM RISE. The verb may be read as an imperfect, "a stream used to rise."

STREAM. *'ēd* occurs elsewhere only in Job 36:27. Albright (1939:102), Speiser (1964:16) and Pope (1965:235–36) have linked Hebrew *'ēd* with the Sumerian ID and the Akkadian *edû* which designates the subterranean waters or the primordial flood or river (Kramer 1961:99–100). N. J. Tromp (1969:22–23) has proposed the translation: " . . . for there was no man to till the ground and to lift the primordial river from the 'earth' and to water the whole surface of the ground." I would suggest rather: " . . . and there was no *'ādām* to work the ground; but the waters below, he (YHWH-God) brought up from the underworld so as to water the whole surface of the ground." *'ereṣ* as "underworld" is well attested in Mesopotamia and at Ugarit. Gunkel (1895) had noted this usage. Dahood (1981) has proposed "rain-cloud" for *'ēd* and renders verse 6: "So he made a rain cloud come up from the nether ocean, and it watered all the surface of the ground."

7. DUST. *'āpār* is the loose earth on the surface of the ground (ThWAT II, 353–56). The material that the potter uses is clay. Hence, the alleged potter metaphor is not to be pressed in this case. God can form, *yāṣār,* Israel (Isa 43:1, 7; 44:2, 24) and the course of history (Jer 18:11).

The theme of the human race made from dust or clay was known at all periods of biblical literature and in the ancient Near East. In an Akkadian version of the Epic of Gilgamesh at the turn of the second millennium we read:

> When Aruru heard this,
>   a double of Anu she conceived within her.
> Aruru washed her hands,
>   pinched off clay and cast it on the steppe.
> On the steppe she created valiant Enkidu (ANET 74:36–39).

And the old Babylonian version of the creation of man by the mother goddess in response to the cry of the gods to be relieved of their burden, reads:

> He who shall serve the gods,
> Let him be formed out of clay, be animated with blood
> (ANET 99:15–15).

The motif of the creation of the first man out of clay or dust or earth is known too among African tribes, even among those who have no knowledge of the art of pottery (Baumann 1936: 203–05). The theme has a long and widespread history.

8. GARDEN. The Hebrew word for garden is rendered in the LXX by *paradeisos,* a Persian word by origin.

EDEN. Millard (1984) proposes that Eden is a west semitic word, built on the root *ʿdn,* with the meaning "pleasure, luxury." Eden may be understood as "blissful Paradise of God." Cf. Ezekiel 28:11-19.

9. THE TREE OF LIFE. The tree of life is known from Assyrian bas-relief and seals as well as in Cretan art as a tree by running waters with two goats on either side eating its leaves (ANEP 619, 706). The motif recurs in both Old Testament and New Testament (Ezek 47:12; Prov 3:18; 11:30; 13:12; 15:4, where it is a symbol of success and happiness; Rev 2:7; 22:2, 14). See further James (1966); Wallace (1985: 101–41).

11. PISHON. The first river (Hebr. *pûš,* to burst forth) is often iden-tified with the Indus, but this is only a good guess. It flows around the land of Havilah (Gen 10:7, 29; 25:18; 1 Sam 15:7, an area in south and northeast Arabia). The Hebrew *ḥul* means sand. Arabia is traditionally the land of precious stones, ointments, and incense as well as of gold (Isa 60:5; Matt 2:11).

13. GIHON. The second river (Hebr. *giaḥ,* to bubble forth) encir-cles Cush, well known as the area of Nubia and Ethiopia. Hence it is identified with the Nile. Gihon is a bubbling spring of water near Jerusalem (1 Kgs 1:33-45).

14. TIGRIS. THE WORD IS *ḥiddeqel;* the river is known by this name in Akkadian; the old Persian is *tigrâ.*

EUPHRATES. Hebrew *pĕrat:* Akkadian *purattu;* old Persian *ūfratūs.* The Hebrew *bārād* means hail; Arabic *barat* means cold. The *pĕrat* (*bārād*) has its source in the high mountains in southeastern Turkey.

The geography here is not very accurate. The origins of the great rivers were something of a mystery to the people of the ancient world, and the sources of the Nile were discovered only in the second half of the nineteenth century (see the late Alan Moorehead's two en-thralling books, *The White Nile* and *The Blue Nile,* London: Ham-ish Hamilton, 1960, 1962). The White Nile has its sources in Lake Victoria and Lake Albert high up in Uganda, the Blue Nile in Lake

Tana in north central Ethiopia; they flow into each other between Khartoum and Omdurman in Sudan. The Tigris and the Euphrates both flow from the Kurdistan mountains in southeastern Turkey, their sources being not far apart. The Indus comes down from the western Himalayas. The imagery of the passage may owe something to the marsh areas in southern Iraq which surround the confluence of the Tigris and the Euphrates at Qurna. Many small tributaries flow into the two great rivers; the Arabs there live on small islands in reed huts and their normal means of transport is a small reed boat ("Reed-hut, reed-hut! Wall, wall! Reed-hut, harken! Wall, reflect"; the god Ea addresses Utnapishtim, the hero of the Babylonian flood story, in his hut on the marshes, ANET 92, Tablet ix, lines 21–22). The area is very green and lush (see the well written and well illustrated book of Wilfrid Thesiger, *The Marsh Arabs,* London: Longmans, Green, 1964 and the beautifully photographed volume of Gavin Young, *Return to the Marshes,* London: Collins, 1977). It has been in danger of destruction since September 1980. An unforgettable summer night sleeping under the moon and stars on the flat roof of a khan overlooking the confluence of the Tigris and Euphrates at Qurna after a journey across the marshes with very friendly Arabs will preserve the area for me.

17. IF YOU DO . . . YOU MUST DIE. *běyôm* does not mean "on the (very) day," but if or when (cf. 2:4b, When *běyôm* YHWH-God . . .). The formula *môt tāmût* (lit., dying you shall die) is derived from the legal codes of the Pentateuch where it denotes a capital offense; e.g., *môt yûmat,* dying, he shall be put to death, Leviticus 20 (nine times); Numbers 35 (five times).

18. A PARTNER EQUAL TO HIM. The Hebrew word *'ēzer* means help or, concretely, helper or savior. A cognate word in Ugaritic *ǵzr* means "youth, warrior" and the verb from the same radicals means "to be strong" (ThWAT II, 257). In Deuteronomy 33:26, 29, *'ēzer* is in parallelism with *ga'ǎwāh,* majesty, and is best understood as "strength." There may be nuances of that meaning in Genesis 2:18 (Freedman 1983). The combination of the preposition *neged,* "in front of, opposite to" with another preposition, *kě,* with the third person masculine singular pronominal suffix, *kěnegdô,* occurs only in Genesis 2:18 and 20 in the MT. BDB (617, *neged,* 2a) renders "a help corresponding to him, i.e., equal and adequate to himself." The meaning derives from the whole context of 2:18-23. *hā'ādām* could not see in the whole of the animal kingdom one that was *'ēzer*

kĕnegdô, i.e., a counterpart to stand before him as his equal, a partner equal to him. In verse 23, he recognizes that equality.

3:1. THE SERPENT. *nāḥāš:* the verb, used in the intensive or *pi'el* form, *niḥēš,* means to practice divination (e.g., Gen 44:5, 15). The bronze serpent that Moses made was known as Nehushtan (2 Kgs 18:4). In Egypt, the serpent played a role in magic (Exod 4:3-5; 7:8-13); it was also a symbol of wisdom and life, as it was in Mesopotamia. In Canaan, the serpent was the symbol of fertility; over recent decades hundreds of small (20-30 centimeters, 10-15 inches) clay figurines representing the fertility goddess, with a serpent around her neck and held by her two hands, have been discovered in Palestine. Plenty of Palestinian pottery has a serpent decoration on the handle. At Ain Samiyā, northeast of Rammallah, a silver cup was found in a tomb (c. 2250-2000 B.C.E.); it is decorated in two scenes, with a serpent in each; in the left hand area, an upright snake faces a janiform figure (i.e., a figure with two faces turned in opposite directions) with a human head and an ox-shaped body, each hand grasping a plant (Avi-Yonah 1975, II: 357-58). From Beth Shean, just south of the lake of Galilee, come cult stands from the eleventh century with the serpent motif entwining them. And Hazor, north of the lake, has given up a silver plated cult stand of bronze with two serpents upright (Avi-Yonah, 1975, II:477). The Canaanites of Palestine and the people of Israel who lived among them were very familiar with the serpent motif. But the serpent of Genesis does not represent any of these. Nevertheless, though the story of Genesis 2-3 is concerned with *hā'ādām,* the human race, and not primarily with Israel, the serpent would have evoked associations with the Canaanite fertility cult in the minds of Israelite listeners and readers.

15. ENMITY I PUT BETWEEN YOU AND THE WOMAN. This verse has been known since medieval and Reformation times as the *protoevangelium,* "the beginning of the gospel." Irenaeus of Lyons (d. c. 200), who was educated in the east, was the first to introduce the Eve-Mary antithesis. But many of the great Fathers of the Church comment on the verse without touching on its messianic, let alone its mariological, significance—in the east, Basil, Gregory of Nazianzen, Chrysostom; in the west, Ambrose, Augustine, Jerome, Gregory the Great (Drewniak 1934).

The Hebrew text reads literally.

Enmity I put between you and the woman,
between your seed (*zera'*) and her seed (*zera'*),
it (the seed) will *šûp* your head and you will *šûp* its heel.

The Hebrew *zera'*, seed, is masculine; hence the Hebrew pronoun, *hû'*, is masculine (there are only the two genders in Hebrew). The LXX renders the Hebrew *zera'* by *sperma*, which is neuter; it renders the Hebrew *hû'*, masculine, by *autos*, he, also masculine, and not by *auto*, it, neuter, in agreement with *sperma*. Hence there is a basis for a messianic interpretation. The Old Latin (OL), a translation of the LXX, read in the early Church, especially in northwest Africa, translates by *ipse*, he. The Vulgate reads *ipsa*, she.

At the time of Jerome's literary activity (380–420) very many Latin manuscripts read *ipsa*, feminine. But Jerome had before him the text: *"Ipse servabit caput tuum, tu servabis ejus calcaneum"* (he shall serve your head, you shall serve his heel); he adds at once that the Hebrew is better: *"Ipse conteret caput tuum, et tu conteres ejus calcaneum"* (he shall crush your head and you shall crush his heel). The Latin text continues: *quia et nostri gressus praepediuntur a colubro; et Dominus conteret Satanam sub pedibus nostris velociter"* (because our feet too are entangled by the snake, so the Lord will crush Satan quickly under our feet), (*Patrologia Latina* 23:991, *Liber Hebraicarum Quaestionum in Genesim*). It seems that *ipsa*, the feminine, consolidated its place in the Latin through the influence of Ambrose of Milan (339–397). Hence the basis for a mariological interpretation. The difficult Hebrew word *šûp* has been rendered crush, bruise, attack, snap at, pursue, strike at. The only other certain use of *šûp* is in Job 9:17: "He would crush with a tempest." It has been proposed that there are two words, *šûp*—grind, crush, bruise—and a by-form of it—*šā'ap*—snap at, seek after—and that both meanings are present (Westermann 1984:259-60). W. von Soden has contested this (1981); he maintains that *šā'ap* is not a variant of *šûp;* he renders "strongly attack."

24. CHERUBIM: Akkadian *kâribu* or *kârubi*. The cherubim of Assyria were enormous composite beings with the body of a lion or bull, wings, and a human face. Their form varied at different stages of Mesopotamian civilization. They may be seen in the National Museum in Baghdad, the Louvre in Paris, and the British Museum in London. The cherubim that guarded the ark of the covenant in Solomon's temple are described in 1 Kings 6:23-28. They were made of olive wood overlaid with gold, and were about five meters (twenty

feet) high with a total wing span of about ten meters (thirty-six feet). Yahweh as it were sat enthroned invisibly on the "mercy seat" formed by the wings of the two cherubim touching tip to tip. Yahweh is said to have "rode on a cherub and flew; he came swiftly on the wings of the wind" (Ps 18:11 [10]); he is "the rider on the clouds" (Ps 68:5 [4]). The background imagery is from the Ugaritic mythology of Baal and Anat (ANET 132; iii, 10–11). R. S. Hendel (1985) has proposed that the passage about the cherubim be rendered: YHWH-God stationed "the cherubim and the flame of the whirling sword to guard the way to the tree of life." The flame would then be "an animate divine being, a member of Yahweh's divine host, similar in status to the cherubim; the 'whirling sword' is its appropriate weapon, ever-moving, like the flame itself."

5. ". . . The Primal Eldest Curse . . . A Brother's Murder" (Hamlet III, 2) (4:1-16)

[1]Now *hā'ādām* knew his wife Eve and she conceived and bore Cain and said: I have created a man together with YHWH.

[2]And she also bore his brother Abel. Now Abel was a shepherd of sheep and Cain was a worker of the ground. [3]In the course of time, Cain brought the produce of the ground as an offering to YHWH. [4]And Abel too brought from the choicest of the firstborn of his flock. And YHWH looked with favor on Abel and his offering; [5]but on Cain and his offering he did not look with favor; and Cain was very angry and his face fell. [6]And YHWH said to Cain: Why are you angry and why has your face fallen? [7]Surely, if you do good—acceptance, but if you do not do good—sin is a lurker at the door and is intent on you, but you must master it.

[8]Cain said to his brother Abel: Let us go out into the field. When they were out in the field, Cain attacked his brother Abel and killed him. [9]Then YHWH said to Cain: Where is your brother Abel? But Cain said: I don't know! Am I my brother's keeper? [10]And he said: What have you done? The voice of the blood of your brother is crying out to me from the ground. [11]Cursed then are you from the ground that has opened its mouth to receive the blood of your brother from your hand. [12]When you work the ground, it shall no more yield its produce; you shall be a restless wanderer on the earth. [13]Cain said to YHWH: My punishment is too great to bear. [14]Now that you have driven me from the ground and your presence, I shall hide myself from you and become a restless wanderer on the earth, and anyone

who finds me will kill me. ¹⁵But YHWH said to him: Not so! If anyone kills Cain he shall be avenged sevenfold; so YHWH put a mark on him lest anyone who should come across him kill him. ¹⁶And Cain went from YHWH's presence and settled in the land of Nod, to the east of Eden.

Comment

This unit or episode defines itself clearly in the biblical text. That there was an independent story about two brothers, one of whom killed the other, is beyond doubt, though we do not know precisely what form it took. Agriculture and cattle breeding were advanced, there were others around who might take vengeance on Cain and, in the following unit, verses 17-26, a wife was available for Cain who could build a city and name it after his firstborn. Whatever the form of the story, it is now drawn into primeval time as the story of the first brothers without any attempt to smooth out what are to us, heirs of enlightenment and historical science, incongruities. The story is about *hā'ādām*. It begins, "Now *hā'ādām . . . ,*" the *hā'ādām* who was driven out of the garden (3:24). The narrative moves through tension verses 3-7, to climax verses 8-12, and resolution, verses 13-16, grim and gloomy though the resolution is.

hā'ādām "knew" (see *Notes*) his wife. The word used here for create, *qānāh*, often means acquire. Eve rejoices that she has done this with YHWH. I see no sign of any *hybris* in her cry. The name Cain, *qayin*, is a play on *qānāh*. Eve calls her baby son *'îsh*, a man seeing in him the future man. The second son is Abel, *hebel*, which means a vapor or mist that is dispersed quickly. "*'ādām* is like a *hebel*, his days like a passing shadow" (Ps 144:4). It is the "vanity of vanities," *hăbēl hăbālîm*, of Qohelet (1:2). Abel (this is the only occasion in the Bible that *hebel* is used as a proper name) is "a passing shadow"; he is the brother (v. 2); his brother twice, my brother once, your brother three times (vv. 8-11). Abel was the brother who was born, was a shepherd, was murdered by his brother. No more.

The brothers offer sacrifice. The offering of the fruits of the flock and the field are the shepherd's and the farmer's spontaneous response to the effects of God's blessing at work in creation. There is no institution of sacrifice by God.

Sacrifice is the essential act of external worship. It is prayer which is acted, a symbolic action which expresses both the interior of the person offering it, and God's response to this prayer . . . it is essential that the external action should express the true inward feelings of man, and that it should be favorably received by God. Failing this, sacrifice is no longer a religious act (de Vaux 1961:451).

The biblical text says nothing of the interior dispositions of the brothers nor of the reason why the sacrifice of the one was accepted and of the other rejected. The early Church reflected further on Cain and his dispositions (Matt 23:35; 1 John 3:12; Heb 11:4; 12:24; Jude 11). The interpretations in each case run parallel to late rabbinic interpretations in which Abel is presented as the just one and Cain as the evil one. The story states simply acceptance and non-acceptance, though something may be implied in verse 7. Cain's reaction is natural. He now stands angry between self-mastery and being mastered (cf. Job 11:13-16). Sin is a lurker or croucher at the door, its intent set on him. Cain has been warned. He is responsible for his actions.

The narrative hastens to its climax. Not a word is wasted. The murder is committed. The interrogation, the declaration, and the punishment rise in an unbroken crescendo, echoing and even drowning out 3:9-13. Cain takes cover under a lie. But nothing can be hidden from the all-seeing eye of God. " . . . the voice of the blood of your brother is crying out *to me* from the ground" (v. 10); "for the life of the flesh is in the blood" (Lev 17:11; cf. Gen 9:4; Lev 7:26; Deut 12:23), and " . . . blood pollutes the land, and no expiation can be made for the land, for the blood that is shed in it, except by the blood of him who shed it" (Num 35:33). Cain is cursed or banned from that very ground that has drunk a brother's blood— *'ădāmāh,* is repeated three times in verses 10-12. Cain has shed blood, taken life; the blood, the life in it, cries out for vengeance. But vengeance is reserved to God (v. 15). Murder is forever the murder of a brother/sister. Banned from the ground, Cain is to be a restless wanderer, literally a staggerer, *nā',* and a wanderer *nād* (both participles); Cain, a wanderer, *nād,* is to live in the land of Nod (v. 16). Cain's punishment is too great to bear; *'āwôn* means punishment, guilt, and sin; punishment is to the fore here, with connotations of the other two. In the midst of Cain's despair, God intervenes with a protecting mark which he puts on Cain. We do not know what form the mark took. It was put on Cain personally, as he alone was responsible for the murder, and it was a protecting sign so that Cain should not be "open season" to all. Vengeance is God's (to be defied by Lamech in vv. 23-24). Cain is at the same time under God's curse (v. 11) and protection (v. 15). He is a murderer; but no one may usurp God's prerogative over life. He is to live "east of Eden," a life alienated from God. One can as much locate Nod and "east of Eden" as one can Eden itself. We are in primeval time. The story follows the same pattern as chapters 2–3. Life comes from and belongs to God (v. 1) who has dominion over *hā'ādām;* Cain takes life, transgresses a limit, usurps God's right; God intervenes with punishment and protection. It is crime and punishment again. The trial of Cain with the interrogation (4:9-12) runs parallel to the trial and interrogation of the man and the woman in 3:9-19.

Notes

1. KNEW. As we saw in 3:5, to know in Hebrew is not just an intellectual exercise; it is empirical, experiential, and often involves the whole person. It is used therefore at times to describe sexual relations. But this use must not be exaggerated. *yd'* occurs 1068 times in the Hebrew text (fifty-one times in the Aramaic sections) of the Bible (ThHAT, I, 682–701). It refers to sexual relations seventeen times, i.e., approximately 0.6 percent, scarcely a regular word to describe the act: five times it is used of normal relations between husband and wife (Gen 4:1, 17, 25; 24:16; 1 Sam 1:19); six times of those who have or have not had intercourse (Num 31:17, 18, 35; Judg 11:39; 27:11, 12); two times of sodomy (Gen 19:5; Judg 19:22); one time of David's impotence in old age (1 Kgs 1:4); one time in reference to Judah and Tamar (Gen 38:26); two times of abusing a woman (Gen 19:18; Judg 19:25).

2. I HAVE CREATED. The word *qānāh* means gain, acquire, and sometimes create, e.g., Genesis 14:19, 22; Exodus 15:16; Psalms 78:54; 139:13; a Ugaritic cognate is *qnj* = create (see further discussion in note on 14:19-20). *qānāh* is a play on the name Cain, *qayin*. Cain is the eponymous ancestor of the tribe known as the Kenites; the link is obvious when the names are written in transliteration of the Hebrew characters—Cain is *qayin*, Kenite is *qênî*, Moses' mother was a Kenite (Judg 1:16, LXX), the daughter of Hobab (Judg 4:11). The Kenites were a non-Israelite clan closely associated with Judah. They settled with Judah in the region of Arad to the east of Beer-sheba and remained always friendly with the Israelites. There was a town of Judah named Cain (Josh 15:27). According to 1 Chronicles 2:55, the Rechabites, fervent Yahwists (2 Kgs 10:15-27;

Jer 35:1-11), were descendants of the Kenites. But there is no sign that the Kenites were worshippers of Yahweh. The word *qayin* seems to be associated with the trade of the smith. Long before the story of Cain was given its biblical form, many associations had accumulated around his name: he was the first murderer, the founder of a city, the ancestor of those from whom many streams of civilization originated (4:17-22).

3. OFFERING. *minḥâ,* later a technical sacrificial term for a grain offering.

7. A LURKER. *robēṣ,* a participle, "crouching"; an animal ready to spring. The word for sin *ḥaṭā't* is feminine, the participle is masculine. The root *rbṣ* has been linked with the Assyrian *rabiṣu,* a demon (Gressmann 1928:26).

8. CAIN SAID . . . LET US GO OUT INTO THE FIELD. The words "let us . . . field" are missing from the Hebrew text, but are supplied from the LXX, other Greek versions, the Samaritan, the Syriac, and the Vulgate. Dahood (1977) has proposed that the Hebrew word *'mr,* said, be understood in the light of the attested Ugaritic *'amr,* see, and that verse 8 be read: "Qayin was watching for his brother Abel." In this case, there is no need to supply a missing half-verse. Dahood quotes the Lexicon of Brown-Driver-Briggs (1907:56a, end of column) which proposed several cases where *'mr* is better understood as "to think, expect;" thence "to look at, aim."

6. The Beginnings of Civilization and The Song of the Sword (J. G. Herder) (4:17-26)

[17]Now Cain knew his wife and she conceived and bore Enoch; and he built a city and called the name of the city by the name of his son, Enoch. [18]To Enoch was born Irad, and Irad begot Mehujael, and Mehujael begot Methushael, and Methushael begot Lamech. [19]Now Lamech took two wives, the name of the one was Adah and the name of the other was Zillah. [20]Adah bore Jabal, the father of the tent-dweller and cattle breeder. [21]The name of his brother was Jubal, and he was the father of all who play the lyre and the flute. [22]And Zillah too, she bore Tubal-cain, the forger of all instruments of bronze and iron.

²³Lamech said to his wives:
Adah and Zillah, listen to my cry;
Wives of Lamech, give ear to my word:
Yes, I have slain a man for wounding me,
a youth for striking me;
²⁴If Cain is avenged seven-fold,
then Lamech seventy-seven-fold!

²⁵Adam knew his wife again and she bore him a son and she called his name Seth because "God has appointed me another child in place of Abel, because Cain slew him." ²⁶To Seth too a son was born and he called his name Enosh. At that time they began to call on the name of YHWH.

Comment

The passage contains a broken genealogy in both the direct and collateral lines (vv. 17-22, 25-26a), a two verse song of vengeance (vv. 23-24), and a statement about worship in the early stages of the human race (v. 26b). There are seven generations in the primeval period—Adam, Cain, Enoch, Irad, Mehujael, Methushael, Lamech (vv. 17-18); Seth and Enosh appear in (vv. 25-26). These are all in the direct line. With Lamech, the genealogy moves into the collateral line through his two wives Adah and Zillah (vv. 19-22).

Civilization had begun with Cain and Abel who initiated farming and cattle breeding. Cain founded the first city. His descendants through Lamech made further advances. Adah's two sons Jabal and Jubal were the fathers of Bedouin or "semi-nomadic" life and music respectively; Zillah's son Tubal-cain was the first to work in iron and bronze, and her daughter Naamah (*na'ămâ*), a feminine formation from a verb *nā'ēm,* was the pleasant, lovely, or delightful one. The history of human development is a necessary part of human history in the historical understanding of the writer. Israel was the heir to these advances begun in primeval time. It was from the human race that civilization began, not from a special intervention of the gods (see note on vv. 20-22). It is *hā'ādām* who, following the command to subdue the earth (Gen 1:28), initiates everything in the world into which he has been put by God. Abel was the first shepherd and Cain the first farmer (4:1-2); Cain the first city builder (4:17); Jabal was the first of those who lived in tents with flocks and his brother Jubal was the first harpist and flautist (4:20-21); Tubal-cain was the first to forge in iron and bronze (4:22); Noah was the first to plant the vine (9:20); and Nimrod was the first hunter (10:8-9). *hā'ādām* of the biblical book of origins is already liberated and secularized. The earth, the universe, is his; and he must control it and search out its secrets.

These very brief narrative notes within the genealogies would probably have existed independently of the flood story. What happened to civilization with the flood? As all was wiped out, all would have to begin again. The difficulty would only arise when the notes and the flood story were brought together.

The cry of vengeance of Lamech (vv. 23-24) may, with 6:1-4 and 9:20-27, be included under "further transgressions." It is rather loosely connected with what has gone before. It deals with vengeance in general and its original setting was most likely the boast of a man before his wife that his honor will be maintained. In the context of the primeval story, Lamech shouts defiance at God, usurps God's position (4:15); the "song" points to the dire consequences of the murder of a brother.

The linear genealogy of *hā'ādām,* interrupted after the birth of Abel (4:2), is resumed in verse 25 with another word play. The Hebrew *šāt* means "he put, constituted, appointed"; hence the third son, to replace Abel, is S(h)eth who, with the next son, Enosh, brings the number of generations to nine. The writer says in conclusion that religion, the worship of God, began with the beginning of the race, verse 26b. Something is happening between God and the human person. The divine name, YHWH, was revealed to Moses (Exod 3:1-15; 6:2-3). For the writer, the cult of the one true God was there from the origins.

Notes

20. THE FATHER OF THE TENT-DWELLER. In the Bible, the human race is the initiator of all progress in civilization. It is quite different in other parts of the ancient Near East. In the Sumerian myths, for example, the god not only creates the universe and the human race, but also supplied the race with cultivated land, artificial irrigation, and the tools of the farmer and the craftsman. The god Enlil creates two gods to take care of the watering and the grain, and supply fresh water. There is also a myth of the creation of the pickaxe (Kramer 1963:151; 1972:15; Pettinato 1971:74–79; Westermann 1984:56–60, 326–34, 341–42).

25. ADAM. As this is a genealogical fragment, '*ādām* is used as a proper name for the first time by the storyteller. BHS proposes that the definite article, *hā*, be read with '*ādām*.

7. From Adam to the Flood
(5:1-32)

¹This is the book of the descendants of Adam.
When God created '*ādām* he made it in the likeness of God.
²Male and female he created them and he blessed them
and called their name '*ādām* when they were created.

³When Adam had lived one hundred and thirty years, he begot (a son)
in his likeness and image and called his name Seth.
⁴After the birth of Seth, Adam lived eight hundred years,
        and begot sons and daughters.
⁵So Adam's life spanned nine hundred and thirty years.
        And he died.

⁶When Seth had lived one hundred and five years, he begot Enosh.
⁷After the birth of Enosh, Seth lived eight hundred and seven years,
        and begot sons and daughters.
⁸So Seth's life spanned nine hundred and twelve years.
        And he died.

⁹When Enosh had lived ninety years, he begot Kenan.
¹⁰After the birth of Kenan, Enosh lived eight hundred and fifteen
    years,
        and begot sons and daughters.
¹¹So Enosh's life spanned nine hundred and five years.
        And he died.

¹²When Kenan had lived seventy years, he begot Mahalalel.
¹³After the birth of Mahalalel, Kenan lived eight hundred and forty
    years,
        and begot sons and daughters.
¹⁴So Kenan's life spanned nine hundred and ten years.
        And he died.

¹⁵When Mahalalel had lived sixty-five years, he begot Jared.
¹⁶After the birth of Jared, Mahalalel lived eight hundred and thirty
    years,
        and begot sons and daughters.
¹⁷So Mahalalel's life spanned eight hundred and ninety-five years.
        And he died.

¹⁸When Jared had lived one hundred and sixty-two years, he begot Enoch.

¹⁹After the birth of Enoch, Jared lived eight hundred years,
and begot sons and daughters.

²⁰So Jared's life spanned nine hundred and sixty-two years.
And he died.

²¹When Enoch had lived sixty-five years, he begot Methuselah.

²²After the birth of Methuselah, Enoch walked with God three hundred years,
and begot sons and daughters.

²³So Enoch's life spanned three hundred and sixty-five years.

²⁴And Enoch walked with God, and he was no more, because God took him.

²⁵When Methuselah had lived one hundred and eighty-seven years, he begot Lamech.

²⁶After the birth of Lamech, Methuselah lived seven hundred and eighty-two years
and begot sons and daughters.

²⁷So Methuselah's life spanned nine hundred and sixty-nine years.
And he died.

²⁸When Lamech had lived one hundred and eighty-two years, he begot a son

²⁹and called his name Noah, saying: This one shall bring us relief from our work and the toil of our hands from the ground that YHWH has cursed.

³⁰After the birth of Noah, Lamech lived five hundred and ninety-five years,
and begot sons and daughters.

³¹So Lamech's life spanned seven hundred and seventy-seven years.
And he died.

³²After Noah became five hundred years, he begot Shem, Ham, and Japheth.

Comment

The priestly account of the beginnings continues in chapter 5 with a list of the descendants of Adam in ten generations. In verses 1a and 3a, *'ādām* is used for the first time as a proper name in the priestly writing. Verses 1b-3 resume the language of 1:26-27 and 2:4a. God created (*bārā*) *'ādām* (1:27; 5:1b) in his likeness (*děmût,* 1:26; 5:1b); "male and female he created them and blessed them" (1:27c-28a; 5:2a); "when they were created" (lit., in their having been created, *hibbārĕ'ām,* 2:4a; 5:2b); "in our image and likeness" (1:26) and "in his likeness and image" (5:3b), the prepositions *bĕ* and *kĕ* being interchanged (see comment on 1:26).

The genealogy of the ten "begetters" before the flood follows a strict pattern:

When (patriarch) A had lived x years, he begot (patriarch) B.
After the birth of B, A lived x years, and begot sons and daughters.
A's life spanned X + X years. And he died.

There are additions in the cases of Adam, Enoch, and Lamech. Adam begot "(a son) in his likeness and image and called his name. . . . " (v. 3b); "Enoch walked with God . . . and Enoch walked with God, and he was no more, because God took him" (vv. 22b, 24); Lamech begot "a son and called his name Noah, saying: This one shall bring us relief from our work and the toil of our hands from the ground that YHWH has cursed" (v. 29; cf. 3:17). If these verses are removed temporarily (simply for the purpose of the exercise, of course, for they belong to the text), the pattern remains fixed. The Noah pattern, which is slightly different, is split after 5:32. The accounts of the flood, the covenant, and Ham's impiety are inserted (6:1-4 + 6:5-9:7; 9:8-17; 9:18-27) and Noah's life span is resumed in 9:28-29. So we have:

5:32   After Noah became five hundred years, he begot Shem, Ham, and Japheth.
9:28   After the flood, Noah lived three hundred and fifty years.
9:29   Noah's life in all spanned nine hundred and fifty years.
           And he died.

The comment on Lamech in verse 29 accords more with the storyteller; the name YHWH is used and the verse refers back to 3:17 and looks forward to 9:20-21. As for Enoch, verses 21-24, he did not die in the way of mortals. After a life which was short in comparison with the other patriarchs of chapter 5, a mere 365 years, God took him. The tradition has it that one day he was not around anymore. He had "walked with God" (vv. 22, 24), as did Noah later (6:9b). Are there two different traditions about Enoch? " . . . he was no more" and "God took him." One who walked with God was just and righteous (Ps 1).

The main interest in chapter 5 is all too often the great ages of the patriarchs, their names, and the relationship of the genealogy to the Babylonian king lists (see *Notes*). These interests have their place, but are not the main concern of the biblical writer. The function of verses 1-5 is to tie the generations from Adam to Noah to the creation of the human race. The writer is looking at the unity of the race which stems from the first man and woman, and the effective working out in time of the blessing bestowed on them at creation (1:28). This blessing is repeated at the "new creation" after the flood (9:1, 7). *hā'ādām* is not just created and left. God's creative power continues in the blessing which enables the couple and their progeny to extend themselves in time. There are two basic elements in the genealogy, the constant and the variable. The constant comprises the begetting, the length of life before and after the first son, more sons and daughters, and "he died" (even the hero of the flood, Noah, 9:29). The monotonous formulas hammer home the fate of each person, just as the repeated formulas in chapter 1 hammer home the effective action of the word of God. The variable consists in the succession of different names and numbers. The constant and the variable are woven together in the course of human life. The priestly writer, whose goal is the erection of the holy place in Jerusalem, looks back to the creator, the creation, and the creation blessing and sees the human race deriving from it.

The first three names in the genealogy of chapter 5, Adam-Seth-Enosh, are the last three in chapter 4. The remaining seven names in the genealogies of both chapters correspond to each other, with variations in spelling and two variations in order (Enoch is the fifth in the succession in 4:17, but the seventh in 5:21; Mehujael is the seventh in 4:18 and Mahalalel [a variation] the fifth in 5:15). Cain (*qayin,* 4:17) and Kenan (*qênān,* 5:12) are variants, as are Methushael (4:18) and Methuselah (5:25), and Irad (4:18) and Jared (5:18). Noah of 5:29 belongs to a different genealogy. Both the storyteller and the priestly writer had before them a common tradition of ten patriarchs who preceded the flood and each used it for his own purposes.

Notes

1. BOOK OF THE DESCENDANTS. *tôlĕdôt,* cf. 2:4a. The function of genealogies in anthropology, and the application to the biblical world, has been studied by Wilson (1975; 1978) and Johnson (1969); see also Westermann (1984:6–18).

Gunkel (1910:131–37), relying on documents available at the beginning of the century, linked the number of generations in Genesis 5 (ten) with the number of generations before the flood in the Old Babylonian King Lists. He also looked for philological connections between the names. But much material has been discovered since that time. It is now questioned whether the Babylonian king lists before and after the flood form a unity; they may well have been combined later. The names in the king lists are now known to be Sumerian and have no connection with the biblical names. The context of the Babylonian lists is historical-political and is concerned with "after kingship had descended from heaven" (Kramer 1963:43–52, 328–31); the biblical context is genealogical (Westermann 1984:347–54). Both the king lists and the genealogy of Genesis 5 are set in primeval time or "before history." The length of the reigns of the Babylonian kings is astronomical—"In Eridu Alulim reigned 28,800 years as king; Alalgar reigned 36,000 years . . . " The great ages of the biblical pre-flood patriarchs, young compared with the primeval Babylonian kings, are a puzzle. And to compound the puzzle, the numbers from the creation to the flood when added up in the different versions, do not agree: the Hebrew text amounts to 1656 years, the Septuagint to 2242, and the Samaritan Pentateuch to 1307 (Westermann 1984:352; Vawter 1977:107). No conclusions follow from exercises in addition and subtraction of these numbers and, as Vawter (1977:108) has noted, "there are other pursuits more rewarding."

21. ENOCH. The mysterious fate of Enoch has given rise to a considerable amount of intertestamental literature extant mainly in Ethiopic (more than forty manuscripts of 1 Enoch are known), with substantial portions in Greek, and fragments in Aramaic from cave four of Qumran (Milik 1976; Knibb 1978; Isaac 1983; Black 1985).

29. NOAH. The meaning of *noaḥ* is uncertain; comfort or console is probably nearest. The verb with its pronominal suffix, *yĕnaḥăm-ēnû*, has been rendered "shall bring us relief"; Psalm 104:15 speaks of wine which "brings joy to or comforts," *yĕśammaḥ,* the heart of a man (cf. 9:20-21); Noah discovers wine and its effects.

8. Introduction to the Flood.
The Corruption of the Race
(6:1-8)

¹When *hā'ādām* began to increase over the face of the ground, daughters were born to them. ²The sons of the gods saw how beautiful the daughters of *hā'ādām* were and took to themselves wives from them

as they chose. ³And YHWH said: My spirit shall not remain in *hā-'ādām* forever inasmuch as it is flesh; its days shall be a hundred and twenty years. ⁴The giants were on the earth in those days; now after the sons of the gods went to the daughters of *hā'ādām,* they bore children to them; these were the warriors who were the men of renown of old.

⁵Now YHWH saw how great was the evil of *hā'ādām* on the earth and that the whole drive of its planning and striving was continually but evil. ⁶YHWH repented that he had made *hā'ādām* on the earth and was grieved to the heart. ⁷YHWH said: I will wipe out *hā'ādām* that I have created from the face of the ground, from *'ādām* to beast, to reptile, to bird of the sky, because I repent that I have made them. ⁸But Noah found favor in the eyes of YHWH.

Comment

An account of the general corruption of the race precedes the story of the flood.

Verses 1-4 are another story about *hā'ādām. hā'ādām* began to increase over the *'ādāmâ* and daughters were born to them (v. 1), just as in 1:26 God said "let us make *'ādām* . . . and let *them* rule . . ." Together with 4:23-24 and 9:20-27 the story can be grouped under the heading of "further transgressions." These four verses are not part of the traditional flood material from Mesopotamia where no parallel to them appears. Rather, the writer uses a myth or a mythical fragment, perhaps from Canaanite sources, and adapts it to his own purposes. It is likely that the myth gave an account of the origin of the giants, the *nĕphilîm* (v. 4; Num 13:33) or the heroes or warriors of old. Gunkel (1910:1xvi) describes the text as it stands as a "mythological torso." There is something substantial, but many important elements are missing. It is as though a classical archaeologist had discovered on an Aegean island the torso of a statue bereft of head, arms, and legs. Again, there is something substantial, but important pieces are missing. The archaeologist would not know whether the subject was Poseidon or Apollo, or whether it was hurling a thunderbolt or raising its arms in supplication. Neverthless, the four times repeated *hā'ādām* (twice in the combination "daughters of *hā'ādām*") and the redactor's own verse 3 give us the clues to some understanding of the passage. "Sons of the gods (or, of god)," i.e., divine beings, unite with completely human females, "daughters of *hā'ādām*." In Greek mythology, Heaven and

Earth (*Ouranos* and *Gē*) united to give birth to the Titans. The divine beings used force; they "took to themselves wives from them as they chose" (v. 26). The women then bore children to them (v. 4b). Even though the sons of the gods were the aggressors, the biblical writer understood this mingling of the divine and the human as a grasp at immortality on the human side and so he has YHWH intervene (v. 3). "My spirit," that is, the breath of life breathed into the human being at creation (2:7), shall not remain in *hā'ādām* forever (*lě'ōlām*). There was already the danger that the human race might reach beyond itself for immortality, the prerogative of God (3:22). But its life span is now limited to three generations, a hundred and twenty years (3 x 40), inasmuch as the race is flesh (*bāśār*). The question at issue is immortality. Petersen (1979:59, 56–67) has written that the story "depicts Yahweh as acting arbitrarily so as to emphasize his goodness in contra-distinction to humanity which had, for a moment, acquired the potential to live *lě'ōlām* . . . the author used another language, that of arbitrary action, to emphasize Yahweh's Godhead," and that "what is crucial is not humanity's morality, but its immortality." But *hā'ādām* is not God (1:26-27; 2:4b-7, 16-17), and must live within the limitations of one's being which, for *hā'ādām*, "not-God," does not include immortality. There is no sign of any arbitrary action on God's part, nor that *hā-'ādām* had, even for a moment, "acquired the potential to live *lě'ōl-ām*." *hā'ādām* was striving for something that was God's, and only God's. The question of proper bounds, and so morality, runs right through Genesis 1-11—(2:4b-3:24; 4:1-16; 6:5-8; 9:20-22; 11:1-9)—and 6:1-4 is set in the middle of all this.

The children born of the union of the divine and the human (v. 4b) were the warriors, i.e., the men of renown of old (v. 4c); it is not said that these are the giants (v. 4a). Verse 4b, "now after the sons of god went to the daughters of *hā'ādām*, they bore children to them," describes an action and follows easily after verse 2. Verses 4a and 4c are statements; the *něphilîm* were around at that time (v. 4a); the offspring of the sons of God and the daughters of *hā'ādām* were the ancient heroes (v. 4c)—the equivalent of the Titans, the offspring of *Ouranos* and *Gē* (?).

There are overtones to the story which would have evoked associations as it impinged on Israelite ears. The Old Testament, in particular the Deuteronomic and Deuteronomistic writers and the prophets, condemned cultic prostitution which was practiced by the Canaanites and which perverted Israelite religious practice through history. The union with the cultic prostitutes, male and female (2 Kgs 23:5-8), was a union with the divine. But Israel's meeting with the divine was in the covenant and God's acts in history. The story as it comes from the biblical writer is not directed immediately at cultic prostitution; but the associations are inevitable. The writer is using the material at hand to him as an example of complete corruption that leads to the flood (6:5-8).

The biblically edited "mythological torso" tells that *hā'ādām* began to increase (*rob*) over the face of the ground. Verses 5-8 narrate in general terms that the wickedness of *hā'ādām* was great (*rābāh,* v. 5). The spread of the human race over the face of the ground means the spread of wickedness; the two are linked (vv. 1 and 7). The whole bent of *hā'ādām,* "its planning and striving" (v. 5), is towards evil. The writer underscores the wickedness of *hā'ādām* and this, in the biblical perspective, leads to the decision of YHWH to wipe out the race. YHWH reflects: " . . . I will wipe out *hā'ādām* that I have created (*bārā'*) . . . ," taking up the language of 1:27; *hā'ādām* is to be wiped from the face of the *'ādāmâ* out of which it was made (2:7; 3:19, 23). YHWH repents that he had made (*'āśāh,* vv. 6, 7) *hā'ādām.* The biblical flood story is tied to the creation story. But this raises a problem. God has created; now he destroys his creation. Why? God acts on and reacts to the human race (Westermann 1984:409-11). Wickedness has spread over the earth through the human race; punishment must be coterminous with it. The animals are taken up into the punishment not because they are guilty but because they are associated intimately and inseparably with *hā'ādām* in life on earth (1:28; 2:18-20). The words of verse 5 about the tendency of *hā'ādām* to evil are resumed at the end of the catastrophe when YHWH gives assurance of permanent stability in the cycle of nature (8:20-22). The story of the flood is set within an inclusion (6:5 and 8:21) that underlines the tendency to evil in *hā'ādām* which remains the same before and after. Noah found favor with YHWH (6:8); as we shall see, he was *ṣaddîq,* just (6:9; 7:1).

Notes

2. THE SONS OF THE GODS. The *běnê 'elohîm,* the sons of (the) god(s), are divine beings, those who are of the realm of the gods, who partake of divinity (Cooke 1964:24). They appear in the Old Testament as members of the heavenly court or council or as divine messengers (Gen 28:12; 1 Kgs 22:19-22; Job 1:6; 2:1; 38:7; Pss 29:1;

82:1,6; 89:7 [6]). In the history of exegesis they are angels (*Book of Enoch,* Knibb 1978), the sons of Seth (Augustine), sons of the overlords or nobles who took by force the young girls among the common people (*'ādām*) who took their fancy (J. J. Astruc 1753), the males in general of the human race (Closen 1937), the *bn ilm* of Ugarit, i.e., the "heroes" or mighty warriors of old (Dexinger 1966). The influence of Augustine on the identity of the actors in the story, and hence on the general interpretation, has been lasting. The sons of God were the sons of Seth. The daughters of men were "the women who had been depraved in morals in the earthly city, that is, in the community of the earth-born, were loved for their physical beauty by the sons of God, that is, the citizens of the other City, on pilgrimage in this world. Such beauty is certainly a good, a gift of God; but he bestows it on the evil as well as on the good for this reason, for fear that the good may consider it an important good." The sons of Seth, good, were corrupted by the daughters of Cain, depraved (*City of God,* bk. 15, chs. 22–23). The Church Fathers after Augustine adopted this interpretation. Many of the Fathers who preceded him, e.g., Justin, Cyprian, Ambrose, understood the "sons of God" in this passage as the bad or fallen angels. When the spiritual nature of these beings was better understood, this interpretation was abandoned. The vast literature on the subject may be found in Cooke (1964), Dexinger (1966), JSOT (1979), Westermann (1984:363–64).

3. SHALL NOT REMAIN. *yādôn.* BDB lists the word under *dîn* with the note that "will not abide" best suits the context. The LXX reads *ou mē katameinē,* and the Vulgate, *non permanebit,* both following this interpretation.

INASMUCH AS. The Hebrew *bĕšagām* is very uncertain. It may be analyzed as: *bĕ,* a preposition, because (?), *š,* a relative (though *š* as an abbreviation of the regular relative *'ăšer* is not attested in the Pentateuch), *gām,* adverb, also—"because he is also." The LXX reads, *dia to einai autous sarkas,* "because of them being flesh;" the Vulgate, *quia caro est,* "because he is flesh."

A HUNDRED AND TWENTY YEARS. Moses died at 120 (Deut 34:7). Herodotus (III, 23) says of the Ethiopians that "most of them lived to be a hundred and twenty, and some even more, and that they ate boiled meat and drank milk."

4. THE GIANTS. *nĕphilîm.* One may note Astruc's (cf. note on v. 2) interpretation: the *nĕphilîm* are thieves and robbers who are usually begotten by the overlords (sons of god) on their wanderings.

5. DRIVE OF ITS PLANNING AND STRIVING. (Westermann 1984:410). The Hebrew reads literally: " . . . the frame of the thoughts of his heart were only evil always." The RSV renders: " . . . every imagination of the thoughts of his heart was only evil continually." The noun *yēṣer* (the verb *yāṣār* means to form or fashion, cf. 2:7), framing, form, purpose, comes to mean a steadfast purpose or a frame of mind. *yēṣer* and the word for thought, *maḥăshābâ,* mean practically the same.

9. The Flood
(6:9-9:17)

⁹This is the story of Noah. Noah was a fully just man in his era; Noah walked with God. ¹⁰Noah begot three sons, Shem, Ham, and Japheth. ¹¹Now the earth was corrupt before God and the earth was full of violence. ¹²God saw how corrupt the earth was and that all flesh had corrupted its way upon the earth. ¹³God said to Noah: The end of all flesh has come before me because the earth is full of violence because of it (lit., them); I will destroy it (lit., them) with the earth. ¹⁴Make yourself an ark of teak wood; of reeds make the ark, and cover it inside and outside with pitch. ¹⁵Make it in this way: its length three hundred cubits, its breadth fifty cubits, its height thirty cubits. ¹⁶Make a roof for the ark and extend it out a cubit from the top, put a door in the side of the ark, and make a lower and a second and a third floor. ¹⁷And I am going to bring the flood waters upon the earth so as to destroy all flesh that has the breath of life in it under heaven; everything on the earth will perish. ¹⁸But I am establishing my covenant with you and you will go into the ark together with your sons and your wife and the wives of your sons. ¹⁹Bring into the ark with you two of all living beings of all flesh, male and female, to keep them alive with you, ²⁰birds of every kind and animals of every kind and every reptile of the ground of every kind—two of every kind shall go in to you to keep them alive. ²¹And you, take with you every kind of food that is eaten and store it up for yourself; it will be food for you and them. ²²And Noah did exactly all that God commanded him.

7:1 Then YHWH said to Noah: Go into the ark, you and your household; indeed, I have perceived that you are just in my eyes in this era; ²take seven pairs, the male and its mate, of all clean animals, and one pair, the male and its mate, of unclean animals; ³take also seven pairs, male and female, of the birds of the heavens to keep their line alive upon the face of the whole earth; ⁴for in seven days from now I will rain upon the earth for forty days and forty nights and I will wipe every existing thing that I have made from the face of the ground. ⁵And Noah did all that YHWH commanded.

⁶Noah was six hundred years old when the flood waters came upon the earth. ⁷Now Noah together with his sons and his wife and the wives of his sons went into the ark to escape from the waters of the flood. ⁸Of clean animals and of unclean animals and of birds and of everything that crawls upon the ground, ⁹a pair, male and female, went with Noah into the ark as God commanded Noah. ¹⁰After seven days the waters of the flood came upon the earth.

¹¹In the six hundredth year of Noah's life, in the second month, on the seventeenth day of the month, on that day, all the fountains of the great deep burst forth and the windows of the sky were opened; ¹²and there was rain upon the earth for forty days and forty nights. ¹³On that very day Noah together with Shem, Ham, and Japheth, Noah's sons, and Noah's wife, and the wives of Noah's sons, went into the ark, ¹⁴they and all living beings of every kind and animals of every kind and every kind of reptile that crawls upon the ground, every bird, every winged thing. ¹⁵They went into the ark with Noah, a pair of all flesh that had the breath of life in it. ¹⁶Everything going into the ark, male and female of all flesh, went in as God commanded it; and YHWH shut him in.

¹⁷The flood was forty days upon the earth;
and the waters increased
    and bore the ark up and it was high above the earth;
¹⁸and the waters prevailed and increased greatly
    and the ark went upon the surface of the waters;
¹⁹and the waters prevailed more and more upon the earth
    so that all mountains and hills under heaven were covered;
²⁰the waters prevailed
    so that the mountains were covered by fifteen cubits.
²¹And all flesh perished—
    creeping things upon the earth,
    bird, animal, wild animal, every swarm swarming upon the earth,
    and all *hā'ādām.*
²²All living things on dry land that had the breath of life in its nostrils died.
²³He wiped out every existing thing from the face of the ground—
    'ādām, animal, reptile, bird of the heavens—
    they were wiped out from the earth.

Only Noah and those with him in the ark were left.
²⁴The waters prevailed upon the earth a hundred and fifty days.

8:1 Then God remembered Noah and all the beasts and animals that were in the ark with him, and God sent a wind upon the earth and the waters began to abate. ²The fountains of the deep and the windows of the sky were stopped, and the rain ceased to fall from the sky, ³and the waters began to recede from the earth gradually, and at the end of a hundred and fifty days the waters subsided. ⁴In the seventh month, on the seventeenth day of the month, the ark came to rest on the mountains of Ararat. ⁵The waters subsided gradually until the tenth month; in the tenth month, on the first day of the month, the tops of the mountains appeared.

⁶At the end of forty days Noah opened the window of the ark that he had made ⁷and sent out the raven and it went to and fro until the waters were dried up from the earth. ⁸Then he sent out the dove to see if the waters had subsided from the surface of the ground. ⁹But the dove found nowhere to rest her foot and so returned to Noah in the ark because the waters were still on the surface of the earth, and Noah put out his hand and took her into the ark. ¹⁰He waited another seven days, and sent the dove out again from the ark, ¹¹and she returned to him in the evening—and there was a twig of fresh olive leaves in her mouth, and Noah knew that the waters had subsided from the surface of the earth. ¹²Noah waited another seven days and sent out the dove and she returned to him no more.

¹³In the six hundred and first year, on the first day of the first month, the waters had dried up from the earth and Noah removed the covering of the ark and saw that the surface of the ground was dry. ¹⁴In the second month, on the twenty-seventh day of the month, the earth was dry. ¹⁵God said to Noah: ¹⁶Go out of the ark, you, together with your wife and your sons and the wives of your sons. ¹⁷Bring out with you every living being of all flesh—birds, animals, every reptile that creeps on the earth that they may swarm upon the earth; increase and multiply upon the earth. ¹⁸So Noah went out together with his sons and his wife and the wives of his sons. ¹⁹Every living being, every reptile and every bird and everything that creeps upon the earth, went out of the ark by their families. ²⁰Then Noah built an altar to YHWH. He took of every clean animal and of every clean bird and offered whole burnt-offerings on the altar. ²¹When YHWH smelled the soothing smell, YHWH said in his heart: I will never again curse the ground because of *hā'ādām* even though the drive of the planning of *hā'ādām* is evil from its youth and I will never again destroy every living creature as I have done.

²²As long as the earth is, sowing and harvest and cold and heat, and summer and winter and day and night shall not cease.

9:1 God blessed Noah and his sons and said to them: Increase and multiply and fill the earth. ²The fear and terror of you shall be upon every beast of the earth and upon every kind of bird of the heavens and upon everything that creeps on the ground and on all the fish of the sea; they are given into your hands. ³Everything that lives and moves shall be food for you, and as I gave the green plants to you, I give you all. ⁴However, flesh with its life, its blood, you shall not eat.

⁵Indeed, your blood, yes, your lives I will demand,
from every living being I will demand it,
from *hā'ādām,* from each person, I will demand the life of
hā'ādām.

⁶Who sheds the blood of *hā'ādām*
on behalf of *hā'ādām* shall his blood be shed
for God has made *hā'ādām* in his image.
⁷But you, increase and multiply, spread on the earth and multiply on it.

⁸Then God said to Noah and to his sons with him: ⁹See, I am establishing my covenant with you and your descendants after you, ¹⁰and with every living being that is with you, with bird, with animal, with every living thing on the earth with you, with everything coming out of the ark, with every living thing on the earth. ¹¹I am establishing my covenant with you that never again shall all flesh be cut off by the waters of the flood and that never again shall there be a flood to destroy the earth. ¹²And God said: This is the sign of the covenant that I am making between myself and you and every living being that is with you, for every generation. ¹³I have put my bow in the cloud and it will be a sign of the covenant between myself and the earth. ¹⁴When I cloud over the earth and the bow is seen in the cloud, ¹⁵then I will remember my covenant between myself and you and every living being and all flesh that there shall never again be flood waters to destroy all flesh. ¹⁶When the bow is in the cloud, I will see it and remember the eternal covenant between God and every living being and all flesh that is on the earth. ¹⁷And God said to Noah: This is the sign of the covenant that I have established between myself and all flesh that is on the earth.

Comment

The story (*tôlĕdôt,* 6:9) of Noah who had been introduced in 5:29-32, is, in the biblical perspective, the story of the flood, with the addition of the account of the impiety of his son, Ham, and the consequent curses (9:20-29). Another story (*tôlĕdôt*), that of Noah's sons, begins in 10:1. God is the prime mover throughout; Noah is the human instrument through whom God effects his saving action and is an important player in the drama; his name occurs five times in the first five verses (vv. 9-13) and thirty-three times in the whole story (6:9–9:29).

The story opens and closes with two long addresses by God (6:13-21; 9:1-17). The formula "I am establishing my covenant" (6:18) is resumed three times in the concluding address (9:11, 12, 17). The story is dominated by divine addresses (6:13-19; 8:15-17; 9:1-17). Add the address of 7:1-4 and twenty-nine (over one third) of the seventy-seven verses of the flood story are divine addresses. A large part of the narrative consists of enumerations of the people and the animals that went into and came out of the ark together (6:18-21; 7:2-3, 7-9, 13-16; 8:16-19; 9:9-10); these make nineteen verses in all, almost a quarter of the whole. One may add 8:1, when God remembers Noah and all in the ark, and 7:21-23, where there is an enumeration of all the animals that with *'ādām,* were obliterated from the face of the ground. Four times the writer notes either that Noah did all that God/YHWH commanded him (6:22; 7:5 [YHWH]) or that all entered the ark as God commanded Noah (7:9b, 16a). The description of the flood itself occupies ten verses (7:11-12, 17-24); the aftermath of the flood, i.e., the passages that precede the formal conclusions, cover nineteen verses (8:1-19); the gradual recession of the waters is narrated in two blocks of five and seven verses (8:1-5, 6-12).

The many repetitions, incongruities, and sutures, real or apparent (to the Western mind of the post-Enlightenment), together with the variation in the use of the names for God, *'Elohîm* (fourteen times) and YHWH (five times), have convinced a very large majority of exegetes over the last hundred years or more that the biblical flood narrative is a composite work put together from two already existing written Israelite accounts, themselves dependent on other accounts that derive ultimately from Mesopotamia. That there were flood traditions in ancient Israel is beyond dispute. That these traditions derived from, or at least had affinities with, the Mesopotamian accounts, very few would contest; and these accounts may well have passed through a Canaanite filter. But that there were two complete and separate written accounts, one by a writer known as the Yahwist (J) and one by a priestly writer (P), is another matter. The writer, editor, or redactor of the biblical account used these traditions; but he neither sewed together a patchwork nor cut his story from whole cloth; he received, contributed (in a very large measure), and handed on. The following table is a widely accepted division of the flood story into two sources:

	J	P
the general corruption	6:5-7	6:11-13
announcement of the flood	7:4	6:13, 17
Noah ordered to enter ark	7:1-3	6:18-20
Noah obeys	7:5	6:22 (7:9b, 16a)
Noah enters the ark	7:7	7:13
7 pairs of clean and 1 pair of unclean animals enter	7:2	
1 pair of each, clean and unclean, enter		6:19-20; 7:15-16
the deluge commences	7:10	7:11
it rains	7:4, 12; 8:2b	
windows of firmament are opened waters of deep burst forth		7:11; 8:2a
waters rise and lift ark	7:17	7:18
all living things die	7:22-23	7:21
waters subside	8:3a	8:1a
God's promise	8:20-22	9:8-17

Exegetes separate the text into sources following the accepted criteria for literary criticism: 1) style and language, 2) the different names for God, 3) contradictions and discrepancies, 4) doublets and repetitions, 5) theological differences and different perspectives. But these criteria are not always adequate. For example, the repetitions of words, phrases, and story elements in 7:17-24 are much more likely intended as a literary heightening of effect to produce a crescendo than a combination of disparate documents or sources. There will be comment below as these matters occur in the text.

Westermann (1984:430-35), making use of the criteria of literary criticism, has studied carefully the priestly section of the flood story in 7:1-8:19. As an exercise in method he has separated out the peculiarly "priestly" contribution so as to arrive at the story as it may have lain at hand to the priestly writer of the biblical text. He concludes that the main contribution of the priestly writer was the chronology of the flood (see below), the length of the flood (150 days), and the enumeration of the people and the animals that entered and left the ark, and, like Gunkel and Cassuto, that what was at hand to the writer was a narrative poem. The only deposit in the biblical story of the alleged J account of the flood is a few verses from 7:1-10; the heavy rain (v. 12); YHWH shuts the door (v. 16c); the effect of the flood (vv. 22-23), and, of course, the sending out of the birds. Westermann insists, however, that one must not exegete the accounts separately but that the "composite narrative has something important of its own to say, and that the scope of its effect belongs neither to J nor to P but to R" (redactor; 1984:431).

Before going on to study the text, it will be useful to have an overall view of the chronology of the flood. It is as follows:

7:11   In the 600th year of Noah's life
        in the second month, on the seventeenth day of the month,
        . . . the fountains of the great deep burst forth. . . .
8:4   in the seventh month, on the seventeenth day of the month,
        the ark came to rest. . . .
8:5   in the tenth month, on the first day of the month,
        the tops of the mountains appeared.
8:13   In the 601st year
        in the first month, on the first day of the month,
        the waters had dried up. . . .
8:14   in the second month, on the twenty-seventh day of the month,
        the land was dry.

In 7:4, God tells Noah that he will send the rains that bring the flood in seven days; on the seventeenth day of the second month (7:11) the fountains of the great deep burst forth and the rain comes. God, therefore, spoke to Noah (7:1) on the tenth day of the second month. No date is given for God's first address to Noah (6:13), but one may conjecture (and it is no more than this) that the date was forty days earlier, namely the first day of the first month of Noah's 600th year. So Noah was most likely forty days building the ark and making preparations, though this is not stated in the text. The waters and the rain came on the seventeenth day of the second month in Noah's 600th year, and on that day Noah entered the ark (7:11-13.) The land was dry again on the twenty-seventh day of the second month in Noah's 601st year (8:14) and Noah left the ark at God's command (8:15). So Noah was in the ark for a full solar year of 365 days, counting inclusively. (A solar year consists of twelve lunar months, six of twenty-nine days and six of thirty days alternately—354 days, plus eleven supplementary days; to be precise, a lunar month is twenty-nine days, twelve hours, forty-four minutes, three seconds.) The following is the distribution of time spans within the flood chronology:

7:4	in seven days from now I will rain forty days and forty nights upon the earth.
7:10	after seven days the waters of the flood came upon the earth.
7:12	there was rain upon the earth for forty days and forty nights.
7:17	and the flood was upon the earth for forty days.
7:24	the waters prevailed upon the earth 150 days.
8:3b	at the end of 150 days the waters subsided.
8:6	at the end of forty days Noah opened the window of the ark.
8:10, 12	he (Noah) waited another seven days. (These *"another* seven days" may imply a seven days at the beginning of v. 8.)

The waters prevailed (*gābār* 7:18, 19, 20, 24) upon the earth for 150 days (7:24). The flood is described as a return to primeval chaos (the foundations of the great deep, *tĕhôm rābbāh,* and the windows of the sky, 7:11; 8:2, cf. 1:2, *tĕhôm*). The waters of chaos were increasing over the earth all this time (7:17-20). The traditional numbers seven (7:4, 10; 8:10, 12) and forty (7:4, 10, 12, 17; 8:6) are very often typological numbers in the Bible indicating a notable and a very notable period of time. Even so, the forty days during which the rain fell would be included within the 150 days during which the waters prevailed upon the earth (7:24; 8:3b). The number 150 covers, in round figures (29 + 30 + 29 + 30 + 29), the five months from the seventeenth day of the seventh month (8:4). The rain began on the seventeenth day of the second month of Noah's 600th year. The rain ceased after forty days, that is, on the twenty-seventh day of the third month. The land was dry on the twenty-seventh day of the second month of Noah's 601st year. And so the day on which Noah came out of the ark was exactly one solar year from the day on which he entered it. It was also eleven lunar months from the day on which the rain ceased to fall.

The story of the flood begins in verses 9-22. The verses take up the people mentioned in 5:32 and this interrupted genealogy is resumed and concluded in 9:28-29. Noah was fully just, i.e., he comported himself as was proper in the society in which he lived. He walked with God, as had Enoch (5:22, 24). God took Enoch, and God took Noah and his family into the ark of salvation. Both Enoch and Noah were separated from the rest of the human race (to be separate or apart is to be holy). Separateness is a characteristic theme of the priestly theology. Noah's sons, Shem, Ham, and Japhet are mentioned four times in that order (5:32; 6:10; 9:18; 10:1; the order is reversed in the detailed table of the nations, 10:2-32). The earth was corrupt (*šāḥat*) in God's sight (6:11, 12), and all flesh had corrupted its way on earth (6:12). The earth was corrupt and filled with revolt (*ḥamas,* 6:11, 13). This is the first mention of "sin" in the priestly writing which frames Genesis 1-11. If there was a complete priestly story of the flood and the events that preceded it, then the account of the corruption of *hā'ādām* has been omitted. An equally reasonable explanation of the text is that the priestly writer is the final editor of material at hand to him and so, with the storyteller's account of sin before him (2-3; 4; 6:1-8), he had no need to repeat it. God is to make an end of all flesh, *kôl baśār,* which occurs thirteen times in the priestly account. The phrase covers the human race (6:12, 13), the human race and the animals (6:17; 7:21; 8:17; 9:11, 15 [two times], 16, 17), the animals (6:19; 7:15, 16). It denotes all these creatures in their weakness as flesh. Verses 12-22 are an address by God to Noah instructing him how to build the ark and who and what to bring into it. The ark is to measure 130-150 meters by 22 meters by 12 meters (400-450 feet long, 70 feet broad, 40 feet high [see *Notes*]). God is to cause the flood (*hammabûl,* v. 17). The word seems to be the proper name for the flood in the priestly tradition of the primeval story. Outside Genesis 6-11 it is found only in Psalm 29:10, "YHWH sits enthroned over the flood." In 6:17 and 7:6 waters (*mayyîm*) is used in apposition. The waters of the *mabbûl* are above the firmament and below the earth. Hence they burst forth (7:11; 8:2). Except in 9:11, 15, the reference is always to *the* flood. God establishes his covenant (*běrît*) with Noah (6:18), i.e., he gives Noah a "solemn assurance." The phrase "establish my covenant" is taken up three times in the priestly conclusion (9:9, 11, 17). God is the only speaker in verses 9-22 just as he is the only speaker in 9:8-17 (in 17:1-22, where *běrît* is used thirteen times and where God is again the only speaker, except for two half-verse interruptions by Abraham verses 17b, 18b, its meaning is again "solemn assurance"). God promises solemnly that he will save Noah, his immediate family, and the pairs of animals. This is the meaning of covenant in the context. There is no mutual treaty or covenant making. The action is all from God and Noah is God's obedient instrument (6:22; 7:5c, 9c, 16a).

YHWH now instructs Noah further (7:1-5). Noah is just (*ṣaddîq*) in his era, i.e., he has acted as he should, and so he is YHWH's instrument through which the saving action is to take effect and thus assure that that family of the human race which survives the flood is continuous with the human race that was created at the beginning. YHWH has seen that Noah is the proper person through whom the race is to be preserved. Noah is to take into the ark seven pairs of clean animals and one pair of unclean (7:2). He will need more than one pair of clean animals as there is to be sacrifice after the flood and only clean animals may be sacrificed and the species must continue. He takes seven pairs of the birds of the heaven with no distinction made between clean and unclean. The first bird that he is to send out later to test the level of the flood waters is an unclean bird, the raven (8:7). It was not to return, and its species had to be continued. In 6:20 (cf. 7:15, 16), all animals (no distinction between clean and unclean) *went* into the ark. Noah did not *take* them, as in 7:2. The stereotyped seven days and forty days and nights appear for the first time (7:10, 12, 17; 8:6). In verse 4, YHWH is to cause the rain upon the earth and, just as in 6:17, it is he who is to bring about the flood. The whole action is under the hand of the deity, and the destruction outside the ark is to be total, all that exists (*kôl hayĕqûm*). Noah is under God's direction; he did all that YHWH commanded him (v. 5), just as in 6:22.

The priestly chronology (7:6, 11b) frames the first part of the next section (7:6-16). To our way of thinking, verses 10 and 12 should follow verses 4 and 5: " . . . in seven days from now I will rain upon the earth for forty days and forty nights (v. 4) . . . and Noah did all that YHWH commanded (v. 5) . . . after seven days the waters of the flood came upon the earth (v. 10) . . . and there was rain upon the earth for forty days and forty nights (v. 12).'' The priestly chronology (v. 6), a further enumeration of those who entered the ark (vv. 7-9), and the description of the beginning of the flood as the return to primeval chaos (v. 11b), interrupts the sequence. The interruption of chaos is described in traditional expressions: " . . . all the fountains of the great deep (*tĕhôm rabbāh*) and the windows of the heavens (*'ărubbot haššāmayîm*). . . . " (the great deep, Amos 7:4; Isa 24:18; Mal 3:10). These are the waters that rain upon the earth (v. 12). There is another enumeration of the humans and animals that enter the ark and a further statement of Noah's obedience to God (vv. 13-16a). Then comes the simple note that "YHWH shut him in" (v. 16b).

Verse 17a resumes the forty days tradition (7:4, 10; 8:6). Verses 17b-22 are locked together (see translation) by the waters, which is the subject of the verbs "increased" (*rābāh,* verses 17b, 18a) and "prevailed" (*gābar,* vv. 18a, 19a, 20a, cf. v. 24). There is a crescendo which, when it reaches its climax, is maintained there by an enumeration of all living things that perished (vv. 21-23a), and the statements that only Noah and those with him in the ark were left (v. 23b), and that the waters prevailed for 150 days (v. 24). The writer has packed together tightly whatever sources were at his disposal so as to achieve a mighty climax. Neither God nor YHWH is mentioned in verses 17-24; but the deity is in control of all (6:17; 7:4). The subject of "he wiped out," *wayyimaḥ* (v. 23) is YHWH who "shut him in" (v. 16), and who said "I will wipe out *hā'ādām"* (6:7) and "every existing thing" (7:4). The crescendo, held at its climax, now stops. God remembers Noah and the animals he has saved (8:1). The waters abate gradually before the wind that God sends. Five months to the day after the flood began (7:11) the ark comes to rest on the mountains of Ararat (8:4, see *Notes*). The rain had fallen for forty days; the flood waters cover the earth and the mountains for five months (150 days) to subside for a further two and a half months until the tops of the mountains appear (8:5). But Noah has to wait yet another two months until the waters are dried up (8:13). Verses 2-3a take up 7:11b-12; the process of destruction is reversed.

The writer now takes up the tradition according to which the hero of the flood uses birds to test the level of the flood waters (8:6-12, see *Notes*). Noah sends out the raven, an unclean bird, which does not return but circles around until the waters are dried up. He sends out the dove three times. After the second excursion it returns with a twig of fresh olive leaves in its mouth, a sign that order has finally returned to the earth. YHWH/God is not mentioned in these seven verses.

Though the waters had dried up on the first day of the first month in the six hundred and first year (v. 13), Noah must wait until the twenty-seventh day of the second month before leaving the ark (vv. 14-16), thus having completed a full solar year in it. God orders him to disembark and commands all creatures, human and animal listed in detail, into a new life with the renewal of the blessing of creation "increase and multiply" (v. 17d; cf. 1:28; 9:1, 6).

It is important in the biblical perspective that Noah responds to God's saving action with sacrifice (see *Comment* on 4:4-5). It is not a sacrifice of propitiation but a recognition of supremacy. The expression "YHWH smelled the soothing smell" is standard for the gracious acceptance of sacrifice (Exod 29:18, 24, 41; Lev 1:9; often in Lev and Num; cf. Ps 141:2). The response of YHWH resumes 6:5 with the reflection that *hā'ādām* has not changed (v. 21b). YHWH will never again curse the *'ādāmâ* because of *hā'ādām* as he had done in 3:17 even though *hā'ādām* remains as it was in 6:5.

YHWH's pronouncement (vv. 21b-c, 22) is an abolition of the decision of 6:6-7. The reflection of verse 21b not only resumes 6:5 but also bridges the whole period between 3:17 and 6:5. YHWH pledges that the regularity of nature will never be disturbed again.

The priestly writer now adds a lengthy conclusion to the flood story (9:1-17). The new life announced in 8:18-19 is now made a reality. The blessing of creation (1:22, 28) is renewed and frames the first part (vv. 1-7): "Increase and multiply and fill the earth. . . . " (v. 1), "increase and multiply, spread on the earth. . . . " (v. 7). As God gave all vegetables and fruit to *hā'ādām* for food at the beginning (1:28-29), so now he gives meat as well (vv. 2-3). God gave *hā-'ādām* dominion over the animal kingdom at the beginning (1:28); now he extends this dominion to flesh for food, and the element of fear and dread between the human and the animal world is introduced. An explanation of a present situation is projected back into the immediate post-flood period. An ancient taboo is now introduced (v. 4). It is elaborated in Leviticus 17:10-14. There was an ancient belief that life resided in the pulsating blood. It is a question of blood insofar as and so long as it is the life of an animal. An ancient prohibition against eating blood has been put into the context of the concession of *hā'ādām* to eat flesh. *hā'ādām* may eat the flesh of animals, but with the flesh may not eat the life, for "the blood is the life" (Deut 12:23). Verses 5-6 become a little clearer when set out as in the translation above. God is speaking and is the subject of the verb demand (*dāraš*) three times. That is, vengeance belongs to God. The priestly tradition expounds in legal principles what Genesis 4:1-16 tells in story. Verse 5a has been translated literally, "Indeed (OR but, yet), your blood, yes your lives I will demand." The statement, together with verse 5b, "from every living being (beast?) I will demand it," is very probably to be understood in the context of the domestication of animals and the steps to be taken when an animal has killed or injured a member of the household (Exod 21:28-32). The animal is part of the household and retribution is to be taken upon it as prescribed in the legal codes. The shedding of human blood is the shedding of human life. Because *hā'ādām* is made in God's image, murder is a direct affront to God and retribution is to be taken as God prescribes. God alone is speaking and is in charge throughout. God is not giving *hā'ādām* the right to take vengeance. Noah and his sons are taken up into the creation blessing of 1:28 (v. 7).

The seven times repeated *bĕrît,* covenant (vv. 9, 11, 12, 13, 15, 16, 17), dominates the final passage (vv. 8-17). God is the speaker throughout. It is he who establishes (vv. 9, 11, 17) or makes (v. 12, lit., "gives") the covenant. God established his covenant with Noah when he announced the flood (6:18). He now establishes it with Noah's descendants, all living creatures (vv. 9-10), and all flesh (v. 17). The meaning of *bĕrît* emerges from the context. God, the only active party in the passage, is giving a solemn assurance (cf. Gen 17); he accepts and approves the whole of creation. As the first assurance is to last "as long as earth is" (8:22), so this solemn assurance is a *bĕrît 'ôlām,* an eternal covenant, a typical priestly expression (Gen 17:7, 13, 19; Exod 31:16; Lev 24:8; Num 18:19; 25:13). The sign of the covenant is the (rain-)bow, as God announces solemnly twice: "This is the sign of the covenant. . . . " (*zo't 'ôt habbĕrît,* vv. 12, 17). The bow is the rainbow and not the bow of the warrior that God lays aside in the heavens after shooting at his enemies. God (*YHWH, šadday*) is certainly the warrior who shoots arrows from his bow in a number of passages in the Old Testament (Deut 32:23, 42; 2 Sam 22:15; Pss 38:3 (2); 77:18 (17); 144:6; Job 6:4; Hab 3:9-11; Lam 2:4; 3:12). But there is no sign of war or struggle or personal harrassment here. The storm has ceased, the waters have abated, the bow appears in the heavens, and peace and security are assured. The function of the bow is described twice (vv. 13-15, 16). It is doubtful that there is an etiology here, i.e., that there is a story to explain the appearance of the rainbow. Many scholars are of the opinion that there are doublets in these verses, that the writer has preserved two formulations that lay before him, and that there are several layers in the text (vv. 13, 15, 16, 17). This may be. But it is more satisfactory to look to the repetitions of the words and phrases and the general rhetorical effect they produce. "I am establishing my covenant . . . " (vv. 9, 11) and "I have established . . . " (v. 17) frame the passage; *bĕrît* is repeated seven times; the rainbow four times (vv. 13, 14, 16, 17), and its function as a sign is set in emphatic positions (vv. 12, 17). The covenant is with all living beings (vv. 10, 12, 15, 16) and with all flesh (vv. 11, 15 [two times], 16, 17). Though the arrangement is not systematic and symmetrical, the final effect is to underscore God's solemn assurance that life, human and animal, will never be destroyed again. The human race can now expand with surety in the new creation which is linked, through Noah, with the first creation.

Notes

(In the following notes the references to the Gilgamesh Epic are given by the page and line[s] of the text in ANET.)

On December 3, 1872, George Smith (1840-1876) read a paper to the Society of Biblical Archaeology in London before an audience that included the British Prime Minister, W. E. Gladstone. It caused a sensation. Smith had discovered among the thousands of tablets that had been brought to the British Museum from northern Iraq a Babylonian version of the flood story which bore marked similarities to the biblical flood story. The paper was published in the transactions of the society in the following year. In his book, *The Chaldean Account of Genesis* (1876), Smith gave a general description of the tablets and fragments and was able further to piece together and translate substantial parts of an epic known today as the *Epic of Atrahasis* (Lambert and Millard 1969:1-41). The tablets had been discovered at Kuyunjik on the east bank of the Tigris on the site of ancient Nineveh, opposite the modern Mosul, and were from the library that the Assyrian king Ashurbanipal (688-627 B.C.E.) had assembled. The diggings were conducted mainly by A. H. Layard and his local helper, Hormuzd Rassam, in the 1840s and 1850s. Virtually all the tablets and fragments were brought to the British Museum.

George Smith was an apprentice engraver who had had no formal training in oriental languages and who, by hard work and his own genius, had gained a mastery over cuneiform texts. In 1862, the Museum hired him to help piece together the broken texts. In 1866, he was appointed assistant in the Department of Oriental Antiquities to help publish the texts. Smith made three trips to Mosul in 1873-1876, financed by the London Daily Telegraph, where he discovered thousands more fragments including a missing fragment of the flood story. He died in Aleppo on August 19, 1876, having fallen ill with dysentery during an overland journey from Mosul to the British consul there (Hoberman 1983).

In what follows, I depend heavily on the comprehensive and detailed work of Jeffrey H. Tigay (1982) and Lambert and Millard's critical edition of Atrahasis (1969).

The flood story that was the subject of Smith's famous paper in 1872 was from Tablet XI of the late neo-Babylonian (1000-400 B.C.E.) version of the Epic of Gilgamesh. There was in fact a king of Uruk (Erech, Warka) in the land of Sumer on the lower Euphrates named Gilgamesh who lived 2700–2500 and was remembered for building the walls of Uruk and the temple. By about 2100 Gilgamesh had become a hero or god. There was a series of independent stories about Gilgamesh circulating in Sumerian which correspond to parts of the later Babylonian epic. By the Old Babylonian period (2000–1600) a coherent form of the Gilgamesh Epic was in existence, but without the flood story. Gilgamesh does meet the hero of the flood, Utnapishtim, but the latter gives no account of the flood and his survival of it. The epic had wide circulation and was translated into other languages, e.g., Hittite and Hurrian, of which fragments from the fourteenth century survive. Fragments in Akkadian from the mid-Babylonian period (1600–1000) have been found at Boghaz-Koi, the ancient Hittite capital in north central Turkey, and at Megiddo in central Palestine (this fragment is in the Israel Museum in Jerusalem and is classified "Middle Canaanite 11b, 1750–1500 B.C.E."). The latest version is from the neo-Babylonian period (1000–400). It consists of twelve tablets. The most notable additions in it to the other known versions are Tablet I with the prologue, Tablet XI containing the flood story, and Tablet XII in which, in contradiction to the rest, Gilgamesh's erstwhile companion Enkidu is still alive. The epic had attained its standard Mesopotamian form by the last half or quarter of the second millennium. Tablet XI, the flood story, is best attested; but the only non-Mesopotamian attestation of the flood is an Akkadian text from Ugarit (Lambert and Millard 1969:24, 131–33). In the Gilgamesh Epic, Gilgamesh seeks out Utnapishtim "at the mouth of the rivers" to learn from him the secret of immortality by surviving the flood and then goes on to narrate the story of the flood (Tablet XI).

The other epic mentioned, Atrahasis, was written down about 1600 and from this period come its earliest fragments. The flood story was always an integral part of Atrahasis (for the creation of the human race in Atrahasis, see *Comment, Gen 1:28*). The gods decided to send the flood as a third and final attempt to destroy the human race because, as Enlil said to the great gods, "the noise of mankind has become too intense for me" (Lambert and Millard 1969:73). The Atrahasis Epic proceeds from creation, through the council of the gods, to the revolt of the lesser gods, to the creation of the human race in order to carry the burden of the gods, on to the increase of the race and the din that it raised and the frustrated attempts of the gods to destroy it, and the final unleashing of the flood. Scholars have no doubt that the account of the flood in the

Gilgamesh Epic is dependent on Atrahasis (Lambert and Millard 1969:6, 15; Tigay 1982:216–17; Simoons-Vermeer 1974:23–28). In fact, Gilgamesh is called Atrahasis on one occasion, and one part of the epic clearly presupposes Atrahasis (ANET 95, lines 180–90). The Gilgamesh Epic may be read in ANET (1955:72–99); Heidel (1963); Sandars (1960). Besides the commentaries, the following authors offer a variety of reflections on the biblical flood story: Batto (1987:192–96); Clark (1971); Fisher (1970); Fritz (1982); Frymer-Kensky (1978); Lambert (1965); Lang (1985); Lewis (1984); Loewenstamm (1980; 1984); Millard (1967); Müller (1985); Petersen (1976); Simoons-Vermeer (1974); Wenham (1978).

13. GOD SAID TO NOAH. The god Ea gives instructions to Utnapishtim in the Gilgamesh Epic. Ea was present at the council of the gods which decreed the flood, but he could not reveal to a mortal what had been decided. So he addressed the reed hut in which, presumably, Utnapishtim was living (93:20–22). There are two interesting lines in the epic of which there is no equivalent in Genesis:

> Give up possessions, seek thou life,
> Forswear (worldly) goods and keep the soul alive (93:25–26).

14. MAKE YOURSELF AN ARK OF TEAK WOOD. The word for ark, *tēbâ,* is used elsewhere only to describe the basket, woven out of rushes and sealed with bitumen and pitch, in which the baby Moses was saved (Exod 2:3, 5). It is an Egyptian loan word *ṭb.t* (Vulg. *arca,* whence the English "ark"). The Hebrew for teak is *goper,* transliterated in RSV (LXX *kyparissos*).

MAKE THE ARK WITH REEDS. The word *qinnîm* is rendered "rooms" in the RSV; literally, "nests." The translation follows Driver (1954:243) and others (Loewenstamm 1980:115, n. 34) reading *qā-nîm* from *qaneh,* reed. Verse 14a forms a chiasmus:

> make yourself an ark of teak wood,
> of reeds make the ark.

"Teak wood" and "reeds" are used in an instrumental sense. Both materials are to be used in the construction of the ark. The *tēbâ,* "ark," basket, or chest in which Moses was saved was made with rushes (*gome'*) and sealed with mortar or clay (*ḥomer*) and pitch (*zepet*). To this day the Marsh Arabs in southern Iraq make their huts and boats from reeds that grow to five meters (fifteen feet) or more (Thesiger 1964; Young 1977). The word for pitch is *koper,* an Akkadian loan word (93:65). Both *goper* and *koper* are found only here in the Old Testament.

15. THREE HUNDRED CUBITS. The cubit was the length from the extended fingertips to the elbow, forty-five and seven tenths centimeters (eighteen inches). The older cubit was fifty-three centimeters (twenty-one inches). Utnapishtim's boat was a cube of fifty-two meters (165 feet) with six decks above the main deck, a floor plan divided into nine parts, water-plugs, and was sealed with bitumen. The instructions are more detailed than those given to Noah (93:57–69).

16. ROOF. ṢOHĀR. (Vulg. *fenestra,* window). The Arabic cognate means the back of the hand, the human back, and hence the top or roof of the ark (Armstrong 1960; RSV). It does not mean window. The roof is to project one cubit (about a one-half meter or one and one-half feet) horizontally all round. The Hebrew is awkward and by no means clear, and there are other explanations, e.g. "Make a skylight for the ark and bring it to within a cubit of the top" (Speiser 1964:47). In 8:6 Noah opens the window (*ḥallôn*) in the ark; in 8:13, he removes the covering (*mikseh*). Neither of the two is mentioned in the construction of the ark. But Noah does make a door in the side of the ark (*petaḥ,* v. 16b).

18. COVENANT. There is nothing equivalent to the covenant (*bĕrît*) in the Gilgamesh Epic, or to the repeated and detailed enumeration of the family and the animals. Utnapishtim narrates how "all my family and kin I made go aboard the ship. The beasts of the field, the wild creatures of the field, all the craftsmen I made go aboard" (94:85-87). He took as well all the gold and silver that he had. Also on board was the boatman, Puzur-Amuri (94:95).

7:4. IN SEVEN DAYS. The deluge in Gilgamesh lasted seven days (94:108, 128-29).

16. AND YHWH SHUT HIM IN. Utnapishtim "battened up the entrance" when he boarded the ship (94:93).

17-24. THE FLOOD WAS UPON THE EARTH FORTY DAYS. The description of the onslaught of the flood is very different in Gilgamesh. As the winds gathered force and the rains came "the gods were frightened by the deluge . . . the gods cowered like dogs crouched against the outer wall" (94:114-16).

8:1-2. THEN GOD REMEMBERED NOAH. "When the seventh day arrived, the flood (-carrying) south-storm subsided in the battle . . . the sea grew quiet, the tempest was still, the flood ceased . . . all of mankind had returned to clay" (94:129–34).

4. ARARAT. Akkadian, *Urartu;* Babylonian, *Urashtu;* the mountainous region where Soviet Armenia, northwest Iran, and eastern Turkey come together, between Lakes Van (Turkey) and Urmia (Iran). The highest peak there is Büyük Agi Dag (5014 meters; 16,946 feet), very close to the Soviet border in east Turkey. The murderers of Sennacherib escaped to the "Land of Ararat" (2 Kgs 19:37); Jeremiah mentions it (Jer 51:27). Utnapishtim began his voyage at Shuruppak (93:24) in the south of Mesopotamia between the two rivers; his ark came to rest on Mount Nisir (94:140–45), modern Pir Omar Gudrun, in Kurdistan, 450 kilometers (280 miles) to the north, south of the lower Zab. A mountain in this area in Iran is known as Kuh-i-Nuh, Noah's mountain. H. M. Teeple (1978) and L. R. Bailey (1977) have written amusing accounts of the continued attempts by enthusiasts to locate the ark in this area.

5. THE TOPS OF THE MOUNTAINS WERE SEEN. In the Gilgamesh Epic, too, the mountains emerge into view before Utnapishtim sends out the birds.

6-12. AT THE END OF FORTY DAYS. When "Stillness had set in," narrates Utnapishtim, "I opened a hatch," just as Noah opened the window. He then waited seven days after the ship had come to rest:

> When the seventh day arrived,
> I sent forth and set free a dove.
> The dove went forth, but came back;
> Since no resting-place for it was visible, she turned round.
> Then I sent forth and set free a swallow.
> The swallow went forth, but came back;
> Since no resting place for it was visible, she turned round.
> Then I sent forth and set free a raven.
> The raven went forth and, seeing that the waters had diminished,
> He eats, circles, caws, and turns not round (94:145–54).

The Mesopotamian tradition about the sending out of birds was known before the discovery and translation of the cuneiform tablets. Berossos, a Babylonian priest (340s–260s B.C.E. dates very approximate) who had settled on the Island of Cos, wrote an account of

Babylonian history and antiquities. The work is lost, but is quoted extensively in the first century C.E. and these quotations are quoted in turn by Eusebius in the fourth century C.E. (Lambert and Millard 1969:134–37). They tell that when the waters of the flood had subsided, Xisthros (Ziusudra), the hero of the flood, sent out birds which returned to the boat because they could find neither food nor resting place. He sent them out again a few days later and they returned with their feet covered in mud. He let them out a third time and when they did not return he concluded that land had appeared.

20. THEN NOAH BUILT AN ALTAR TO YHWH. Utnapishtim, like Ziusudra (44:211) and other well known survivors of a flood—Deukalion, Manu—offered sacrifice:

> Then I let out all to the four winds
> and offered a sacrifice.
> I poured out a libation on the mountain.
> Seven and seven cult-vessels I set up,
> Upon their pot-stands I heaped cane, cedarwood and myrtle.
> The gods smelled the savor,
> The gods smelled the sweet savor,
> The gods crowded like flies about the sacrificer (95:156–60).

21. EVEN THOUGH. The particle *ki* is read as a concessive (Wöller 1982:637–38; Aejmelaeus (1986:207).

Conclusion to the Flood Story

There was a tradition of a primeval flood in ancient Israel which may well have been passed on with variations. There may have been a primeval flood epic in verse form (Gunkel 1910; Cassuto 1964), though this is no more than conjecture. The similarities between the biblical story and the Gilgamesh Epic both in general and in details lead to the conclusion that the Mesopotamian account was known either directly or through Canaanite sources in Israel. These similarities, as well as the many and important differences, have been noted above (a long list of points of contact and contrast may be found in the study of E. Fisher [1970:402–03]). The biblical writer who produced the final text as it lies before us did not fit together parts of a jig-saw puzzle. In my view, he was a member of the priestly tradition who made a substantial contribution of his own while using material at hand to him (see *Comment* above). In the biblical perspective the flood is clearly a punishment inflicted by God on the human race because it had revolted against him. Throughout, God is in control of the elements of nature and of those who are saved. There is nothing or no one in opposition to him. He carries through the punishment, saves, accepts the sacrifice that acknowledges his supremacy, promises security for the future, and renews the blessing that he gave at creation. The flood is the climax of the primeval story of which it takes up four of the eleven chapters. But *hā'ādām* remains the same after it as before it (8:21; 9:20-27; 11:1-9). *hā'ādām,* through the survivors of the flood, now divides into its different branches and from the branch of Shem there emerges the one who is to be the father of God's special people.

10. Noah Is Mortal
(9:18-29)

[18]The sons of Noah who went out of the ark were Shem, Ham, and Japheth, and Ham was the father of Canaan. [19]These three were the sons of Noah and from them the whole world was peopled.

[20]Noah, as the first tiller of the ground, planted a vine. [21]He drank of the wine and became drunk and was uncovered in his tent. [22]When Ham, the father of Canaan, saw the nakedness of his father, he told his two brothers outside. [23]But Shem and Japheth took the cloak and put it on the shoulders of each of them, walked backwards, and covered the nakedness of their father; their faces were turned away so that they did not see the nakedness of their father. [24]When Noah awoke from the effects of the wine and became aware of what his youngest son had done to him, [25]he said:
Cursed be Canaan, slave of slaves may he be to his brothers.
[26]And he said:
Blessed be YHWH the God of Shem, may Canaan be slave to him.
[27]May God enlarge Japheth, may he dwell in the tents of Shem, may Canaan be slave to him.
[28]After the flood, Noah lived three hundred and fifty years.
[29]Noah's life in all spanned nine hundred and fifty years.
And he died.

Comment

Verses 18-27 are the non-priestly sequel to the flood story and comprise two independent parts linked artificially by "the father of Canaan'' (vv. 18b and 22a). The incongruities in the text have not yet been explained. Verses 28-29 are the conclusion of the priestly genealogy interrupted after 5:32.

The three sons of Noah, Shem, Ham, and Japheth belong together in genealogical tradition (5:32; 6:10; 7:13, P). They remain together in the non-priestly tradition. Verse 18a looks back on the flood story, verse 19 looks forward to the survey of the descendants of the three sons in chapter 10. Canaan is usually the name of the land that Israel took possession of. Here it is the name of an individual. Some of the older literary critics met the difficulty by deleting "father of Canaan" from verses 18 and 22. The thrust of the story is determined by the three times repeated "the nakedness of his (their) father" (vv. 22, 23). Nakedness usually denotes a loss of human and social dignity (Bailey 1970:145). Noah had cultivated the vine and had become drunk with the wine. It is not a question of narrating the sin of the primeval ancestor(s) or of condemning drunkenness; nor does one have to excuse Noah because, as the first cultivator of the vine, he did not know the strength of its products. The story just makes a simple statement so as to set the scene. drunkenness in Israel and the ancient Near East was a social solecism. Israel regarded wine as the product of human industry (cf. 4:17-21, human industry and the advance of civilization) and not to be feared; it is a gift from God who gives growth and enables man to "bring forth fruit from the earth and wine to gladden the heart of man. . . ." (Ps 104:15). Wine was not the invention of a god, as it was of Dionysus in ancient Greece. The story says that Ham saw the nakedness of his father and told his brothers outside—no more. To look for more, to look for an act of incest is to read into the text what is not there and what the text is not concerned with. Even when a restrained author like Susan Niditch, for example, speaks of "the incestuous character of Ham's actions . . . ," " . . . the seeing of his nakedness is itself a sexual act, an act of control, an act of incest. . . . " (1985:53), this is to over-read the text, despite the number of scriptural passages advanced. Ham was guilty of an act of impiety. He should have covered his father's nakedness, as did Shem and Japheth. The son, especially when sharing the household with his father, is bound by obligations of filial piety. In the Aqhat story from Ugarit, Baal laments that Daniel "hath no son like his brethren." He enumerates the duties that the son performs for his father. The dutiful son is the one

Who takes him by the hand when he's drunk,
Carries him when he's sated with wine (ANET 150:32-33).

Ham failed on two counts: 1) he did not cover his father's nakedness, that is, he did not take away his shame; 2) he did not assist his father in his drunkenness as a dutiful son should. But Shem and Japheth did their duty.

To ask how Noah found out what had happened when he was under the influence of the wine is to ask a meaningless question and to misunderstand the function of story.

We do not know the source, if any, of the oracles of curse and blessing in verses 25-27. It has been proposed that there were two traditional lists of Noah's sons—Shem, Ham, Japheth, and Shem, Canaan, Japheth, and that they have been brought together. If so, this is a rare passage where Canaan is used as the name of an individual (vv. 18b, 22a, 25-27). There was no promise or oracle that the people of Canaan were to be slaves of the conquering Israelites, but the Canaanites were to be driven or exterminated from the land. Canaan and Ham are equated. Canaan (Ham) is to be the meanest slave to his two brothers (v. 25) and is to serve each individually (vv. 26, 27). Many Canaanite practices were an abomination to Israel. Perhaps the writer, or the tradition he used, wanted to trace these back to the impious son of Noah. There is a word play in verse 27: the verb *pātāh* means to be spacious or wide open; the jussive form, *yapt,* may he make wide, sounds almost the same as the name Japheth, *yepet* (may God make wide for Japheth, i.e., give him an extensive heritage). Many exegetes make Japheth the subject of verse 27b, "may he dwell in the tents of Shem"; who is this Japheth, how does he dwell in the tents of Shem? (Westermann 1984:493). But surely God is the subject, as he is in verse 27a, and so continues his blessing on Shem (BDB 1015, 2. c.). The problem is, how did the text achieve its final form?

Verses 28-29 close the genealogy that was interrupted at 5:32; Noah dies like all mortals. The flood story is enclosed within the genealogy of Noah.

Notes

18. HAM WAS THE FATHER OF CANAAN. The words Ham, *ham,* and Canaan, *kĕna'an,* are in no way linked philologically.

20. VINE, WINE. Wine had its origin in the area of Pontus on the Euxine Sea in Asia Minor. The form of the word has remained remarkably stable in its passage through time and languages: *yayin* (Hebrew), *voino* and *oinos* (Greek), *vinum* (Latin), *Wein, vin, wine.* On the history of wine in a sacral context, see Karl Kircher (1910); for reflections on wine in the Old Testament, W. Dommershausen (1975), O. H. Steck (1977).

28-29. AFTER THE FLOOD. At the end of the flood and after the gods had ceased quarrelling about Utnapishtim and those who had been saved with him, "because no man was to survive the destruction" (95:175), the god Enlil went aboard the ship. Utnapishtim relates that:

> Holding me by the hand, he took me aboard,
> He took my wife aboard and made (her) kneel by my side.
> Standing between us, he touched our foreheads to bless us:
> "Hitherto Utnapishtim has been but human.
> Henceforth Utnapishtim and his wife shall be like unto us gods.
> Utnapishtim shall reside far away at the mouth of the rivers!"
> (95:190-95)

Ziusudra in the Sumerian story is also made immortal (44:252-60). But Noah dies like all *hā'ādām.*

11. The Nations: The Unity of the Race (10:1-32)

¹These are the descendants of the sons of Noah, Shem, Ham and Japheth: sons were born to them after the flood.

²The sons of Japheth:
  Gomer, Magog, Madai, Javan, Tubal, Meshech, and Tiras.
    ³The sons of Gomer: Ashkenaz, Riphath, and Togarmah.
    ⁴The sons of Javan: Elishah, Tarshish, Kittim, Dodanim.
    ⁵From these the coastland peoples spread.
  (These are the sons of Japheth) according to their lands, each with its own language, according to their clans within their nations.

⁶The sons of Ham:
  Cush, Egypt, Put, and Canaan.
    ⁷The sons of Cush: Seba, Havilah, Sabtah, Raamah, and Sabteca.
    The sons of Raamah: Sheba and Dedan.

⁸Cush begot Nimrod and he was the first man of might on earth.
⁹He was a mighty hunter before YHWH. And so it was said:
Like Nimrod, a mighty hunter before YHWH.
¹⁰Now the beginning of his kingdom was Babel and Erech and
Akkad and Calneh in the land of Shinar. ¹¹From this land he
went up to Asshur and built Nineveh and Rahoboth-Ir and
Calah,
¹²and Resen between Nineveh and Calah that is the great city.
¹³Misraim (Egypt) begot the Ludim, the Anamim, the Lehabim,
              ¹⁴the Pathrusim, the Casluhim, the Caphtorim,
              from whom the Philistines came.
¹⁵Canaan begot Sidon, his first-born, and Heth;
              ¹⁶and the Jebusites, the Amorites, the Girgashites,
              ¹⁷the Hivites, the Arkites, the Sinites,
              ¹⁸ᵃthe Arvadites, the Semarites, and the Hamathites.
¹⁸ᵇAfterwards the clans of the Canaanites spread abroad,
¹⁹so that the territory of the Canaanites extended from Sidon
toward Gerar as far as Gaza and toward Sodom and Gomorrah and Adamah and Zeboim, as far as Lasha.

²⁰These are the sons of Ham, according to their clans, according to
their languages, within their lands, within their nations.

²¹To Shem also (sons) were born, to him the father of all the sons
of Eber, to the elder brother of Japheth.

²²The sons of Shem:
Elam, Asshur, Arpachshad, Lud, Aram.
              ²³The sons of Aram: Uz, Hul, Gether, Mash.
              ²⁴Arpachshad begot Shelah, and Shelah begot Eber.
              ²⁵And to Eber two sons were born, the name of one was Pe-
leg, for in his days the earth was divided, and the name of the
other was Joktan.
              ²⁶Joktan begot Almodad, Sheleph, Hazamarveth, Jerah,
              ²⁷   Hadoram, Uzal, Diklah,
              ²⁸   Obal, Abimael, Sheba,
              ²⁹   Ophir, Havilah, and Jobab.
              All these were the sons of Joktan.
              ³⁰And their territories extended from Mesha toward Sephar,
as far as the mountains in the east.
³¹These are the sons of Shem, according to their clans, according to
their languages, within their lands, within their nations.

³²These are the clans of the sons of Noah, according to their descendants, within their nations, and from them the nations spread on the
earth after the flood.

Comment

The human race continues in time and spreads in space through the sons of Noah, Shem, Ham, and Japheth, the survivors of the flood through whom the renewed creation blessing (9:1, 7) is effective. This "genealogy" is the most remarkable expression of the effect of the blessing in the whole Bible. All peoples belong to the race of *hā'ādām*. The human race after the flood is linked with the human race before the flood (5:32), which is derived from *hā'ādām* of the first creation (1:27; 5:1-5). The whole table is contained within the inclusion "after the flood" (10:1b and 32b). Commentators usually divide the chapter more or less as follows:

P	vv. 1a	2-5, 6-7		20		22-23		31, 32
non-P		1b	8-19		21		24-30	

The priestly writer introduces the *tôlĕdôt*, the descendants of the sons of Noah—the sons of Japheth (vv. 2-4), peoples to the north; of Ham (vv. 6-7), peoples to the south; of Shem (vv. 22-23), peoples to the east. Each list ends with a summary and general description of what a nation or people is: "These are the sons of (Japheth, Ham, Shem) according to their lands, each with its own language, according to their clans, within their nations" (vv. 5, 20, 21). The whole is summed up in a closing formula (v. 32). The formulas are virtually the same each time. Two large blocks (vv. 8-19 and vv. 24-30), themselves composite, and an introductory verse (v. 21) have been brought into the more regular priestly arrangement. Only Japheth, Ham, and Shem are personal names, the rest being the names of peoples, countries, or regions, though Arpachshad, Shelah, Eber, and Peleg (v. 24) appear as personal names in 11:10-15. The list is an extraordinary combination of system and lack of system. It comprises the world known to Israel about the time of Solomon (mid-tenth century B.C.E.). The writer has used the medium and form of a family genealogy to convey the origin and disposition of peoples. For all the disadvantages, it has the advantage of presenting the human race as a family.

A number of the peoples or nations mentioned have made considerable contributions to civilization and commerce. Israel is but one among them. If Israel has any claim, it is not due to itself or its accomplishments, but to God's election (Deut 7:7-8).

Notes

2-4. These widely dispersed peoples are all to the north of Israel. *JAPHETH.* cf. Comment 9:27. Iapetos was one of the Titans, a son of *Ouranos* and *Gē,* in Greek mythology.

THE SONS OF JAPHETH. These belong to the regions of Asia Minor and Armenia.

GOMER. In Greek, the Cimerians, on the north coast of the Black Sea between the Don and the Danube; an Indo-European group (Ezek 38:6).

MAGOG. It is very uncertain who is meant, though many refer the name to the Scythians (Ezek 38:2; 39:6).

MADAI. The Medes (2 Kgs 17:6; 18:11; Isa 21:2; Jer 25:25; 51:11, 28).

JAVAN. The Ionians; a general name in the east for the Greeks (Isa 66:19; Ezek 27:13; Dan 8:21; 10:20; 11:2).

TUBAL AND MESHECH. Generally named together in the Old Testament, and located in the east of Asia Minor (Ezek 27:13; 32:26; 38:2; 39:1; cf. Ps 120:5).

TIRAS. Only mention in Old Testament; Tyrrhenians, Etruscans, Thracians?

ASHKENAZ. Called with the kingdoms of Ararat and the Minni to make war against Babylon (Jer 51:27). The Scythians?

RIPHATH. Not known elsewhere.

TOGARMAH. Somewhere in central Asia Minor (Ezek 27:13; 38:3-6).

ELISHAH. Purple is brought from Elishah to Tyre (Ezek 27:7); probably Cyprus.

TARSHISH. Tartessos in Spain? Sardinia? (Isa 66:19; Ps 72:10); a distant place? (Jonah 1:3; 4:2) ships of Tarshish (1 Kgs 22:49; Ps 48:8; Isa 2:16; 60:9). Could refer to more than one place?

KITTIM, DODANIM. Plural names; very probably Greek settlements on the islands of Cyprus and Rhodes.

6-7. THE SONS OF HAM. These countries and regions are to the south of Israel.

CUSH. The area of southern Egypt, Nubia, and Ethiopia (Isa 11:11; Jer 13:23).

EGYPT. Miṣraim is the general semitic name for Egypt.

PUT. Very probably Libya (Jer 46:9; Ezek 30:5; Nah 3:9).

CANAAN. Palestine, west of the Jordan.

The names of the five sons of Cush and the two sons of Raamah designate areas to the far south and are located in Arabia. On Havilah, see *Note* on 2:11.

8-12. CUSH BEGOT NIMROD. Cush, a Hamite of the region of Nubia, becomes here the father of Nimrod, a Semite, of northern Mesopotamia. The four verses concern Nimrod and his founding a kingdom. They are like the elaborations in the genealogies in 4:20-22 and 5:29. The etymology of Nimrod, found also in Micah 5:5 (6) in the context of Assyria, is uncertain. Dahood (1978:275) has proposed that the name consists of an animal name plus the name of a god: *nāmēr,* Hebrew leopard or panther, plus *hd; hdd* is another name for the Canaanite storm god, Baal; hence "the panther of Hadd." He proposes, among other analogies, the Ugaritic *ni-mi-ri-yà,* "the panther of Yah." The writer is using here a tradition about Nimrod as a mighty hunter. The word rendered by "might" or "mighty" is the Hebrew *gibbor* meaning a warrior. Bas-reliefs from Assyria in the later periods portray the king as a hunter. Verses 8-12 sketch the foundation and expansion of the empires of Mesopotamia.

BABEL. bāb-ilu, the gate of the god.

ERECH. Uruk (Bab.), the modern Warka, 200 kilometers (125 miles) southeast of Babylon, on the Euphrates. As we have seen in the *Notes,* on the flood story, it was the city of a real ruler named Gilgamesh.

ACCAD. Akkada (Bab.), Agado (Sum.), founded by Sargon 1 about 2500 B.C.E.

CALNEH. No city of this name is known. Some (RSV) divide the Hebrew word *kal-neh* so as to render "all of them"; but this is dubious.

SHINAR. The more southern area of Mesopotamia covering both Sumer and Akkad.

ASSHUR. Assyria, in the north of Mesopotamia, also the city of Asshur on the west bank of the Tigris, later the religious capital of Assyria.

NINEVEH. The administrative capital of Assyria; the "great city" of Jonah; now the small city of Ninna on the east bank of the Tigris opposite the modern Mosul.

RAHOBOTH-IR. A Hebrew formation, otherwise unknown.

CALAH. Nimrud, the military capital of Assyria, some twenty kilometers south of Mosul.

RESEN. Not known.

13-14. Mıṣraım. These are the names of seven peoples (eight, including the Philistines) who border on or have some relationship with Egypt. The names have been stylized so as to have each end with the Hebrew plural form—*îm*. The *Ludim* are mentioned in Jeremiah 46:9 and Ezekiel 30:5; the *Patrusim* in Isaiah 11:11; Jeremiah 44:1, 15; Ezekiel 30:14; the *Caphtorim* are Cretans, whence the Philistines have their origin. The others are not known with certainty.

15-19. Canaan. *Sidon* stands for Phoenicia; *Heth* for the Hittites (see *Notes* ch. 23). The four names in verses 16-17a, Jebusites, Amorites, Girgashites, Hivites, refer to groups of pre-Israelite peoples in Canaan. The next five names, verses 17b-18a, from Arkites to Hamathites, refer to Phoenician cities whose names have been stylized so as to conform to the formation of the previous four names in verses 16-17a.

Jebusites. The pre-Israelite inhabitants of Jerusalem.

Amorites. An early Babylonian name (Amurru) for peoples living to the west in Syria and Palestine.

Girgashites. Genesis 15:21; Deuteronomy 7:1; Joshua 3:10; 24:11; Nehemiah 9:8, and in Phoenician inscriptions; nothing more is known of them.

Hivites. Joshua 9:7; 11:19; in central Palestine, near Gibeon.

The five Phoenician cities from which the names in verses 17b-18a are formed are well attested and identified outside the Old Testament.

18b-19. The purpose of these verses is no more than to identify a few important points on the border of Canaan.

21-30. The sons of Shem. The title "father," *'ab,* given to Shem in verse 21, is very likely honorific.

22-24. The five names refer to regions well to the east of Israel. *Elam* is that western area of modern Iran that borders on Iraq. Its ancient capital was Sousa, the modern Shush. *Aram* is the northern region between the two rivers. Nothing is known of *Hul* and *Gether.* Job (1:1) was from the land of *Uz.* Uz and Buz were sons of Abraham's brother, Nahor (Gen 22:21). *Mash* may be Mt. Masius, north of Nisibis (modern Kameshli in northeast Syria, on the border between Turkey and Syria). The succession Arpachshad-Selah-Eber-Peleg is found in 11:10-17, where the names are personal. The verb *pālag* (whence Peleg) means to divide; perhaps a witness to the division that comes in 11:1-9.

26-30. The four names of the thirteen in verses 26-29 that can be identified, namely *Hazamarveth, Sheba, Ophir,* and *Havilah,* all lie in the Arabian peninsula, which indicates the same region for the other nine names. *Hazamarveth* is the modern area of Hadramut stretching along the southwest coast of Arabia from Yemen to Oman. It is mentioned in Sabean inscriptions. *Sheba* was a well-known Arabian city, and could refer as well to the whole Arabian peninsula. For *Havilah,* see verse 7 (Gen 2:11). *Ophir* could be anywhere from east Africa to India (1 Kgs 9:28; 22:49; Isa 13:12; Ps 45:10; Job 22:24; 28:16). Joktan is found as a personal name in Arabic. The geography of verse 30 cannot be explained.

12. The Tower of Babel
(11:1-9)

[1]Now there was a time when the whole earth had one language and one vocabulary. [2]And it was then as they journeyed eastward that they found a plain in the land of Shinar and settled there. [3]And they said to each other: Come, let us make bricks and fire them thoroughly. And so they used brick for stone and bitumen for mortar. [4]And they said: Come, let us build ourselves a city with a tower with its top touching the heavens and let us make a name for ourselves lest we be scattered over the face of the whole earth. [5]Then YHWH came down to see the city with the tower that the sons of *hā'ādām* had built. [6]And YHWH said: See, they are one people and all of them have one language; yet this is the beginning of their doing; and now nothing that they plan to do will be impossible for them. [7]Come, let us go down and confuse their language there so that no one understands the language of his neighbor. [8]And YHWH scattered them from there over the face of the whole earth and they left off building the city. [9]And so its name was called Babel because there YHWH confused the language of the whole earth and from there YHWH scattered them over the face of the whole earth.

Comment

The story entitled "The Tower of Babel" is a unity in its biblical form, whatever its sources. It has an obvious frame: " . . . there was a time when the whole earth had one language . . . " (v. 1), and " . . . YHWH confused the language of the whole earth. . . . " (v. 9). There is clearly a beginning and an end. The theme of (one) language, *śāpâ,* occurs five times (vv. 1, 6, 7 [two times], 9); that of the whole earth four times (vv. 1, 4, 8, 9), in the phrase "over the face of the earth" three times (vv. 4, 8, 9). The story is again about *hā'ādām;* the sons of *hā'ādām* take the initiative (v. 5). The *běnê hā'ādām* are the "they" of verses 2-4. Verses 2-4 describe the reflections and action of *hā'ādām,* verses 5-8 the reflections and action of God. There is no dialogue between God and *hā'ādām,* nor does God address *hā'ādām.* There are three distinct and disparate motifs: (1) the building of a city with a tower, (2) the unity and confusion of language, (3) the dispersion of the race. But these motifs must be read in the unity of the story as it stands in the context of chapters 1-11.

Gunkel proposed that two stories have been fused together, one relating to the building of a city, so that mankind might not be dispersed (vv. 1, 3a, 41-c, 6a, 7, 8b, 9a), the other relating to the building of a tower, so that *hā'ādām* might make a name for himself on earth (vv. 2, 4b, 5, 6b, 8a, 9b), the latter being the older. Klaus Seybold (1976) has suggested that the basic text consists of verses 1-4a, 5-7, 8b-9a, into which have been inserted the three passages about the scattering (Hebr. *pûṣ*) of the race over the face of the earth (vv. 4b, 8a, 9b). But as with chapters 2-3, the sources have been formed into a unity, though not honed as smoothly as some moderns might wish.

Though the story is still in the primeval period a definite geographical region is mentioned, a plain in the land of Shinar in southern Mesopotamia. And Babel (Babylon) is identified in a word play (*bālal* vv. 7, 9). The movement into the framework of history is beginning.

After the flood, the drive of the planning and striving of *hā'ādām* was still evil (6:5; 8:21). This is true both of the individual, like Ham (9:20-27), and of the human race in general (11:1-9). The sons of *hā'ādām* (v. 5) want to build to the heavens and so make a name for themselves. A name, of course, is the source of reputation. Name, *šem,* together with make, *'āsāh,* is confined to the king (2 Sam 7:9; 8:13) and to God working wonders in Egypt (Jer 32:20; Isa 63:12, 14; Dan 9:15; Neh 9:10; Westermann 1984:548). There is nothing wrong in building, even in building to the heights; it is the motivation that is at fault. *hā'ādām* will challenge the name of God. God has already reflected on the attempt of *hā'ādām* to reach for equality with him (3:2-6, 22-24); what will he do next? Reach for immortality? (3:22). So too here—*hā'ādām* will stop at nothing (11:6b). So the race is scattered and its language confounded. *hā'ādām* has again reached beyond his limits. There is for a fourth time the pattern of crime and punishment (3; 4:1-16; 6:5-8:22). But where, this fourth time, is God's saving act? After ten generations, in the choice of Abraham (11:27-12:3).

The story as a whole is etiological; it is not made so by verse 9. There was a time, inaccessible, when the relations within the human race were other than the experience of the writer. The human race was together and could communicate (v. 1). It is no longer together and can no longer communicate (v. 9). This primeval story tells how this happened in the primeval period.

Notes

It is often claimed that the story of The Tower of Babel has its origin in Mesopotamia. This is reasonable, though it is to be noted that (1) there is no clear parallel from this region, (2) the three motifs of the building of a tower, the confusion of languages, and the dispersion of the human race, are independent and disparate motifs, (3) the dispersion of the human race is a common conclusion to flood stories, and the building of a tower to the heavens is a motif in African, Indian, and other stories, which is not connected with the confusion of languages (Westermann 1984:535-36).

A. Frenz (1969) has discussed some Vedic parallels to the story. The demons (Kalakanjas) piled stones on top of each other so as to mount to heaven. Two of them reached heaven. Then Indra (Indian Zeus), who had contributed his own tile to the pile, pulled it out and the demons fell down (there are variations of the story). In other versions, the demons piled a fire altar(s) to reach to heaven. "With this we shall climb to the heavens." It was an attack on the gods who had to defend themselves. The god and the demons strive for precedence. Again Indra pulls out his own tile. There is some agreement with Genesis 11:5-6. People build a tower to climb to heaven. There is a threat to the divinity (Gen 11:6b?). The high god must intervene. Indra intervenes literally and personally; God of the Bible uses other means. The Vedic attackers are destroyed; the sons of *hā'ādām* of Genesis survive to be dispersed. The Vedic story is dated 1000-750 B.C.E.

Some scholars have linked the tower with the remains of various ziggurats or towers in Mesopotamia where the remains of some thirty-three have been found. These are well illustrated in Beek's *Atlas of Mesopotamia* (1962:33, 43, 141-44, 151). When Nebuchadnezzar II (605-563 B.C.E.) was to rebuild the ziggurat of E-temenan-ki, he was "to fix its foundation in the womb of the earth and make its summit touch the heavens" (Herodotus 1:178ff.). It was to be 90 meters (297 feet) high. According to Kraeling (1920:281) the story of the tower in Genesis was originally a cult story of Ezida, the name of the temple dedicated to Nebo at Borsippa, just south of Babylon. It was at the time a popular Aramean legend, then a Babylonian reminiscence of a Hebrew traveller, and eventually a vehicle of deep religious and philosophical thought; such was the evolution of the biblical story of the Tower of Babel. Another candidate for identification with the Tower of Babel is the ziggurat of Choga-Zambil (Tchoga-Zanbil, and other variant spellings) in southwest Iran, forty-two kilometers (twenty-six miles) southeast of Sousa (modern Shush), on the river Dez (my visit was by courtesy of the Iranian military police of Haft-Tepe, Seven Hills). The town and temple, Dur-Untashi, was built about 1250 B.C.E. and named after an Elamite king, Untash-Huban. It was destroyed by Ashurbanipal about 650. The site had been covered by centuries of desert sand and was rediscovered in 1935 by geologists prospecting for the Anglo-Persian Oil Company. Serious excavations began in the winter of 1951 and continued for seven successive winters, hindered always by the excessive heat, labor problems, and difficulty of access. The building is surrounded by a wall 1300 meters (4200 feet) by 900 (2925 feet). There is also an inner wall enclosing the sacred quarter 440 meters (1430 feet) square. The tower itself was 110 meters (346 feet) square and rose to a height of fifty-three meters (174 feet), and consisted of five stories surmounted by a temple. The present ruin rises only to about 25 meters (80 feet). The stories are built inside each other, not on top of each other, so that each had its foundations on ground level. They formed a series of hollow boxes, fitting tightly into each other, the inner story being taller than the next outside it. The fifth was not hollow; it had a terraced roof about thirty-six meters (115 feet) square. The whole was made of mud brick cased in baked brick. On every floor at eye level was a continuous row of bricks inscribed in cuneiform. Each face had at its center a monumental doorway. There was a maze-like pattern of stairways and platforms leading from storey to storey. Many objects were found—clubs in marble, alabaster, daggers, cups, vases, most of them inscribed (*Guide Bleu: Iran-Afghanistan,* 1974:242–44; Labat in CAH, 197:393–94).

A seal 3.81 centimeters (1.5 inches) high from Mesopotamia from the period 2254–2154 B.C.E., carries on its right and left sides the impression of a god carrying mortar on his head as he mounts a ladder to the top of a tower; two other gods on the top of the tower add bricks; the gods in the center are waging war, wearing horned headdress. Is it a representation of the epic of creation? Are the gods constructing a temple for Marduk in thanks for his victory over the powers of chaos? (Shanks 1985:23).

All this, however, can be no more than interesting and useful background to the biblical story which must be accepted and read on its own merits within the context of Genesis 1–11.

3-4. Literally, "Let us brick bricks and burn brands." Probably a stereotyped phrase. The writer had accurate information about the building materials of Mesopotamia. In Palestine, stone and mortar were used and archaeologists attest that there is no evidence that bitumen was ever used as a cement there. In the Enuma Elish epic we read:

> Let its brickwork be fashioned. You shall name it The Sanctuary.
> The Anunnaki applied the implement;
> For one whole year they molded bricks.
> When the second year arrived
> They raised the head of Esagila equalling Apsu (ANET 68:58–62).

The ritual for the building of a tower is given in detail in Frankfort (1948:272–74).

4. WITH A TOWER. Literally, "and a tower." The word for tower, *migdol,* described part of the fortification of a city. It is used also for the wooden structure that serves as a watchtower in a vineyard (Isa 5:2).

7. CONFUSE. THE WORD IS *bālal,* cf. verse 9.

9. BABEL. The Akkadian *babili* means the gate of the god; *babilam* the gate of the gods (the name of the city); *bâb ilânu* means the door of the gods; alternatively, a popular etymology of a pre-Akkadian name (Gelb 1955; cf., *EBB* 37 [1956] 140–41).

13. From Shem to Abraham
(11:10-26)

[10]These are the descendants of Shem.
When Shem was a hundred years old, he begot Arpachshad,
two years after the flood.

¹¹After the birth of Arpachshad, Shem lived five hundred years,
and begot sons and daughters.
¹²When Arpachshad had lived thirty five years, he begot Shelah.
¹³After the birth of Shelah, Arpachshad lived four hundred and three
years,   and begot sons and daughters.
¹⁴When Shelah had lived thirty years, he begot Eber.
¹⁵After the birth of Eber, Shelah lived four hundred and three years,
and begot sons and daughters.
¹⁶When Eber had lived thirty four years, he begot Peleg.
¹⁷After the birth of Peleg, Eber lived four hundred and thirty years,
and begot sons and daughters.
¹⁸When Peleg had lived thirty years, he begot Reu.
¹⁹After the birth of Reu, Peleg lived two hundred and nine years,
and begot sons and daughters.
²⁰When Reu had lived thirty two years, he begot Serug.
²¹After the birth of Serug, Reu lived two hundred and seven years,
and begot sons and daughters.
²²When Serug had lived thirty years, he begot Nahor.
²³After the birth of Nahor, Serug lived two hundred years,
and begot sons and daughters.
²⁴When Nahor had lived twenty nine years, he begot Terah.
²⁵After the birth of Terah, Nahor lived a hundred and nineteen years,
and begot sons and daughters.
²⁶When Terah had lived seventy years, he begot Abram, Nahor, and
Haran.

Comment

The priestly writer now traces the genealogy of Shem. This genealogy is not a continuation of that in chapter 5 which was concerned
with the human race from the first couple to the flood; it is concerned with a particular branch of the race. It traces Abraham back
to one of the survivors of the flood, and hence to the beginnings
of the human race. Chapter 5 is in the primeval period, "before history"; chapter 11 is moving into the framework of history.

The form of the genealogy is like that of chapter 5, but with some
differences. It does not give the total life span of the patriarch (as
in 5:5, 8, 11 . . .), nor does it note that "he died" (5:5, 8, 11 . . .).
The LXX adds "and he died" at the end of verses 11, 13, 15, 17,
19, 21, 23, 25; it also adds a hundred years to the ages of the patriarchs in verses 12, 14, 16, 18, 20, 22. There are other discrepancies
in the numbers as well. Finally, the LXX reads as follows in verses
12-13.

¹²When Arpachshad had lived a hundred and thirty five years, he begot Kenan.

¹³After the birth of Kenan, Arpachshad lived four hundred and thirty years,   and begot sons and daughters, and he died.

When Kenan had lived a hundred and thirty years, he begot Shelah.

After the birth of Shelah, Kenan lived three hundred and thirty years, and begot sons and daughters, and he died.

So the LXX has ten generations from Shem to Terah (as ch. 5 has from Adam to Noah), whereas the Massoretic Text has only nine.

The genealogy of Noah ends with his three sons from whom the human race comes (5:32; 9:18-19). The genealogy of Shem ends with Abram, Nahor, and Haran, from whom the patriarchal narrative derives.

The priestly writer makes the transition from "before history" to "history." God's creation blessing, renewed after the flood (9:1, 7), is working effectively. The forefathers of Israel, in the biblical perspective, "lived of old beyond the Euphrates . . . and they served other gods" (Josh 24:2). God's blessing was at work among them.

Notes

10-13. ARPACHSHAD. In 10:22 he is listed as the third son of Shem where his name is really that of a people, place, or region.

14-17. SHELAH-EBER-PELEG. Cf. 10:24-25.

18-22. REU-ERUG-NAHOR. Reu and Serug are the only names appearing in chapter 11 which do not appear in chapter 10. Both are unknown elsewhere in the Old Testament. Reu has been linked with Reuel (Exod 2:18; Num 10:29). Serug, Akkadian Sarugi, was a city and an area between Haran and Carchemish. In the priestly tradition, Nahor is both the grandfather and the brother of Abraham (Gen 11:24-26). In Genesis 22:20-24, Nahor is a well known Aramean line; in 24:10, there is the city of Nahor; in 27:43; 28:10; 29:4, the family of Nahor lives in Haran. The Mari texts attest a city of Nahor near Haran.

24-26. TERAH. A semitic name meaning a deer or antelope: Akkadian tarḥu/turaḥu. Nahor and Terah are both place names in the area of Haran, and personal names; perhaps the city is named after the founder.

The Statement of Genesis 1–11

The biblical text is Israel's statement on the universe, the human race (*hā'ādām*) and the interaction between God and *hā'ādām*. The word *(hā)'ādām* occurs forty-six times in these chapters (twenty-four times in 2:4b–3:24). The statement is only complete when the text as it lies before us is read as a whole. The priestly writer is the systematizer, the non-priestly writer is the storyteller who narrates the wickedness of *hā'ādām* in a series of stories. The priestly writer presents God's universe, "the heavens and the earth" (1:1; 2:1), as the theater in which man and woman, made in God's image and likeness, and so with a special relationship to him, are to play out a responsible existence. He has God direct them toward the universe (1:28b), and God is their point of reference. He underscores God's blessing (1:28a) and sees it working itself out in time (5:1-32; 11:10-26) and space (ch. 10). Though he knows that the earth has become corrupt in God's sight (6:11-12), he gives no account of the revolt of *hā'ādām*. But the storyteller does. Well aware that "YHWH-God made earth and heavens" (2:4b), he speaks from the world of the revolt of *hā'ādām* against God (2:4b–3:24). He does not use the word "sin" in these chapters, but gives a complete account of what sin is, defiance of God (2:16-17; 3:1-7, 9-13, 19). He has experienced the revolt of brother against brother (4:1-16) and he knows that the human being has not mastered sin (4:7). He has experienced the general revolt of the race against the creator: "YHWH saw how great was the evil of *hā'ādām* . . . YHWH said: I will wipe *hā'ādām* that I have created (*bārā'*) from the face of the ground. . . . " (6:5-7). This is the only time that the storyteller uses the priestly writer's *bārā'*. God destroys the order that he has created by the flood. The priestly writer understands the flood as a return to primeval chaos (7:11; 8:2a). Both writers record that God effects a return to the stability and order of creation (8:22; 9:12-16). God renews the primeval blessing (9:1, 7). But *hā'ādām* after the flood (8:21) remains *hā'ādām* before the flood (6:5). He remains perverse (9:20-27). His *hybris,* spurring him to make a name for himself (11:4), leads to defiance of God with the consequent multiplication of languages and dispersion over the earth. The storyteller narrates the state of *hā'ādām* through a pattern that fits broadly the scheme of crime and punishment (2:4b–3:14; 4:1-16; 6:1–8:22; 11:1-9). There are limits to the human state; *hā'ādām* oversteps them; God intervenes with punishment; God also intervenes with a mitigating or saving action (3:21; 4:15; the ark and the assurance in 8:21b, plus the remembrance in 8:1 and the solemn assurance in 9:8-17; 11:27-32). *hā'ādām* is the essential farmer throughout, ever bound to the ground (*'ădāmâ;* 2:4b-3:24; 4:2, 3, 10, 11, 12, 14; 6:7; 9:20). He is also the *hā'ādām* of the priestly writer. Genesis 1–11 is a comprehensive description of the human condition (Crüsemann 1981:26; Moran 1971:58). Such then is *hā'ādām;* such has *hā'ādām* always been and always will be. The events take place in the primeval period, "before history." But for the biblical writers they are events that really happened. They are history.

2

The Abraham Cycle
(11:27–25:18)

The themes of the barrenness of Abraham's wife Sarah, the promise of a son, and the assurance of blessing dominate the Abraham cycle. The barrenness theme is sounded at the beginning of the cycle as strikingly and as firmly as the opening theme of Beethoven's fifth symphony: "Now Sarai was barren, she had no child" (11:30). It rings out clearly from the genealogical and itinerary matter in which it is set. As counterpart to the theme of barrenness, the theme of blessing is heard immediately (12:1-3). It too rings out and counterbalances its opposite. Blessing is effective in the continuation of the family through myriads of descendants, in the family's well-being, and the well-being of all groups that have contact with it. Abraham is to prosper under God's blessing "and so all the clans of the earth shall find blessing through you" (12:3). This assurance is repeated twice in the Abraham cycle (18:18; 22:18) and twice in the Jacob cycle (26:4; 28:14; see *Comments*). In fact, blessing could well be called the "signature tune" of the patriarchal story.

Immediately after arriving in the land to which he has been sent and which has been promised to him (12:7), Abraham puts the promise in danger in a deception which exposes Sarah to the power of the Egyptian court (12:10-20), an episode which is set in the framework of Abraham's itinerary (12:9-10; 13:1-4). The theme "no son" recurs in chapters 15 and 16, and in the accumulation of promises in chapter 17 (vv. 16-22). Next, messengers assure Abraham that he will have a son and specify the time when the son is to be born (18:1-15). The promise and its fulfillment is left, as it were, hanging in the air during a theological reflection, a theological discussion, and the story of Lot and his involvement in the destruction of the cities (18:16-19:38). Abraham puts the promise in danger again by exposing Sarah this time to the power of a Philistine potentate (20:1-18). Finally, the son of the promise is born (21:1-7). The Abraham story has reached its goal. It could well end at this point. But three more stories about Abraham are added (chs. 22–24). The Abraham cycle closes as it had begun, with genealogies (25:1-6, 12-18), and a record of the death of Abraham (25:7-10) who is buried in peace by his two sons Isaac and Ishmael (25:9).

The blessing theme covers the promise of the land (12:1, 7; 13:14-17; 15:7, 13, 16, 18; 17:8; 22:17) and of descendants (12:2, 7; 13:15; 15:4-5, 13, 16, 18; 16:10; 17:2, 4-7, 16, 19-20; 21:12-13, 18; 22:16-19a). All the promises are brought together in the middle of the cycle (13:14-17; 15:1-6, 7-21; 16:10; 17; 18:1-16, 18); and the promise of descendants is repeated in the stories that follow the birth of the son of the promise (21:8-14). The promise of the son belongs to the ancient Abraham traditions. It constitutes the Abraham cycle which is unintelligible without it. Each of the other promises in the Abraham cycle has its own history in the tradition (see Excursus, Promises).

The tradition about Lot has been joined to the Abraham tradition. Lot is first introduced as a nephew of Abraham and a member of his caravan (11:27, 31; 12:4-5; 13:1). He becomes, like Abraham, the owner of large herds and flocks which, for reasons of pasture, require him to separate from Abraham; so he settles in the Jordan valley. He later sojourns in Sodom (13:5-12). The writer sounds at once the theme of the wickedness of Sodom (13:13) which is taken up and developed in 18:20-21, 23-33; 19.

The Abraham story as it lies before us is the final result of a long process of development. This process of growth was, in its broad lines, something like this: there was a tradition that the father of the people that became Israel came to Canaan from somewhere beyond the Euphrates, be it Haran in northeast Mesopotamia, or Ur, just west of the marsh area in the south, some one hundred thirty kilometers (eighty-five miles) west of the confluence of the two rivers. There were individual narratives about Abraham which were brought together, and a strong tradition that Abraham was for a long time childless. These traditions and stories were theologized and reworked with the promise traditions, each of which had its own origin and growth in the course of the clan's settlement in Canaan and within the origin, development, and history of the monarchy. There was

The Abraham Cycle **Genesis 11:27–25:18**

BIRTH OF SON	LOT	PROMISES	
11:30 NO SON: BARREN	11:27 (P), 31 (P), 12:4-5 (P) (no narrative about Lot)	12:1-3 blessing	
itinerary (P 4b-5 12:4-9 (= 11:31 12:10-20 = 20:1-18 = 26:1-11 promise in danger		(12:7)	
	13:1, 2-12, 13 (link with ch. 19)		ch. 14
	(14:12-16)	13:14-17	Death of Abraham 25:7-10 (11) P:
		15:1-6, 7-21	prefaced & followed by
(15:1-7 no son)		(two narratives constructed around the promises)	two genealogies 25:1-6 (ad hoc creation?),
16:1-14 no son (P-frame vv. 1[a], 15-16)		(16:10) 17 (P: accumulation of promises)	25:12-18 P.
18:1-16a son promised		(18:1-16a) (promise integral to narrative)	
	18:16b-33 (link piece) 19:1-29, 30-38	(18:18)	
(20:1-18 = 12:10-20 = 26:1-11)			
21:1-7 BIRTH OF SON			
21:8-21 = 16:1-14 21:22-34 = 26:12-33		21:12b-13, 18	
22:1-14, 19 (P vv. 20-24) (promise in danger)		22:15-18	
23 family grave (P-frame vv. 1-2, 19)			
24 a wife for the son, J			

Genealogy
and
Itinerary.

11:27-32 (P & J)

(P 27a, 31-32)

Figure 2

a common editing of the patriarchal traditions both about Abraham and Jacob as the common language, formulas, and outlook of the promise material show. It is misleading to call the promise material "secondary" to the narrative material. Secondary it is to the narrative traditions before they became part of the biblical text, but it is not secondary to the biblical text. It is an essential part of it. It is the biblical text that one must exegete, always bearing in mind the long and at times massive process of formation that lies behind it. Further, it is misleading to state that there is very little left in the Abraham cycle when everything that has to do with Isaac has been removed from it. The Abraham story is in essence the story of the leader and father of a clan who is childless and whose itineraries and experiences revolve around the hope for the future through a son. The future son is constitutive of the Abraham tradition and inseparable from it. When the son is born after years of waiting, Abraham is a hundred (17:17; 21:5) and Sarah ninety (17:17). And the son of the promise is just that, namely promise, the channel through which the promises made to Abraham pass on to Jacob-Israel.

The Abraham tradition continued to live on in Israel, pre- and post-exilic, and the stories in chapters 22 to 24 catch it and crystallize it in writing at a stage which becomes the biblical text. It continues in Judaism and in the Genesis Apocryphon of the Dead Sea Scrolls.

1. Abraham: Family, Sending, Blessing (11:27–12:9)

[27]Now this is the story of Terah.
Terah begot Abram, Nahor, and Haran, and Haran begot Lot.
[28]And Haran died in the lifetime of his father Terah, in the land of his kindred, in Ur of the Chaldeans.
[29]And Abram and Terah took wives to themselves; the name of Abram's wife was Sarai, and the name of Nahor's wife was Milcah, the daughter of Haran, the father of Milcah and Iscah.
[30]Now Sarai was barren; she had no child.
[31]Terah took Abram his son, and Lot the son of Haran, his grandson, and Sarai his daughter, the wife of his son Abram, and they went with them from Ur of the Chaldeans to go to the land of Canaan; But when they arrived at Haran, they stayed there.

³²Terah's life spanned two hundred and five years, and Terah died in Haran.

12:1 Now YHWH said to Abram:
Go your way from your land and your kindred and your father's house to the land that I will show you. ²And I will make you a great nation, and I will bless you, and I will make your name great, so that you will be a blessing. ³I will bless those who bless you, and him who despises you, I will curse. And so all the clans of the earth shall find blessing through you. ⁴So Abram went as YHWH told him, and Lot went with him. Now Abram was seventy-five years old when he went from Haran. ⁵And Abram took Sarai his wife and Lot his brother's son, and all the possessions that they had gathered, and the personnel that they had acquired in Haran, and they went to go to the land of Canaan. When they arrived at the land of Canaan, ⁶Abram passed through the land to the place of Shechem, to the oak of Moreh. The Canaanites were in the land at that time. ⁷Then YHWH appeared to Abram and said: "To your descendants I will give this land." So he built an altar there to YHWH who had appeared to him. ⁸From there he moved to the mountain eastward, to Bethel, and pitched his tent with Bethel to the west and Ai to the east, and he built an altar there to YHWH and called on the name of YHWH. ⁹And Abram journeyed on, moving in stages toward the Negeb.

Comment

The first part of this section, the removal of Terah and his family from Ur to Haran, has a clear beginning and end: "Now this is the story of Terah" (v. 27), and "Terah died in Haran" (v. 32). Terah the father, Abram, Nahor, and Haran had been named in verse 26; the names are resumed in verse 27. The formulas of genealogy and itinerary are combined: genealogy—begot, the names of the sons and the wives, died; itinerary—took, went, to go, arrived, stayed (11:31; cf. 12:5). The function of the passage (11:27–32) is: (1) to provide a transition from a branch of the family that had survived the flood to the ancestors of Israel, to move from the primeval period into the framework of history; (2) to underscore the tradition of the Mesopotamian origin of the ancestors (Josh 24:2); (3) to sound the theme of childlessness that runs through the Abraham cycle of stories (v. 30). This last verse is most important. Sarah's barrenness is the point of departure of a succession of stories, chapters 15, 16, 17, 18. Gunkel wrote long ago: "Sarah's childlessness is the precondition for almost all the narratives that follow, as well as for the emigration; Abraham's faith in God's promise that he will become a great people (12:2) is all the more astounding as at that time he did not have even a single son" (1910:162). Von Rad plays down verse 30: "Sarai's barrenness is mentioned in passing. The narrator had to do that not only to prepare the reader for the event that is conditioned by the fact, but, above all, to make him conscious of the paradox of God's initial speech to Abraham" (1972:158–59). But verse 30 is not a passing mention; rather, it sounds the theme that is to re-echo through the Abraham cycle.

Abraham, still a traveller or a wanderer or a nomad of sorts, has settled at Haran. But in the biblical perspective he is still "on the way." To set him and his family "on the way" again, the author has YHWH intervene and command. Abraham is sent and blessed. The sending and the blessing go together. It is in Abraham's sending that the blessing carries on its effect. Verses 1-3 must not be isolated from what has preceded and what follows, but must be read in the whole context of 11:27–12:9. God (YHWH) is the prime mover. He gives the command to go (v. 1b), he will show Abraham the land of destiny (1c), he is the subject of the five verbs in verses 2-3a. God's blessing proceeds from his will to form a relationship between himself and Abraham and through Abraham with his descendants and "all the clans of the earth"; it is not due to any merit of Abraham nor is it a reward for good conduct. When God blesses, he commands that dynamism to increase, which is inherent in living beings as a constituent part of their created state, to move into action under his protection; but not only this; he assures greatness, prosperity, and well-being, and makes Abraham the mediator of it all. (The blessing-curse formula is used in Gen 27:29b and Num 24:9b with variations in number and order.) These blessings and promises are, as it were, a rack on which the patriarchal story is stretched. The descendants of Abraham will become a great nation (12:2; 17:16, 20; 18:18; 46:3) and will be "greatly multiplied" (16:10; 17:2, 20; 22:17; 26:4, 24); they will be as countless as "the dust of the earth" (13:16; 28:14) and as numerous as "the stars" (15:5; 22:17; 26:4) and as "the sand which is on the sea shore" (22:17); Abraham, and later Jacob, is the instrument through whom "all the clans of the earth shall find a blessing" (12:3; 18:18; 22:18; 26:4; 28:14). Ishmael too, though not the son of the promise, is blessed because he is from Abraham (17:20; 21:13). The blessing reaches its goal in all the clans of the earth. It is universal. The promises stand under the blessing. "Blessing is a continual activity of God that is either present or not present" (Westermann 1978:4). P. D. Miller (1984:475) has expressed very well the importance of the blessing at the beginning of the patriarchal story:

> Popular understanding of the God of the Bible often conceives of the deity as a God of love and wrath, a God of mercy and judgment, as these were the two parts of the character of God or the two sides of the divine activity and purpose. The call of Abraham helps to make clear that the God of biblical faith, in contrast to such a popular notion, is clearly bent toward blessing and mercy toward the human creature. Judgement takes place when the loving purposes of a compassionate God are thwarted or opposed. But the divine way and purpose are not any less loving or set for blessing. When Yahweh sent Abraham out, it was to bring about blessing, not curse. That is the good report which the Bible transmits to each generation.

Von Rad (1962:60–65; 1972:25, 158–61) understands 12:1-3 as the end of the primeval story and the key to it. The promise of blessings, he maintains, renders the first eleven chapters understandable, especially the work of the storyteller or Yahwist. This approach is taken and endorsed by Wolff (1964:137–51). However, with Crüsemann (1981), I do not think that 12:1-3 comes from the same hand as the work of the storyteller in chapters 2 to 11 for the following reasons: (1) because the primeval story is a tightly knit and independent unit with a series of cross references which bind it together; (2) the story of the tower of Babel leaves the human race as the writer experiences it, divided, dispersed and speaking a variety of languages; (3) the words *ereṣ* and *'ădāmâ* are used in different senses; in 12:2 *ereṣ* is a definite land or region, while throughout chapters 2 to 11 it means always and often the whole world; in 12:3 "all the clans of the earth (*'ădāmâ*)" are to find blessing, while in chapters 2 to 11 *'ădāmâ* is the soil of the fertile land (twenty-seven times; 6:1 is perhaps the sole exception) to which *hā'ādām* is bound and from which Cain is banned (4:11). The same author would not have used both words with such different meanings in a continuous piece; (4) the promise of 12:1-3 is a promise of blessing, not of salvation. It is a promise made to a person and his clan, not to a people; it is universal in its amplitude. The divine command and promise of 12:1-3, however, remains both a link with what has gone before and a heading or "entrance hymn" to the patriarchal story which recurs again and again to the end of the Book of Genesis. As we have said, blessing is the "signature tune" of the patriarchal story.

Abraham obeys, as did Noah (6:22; 7:5). Many, following Gunkel (1910:163–64), understand God's command as a "very harsh command" and "a severe test of faith." But this is a misunderstanding. Abraham is already on the way to Canaan (11:31). God's command is the sign for the next stage of the journey. The journey is necessary for the fulfillment of the promises. Abraham has no option but to obey. The itinerary formula is used again (v. 5: cf. 11:31): went, took, to go, arrived. When Abraham arrived in Canaan he went directly to Shechem, to the oak of Moreh. The writer adds the note that the Canaanites were in the land (v. 6b). So Abraham, in the midst of the Canaanites who did not know YHWH, went to a Canaanite shrine and built an altar to YHWH who appeared to him there (v. 7a). Abraham is not founding a cult nor do we have a typical story of the foundation of a sanctuary or a cult legend, that is, a story that explains why a place is sacred, namely because God appeared there. Abraham's action is both (1) a response to YHWH's promise to give the land to Abraham's descendants and a sign that points to the future possession of the land, and (2) an act of homage to YHWH among a people that did not worship him. The patriarchs did not found cults; Shechem, Bethel, and Beersheba were already holy places.

YHWH appeared to Abraham (12:7), and again to Abraham (17:1; 18:1), to Isaac (26:2; 24), to Jacob (35:9, *elohîm*); each time the formula which announces the appearance, *wayyērā' YHWH ('elohîm*), introduces an address by God. Abraham called on the name of YHWH (12:8b; 13:4; 21:33; 26:25 [Isaac]). Each time there is an altar and an invocation by the patriarch, there is action and word in worship. The patriarchs conduct their own worship; there is no priest or Levite or temple or rite of worship. The human race invoked YHWH from the beginning (4:26). Abraham called on YHWH whom the author of Genesis 4:26 had identified with the God whom the human race called on in the primeval period. YHWH, the God of the patriarchs, the personal God of Israel, is God of the human race. Abraham, still "on the way," continues to move south by stages (v. 9).

Notes

27. STORY. TÔLĔDÔT. See *Comment* and *Notes* on 2:4a.

28. UR OF THE CHALDEANS. Ur, close to the Euphrates, and a short distance from the modern An Nasriya in southern Iraq, was well

known before the excavations of Leonard Woolley (1922–1934) brought it into prominence. The city dates from about 2500 B.C.E. and was a Sumerian foundation. In the centuries that followed, a semitic group, to whom the name Akkadian may be applied, impressed their stamp on it. Scholars agree that the qualification of Ur by "of the Chaldeans" (*Kasdim*) could only come from the neo-Babylonian period (seventh-sixth century B.C.E.). Some have located Ur at Ura, a city in northern Mesopotamia linked with the Hittite merchants (Gordon 1958; contrary, Saggs 1960).

HARAN. The personal name is written with the aspirate *h* (*he*), the name of the city with the unvoiced guttural *ḥ* (*heth*). Haran, the city, is mentioned several times in Genesis (11:31, 32; 12:4, 5; 27:43; 28:10; 29:4) as well as in the texts from Mari on the mid-Euphrates from about 1700 B.C.E.

29. SARAI, MILCAH. The names mean "princess" and "queen" respectively. The Akkadian *šarratu* is the name of the wife of Sin, the moon god, and *malkatu* the name of Ishtar, daughter of the moon god. But there is no sign in the biblical texts of any cult connected with them (cf. Josh 24:2).

12:3. FIND BLESSING. The Hebrew verb "bless" is *bārak*. The form used here, and in 18:18; 28:14, is *nibrĕkû*, a passive or Nip'al form, and in 22:18; 26:4, *hitbārăkû*, a type of reflexive or Hitpa'el form. Both forms are used also in the middle or acquisitive sense, "win or gain a blessing for oneself." The meaning is determined not by grammatical analysis alone, but also by context. Full discussion may be found in Westermann (1985:151–52) and Mitchell (1987:31–36).

6. SHECHEM, THE OAK OF MOREH. Shechem is located at the modern Tell Balatah about two kilometers east of Nablus. There was a city on the site as early as the third millennium. Shechem, which means "shoulder," so named because of its position between Mounts Ebal and Gerizim, is associated with Jacob in the tradition (33:18-20; 34; 35:4). It is the place where Joshua renewed the covenant (Josh 24; cf. Deut 27; Josh 8:30-35; Judg 8:33; 9:4, 46). The oak of Moreh, or the terebinth, or big tree, is probably the same tree as that mentioned elsewhere (Gen 35:4; Deut 11:30; Josh 24:26; Judg 9:26, 37). Abraham planted a tamarisk at Beersheba and called on El 'olam, God the Eternal (21:33). Moreh means teacher or diviner (de Vaux 1961:278–79; 1978:185–86).

8. BETHEL, AI. *bēt'el,* "house of God." Near modern Beitin about twenty kilometers (fourteen miles) north of Jerusalem. It is associated with the patriarchs (13:3; 28:10-20; 35:1-13) and with the conquest by Joshua (Josh 7:2; 8:9, 12, 17; cf. Judg 1:22-25). Ai is always *hā'ai,* "the ruin." In the biblical story it was the second city taken by Joshua (Josh 7:2–8:29). It had been destroyed utterly about 2500 B.C.E.

2. The Ancestress and the Promise in Danger (12:10–13:4)

[10]Now there was a famine in the land, so Abram went down to Egypt to sojourn there because the famine was severe in the land. [11]When he came to cross the border into Egypt, he said to Sarai his wife: "Listen—I know that you are a woman of beautiful appearance. [12]When the Egyptians see you they will say: This is his wife. They will kill me, but let you live. [13]Now say that you are my sister so that it may go well with me because of you, and that my life may be spared on account of you." [14]When Abram entered Egypt, the Egyptians saw what a very beautiful woman she was; [15]and when the courtiers of Pharaoh saw her, they praised her to Pharaoh, and the wife was taken to Pharaoh's house. [16]But as for Abram, he treated him well because of her, and he had sheep and oxen and servants and maidservants and asses and camels. [17]Then YHWH struck Pharaoh and his house with severe plagues because of Sarai the wife of Abram. [18]So Pharaoh called Abram and said: "What is this that you have done to me? Why did you not tell me that she is your wife? [19]Why did you say: She is my sister, so that I took her for my wife? Now here is your wife—take her and go." [20]And Pharaoh gave men orders about him and they sent him and his wife and all that he had on their way.

13:1 So Abram went up from Egypt with his wife and all that he had, and Lot with him, to the Negeb. [2]Now Abram was very rich in cattle, silver, and gold. [3]So he journeyed on in stages from the Negeb to Bethel, the place where his tent had been at first between Bethel and Ai, [4]to the place where he made an altar at the beginning; there Abram called on the name of YHWH.

Comment

The passage is neatly framed with Bethel and Ai, the altar, and the invocation of YHWH, at the beginning and the end (12:8; 13:3-4).

Abraham:

at Bethel and Ai	12:8a
builds an altar	12:8b
calls on YHWH	12:8b
goes to Negeb	12:9
goes down to Egypt	12:10
goes up from Egypt	13:1a
goes to Negeb	13:1b
returns to altar	13:4a
calls on YHWH	13:4b
at Bethel and Ai	13:3b

The frame forms an almost perfect symmetry. The famine drives the wandering Abraham (12:9) further south into Egypt, whither he goes to live as a resident alien (*gûr*). Abraham has been blessed and assured that he will become a great nation. The promise is to be fulfilled through his wife who is barren. Abraham now puts his wife and the promise in danger. The episode is to be understood in the biblical context in which it now stands, so that to object that the promise is not mentioned in the story is to neglect the context. The episode is very carefully honed. It is almost the perfect example of the unadorned folktale (Olrik 1965; Van Seters 1975:160–62, 167–71; Westermann 1984:161–62). The structure is simple: the setting (v. 10), the first dialogue (vv. 11-13), the brief narrative (vv. 14-17), the second dialogue (vv. 18-19), the conclusion (v. 20).

Verse 10 ties what was an independent story to what has gone before. Abraham was on his way south (v. 9); the famine drives him further south. Sarah does not speak in the "dialogue" in verses 11-13 just as Abraham does not speak in the "dialogue" in verses 18-19. Abraham knows that he is putting his wife in danger so as to save himself. He tells Sarah to say that she is his sister "so that it may go well with me *because of you,* and that my life may be spared on *account of you.*" He is fully responsible. Events run their course in verses 14-16 just as Abraham had foreseen. Pharaoh, because his power is absolute, can take a woman as he pleases. And so Abraham fares well. Is it because he has received the brideprice, as he is thought to be the brother? YHWH intervenes (v. 17). There has in fact been a breach of the marriage bond. Pharaoh has taken a married woman into his harem, though he is unaware of her real status (a woman some time in a harem without the potentate summoning her, as the parallel story in chapter 20 notes, "I did not let you touch her" [20:6]). How did he find out who Sarah really was? Gunkel (1910:171–72) and Koch (1969:111–32), for example, think that something like an inquiry by Pharaoh and his courtiers into the cause of the plagues was part of the original story and has dropped out (i.e., that part of the narrative known as the peripeteia, the sudden reversal of fortune in drama or life; the point around which the sudden change revolves [Else 1965:27]). But as the storyteller is always omniscient and the listeners know the situation, the question is irrelevant; no detailed explanation is necessary. Pharaoh has experienced a power behind Abraham that is greater than he. His question: "What is this that you have done to me?," with the further questions, follows the standard pattern of reproach (Gen 3:9-13; 4:9-11; 20:9-10; 26:10; 29:25; Num 23:11). Abraham's deception is uncovered. Pharaoh expels him with "Take your wife and go" (v. 19b). Pharaoh's men escort Abraham and his household to the border. Abraham, with full knowledge, has put his wife and the promise in danger; YHWH, faithful to his promise, has in his providence saved them. The narrative neither glorifies the cleverness of the patriarch, nor extols the beauty of the ancestress (Gunkel; the *Genesis Apocryphon* from Qumran at the Dead Sea), nor tells of the despoiling of the Egyptians (Thompson 1974:246; Coats 1968). But it does underscore the steadfast loyalty of YHWH, as Gunkel also notes.

Notes

The story of a patriarch passing off his wife as his sister when face-to-face with a powerful ruler is repeated twice: Abraham, Sarah, and Abimelech (20:1-18) and Isaac, Rebekah, and Abimelech (26:1-11). The relationship between the stories will be discussed in the *Notes* to chapter 20.

A number of scholars have thought that the documents discovered at Nuzi (ANET 219-20) and some of the legal codes of the ancient Near East such as the laws of Eshnunna, the code of Hammurapi, the Hittite laws, the Neo-Babylonian laws (ANET 161-63, 164-80, 188-96, 197-98), provide parallels to some of the patriarchal customs and have influenced them directly, the present passage being among them. Nuzi, the modern Yorgan-Tepe in northern Iraq, lies east of the Tigris just below the Little Zab, fourteen kilometers (ten miles) southwest of Kirkuk. E. Chiera of the University of Pennsylvania began excavations there in 1925, and the Semitic Museum,

Harvard University, and the American School of Oriental Research, Baghdad, under R. Pfeiffer and E. A. Speiser, continued them. The history of Nuzi goes back to 4000 B.C.E. Thousands of tablets were discovered there from the fifteenth century, the period when the Hurrians of the Mitanni kingdom controlled the city, and were written by Hurrian scribes in Old Babylonian cuneiform. The biblical passages to which parallels from Nuzi and the legal codes have been alleged are: the wife-sister relationship (12:10-20 and parallels); the alleged adoption by Abraham of his servant, Eliezer (15:2-3); covenant and "sacrifice" (15:7-17); the childless wife and the "secondary" wife (16:1-14); Abraham's purchase of a burial place and land from the biblical Hittites (23:1-20); the authority of a brother, Laban, in the marriage of his sister, Rebekah (24:50-61); the right of the first-born (25:29-34); Jacob's marriages (chs. 29–31); Jacob, the shepherd (30:27-34); the teraphim (31:34-35); the terms of Jacob's employment (31:38-40). There will be a short note on each of these passages in the course of the commentary and notes. Full discussions, giving different points of view and ample citations (especially by Thompson and Van Seters), may be found in the commentaries of Speiser (1964), Vawter (1977), and Westermann (1985), as well as in Tournay (1960), Mullo Weir (1967), Thompson (1974:196–297), Van Seters (1975:64–103), de Vaux (221–56), Selman (1980). It may be said by way of anticipation that there is general agreement that the alleged parallels to the biblical passages are not precise and that it is not a case of direct influence on the Bible or of biblical borrowings. However, the customs and laws provide a general and useful cultural background to the patriarchal traditions. Nuzi is not mentioned in the Old Testament.

There was a legal practice or custom at Nuzi whereby a brother, usually the eldest, and when the father was dead, entrusts his sister, under certain conditions and for a consideration, to another man (or agent?). The girl thus becomes the juridical "sister" of the adopter. This adopter or juridical "brother" is to find a husband for his juridical "sister." In one marriage contract, a juridical "brother" has given his juridical "sister" in marriage to a third party, all proprieties having being observed. There is another document in which these same three declare their agreement to the contract. In a third document, with the same three parties, the blood brother gives his sister to the third man "as sister." This "third man," the new "brother," may later want to marry "his sister"; this would require another document. However, there is no discernible influence of the customs of the Nuzi tablets on the biblical text. In the biblical passage, Abraham deceives the Egyptians for his own good. Pharaoh intends that Sarah shall be one of his wives (v. 19a), as Abraham receives a good "price" (v. 16). Hence there is technical adultery, the "great sin" in Egypt and the ancient Near East, and the consequent severe punishment (v. 17). It is unlikely that Abraham is using the word "sister" in an ambiguous sense. The beloved in the Song of Songs uses "sister" as a term of affection when addressing his bride (4:9, 10; 5:1, 2), and in the book of Tobit, Tobit (5:20), Raguel (7:16), and Tobias (8:4) each address their wives as sister. Further, certain Egyptian documents juxtapose or equate wife and sister (Van Seters (175:76).

16. CAMELS. Exegetes usually dismiss the reference to camels with a sentence like, "The *camels* mentioned in verse 16 above and subsequently in the patriarchal history are an anachronism, since it appears to be quite certain that the camel was not domesticated in the Near East until about the thirteenth century B.C." (Vawter 1977:181). Van Seters, though maintaining that "only with the first millennium was the camel fully domesticated as a riding and burden-carrying animal" (1975:17), is much more nuanced when discussing camels in the biblical context: "The camels in such stories as Genesis 24 and 31 are quite integral to the accounts" (Van Seters considers that the patriarchal stories and traditions are late, about the sixth century). De Vaux (1978:222–23) is more reserved, though in basic agreement that the camel was domesticated in the ancient Near East only from the end of the second millennium B.C.E. However, the research of Hilda Gauthier-Pilters and Anne Innis Dagg (1981:115–45), and of Juliet Clutton-Brock (1981:121–29), point in a different direction. The Bactrian camel (two humps) seems to have been domesticated in Iran by 2500 B.C.E., and the dromedary (one hump) in southern Arabia by about 2000 B.C.E. Juris Zarins (1982:251–53), in his summing up of the work of Clutton-Brock, writes:

> In summary then, it would appear that camels were certainly present in the Levantine fringes as a wild form following the Neolithic period, and early domestic forms, derived from nomadic domestication centers to the south, could have been present within the Fertile Crescent as early as the third millennium B.C. On a more intensive and consistent basis, the domestic camel arrived in north Arabia and the Levant by the Iron Period (Judg 6-8).

E. A. Knauf has provided a brief survey of the domestication of the camel from the fourth or third millennium to the middle of the first millennium (1983; 1987). On the general domestication of animals, one can refer with profit to the work of the palaeontologist Richard E. Leakey (1981:6, 197). All this neither proves nor disproves the historicity of the patriarchal narratives, and may seem much ado about very little. Anyway, I became a great admirer of the camel in my journeys and sojourns from Afghanistan across to the Sudan.

3. Abraham and Lot: Promises Repeated
(13:5-18)

⁵Lot, who went with Abraham, also had sheep, cattle, and tents ⁶so that the land was not sufficient for them to dwell together; because their possessions were great, they were unable to dwell together. ⁷Hence, there was strife between the herdsmen of Abram and the herdsmen of Lot. The Canaanites and the Perizzites were dwelling in the land at that time. ⁸So Abram said to Lot: "Please, let there be no strife between me and you, between my herdsmen and yours, for we are kinsmen. ⁹Surely the whole land is before you; separate from me; if you go left, I will go right; if you go right, I will go left." ¹⁰So Lot lifted up his eyes and saw how well watered the winding Jordan valley was before YHWH destroyed Sodom and Gomorrah; it was like the garden of God, like the land of Egypt in the direction of Zoar. ¹¹So Lot chose the winding Jordan valley and journeyed east, and they separated from each other. ¹²Abram dwelt in the land of Canaan and Lot dwelt among the cities of the winding valley and moved his tent as far as Sodom. ¹³Now the men of Sodom were wicked and great sinners before YHWH.

¹⁴Now YHWH said to Abram after Lot separated from him: Lift up your eyes and look from the place where you are now, to the north, to the south, to the east, to the west; ¹⁵for all the land that you see I will give to you and your descendants for ever. ¹⁶I will make your descendants as countless as the dust of the earth; if one can count the dust of the earth, your descendants too shall be counted. ¹⁷Arise, walk through the length and breadth of the land because I will give it to you. ¹⁸So Abram moved his tent and went and dwelt by the oaks of Mamre that are at Hebron; and he built an altar there to YHWH.

Comment

So far, Lot has been given honorable mention three times, as the son of Haran (11:27), and as a member of Abraham's caravan (12:4; 13:1). The writer knows the tradition that links Lot with Sodom and Gomorrah (13:10) and sounds the theme of the wickedness of Sodom (13:13) which is described in detail later (18:16–19:29). Verse 5 picks up verse 1b; verse 2, "Abram was very rich in cattle, silver, and gold," and verse 5, "Lot too who went with Abram had sheep, cattle, and tents," set the stage for the dispute. The wealth of each in livestock gives rise to a dispute among the herdsmen and this leads in turn to a separation between the kinsmen. Separation and independent settlement are the goal of the narrative. All three elements, wealth in livestock, strife, and separation, go together. Both Abraham and Lot, though still leading a type of nomadic life, make their first claim to the land even though the original inhabitants, the Canaanites and the Perizzites, are there. It is not to the point to say that the most important item, the dispute between the herdsmen, is not described. The dispute is functional in the story. The simple fact of the dispute leads directly to the goal. Abraham, as the head of the caravan and final arbiter, solves the dispute by making a simple and peaceful offer. Lot finds the winding southern Jordan valley attractive, as the magnificent photograph in Grollenberg's atlas shows it to be (1957:17). It is to read much into the text to speak of Lot looking down on the valley with lustful and avaricious eyes and so being drawn into his ultimate involvement in the fate of Sodom and Gomorrah. The separation is completed (vv. 11-12). Lot leaves Canaan and moves his tent to Sodom (v. 12), the wickedness of the people among whom Lot settles is anticipated (v. 13), Abraham stays in Canaan and moves his tent to the oaks of Mamre at Hebron (v. 18). Both are still wanderers and living in tents. The text gives no ground to suppose that the story is etiological, that is, that it was composed in order to explain the acquisition of land by the corporate personalities of Abraham and Lot. But before Abraham settles at Hebron, the promise of land and descendants is repeated (vv. 14-17).

There is a new introduction: "Now YHWH said," which is linked with the narrative by "after Lot separated from him" (v. 14a). The writer makes a short scene out of the confirmation of the promises of land and descendants. The land of Canaan, in which Abraham is about to settle, is to belong to him and his descendants for ever

(v. 15b, "for ever," *'ad 'olam,* is repeated in this context in the Pentateuch about forty times). Abraham stands at a vantage point near Bethel from where he can view Canaan to the four points of the compass. As far as his eyes can see, the land is his, and his descendants are to be "as countless as the dust of the earth" (v. 16; 28:13). The author has before him a story about the separation of Abraham and Lot caused by the increase of the livestock. He supplements this story with the renewal of the promise of land and descendants and links it with the story (v. 14) before he reports Abraham's settlement in Hebron.

Notes

7. PERIZZITES. A name for one of the original inhabitants of the land which occurs twenty-three times in the Old Testament, four times together with the Canaanites, and one time in the Amarna letters. No more is known of them. The Hebrew word *perazâ* means an open village.

10. WINDING JORDAN VALLEY. *kikkār,* a round: hence, a round district, loaf, weight. The southern part of the Jordan winds in a remarkable way before it runs into the Dead Sea.

SODOM AND GOMORRAH. The cities are located at the southern end of the Dead Sea.

18. MAMRE. It is both a personal (14:13, 24) and a place (23:17, 19; 25:9; 49:30; 50:13) name and occurs only in Genesis. It is the modern Ramat el-Khalil about three kilometers north of old Hebron. "Long a place of popular Jewish devotion because of a great tree, the site became the focal point of local superstitious practices for pagans" (Murphy-O'Connor 1986:277). Constantine's mother-in-law, Eutropia, built a basilica there, the remains of which have been uncovered.

4. Abraham and the Kings from the East
(14:1-24)

¹Now in the days of Amraphel king of Shinar, Arioch king of Ellasar, Chedorlaomer king of Elam, and Tidal king of Goi-im, ²these made war with Bera king of Sodom, Birsha king of Gomorrah, Shinab king of Admah, Shember king of Zeboi-im, and the king of Bela (that

is, Zoar). ³All these joined forces in the valley of Siddim (that is, the Salt Sea). ⁴They had been subject to Chedorlaomer for twelve years but in the thirteenth year they revolted. ⁵In the fourteenth year Chedorlaomer and the kings with him came and defeated the Rephaim in Ashteroth-Karnaim, the Zuzim in Ham, and the Emim in Shaveh-kiriathaim. ⁶And the Horites in their hill-country of Seir as far as El-paran on the edge of the wilderness. ⁷Then they turned back and came to En-mispat (that is, Kadesh) and they defeated both the Amalekites and the Amorites who dwelt in Hazazon-tamar. ⁸Then the king of Sodom, the king of Gomorrah, the king of Admah, the king of Zeboi-im, and the king of Bela (that is, Zoar) went out and joined battle with them in the valley of Siddim, ⁹with Chedorlaomer king of Elam, Tidal king of Goi-im, Amraphel king of Shinar, and Arioch king El-lasar, four kings against five. ¹⁰Now the valley of Siddim was full of bitumen pits, and as the kings of Sodom and Gomorrah fled, they fell into them, while the rest fled to the mountains. ¹¹They took all the goods and food of Sodom and Gomorrah and went; ¹²and they took Lot, Abram's kinsman, who was living in Sodom, and all his goods and went.

¹³Then one who had escaped came and told Abram the Hebrew who was living by the oaks of Mamre the Amorite, a kinsman of Eshcol and Aner; these were allies of Abram. ¹⁴When Abram heard that his kinsman had been captured, he mustered his retainers, men born in his household, three hundred and eighteen of them, and went in pursuit as far as Dan. ¹⁵He and his men deployed against them by night, defeated them and pursued them as far as Hobah, which is north of Damascus. ¹⁶He brought back all the goods as well as his kinsman Lot with the women and the people. ¹⁷After his return from his defeat of Chedorlaomer and the kings who were with him, the king of Sodom went out to meet him at the valley of Shaweh (that is, the valley of the king).

¹⁸Melchizedek king of Salem brought out bread and wine, ¹⁹and as he was priest of El Elyon he blessed Abram and said:
May Abram be blessed by El Elyon, creator of heaven and earth, ²⁰and may El Elyon be praised who delivered your enemies into your hand. Then Abram gave him a tenth of everything.
²¹Then the king of Sodom said: Give me the people; the goods, keep for yourself. ²²But Abram said to the king of Sodom: I have raised my hand to YHWH, El Elyon, creator of heaven and earth, ²³that I will not take so much as a thread or a sandal-strap or anything that is yours lest you say, "It is I who have made Abram rich." ²⁴For me, only what the young men have eaten and the share of the men who went with me, Aner, Eshcol, and Mamre—let them take their share.

Comment

This chapter, of which de Vaux (1978:219) has written that it "cannot be regarded as historically useful, but it is necessary to explain its origin and character," is best understood if one follows the direction indicated by Emerton (1971) and Westermann (1985) together with Van Seters (1975:296-308).

In verses 1-11 four kings from the east, a west semite or Amorite (Amraphel), a Hurrian (Arioch), an Elamite (Chedorlaomer), and a Hittite (Tidal), join together to subdue a revolt by five insignificant rulers of equally insignificant cities around the southern region of the Dead Sea. One asks at once, at what period in the second millennium B.C.E. would a king of Elam, in the region between the Zagros mountains in southeastern Iran and the Tigris, with its capital at Sousa (modern Shush), have exercised sovereignty in southern Palestine? And how and for what reason would a Hittite, an Amorite, and a Hurrian have joined forces with him? Though the names of the eastern kings are not inventions, only one name, Tidal, is attested historically as a ruler. There are indeed large gaps in our knowledge of the period, the first half of the second millennium, in which the invasion is alleged to have taken place, and there is no indication in documents outside the Old Testament of such an alliance and invasion (though this of itself does not disqualify the account from history). The names of two of the five kings from around the Dead Sea, Bera of Sodom and Birsha of Gomorrah, are artificial names, and the name of one of the five cities, Bela, is a construction. Four of the five cities, Bela being the exception, are mentioned in the table of the nations (Gen 10:19), and in Deuteronomy 29:22 as the objects of God's destroying anger (an exilic text), while the first century book of Wisdom speaks of a righteous man whom wisdom rescued "when the ungodly were perishing; he escaped the fire that descended on the Five Cities" (10:6). The four kings of the east take the well attested historical route along the mountain plateau of Transjordan (the King's Highway, Num 20:17) and make a diversion from the object of their original campaign in which they defeat primeval peoples famed in story, the Rephaim, the Zuzim, and the Emim (v. 5; cf. the antiquarian notes in Deut 2:10-11, 20-21; 3:11, 13b) as well as historical peoples, the Horites, the Amalekites, and the Amorites (vv. 6-7; cf. Deut 2:12, 22).

Leaving aside the long lists of names in verses 1-2, 5b-7, 8-9 (seven of vv. 1-11 are lists), we are left with the frame:

v. 1 "In the days of . . . " date.
v. 4 Reason for campaign; revolt, date.
v. 5 Departure for campaign; date.
v. 8 Lines of battle drawn.
v. 10 The kings of the Dead Sea presumably defeated.
v. 11 The four kings of the east take the booty and depart.

Very similar patterns appear in the Second Book of Kings, e.g., 2 Kings 18: "He [Hezekiah] rebelled against the king of Assyria, and would not serve him" (v. 7b); "in the fourteenth year of King Hezekiah, Sennacherib king of Assyria came up against all the fortified cities of Judah and took them" (v. 13); "and when they called for the king" (v. 18); 2 Kings 24: "In his [Jehoiakim's] days Nebuchadnezzar king of Babylon came up, and Jehoiakim became his servant three years; then he turned and rebelled against him" (v. 1); "at that time the servants of Nebuchadnezzar king of Babylon came up to Jerusalem and the city was besieged" (v. 16); "the king of Babylon took him prisoner . . . and carried off all the treasures of the house of the Lord" (vv. 12b–13a); 2 Kings 24–25: "And Zedekiah rebelled against the king of Babylon" (24:20b); "In the ninth year of his reign . . . Nebuchadnezzar came with all his army" (25:1). The pattern is well known too from Babylonian-Assyrian documents in which the campaign is recorded in the first person.

We have then an easily recognizable pattern, which is standard for describing a campaign, into which two lists of contestants and their realms have been set, together with lists of peoples and places in a diversionary campaign (vv. 5b–7) which takes the invaders down into the southern Negev and back. Verses 1–11 are a self-contained piece in which there is no mention of Abraham and Lot.

In verses 12–17 and 21–24 Abraham appears as a hero after the pattern of the judges, a figure very different from the Abraham of the rest of the cycle. As Gideon with three hundred men (Judg 7:7, 16) defeated the Midianites from the desert, so too Abraham with three hundred eighteen men pursued and defeated four powerful middle eastern kings. The patriarch is exalted as a great warrior who faced successfully the great kings of the east. This hero story is joined to the account of the campaign at verse 12:

v. 11 they took all the goods and food of Sodom and Gomorrah and went;
v. 12 they took Lot, Abram's kinsman who was living in Sodom, and all his goods and went.

The mood of the campaign (vv. 1-11) flows over into and affects the hero story (vv. 12-17, 21-24). Abraham is taken up into the campaign of the kings of the east and emerges as a warrior-hero. The king of Sodom (a new king? cf. v. 10) comes out to meet Abraham on his return (v. 17). The Melchizedek (vv. 18-20) episode interrupts the meeting (v. 21 follows easily after v. 17). It too has its own separate history in tradition.

When Gideon returned from his victorious campaigns against the Midianites, he refused the request of the men of Israel to rule over them, to set up a dynasty, and to aggrandize himself from the booty (Judg 8:22-28). Abraham does the same (vv. 21-24). He has taken an oath, "I have raised my hand to YHWH, El Elyon." He wants only that the young men receive their upkeep and that his kinsmen have their just share.

Melchizedek king of Salem (Jerusalem) goes out to meet the victor. He refreshes Abraham with bread and wine. The victuals are not symbolic of, nor do they connote sacrifice, nor is the word "brought out," *hôṣî'*, in any way a sacrificial term. Verse 18 nevertheless has had profound echoes in Christian tradition as a symbol of the Eucharist, and the author of the Letter to the Hebrews (5:6-10; 6:20; 7:1-28), in an excellent example of midrash, has used the figure of Melchizedek as his point of departure to theologize on Christ the High Priest (see *Notes*). Melchizedek is both king and priest "of God Most High, creator of heaven and earth" (v. 19b). Abraham has been blessed (favored, prospered) by God in his victory and the king-priest prays implicitly that the blessing will continue. He prays too that God be acknowledged for what he has done: "May God Most High be praised." It is not correct to link this blessing with 12:1-3 which is a promise of descendants and greatness and is resumed several times in the patriarchal story. Further, each has a different history in tradition. Abraham pays a tithe to the king-priest and so acknowledges his realm, his God, and his sanctuary. This is not in contradiction to verses 22-23 in the biblical context, as Abraham is not retaining any of the booty for himself, though he is disposing of part of it. Tithes are payable only in a sedentary society and on a regular basis and there is a broad, though not unanimous, consensus among scholars that the passage is introduced to justify the practice under the monarchy or even later. Abraham accepts the name and title of the God of Melchizedek, God Most High, creator of heaven and earth (v. 19b), and equates this God with YHWH—YHWH, God Most High, creator of heaven and earth (v.

22), thus acknowledging that he and Melchizedek worship the one and the same God. The writer thereby clamps the independent Melchizedek tradition (vv. 18-20) into the story of Abraham the warrior-hero.

All aspects of chapter 14 being considered, the following explanation is reasonable: an artificial account of a campaign composed according to a standard and well attested pattern, has been constructed in which the aggressors are four kings from regions in the ancient Near East, and those in revolt are five minor kings from the region of the Dead Sea. It is not known who constructed the account and when. An account of a diversionary campaign by the four kings of the east against both primeval peoples (giants) and historical peoples is included, all these people being mentioned in Deuteronomy 2-3. The accounts of these two campaigns, which do not mention either Abraham or Lot, form a self-contained piece. A story about Abraham as a warrior-hero, after the manner of the Judges, is linked with this campaign by means of verse 12, which runs parallel to verse 11. The Abraham of this story is totally different from the Abraham of the rest of the Abraham cycle. An independent tradition about Melchizedek is built into the account of the return of Abraham, now the victorious warrior-hero, and clamped to it by the equation of the God of Melchizedek with the God of Abraham (vv. 19b, 22). It is unlikely that the account of the campaign of four very different and disparate eastern kings against five very minor kings from southern Canaan narrates an event that took place in the second millennium B.C.E.

Notes

1. AMRAPHEL KING OF SHINAR. We can say with certainty only that the proper name Amraphel is Amorite (west semitic) and so linked with Mesopotamia. The original form would be Amar-pi-el, "the mouth of the god has spoken." Attempts to identify him with Hammurapi of Mari (1792-1750), or with any of three or four contemporary rulers of the same name (in Aleppo or Kurda) founder on virtually insuperable philological difficulties. Shinar (10:10) generally designates Babylon(ia) in other parts of the Old Testament (Akkadian *šumeru*).

ARIOCH KING OF ELLASAR. Arioch is a Hurrian name and this is all that we can say with certainty. Some have proposed that he be identified with Arriwuk, son of Zimri-Lim of Mari. The Nuzi equivalent is Ariuki. The name occurs in the Book of Daniel (2:14, 15, 24, 25). Ellasar has not been explained satisfactorily; the Genesis Apocryphon (21:23) from Qumran identifies it with *Kptwk,* i.e., Cappadocia in Anatolia (Turkey).

CHEDORLAOMER KING OF ELAM. The name comprises two authentic Elamite elements, *Kudu* = protector, *Lagamur* = name of a deity. No such name has been found in historical documents, though Kutur-Nahhunte (*c.*1730) has been suggested. Elam is the region east and northeast of the Tigris valley in and at the foot of the Zagros mountains (modern southwestern Iran). It is mentioned in documents as early as 2700 B.C.E. The code of Hammurapi was discovered in its capital Sousa (modern Shush) in 1900 C.E.

TIDAL KING OF GOI-IM. Tidal is certainly the equivalent of the Hittite cuneiform Tudhaliya (Tudkhaliash). From the late eighteenth century on, there were four or five Hittite kings of this name. Tidal is the only name of these four kings of Genesis 14 that is attested in a historical document. Goi-im is the same as the Hebrew "nations" or "peoples." Speiser (1964:107) and de Vaux (1978:218) look to the seventeenth century cuneiform texts for a possible explanation where *Umman-Manda,* "the peoples of Manda," describes warlike groups from the north who irrupted into Mesopotamia and who were enemies of the Hittite king Hattusilis I. The name was later applied to the Cimerians in the first millennium and later to the Medes in the sixth century.

2. BERA, BIRSHA. *bera'* means "in evil," *birsha'* means "in wickedness," reflection on the ill repute of Sodom and Gomorrah.

SHINAB, SHEMEBER. Shemabad in the Samaritan and Shemya[o]bad in the *Genesis Apocryphon.*

BELA'. "Swallowed" or "a swallowing." It has been suggested that "the king of Bela (that is, Zoar)" is a distortion of "Bela, the king of Zoar" (for Zoar, cf. Gen 19:22, 30).

3. SIDDIM. Seems to be the proper name of the area south of the Dead Sea which was later submerged.

5-7. REPHAIM, ZUZIM, EMIM. Deuteronomy 2:2, 10-11, 20; 3:11, 13. All three are prehistoric races of giants. The Rephaim (Deut 2:11; 3:11, 13) are also the "spirits of the dead" (Isa 26:14, 19; Ps 88:11 [10]). Their city, Asteroth-karnaim, "Astarte of the two horns"

(Amos 6:11), is the capital of Bashan in northern Transjordan. The Zuzim are "the Zamzummim of Ammon" (Deut 2:20), a giant pre-Ammonite race. The name has not been explained, nor has their city, Ham, been located. The Emmim are the Rephaim in Moab (Deut 2:12) and the giant forerunners of the Moabites. Their city, Shaveh-Kiriathaim, the valley of the Kiriathaim, is near Hebron (Num 32:17; Isa 13:19).

HORITES, AMALEKITES, AMORITES. The Horites in the Old Testament are (1) non-semitic Hurrians, (2) semitic predecessors of Seir/Edom (Gen 36:20; Deut 2:12, 22). The Amalekites are the traditional enemies of Israel (Exod 17:8-16; 1 Sam 15; 20). The Amorites, western semites, are one of the pre-Israelite tribes of Canaan. They seem to have been well distributed over the mountain ranges of western Palestine. Mamre, an ally of Abraham, was an Amorite (14:13). In the time of Joshua, Amorite rulers governed western Palestine. Their city, Hazazon-tamar, is identified in 2 Chronicles 20:2 as En-Gedi on the western side of the Dead Sea.

EL-PARAN, EN-MISHPAT, KADESH. El-paran: *'yl* in Hebrew is a terebinth; Paran is the region between the Dead Sea and the Gulf of Aqabah. It may be the port of Elath. En-mishpat is the "spring of decision (judgment)." Kadesh is in the southern Negev, eighty kilometers (fifty miles) south of Beersheba (Exod 15:25; 17:7; Num 20:1; Deut 1:2).

11. GOODS. The word *rekuš,* goods or possessions, is used in verses 11, 12, 16, 17, and refers to movable possessions of all kinds. It is said to be a "late" word used only in the priestly work and postexilic books (e.g., de Vaux 1978:217).

13. ABRAM THE HEBREW. *'ibrî.* In Roman times, "Hebrews" was the term which designated the Jews of Palestine as distinct from the Jews of the Diaspora. It is used in the Old Testament for the language of Canaan (Isa 19:18) and the Judean tongue (2 Kgs 18:26; Isa 36:11; Neh 13:14; 2 Chr 32:18). It is most frequent in the Egyptian narratives: when an Egyptian speaks of an Israelite (Gen 39:17; 41:12; Exod 1:16, 22); when an Israelite speaks of his people to the Egyptians (Exod 1:19; 2:7; 3:18; 5:3; 7:16; 9:1-13); to distinguish Israelites from Egyptians (Gen 43:32; Exod 1:15; 2:11, 13). In the wars against the Philistines under Saul, it is used on the lips of the Philistines (1 Sam 4:6, 9; 13:19; 14:11; 29:3; also in 1 Sam 13:3, 7;

14:21). It is used again in the book of the Covenant in the legislation about freeing Hebrew slaves (Exod 21:2-6; resumed in Deut 15:12-17; Jer 34:9, 14). Genesis 14:13 and Jonah 1:9 are isolated uses. *'ibrî* is always used in an ethnic sense. Scholars have discussed at length the relationship of the Hebrews to the Habiru/Apiru, frequently mentioned in semitic cuneiform documents of the second millennium (an ethnic group or free-booters or mercenaries or raiding parties or fugitives or peoples on the margin of settled societies??): Weippert (1971:63–102); Cazelles (1973:1–28); de Vaux 1978:105–12, 209–16). Loretz (1984) has written a comprehensive monograph on the subject in German which has been assessed by H. Engel (1986).

14. RETAINERS. *ḥānîkîm*. The only occurrence of the word in the Old Testament; it is found in nineteenth century Egyptian execration texts (ANET 328–29) and in a fifteenth century letter from Ta'annach in Palestine.

MEN BORN IN HIS HOUSEHOLD. *yelîdê bêtô*. The phrase explains the previous word, and probably refers to servants born in the household and bound by certain obligations.

15. HOBAH. Otherwise unknown.

18. MELCHIZEDEK. *malkî-ṣedeq* = ṣedeq is my king or my king is upright. In Joshua 10:1 *'adonay ṣedeq* = ṣedeq is my lord or my lord is upright. There is attestation of a west-semitic god, *ṣedeq* (Rosenberg 1965). Other names in the Old Testament formed with *malkî*, my king, are Malki-yah (Malchiah, Jer 38:6; Ezra 10:31) = YHWH is my king, and Malkî-el (Gen 46:17) = El is my king. Melchizedek is mentioned elsewhere in the Old Testament only in Psalm 110, and in the New Testament in Hebrews 5–7. Fitzmyer (1963) has discussed fully the significance of Melchizedek in Hebrews 7 with reference to the *Genesis Apocryphon* and the Palestinian Targum Neofiti 1, with a note on Melchizedek and sacrifice in the Fathers (p. 320, n. 61). F. L. Horton (1976) has given a comprehensive account of the Melchizedek tradition from the Old Testament to the fifth century C.E.

SALEM. Hebrew, *šalem,* is usually identified with Jerusalem. In Psalm 76:3 (2), *šalem* and Sion are used in parallelism: "His abode has been established in Salem, his dwelling place in Zion." In Psalm 110 the Davidic king reigns in the same place as Melchizedek. According to E. Dhorme (*La Bible,* Paris: Pléiade, 1, 45, 1956) Shalem, correctly translated by the LXX and the Vulgate as Salem, is a small village which still bears this latter name about five kilometers east of ancient Shechem (Gen 33:18; RSV, NAB, NEB, JB second edition, all translate *šalem* by "safely"). Shalim is a well attested Amorite divinity (Chaine 1949:204–05) from which the name Jerusalem is usually derived. The oldest form of Jerusalem, U-ru-salim, is attested in seven letters from its king Abdu-heba to the Egyptian ruler at Tell-el-Amarna (1400–1350). "King of peace" (Heb 7:2), linking *šalem* with *šalôm,* is a popular interpretation known to Philo (*De Legum Allegoria* 3, 79).

'EL 'ELYON. God, Most High. El is a proper name for the senior god in the Ugaritic texts; it is also a general word for God. Elyon is an epithet of Baal at Ugarit meaning "most high"; there is also a Phoenician deity of that name. It is a regular epithet or substitute for God in the Psalms (Pss 7:18; 9:3; 18:14; 46:5; 47:3; 50:14; 57:3; 73:11; 82:6; 83:19; 87:5; 91:1, 9; 92:2; 97:5, 9; 107:11; also Deut 32:8). The composite name, *'el 'elyon,* occurs in Psalm 78:35 where it is parallel to *'elohim. Elyon* is in parallelism to *'el* in Psalms 73:11; 107:11, and to both *šadday* and YHWH in Psalm 91:1, 9.

19. CREATOR. The word is *qoneh,* the active participle of the verb *qnh,* primarily "acquire" or "possess," but also "create" (see *Notes* on 4:1). A recent discovery during the excavations in the Jewish quarter in the Old City of Jerusalem provides further background. "Of special interest is a stone-jar fragment bearing a three-line ink inscription in fine Hebrew script. The first two lines seem to have contained names, only one of which, Mikhayahu, is clearly legible. In the third line, there is the word *qn 'rs,* which apparently should be restored to read [*El*] *qoneh 'areṣ*" (Y. Yadin 1975:43). "In our inscription, the expression 'Creator of Earth' appears for the first time in a later Hebrew context, indicating that this was indeed also the epithet of the God of Israel" (N. Avigad 1984:41). A clearer and more complete reading of the inscription indicates that a series of personal names ending in *-yahu* precedes the "[*El*] *qoneh 'areṣ.*" The text may be an acknowledgment of or prayer for the blessing of El or YHWH, creator of earth (Miller 1980). The phrase El-the-Creator-of-the-Earth (*El qn 'rṣ*) is found in Phoenician (eighth century inscription from Karatepe in south central Turkey; translation ANET 499–500); our creator (*qnyn*) occurs in Ugaritic texts (Text

76:111:5-7; Pope 1955:51–52). Cross has noted that "El is the creator God of the Canaanites and *qônê 'arṣ* applies exclusively to him"
(1973:50).

19b-20a. BLESSED . . . PRAISED. The same Hebrew word, *bārûk*,
is used of both Abraham and YHWH, but with different connotations.

5. The Promises of Heir, Descendants, Land:
The Solemn Assurance
(15:1-21)

¹After these events the word of YHWH came to Abram in a vision: Do not fear Abram, I am your protector, I will reward you very
greatly. ²But Abram said: My lord, YHWH, what are you giving me
while I continue childless and a steward is my adopted heir, the
Damascene Eliezer. ³And Abram said: See, you have given me no
descendants, and my adopted heir inherits me. ⁴But the word of
YHWH came to him: This one shall not inherit you, but one who
comes from your own body shall inherit you. ⁵Then he led him outside and said: Look now at the heavens and count the stars if you
can count them. Then he said to him: So shall your descendants be.
⁶So he went on believing in YHWH and reckoned it to him as loyalty.

⁷Then he said to him: I am YHWH who brought you out from Ur
of the Chaldeans to give you this land as your inheritance. ⁸But he
said: My Lord, YHWH, how am I to know that I shall inherit it. ⁹And
he said to him: Bring me a three-year-old bull-calf and a three-year-
old she-goat and a three-year-old ram and a turtle dove and a young
pigeon. ¹⁰So he brought them all to him, and cut them down the
middle, and laid out each part opposite its counterpart; but the birds,
he did not cut. ¹¹But when the vultures swooped down on the carcasses, Abram drove them away. ¹²As the sun was going down, a deep
sleep fell upon Abram, and terror and great darkness fell upon him.

¹³And he said to Abram: Know for sure that your descendants will
be sojourners in a land that is not theirs and they will serve and suffer oppression for four hundred years. ¹⁴But on the people whom they
serve, I will pass judgment and they shall come out with great possessions. ¹⁵But you, you shall go to your fathers in peace and shall be
buried in good old age. ¹⁶But in the fourth generation they shall return here because the wickedness of the Amorites shall not have run
its course till then.

¹⁷When the sun had gone down and the darkness was thick, then a smoking pot and a flaming torch passed between these halves. ¹⁸On that day YHWH gave Abram a solemn assurance: To your descendants I give this land from the river of Egypt to the great river, the Euphrates, ¹⁹[the land of] the Kenites, the Kenizzites, the Kadmonites; ²⁰the Hittites, the Perizzites, the Rephaim; ²¹the Amorites, the Canaanites, the Girgashites, the Jebusites.

Comment

Chapter 15 is central to the biblical portrait of Abraham. It consists of (1) the promises of heir and descendants (vv. 1-5), (2) the underscoring of Abraham's steadfast faith (v. 6), and (3) a solemn ritual assurance of the land (vv. 7-12, 17) into which a theology of history has been incorporated (vv. 13-16). (One should note how the promises are heaped together in the middle of the Abraham cycle, 13:14-17; 15:1-6, 7-21; 16:10; 17:1-22; 18:1-16.) The writer has composed two narratives in which the promises are the theme. They are "factitious" narratives (my translation of Lohfink's "nachgeahmte Erzhlungen"), i.e., artificial narratives constructed around and for the purpose of communicating the promises. Their structures run parallel:

vv. 1-6			vv. 7-21	
The promise of an heir.			*The promise of the land.*	
1a	YHWH speaks word in a vision	7a	YHWH speaks word directly	
1b	YHWH assures reward	1b	YHWH assures the land	
2a	Adonai YHWH	8a	Adonai YHWH	
2-3	Abraham complains	8	Abraham asks how	
3-4	*yrš,* inherit (three times)	7-8	*yrš,* inherit (two times)	
3-5	*zera',* descendants (three times)			
4-5	YHWH assures by sign of stars	9-12, 17	YHWH assures by rite	
		13-18	*zera',* descendants (two times)	
		13-16	outline of theology of history	
6	Abraham accepts in faith YHWH's loyal assurance	18	YHWH repeats assurance of land	

The difference between these stories and many other of the patriarchal stories is that these almost certainly have no history in tradition precisely as stories but are compositions for a specific purpose which center on promises already at hand.

Verses 1-6 have a clear beginning and an end: "The word of YHWH came to Abram" (v. 1) and "he went on believing in YHWH" (v. 6). These sentences frame the dialogue. The introductory words, "After these events," are not merely editorial. What is to be narrated is to follow what has just been narrated, though not in immediate historical succession. It might be paraphrased, "now here is another story about Abraham" (22:1; 22:20; 39:7; 40:1; 48:1, though, as Westermann notes, the last three are in continuous narrative). I do not think that it is correct to see an internal link between this and the previous chapter just because the root of the verb *miggēn,* "has delivered" (14:20), appears as *māgēn,* "shield" or "protector" (15:1b) and because, as claimed at times, Abraham's reward (15:1b) is for his action and renunciation in chapter 14. The phrase "the word of YHWH came" is unique in the Pentateuch, though frequent in the Deuteronomistic history (e.g., 1 Sam 15:20; 2 Sam 24:11; 1 Kgs 12:22; 16:1; 17:2, 8; 18:31) and in the prophetic books, (e.g., Isa 1:1; Ezek 1:1; Amos 1:1; Obad 1:1; Hab 1:1). "The word of the Lord (*děbar YHWH*) is used almost exclusively in the Old Testament for the revelation received by a prophet, or for the oral communication of that revelation as a speech of Yahweh" (Tucker 1977:63). "In a vision" is found only in Ezekiel 13:7 and Numbers 24:4, 16. "Do not fear" (*'al tîrâ*) belongs primarily to the context of the holy war in Israel and is addressed to Moses, Joshua, and the kings of Judah (even to Ahaz, Isa 7:4), as well as to the kings of Assyria and Mesopotamia. It is a regular formula of assurance in the first part of Deutero-Isaiah (41:10, 14; 43:1, 5; 44:8). The writer uses two standard formulas to introduce his brief narrative, one prophetic, the other from the war tradition, but neither of which carry necessarily their original connotations. The RSV renders the last part of verse 1: "I am your shield your reward shall be very great." Other versions are: "I am giving you a very great reward," or "I am your shield, your very great reward" (NEB); "I am your shield, and shall give you a very great reward" (JB second edition). Whatever the exact translation may be (see *Notes*), YHWH is assuring Abraham of his protection and support. But Abraham complains: what is the use of it all if he has no heir and a servant of his household is to inherit him. Though the text of verse 2b does not cohere well and has given rise to a myriad of emendations and transmutations (see *Notes*), the essential meaning is clear: I have no heir, no descendant; one not of my line (an adopted servant?) is to be my heir:

v. 2b   a steward (*ben mešeq*) is my adopted heir ([*ben*] *bêtî*),
the Damascene Eliezer.

         my adopted heir (*ben bêtî*) inherits me.

v. 3b   this one shall not inherit you.

v. 4b   but one who comes from your own body shall inherit you.

The prophetic formula of verse 1a introduces God's word a second time (v. 4a). Abraham shall have a son and heir of his own body and the mother of the son is to be Sarah (11:30; 17:15-21; 18:1-16). YHWH, who directs the action throughout, will see to this (18:14a). Abraham has complained of no descendant (*zera'*, v. 4a); YHWH now promises him descendants (*zera'*, v. 5b) as countless as the stars (cf. 22:17; 26:4).

YHWH has given his word of assurance; so Abraham continues to believe in YHWH and he (Abraham) reckons it (the promise) to him (YHWH) [as] loyalty or fidelity (v. 6). The RSV reads: "And he believed the Lord; and he reckoned it to him as righteousness." Abraham, of course, believed in the Lord; but who reckoned what to whom as what? The LXX reads: "And Abraham believed in God, and it was reckoned (*elogisthē,* aorist passive) to him unto righteousness (*eis dikaiosynēn*)." Paul (Rom 4:3; Gal 3:6) and James (2:23) repeat this rendering. The accepted interpretation of Genesis 15:6 is that Abraham believed in YHWH and he (YHWH) attributed it (the act of believing) to him (Abraham) [as] *ṣĕdāqâ*. Following von Rad's important essay (1966b), many have seen the *background* to this famous verse in the liturgy of the temple. The priest declares the worshiper righteous "who conducts himself properly with reference to an existing communal relationship, who, therefore, does justice to the claims which the communal relationship, makes on him. . . . Man is righteous so long as he affirms the regulations of this communal relationship established by God, say, the covenant and the commandments." The Abraham episode is, of course, not within the realm of cult: "it is transferred to the realm of God's free and personal relationship to Abraham" (von Rad 1972:185). According to von Rad, the author of Genesis 15:6 has YHWH, not a temple official, priest or Levite, make the pronouncement. And YHWH pronounces Abraham to have fulfilled righteousness, to share righteousness, *ṣĕdāqâ*, not by an act or a work, ritual or otherwise, but by faith. Von Rad understands the verse less as a polemic than as a revolutionary statement. Faith sets one right with God, and it is God who reckons this internal act to Abraham as *ṣĕdāqâ*. But the Hebrew allows readily the translation given above. YHWH has promised that Abraham is to be the ancestor of myriads of descendants (12:2-3); but how can Abraham be the ancestor if he has no heir (15:2-3)? Despite appearances to the contrary, YHWH remains faithful to his promise; this fidelity or loyalty is YHWH's *ṣĕdāqâ* which Abraham acknowledges (Gaston 1980; Oeming 1983). Hence, verse 6 is rendered: "So Abraham went on believing in YHWH and he (Abraham) reckoned it (the assurance given in v. 4) to him (YHWH) as (YHWH's) loyalty." The Old Testament theologian who wrote this unit and concluded it with Abraham acknowledging in faith God's faithfulness, was not aware of the problem that Paul faced when writing to the Galatians and Romans, nor of the religious debates of the sixteenth century.

The two actors in the second story have been introduced already so that there is no need to introduce them again. YHWH, who initiates all the action, addresses Abraham directly and promises him the land (v. 7). The introductory formula, "I am YHWH," and the pattern of the address occurs with reference to the deliverance from Egypt in Leviticus 25:38: "I am YHWH your (plural) God who brought you (plural) out from the land of Egypt to give you (plural) the land of Canaan." Abraham is the representative of Israel in the Genesis passage. Abraham, despite his persisting faith (v. 6), asks for assurance (v. 8). YHWH gives him the assurance: "Know for sure" (v. 13), and confirms it by means of the solemn and strange ritual (vv. 9-12, 17). The primary purpose of this second factitious narrative is not to describe a sacrificial action, but to present in narrative form God's solemn promise of the land assured by a solemn ceremony which constitutes God's oath. The ceremony has a clear beginning (v. 9) and an end (v. 18). It is interrupted by verses 13-16 where God communicates to Abraham in a "trance" (*tardēmâ*, "dream," "deep sleep," cf. Gen 2:21) an outline of a theology of history. This episode has its own introduction, "a deep sleep fell upon Abram" (v. 12b), and is tied into the rite by "As the sun was going down" (v. 12a) and "when the sun had gone down" (v. 17a). The feeling of awe and solemnity is heightened by the swooping vultures (v. 11a), the terror and great darkness (v. 12b), and the thick darkness (v. 17a). Scholars have not been successful in elucidating the "swooping vultures"—birds of ill-omen, evil spirits or, more likely, part of the literary effect.

The three times repeated "three-year-old" (v. 9) echoes the language of an ordered rite, and the mention of the birds recalls Leviticus 1:14-17; 5:7-10 where the birds are not to be divided in the sacrificial rite, but their necks are to be wrung. The ritual of cutting the larger animals in two, laying the parts opposite each other, and passing between them (vv. 10, 17) constitutes a solemn action. In Jeremiah 34:8-24, the Lord upbraids the leaders in Jerusalem because they have broken the covenant they made to free Hebrew slaves (34:8, 10). Hence God's threat: "The men who transgressed my covenant, who did not stand by the words of the covenant which they made before me, I will make the bull-calf which they cut in two and passed between its parts" (34:18-19; there is no "as" or "like," Hebrew *kĕ,* before "the bull-calf"). The leaders and the people made a covenant by cutting a bull-calf in two and passing between the parts. The divided carcasses become a prey to the birds and beasts; so too will the carcasses of the leaders and the people become a prey to the Babylon army. The Lord will make them literally "the bull-calf" that was preyed upon. In Genesis 15, YHWH passes symbolically between the severed animals as "a smoking fire pot and a flaming torch" and so gives a solemn assurance that the promise of the land will be fulfilled (v. 18b). The text does not state that there was formal sacrifice or that the Lord took an oath. However, the theme of the oath to give the land to Abraham and his successors is taken up in 22:16; 26:3; it is characteristically dtn-dtr and it recurs through the Pentateuch (Exod 13:5, 11; 31:13; 33:1; Num 11:12; 14:16, 23; 32:11; Deut 1:8, 35; 6:10, 18, 23; 7:8, 13; 8:1; 9:5; 10:11; 11:9, 21; 19:8; 26:3, 15; 28:11; 30:20; 31:7, 20, 21; and it rounds off the story of Moses, 34:4).

Verses 13-16 are an interpretation of history clothed in the form of a prediction. Verses 13, 14, 16 are about Israel, verse 15 is about Abraham. God controls history; he directs the destiny of Israel and other nations. He also directs Abraham through a blessed life to a blessed death in peace (*šālôm*) with his fathers. This is God's plan in history. Von Rad describes the passage as "a cabinet piece of Old Testament theology of history" (1972:188). He points to (1) the universal aspect, God rules over world history; (2) the nations, who eventually become ripe for judgment in the course of history; (3) God, who follows a special plan in world history for his people; (4) Abraham and Israel, who are to know of God's mysterious plan, and who are not to think of history as a riddle but to understand it in faith (Gen 18:17). The Amorites, one of the pre-Israelite inhabitants of the land, are regarded poorly in the tradition (Deut 9:4-5; Lev 18:24-27; 1 Kgs 14:24). Their lawlessness brings its own retribution in history. Throughout chapter 15, as in Genesis 6:18 and 9:8-17, God is the main actor and the initiator of the covenant. It is he who imposes obligations on himself; it is he, and only he, who gives the solemn assurance. C. T. Begg has studied the subsequent history in Jewish tradition of the animal rites described here (1988).

Notes

1. DELIVERER. The word *māgēn* means shield (Deut 33:29; Pss 18:3, 31; 84:12 [11]; 144:2). Dahood (1964:94; 1968:282-83) has proposed that the participle *mogēn* be read and that the verb be linked with the Ugaritic *mgn* = bestow, and further that the participle of the verb *śākār,* to reward, be read, giving *śokēreka* = one who rewards you; hence the translation: "I am your benefactor, who will reward you very greatly." Psalm 84:12 [11] may be rendered: "Truly sun (king) and benefactor (*mogēn* for *magēn*) is YHWH, God bestowing (*mogēn,* understood) favor and honor." (In the court correspondence of Tell-el-Amarna, fourteenth century B.C.E., *šamšu,* "sun," was used to designate the Pharaoh).

2. A STEWARD IS MY ADOPTED HEIR, THE DAMASCENE ELIEZER. The text of verse 2b reads: *û-ben mešeq bêtî hû dammeśeq 'eli'ezer;* literally, "and the son of mesheq (of) my house, he (or, is) (the) Damascene Eliezer." The words *ben bêtî,* son of my house, occur again in verse 3b without the troublesome *mešeq* interposed between them. Amid the many emendations, rearrangements, and omissions that have been proposed, some of them as justified as that accepted here, I follow for the most part Cazelles (1962:330-31): *ben bêtî* corresponds to the Akkadian *mar bîtî,* son of the house, i.e., a slave given freedom by adoption; the Ugaritic *mšq mlkt* is the drinking cup of the queen (Hebr. *šaqah;* in Hip'il, to give to drink; *mašqeh,* irrigation, drink), and *ben mešeq* is a cup-bearer or steward; hence the rendering: "and a steward (*ben mešeq*) is my adopted heir (*ben* is understood before *bêtî*), (namely) the Damascene Eliezer." Verse 3b reads: "and my adopted heir inherits me," i.e., one who is not descended from my own body. The text does not mention adoption specifically, but it is there implicitly if one equates *ben bêtî* with the Akkadian *mar bîtî.* N. J. Tromp (1969:77-78) has proposed that *bêt,*

house, be understood as meaning *sheol,* grave, and that verse 2 be read: "Lord Yahweh, what could you give me, if I pass away childless and if the one who pours out libations on my grave ("house") is Eliezer. . . . "

Some have thought that the documents from Nuzi (see *Notes* to 12:10-20) may provide a background to verses 1-6. In the ancient Near East a man or woman who was childless could adopt another, free-born or slave. The adoptee would be obliged to care for and bury the adopter and eventually become the heir. In the case of genuine adoption, some of the Nuzi texts provide that if the adopter subsequently begets a son, the adoptee must yield his rights to the first-born and heir of the adopter (ANET 219, Nr. 2; 220, Nr. 3). This form of adoption could be abused so as to evade land laws and to keep the property within the family. The law declared that land was inalienable and must be kept with the family. One who was in financial straits could adopt as his son a wealthy man who would help settle financial matters and so, in recompense, become the heir. The Nuzi documents tell of one named Tehiptilla (ANET 219, Nr. 1), the wealthiest man in the community, who was adopted by a number of people; he gave a gift to each of his "fathers." But there is no provision for caring for them in life or of mourning for them in death. These interesting documents provide a general background against which the Abraham-Eliezer episode may be read; it is not a question of direct influence (Thompson 1974:203–30; Van Seters 1975:85–87; de Vaux 1978:249; Selman 1980:109).

6. HE WENT ON BELIEVING. *wĕhe'emîn* from [*'aman*], to be firm; in Hip'il, to believe. This is a case of the frequentative use of the perfect consecutive (Ges-K 112, 3 [a] [d], ss). The well-known passage from Isaiah 7:9 plays on both meanings deriving from [*'aman*]: "If you stand not in faith, you'll stand not at all," *'im lo' ta'mînû kî lo' tē'āmēnû;* see further Isaiah 28:16: "who stands in faith, runs not around (distractedly)," *hamma'ămîn lo' yāḥîš.*

LOYALTY. The Hebrew *ṣĕdāqâ* is rendered by sixteen different words in the RSV, the most frequent of which is "righteousness," whatever that may mean. God's *ṣedeq* or *ṣĕdāqâ* (no difference in meaning; the words occur forty-nine times and thirty-four times respectively in the Psalms and, all told, thirty-six times in Isa 40-66) is for the most part his saving action towards his people with frequent connotations of loyalty or fidelity. The *ṣedeq* or *ṣĕdāqâ* (often used in coordination with or in parallelism to *mišpaṭ,* order, ordinance, judgment, a regular and proper way of doing something) of the individual or the group in Israel describes the proper order in the life of the people that is put there by God and is the right response to his *ṣedeq* or *ṣĕdāqâ*.

10. CUT THEM DOWN THE MIDDLE. The usual phrase "to make a covenant" is *kārat bĕrît,* "to cut a covenant." It is an idiom, a phrase approved by usage the meaning of which is not deducible from the component parts, i.e., whenever the phrase is used, it does not have to mean that something is in fact cut into parts. The word used here for "cut" is the unusual *bātār,* found elsewhere only in Jeremiah 34:18-19 and Song of Songs 2:17. It has been proposed that in the Song of Songs the words *'al hārê bāter* mean "on the mountains of the parts cut in two," i.e., of the alliance, and that the mountains are those of the land promised to Abraham (Robert-Tournay-Feuillet 1963:128–29). The background of the rite used here is very obscure. A text from Mari (eighteenth century B.C.E.) describes the making of a covenant:

> To my lord say: Thus Ibal-Il thy servant. The tablet of Ibal-Adad from Aslakka reached me and I went to Aslakka to "kill an ass" between the Hanu and Idmaras. A "puppy and lettuce" they brought, but I obeyed my lord and I did not give "the puppy and lettuce." I caused the foal of an ass to be slaughtered. I established peace between Hanu and Idamaras (ANET 482, trans. W. F. Albright; for a modified trans. cf. G. F. Hasel [1981]).

The note in ANET to the translation referring to "kill an ass" says that the expression "is always in Amorite, transcribed in cuneiform *hayaram gatulum* (Hebr. *qāṭol 'ayir*); it means simply 'make a treaty,' which was solemnized by the sacrifice of a young ass." Coming down a thousand years to the treaty between Ashurnirari V of Assyria and Mati'ilu of Arpad (eighth century B.C.E.), we read:

> This spring lamb has been brought from its fold not for sacrifice, not for a banquet, not for a purchase, not for (divination concerning) a sick man, not to be slaughtered for [. . .]: it has been brought to sanction the treaty between Ashurnirari and Mati'ilu. If Mati'ilu sins against (this) treaty made under oath by the gods, then, just as this spring lamb, brought from its fold, will not return to its fold, will not behold its fold again, alas, Mati'ilu, together with his sons, daughters, officials, and the people of his land [will be ousted] from his country, will not return to his country, and not behold his coun-

try again. This head is not the head of a lamb, it is the head of Mati'ilu, it is the head of his sons, his officials, and the people of his land. If Mati'ilu sins against this treaty, so may, just as the head of this spring lamb is torn off, and its knuckle placed in its mouth [. . .], the head of Mati'ilu be torn off, and his sons [. . .] . . . (ANET Supp 96 (532).

Other treaties provide similar but varied backgrounds (Hasel 1981). One does not interpret the rite of Genesis 15 through these treaties which, nevertheless, remain a useful background.

12. A DEEP SLEEP. *tardēmâ.* A deep sleep (trance?), awe, and darkness accompany some sort of communication from above in Job 4:13; 33:16.

18. THE RIVER OF EGYPT. Usually the Nile; but Egypt is not part of the promised land. Here "the river of Egypt" refers to the modern Wadi-el-'Arish which separates Palestine from the Sinai Peninsula. Between the two World Wars El 'Arish was the residence of the British Governor of Sinai. The geographical details in this verse compass the widest possible extent of the land of Israel (1 Kgs 5:1 [4:21]).

19-21. KENITES. They come from somewhere in Sinai or Arabia, southeast of the Gulf of Aqabah. Moses married a Kenite woman and the Kenites settled with Judah in the area of Arad (Judg 1:16). Saul (1 Sam 15:6) and David (1 Sam 27:10; 30:29) encounter the Kenites. Relations between them and early Israel were friendly.

KENIZZITES. Caleb was a Kenizzite (Josh 14:6, 14).

KADMONITES. Literally, "easterners."

HITTITES. Cf. *Notes* chapter 23. The empire of the classical Hittites flourished in Anatolia 1800–1200 B.C.E. (approx.).

PERIZZITES. *Notes* 13:7.

REPHAIM. *Notes* 14:5-7.

JEBUSITES. The ruling Hurrian element in Jerusalem in the Amarna period (c. 1400 B.C.E.).

6. The Child of the Maid Servant
(16:1-16)

¹Sarai the wife of Abram had borne him no children. She had a maid servant, an Egyptian, whose name was Hagar. ²Sarai said to Abram: Seeing that YHWH has prevented me from bearing children, go now to my maid servant; perhaps I shall be built up from her. So Abram listened to the voice of Sarai. ³So Sarai the wife of Abram took Hagar the Egyptian, her maid servant, and gave her to Abram her husband as wife after Abram had been living in the land of Canaan for ten years. ⁴He went to Hagar and she became pregnant. When she saw that she was pregnant, her mistress lost status in her eyes. ⁵So Sarai said to Abram: The outrage on me be upon you. I gave my maid servant to your embrace; now that she sees that she is pregnant, I have lost status in her eyes; let YHWH judge between me and you. ⁶But Abram said to Sarai: Your maid servant is in your hands; do with her as you will. So Sarai made life hard for her, and she fled from her.

⁷The messenger of YHWH found her by a spring of water in the desert, by the spring on the way to Shur, ⁸and he said: Hagar, maid servant of Sarai, from where are you coming and where are you going to? She said: From Sarai my mistress; I am fleeing. ⁹The messenger of YHWH said to her: Return to your mistress and submit to her authority. ¹⁰The messenger of YHWH said to her: I will multiply your descendants greatly so that they cannot be counted for number. ¹¹The messenger of YHWH said to her: See, you are pregnant and shall give birth to a son and you shall call him Ishmael, because YHWH has attended to your hardship. ¹²He shall be a wild-ass of a man, his hand against everyone and the hand of everyone against him. He shall dwell over against his kinsmen. ¹³Then she invoked the name of YHWH who was speaking to her: You are El who sees me! for she said: Have I really seen (God) after he has seen me? ¹⁴And so she called the well, the well of the living one who sees me. It lies between Kadesh and Bered.

¹⁵And Hagar bore a son to Abram, and Abram called his son whom Hagar had borne Ishmael. ¹⁶Abram was eighty-six years old when Hagar bore Ishmael to Abram.

Comment

Verse 1a is the point of departure of the narrative and the point of return (vv. 15-16). The narrative is the story of a childless wife who wants to "build up" (v. 2) her family. In the broad context of the Abraham cycle it is a question of the continuation of the line. The first verse "Sarai the wife of Abraham had borne him no children" echoes "Now Sarai was barren, she had no child" (11:30). The narrative moves from the childless wife, through recrimination and conflict, to its climax in the distressed Hagar on whom it now focuses, and then on to resolution with the birth of an heir, though not the child of the promise. Whatever the sources and editorial history, the alleged "additions" and independent units, this is the narrative that lies before us. The three actors introduced in v. 1 continue active through the first part of the story (vv. 1-6); but only Hagar is there to encounter YHWH in the second part (vv. 7-14). The story cannot end with v. 6; Sarah has not yet achieved her purpose: "Perhaps I shall be built up from her" (v. 2b). The son of the mistress' maid servant is the son and heir of the household and remains heir unless a son is born to the mistress. But a son born and living in the desert, even though blessed by YHWH (v. 10) and whose name is given and tribal life described (vv. 11-12), cannot live as a member of the household. So Hagar must go back to the household to give birth (v. 9). Hagar has encountered God; she reflects on her experience (vv. 13-14). Abraham, without a son at the beginning of the story (v. 1a), is now the father of a son (vv. 15-16).

Chapter 16 as it lies before us brings together several themes and literary formulas. The theme of the childless wife (vv. 1-3) leads to conflict and hardship (vv. 4-6), on to divine concern for the one suffering the hardship (vv. 7-9), and to promise (v. 10). The birth formula (vv. 11-12) is followed by an etiology (vv. 13-14).

The patriarchal stories know, and Sarah acknowledges, that God is in control of birth (16:2, 11; 18:10-14; 20:18; 29:31; 30:22). When Sarah gives her personal maid servant to her husband she is following normal practice in the circumstances in the ancient Near East of the second and first millennium (*Notes*). But Hagar is not a mere bed companion; she shares in the life of the father of the household. Sarah loses caste in Hagar's eyes. Conflict is imminent. She confronts Abraham with a legal formula, "let YHWH judge between me and you" (v. 5c; cf. Gen 31:53; 1 Sam 24:13 [12], 16[15]) because she has suffered an injustice and holds Abraham responsible. So Abraham gives his secondary wife into the power of the mistress of the house.

Hagar is now in the desert by a spring (or well) of water. Van Seters (1975:193) has written that "the well is nothing more than a piece of scenery in the story, the place where strangers meet in the desert." It is "secondary." No; a well is a natural meeting place for strangers, friends, and kinsmen alike (Gen 24:11; 29:2; Exod 2:15-16). Though Hagar is not in mortal danger, as she and the child are in 21:15-16, the well is more than scenery. It is the place where God communicates with her. Because YHWH has seen her (attended to her distress) and she has seen (experienced) him, she gives God and the well a name: "El who sees me" and "the well of the living one who sees me" (vv. 13-14). God communicates through his messenger (*mal'ak*). The messenger is the one who encounters a person and who is there only in the meeting and nowhere else. The *mal'ak* is just there and not there. God is in the message, not in the messenger. It is not a case of "separated spiritual substances" (North 1967). It is not an ontological matter.

Exegetes have been preoccupied with the structure and process of formation of the chapter. Were verses 1-6 and 7-14 originally two independent self-contained narratives which were joined together, the one narrating a conflict between two women, the other giving an account of a birth? Do verses 1a, 3, 15-16, as the work of a (priestly) editor, frame an already existing story, as can be well argued? Did verses 11-12 follow immediately on verse 8 in the original story? Are verses 9, 10, 11, each of which begins with the formula "the messenger of YHWH said to her," independent sayings brought together loosely in the final story? Is the announcement of the birth (vv. 11-12) a unit independent of the original story? Do verses 13-14 contain two independent etiologies which have been brought together (v. 13)? There are almost as many answers to these questions as there are commentators. The one certainty is that the present text is the end product of a process of growth. The way is wide open to more or less convincing, and subjective, conjecture.

It is worthwhile dwelling briefly on the three verses introduced by the messenger formula (vv. 9, 10, 11). Verses 9-10 are described at times as "redactional additions." If so, an addition to what, by whom, and when? Verse 10 directs the promise of numerous progeny (12:2-3; 13:16; 15:5; 21:13) to Ishmael's line, underscoring the patriarch's concern for him (17:20; 21:13). Verse 11 is a birth formula which occurs several times in the Old Testament with slight variations (Gen 17:19; Judg 13:3-5; Isa 7:14; add 1 Kgs 13:2; 1 Chr 22:9) as well as in the New Testament (Luke 1:31; cf. Matt 1:23). However "independent" the sayings may be, they have been brought together in the middle of the Abraham cycle—verse 9 so that Ishmael may live as son and heir, at least for a time, in the household;

verse 10 to record the blessing on Ishmael "because he is your descendant" (21:13); verse 11 to announce the fact of Ishmael's birth, his nature, and his destiny, and to describe the characteristics of the Ishmaelites. For all its pre-history, the text must be read as it lies before us as part of the Abraham cycle. It is the story of a childless wife who takes the measures, normal in her society, to provide an heir, and which leads to conflict and distress. The child born, though not to be heir in the long run, is under the blessing of God. The mother experiences God through conflict and distress.

The tribal explanation, that the story is etiological, answering the question "how did Ishmael become a bedouin?" (v. 12) is marginal (Gunkel 1910:188-89); though, as Gunkel observed, if we had an accurate historical account of Ishmael, we would remain more or less indifferent to it because Ishmael, in the biblical story, has scarcely accomplished anything for the human race; but because poetic imagination has depicted him as a "wild ass of a man" (16:12), he lives on forever. Von Rad has followed Gunkel's romanticism, so fashionable in descriptions of bedouin life in the late nineteenth and early twentieth centuries; the description shows "undisguised sympathy and admiration for the roving Bedouin who bends his neck to no yoke" (1972:194). The story is partly, though by no means wholly, a disputation between women. But the disputation arises only from the means taken to have an heir. The story in its final form is not a story of Abraham, a man of little faith, who uses natural means to anticipate, substitute for, or hasten God's action (von Rad 1972:196). It presents an Abraham tradition different from chapter 15. It is, by and large, a family story. The explanation of the Hagar stories (16; 21:8-21) as grounded in stories of the exposition of a child in which the central motif is symbolic death followed by symbolic resurrection is far from convincing (White 1975).

Notes

2. GO NOW TO MY MAID SERVANT. When Rachel saw that she bore no children to Jacob, she gave him her maid, Bilhah, so that "I may have children through her" (30:1-3). When Leah ceased bearing children, she gave her maid, Zilpah, to Jacob as wife (30:9). The maid servant is not just a slave, but a servant girl attached in a special way to the mistress of the house. Texts from the ancient Near East provide a useful background. An old Assyrian text from the nineteenth century reads:

> Laqipum has married Hatala, daughter of Enishru. . . . If within
> two years she (i.e., Hatala) does not provide him with offspring, she
> will purchase a slave woman, and later on, after she (the slave woman,
> but perhaps Hatala) will have produced a child by him, he may dis-
> pose of her by sale wheresoever he pleases . . . (ANET Supp 543 [4]).

An adoption text from fifteenth century Nuzi provides:

> . . . Kelim-ninu has been given in marriage to Shennima. If Kelim-
> ninu bears (children) Shennima shall not take another wife; but if
> Kelim-ninu does not bear, Kelim-ninu shall acquire a woman of the
> land of Lullu as wife for Shennima, and Kelim-ninu may not send
> the offspring away (OR "shall not have authority over the offspring"
> [Speiser 1964:120]) (ANET 220 [3]).

A section from the Code of Hammurapi from the eighteenth-
seventeenth century is often quoted:

> When a seignior (i.e., a free man) married a hierodule (i.e., a priest-
> ess) and she gave a female slave to her husband and she has then borne
> children, if later that female has claimed equality with her mistress
> because she bore children, her mistress may not sell her; she may mark
> her with a slave-mark and count her among the slaves (ANET 172:146).

Thus the priestess finds a way around the law which forbids her to
have children of her own. Another law from the Code of Hammurapi
reads:

> When a seignior's first wife bore him children and his female slave
> also bore him children, if the father during his lifetime has ever said:
> "My children!" to the children whom the slave bore him, thus hav-
> ing counted them with the children of the first wife, after the father
> has gone to (his) fate, the children of the first wife and the children
> of the slave shall share equally in the goods of the paternal estate,
> with the first-born, the son of the first wife receiving a preferential
> share (ANET 173:170).

And finally the nineteenth century Code of Lipit-Ishtar states:

> If a man's wife has not borne him children (but) a harlot (from) the
> public square has borne him children, he shall provide grain, oil, and
> clothing for that harlot; the children which the harlot has borne him
> shall not be his heirs, and as long as his wife lives the harlot shall
> not live in the house with his wife (ANET 160:27).

This is the varied ancient Near Eastern background out of which Genesis 16:1-6 comes. It neither proves nor disproves a historical background to the biblical story nor, of itself, sets the story in either the second or the first millennium. It is simply what it is—very helpful historical background. Thompson (1974:252–69) and Van Seters (1975:68–71) treat the question in detail.

PERHAPS I SHALL BE BUILT UP FROM HER. *'ibbâneh.* "the life of a woman is an integral whole . . . only when she is a member of a family in which she presents her husband with children" (Westermann 1984:239).

6. SARAI MADE LIFE HARD FOR HER. *te'anneh,* she made life hard, and *'oni* (v. 11), hardship, are from the same root, *'ānāh.*

7. THE MESSENGER OF YHWH. The formulas *mal'ak YHWH* and *mal'ak 'elohim* occur fifty-eight times and eleven times respectively in the Old Testament. It is best to avoid the translation "angel of the LORD" because of later associations with intermediary figures in the intertestamental period and representations in medieval and renaissance Christian art. God speaks in the messenger.

SHUR. Hagar went southwards to Shur (lit., a wall, cf. 20:1; 25:18). It may not be a place name, but the wall of defense built on the Egyptian frontier to control the "Asiatics."

11B. BECAUSE YHWH HAS ATTENDED TO YOUR HARDSHIP. The name Ishmael, *yišma' 'el,* means "God hears." Dahood (1968, 1980) has proposed that verse 11b be read as: "For YHWH has heard you, El has answered you" (*kî yišma' YHWH, 'el 'anayakî*), which requires no change in the consonantal text.

12. HIS HAND AGAINST EVERYONE. Referring to the way of life of the Ishmaelites. They shall be raiders against their kinsmen.

13-14. YOU ARE EL WHO SEES ME. There are many versions of these difficult verses. Verse 13a, "you are El who sees me," or "you are the God of seeing" is clear enough. Verse 13b reads: *hagam hălom ra'îtî 'ahărê ro'î,* which is literally "also here have I seen after his seeing me." God has seen, listened to, attended to, Hagar; Hagar has seen, experienced God; she utters an exclamation of praise. Various emendations of the text have been made, the best known being that of Wellhausen, "Did I really see God and yet remained alive?" (*hgm 'elhm r'yty w'hy*). Speiser (1964:117) translates: "Did I not go on seeing here after he had seen me?'' Another version reads: ''Would I have gone here indeed (thither) looking for him that looks after me'' (Booij 1980). Hagar names the well ''the well of the living one who sees me.'' The name records her experience.

KADESH. About ninety-five kilometers (sixty miles) south of Beersheba.

7. The Covenant and Its Sign
(17:1-27)

[1]When Abram was ninety-nine years old YHWH appeared to Abram and said to him: I am El šadday. Walk before me with integrity. [2]I am making my covenant between me and you and will multiply you very greatly. [3]Then Abram fell on his face and God spoke to him saying: [4]See, I make my covenant with you so that you will be the father of a great number of nations. [5]No longer shall your name be called Abram, but your name shall be Abraham because I make you the father of a great number of nations. [6]I will make you very fruitful and I will make nations of you and kings shall come from you. [7]And I establish my covenant between me and you and your descendants after you through their generations as an everlasting covenant to be God to you and your descendants after you. [8]I give you and your descendants after you the land where you sojourn, all the land of Canaan as an everlasting possession, and I will be God to them.

[9]And God said to Abraham: And you, you are to keep my covenant, you and your descendants after you through their generations. [10]This is my covenant between me and you and your descendants after you that you are to keep: Every male among you shall be circumcised. [11]You shall circumcise the flesh of your foreskins so that it shall be a sign of the covenant between me and you. [12]A boy eight days old among you shall be circumcised, every male of your generations born in the household or bought with silver from a foreigner who is not from your descendants. [13]He who is born of your household and he who is bought with silver shall be circumcised, and so my covenant in your flesh shall be an everlasting covenant. [14]An uncircumcised male who is not circumcised in the flesh of his foreskin, this person shall be cut off from the people he has broken my covenant.

[15]Then God said to Abraham: Sarai your wife—her name shall not be called Sarai, but her name shall be Sarah. [16]I will bless her and will give you a son from her; I will bless her and she shall issue into nations; kings of peoples shall come from her. [17]And Abraham fell

on his face and laughed and said to himself: Shall a child be born to one who is a hundred years old? And shall Sarah bear at ninety? ¹⁸Then Abraham said to God: If only Ishmael would live under your care! ¹⁹And God said: No, Sarah your wife shall bear a son, and you shall call him Isaac. And I will establish my covenant with him and his descendants with him, an everlasting covenant. ²⁰As for Ishmael, I have heard you; yes, I will bless him and make him fruitful and multiply him very greatly; he shall beget twelve princes and I will make him a great nation. ²¹But my covenant I will establish with Isaac whom Sarah shall bear to you at this time next year. ²²When God had finished speaking with him, he went up from Abraham.

²³Then Abraham took Ishmael his son and all born in his household and all bought with silver, all males of Abraham's household, and circumcised the flesh of their foreskins that very day as God had said to him. ²⁴And Abraham was ninety-nine years old when he circumcised the flesh of his foreskin. ²⁵Ishmael his son was thirteen years old when he was circumcised in the flesh of his foreskin. ²⁶On that very day Abraham and his son Ishmael were circumcised, ²⁷and all the men of his household, those born there and those bought with silver from a foreigner were circumcised with him.

Comment

The unit 17:1-22 defines itself clearly: "YHWH appeared to Abram" (v. 1a) is the beginning and "When God had finished speaking with him, he went up from Abraham" (v. 22) is the end. Abraham then carries out the divine command (vv. 23-27). God is the main speaker throughout (vv. 1b-2, 3b-16, 19-21); Abraham falls prostrate (vv. 3a, 17a), laughs and doubts (v. 17b), and expresses a wish about Ishmael (v. 18). The passage is not a narrative, but a divine speech in which God gives a solemn assurance, as in 9:8-17. The word *běrît,* usually translated by covenant, occurs thirteen times: in the preamble (vv. 1b-3a; one time), in the first series of promises (vv. 3b-8; three times), in the command to make circumcision the sign of the covenant (vv. 9-14; six times), in the promise of a son (vv. 15-21; three times). The passage is entirely theological. The writer is heir to the promise material in Israel and reworks the traditions at hand to him (12:1-3; 15; 18:1-15; traces of 16; 21). The promise of increase or a multitude of descendants dominates and is distributed throughout the divine speech: "I will multiply you very greatly (vv. 2b, 20a); "I will make you very fruitful" (vv. 6a, 20a); "you will be the father of a great number of nations" (vv. 4b, 5b); "kings shall come from you" (vv. 6b, 16b, 20b); "I will bless her (him) and make her (him) fruitful" (vv. 16b, 20a); "I will make him a great nation" (v. 20b). Then there is the promise of the land (v. 8), and the assurance of the divine presence (vv. 7b, 8b), which is characteristic of the Jacob cycle. The promise of the son and heir is given solemnly in verses 15-21. The writer, usually designated the priestly writer (P), is not attending to a single event but is looking to the Abraham story as a whole, the essence of which is promise with verse 7 as its center. God is the main actor, in fact the sole actor; Abraham is the passive recipient. God binds himself and Abraham; Abraham does not, and cannot, bind God; he can only respond to God.

Between the promises of descendants and divine presence (vv. 2-8) and the promise of a son (vv. 15-21) comes the prescription of circumcision, the sign of the covenant (vv. 9-14). Circumcision is brought into relationship with the covenant (vv. 10b, 11b, 13b). We do not know how circumcision became a sign of the covenant and a condition for belonging to the worshipping community of Israel. Originally, the rite had no connection with the worship of God in Israel. The writer wants to ground circumcision in the patriarchal period, in the era of Israel's first fathers. During the exile, Israel lived among people who did not practice circumcision. Hence, Israel made it the distinctive mark of the male who belonged to Israel and YHWH.

It is very likely that the chapter was composed for and addressed to the post-exilic community to help it to find its identity by anchoring circumcision in the tradition of the covenant with Abraham. The account of the execution of the divine command (vv. 22-27) is an exhortation to action.

There are three names for God in the first three verses: YHWH, El šadday, and Elohim (v. 3). Elohim only is used throughout the rest of the chapter. Most exegetes attribute chapter 17 to the priestly writer, so that many ascribe the proper name YHWH to a redactor or to a scribal error because in the priestly tradition the divine name YHWH is first revealed to Moses (Exod 6:2-3). But this procedure smacks of the *deus ex machina*. Some think that the name YHWH is equated with El šadday, just as it is with El Elyon (14:22) and El Ro'i (16:13). Westermann (1984:252) suggests that the priestly writer is passing on an ancient patriarchal promise in which the divine name is given as YHWH, an explanation which, though not entirely convincing, is least open to objection.

Covenant, *běrît,* repeated thirteen times in 9:8-17, is here a "solemn assurance" given by God. Abram is no longer Abram but Abraham, just as Sarai is no longer Sarai but Sarah (v. 15). A change in name meant a change in destiny for the ancient. Abraham and Sarah are to be the father and mother of nations and, under God's direction, the father and mother of his people. Later, Jacob becomes Israel (32:29 [30]; 35:10), the name of God's people in the context of election.

Abraham has been constituted the father of many, "I make you" (v. 5b). The solemn assurance is everlasting (v. 7; cf. vv. 9b, 13, 19; cf. 9:16). The covenant of Sinai is everlasting (Exod 31:16); the house of David is to last forever (2 Sam 7:16, 24-29; Pss 89:29-30 [28-29]; 132:12). The prophets of the exile later speak of the "everlasting covenant" (Isa 55:3; 61:8). After the disaster of the destruction of Jerusalem and the agonies of the exile, the prophets and singers of Israel wanted to assure the people that God had not abandoned them. The name of the son of the solemn promise or assurance is to be Isaac, *yiṣḥaq* (v. 19b). Abraham had laughed, *way-yiṣḥaq* (v. 17), hinting at the name. The *yiṣḥaq* theme continues through chapter 18 where Sarah laughs, *wat-tiṣḥaq* (18:12, 13, 15), and chapter 21, where Sarah says "God has made laughter (*ṣehoq*) for me; every one who hears will laugh over me (*yiṣḥaq*)" (2:16), and then sees Ishmael playing (*meṣḥēq*) with Isaac (21:9).

Notes

1. EL ŠADDAY. *El šadday* occurs forty-eight times in the Old Testament, eight times in the "long form," i.e., with El as *El šadday,* on other occasions simply as *šadday.* The "long form" is restricted to Genesis 17:1; 28:3; 35:11; 43:14; 48:3; (49:25, BHS ?); Exodus 6:3, all generally regarded as priestly passages; and Ezekiel 10:5 (cf. 1:24). *šadday* occurs by itself thirty-one times in the Book of Job (Weippert 1976). In Psalm 91:1 (the other psalm occurrence is in Psalm 68:15 [14]) it occurs in a group of four names for God: "He who dwells in the shelter of Elyon, who abides in the shadow of El šadday, will say to YHWH: My refuge and my fortress; Elohim, in whom I trust." Jerome's Vulgate version, *omnipotens,* has established "almighty" as the equivalent in the western tradition. Scholars have discussed *šadday* in detail, deriving it from *šdd, šd',* = to deal violently with, to destroy, hence, "destroyer" or "all

powerful"; from *šaday/šadeh* = field, hence, "God of the plain, of the field, of the steppe"; from *šad* = breast, hence, "the God of the breasts" (Biale 1981/82). It has been proposed also that El *šadday* was a lunar deity (Abel 1973). Cross (1973:52-60) and de Vaux (1978:263-65) had each suggested independently that the name had a northwest semitic or Canaanite or Ugaritic origin; Weippert concluded his discussion: "We have to do with a pre-Yahwistic (Canaanite?) name for God, about the history and original nature of which we can scarcely say anything more." More recently, Loretz (1980) published a Ugaritic text which confirms that these scholars were pointing in the right direction. The text reads: *il šd yṣd,* "El of the field (who) hunts." One may conclude then that El *šadday* is of Canaanite origin, deriving from the fourteenth-fifteenth century at the latest and meaning "God of the steppe or field." It is likely that El *šadday* came to southern Palestine from the north after the thirteenth century; but "how" is another question (Knauf 1985).

INTEGRITY. *tamîm.* Literally, "be whole or integral." Luther rendered by "pious," moderns by "blameless." But the word means rather "be whole." Integrity is the best equivalent as the writer is saying that one belongs to God only when there is no reservation or condition.

2. COVENANT. The Hebrew word *běrît* occurs 287 times in the Old Testament, never in the plural. The LXX renders it 267 times by *diathēkē* (the word used in the New Testament for the "new covenant" [Mark 14:22-26; Matt 26:26-30; Luke 22:15-20; 1 Cor 11:23-25]). Jerome renders it 135 times by *foedus* and 96 times by *pactum.* The etymology of the word remains unresolved. But, as J. Barr has noted (1977:24), one must ask (1) whether this or that etymology is in fact correct; (2) whether it has any real value for understanding the semantic function of the word as employed by speakers and writers about ancient Israel.

The phrase "to make a covenant" is *kārat běrît,* literally, "to cut a covenant," which occurs eighty times in the Old Testament (other phrases, far less frequent, are to establish, to order, to give, to set up, to announce a covenant). What may well be the background of "cut a covenant" is found in Genesis 15:7-21; Jeremiah 34:18-20; but literal "cutting" is not necessarily inherent in the idiom. The word *běrît* describes a variety of actions or ceremonies. There are secular agreements between Israel and the Gibeonites (Josh 9:1-10:1), Jabesh-Gilead and Nahash (1 Sam 11:1-3), Jonathan and David (1

Sam 18:1-4 and 20:5-8; 1 Sam 20:11-17 and 23:16-18), Abner and David (2 Sam 3:12-21), David and Israel (2 Sam 3:21; 5:1-3), Ahab and Ben Hadad (1 Kgs 20:31-34), Jehoida and Joash (2 Kgs 11). There are treaties or covenants in the Book of Genesis between Abraham and Abimelek (21:22-24, 27, 31 and 21:25-26, 28-30, 32-34), Isaac and Abimelek (26:26-33), Jacob and Laban (31:44-45, 49-50, 53b-54 and 31:46, 51-53a). David and Hiram of Tyre assume mutual obligations (1 Kgs 5:26 [12]). YHWH is the one who initiates the covenant with Moses and the people and imposes the obligations (Exod 24:7; 34:27).

Bĕrît describes actions and rites, at times with meals and the taking of oaths in which (1) one takes an obligation upon oneself, (2) imposes an obligation upon another, (3) there is mutual acceptance of obligations, (4) an obligation is imposed by a third party. The obligations set up relationships and commitments.

bĕrît was originally a secular arrangement involving relationships and obligations. It was later used to describe obligations in the religious area. The *bĕrît* between Israel and YHWH may be described as bilateral or mutual. YHWH puts himself under obligation and Israel is to respond; Israel cannot put YHWH under obligation. In Genesis 6:18; 9:8-17; 15:18; 17:1-22, YHWH/God gives a solemn assurance, binding himself. In Genesis 17, God obliges Abraham, and so Israel, to the duty of circumcision in the context of his own solemn assurance; Israel must circumcise to fulfill the obligation; YHWH binds himself to fulfill his solemn assurance; but Israel cannot bind him to this.

bĕrît is not a simple, univocal word; it describes a variety of acts and ceremonies with an equal variety of obligations and relationships. It describes too the solemn assurance given by God to the three key figures in the religious history of Israel: Abraham, Moses, and David. Further details may be found in McCarthy (1964; 1972a; 1972b; 1981), Kutsch (1976, THAT 1:339–51), Nicholson (1986).

5. ABRAM, ABRAHAM. "Linguistically the medial -*ha* is a secondary extensive in a manner common in Aramaic" (Speiser 1964:124). The name means "the father (*'ab*) is exalted (*rām*)."

9-14. CIRCUMCISION. Circumcision was a very ancient rite in the ancient Near East and is attested on Egyptian bas-reliefs as early as the third millennium and was known in Syria in the same epoch. It is difficult to determine how widespread it was. It was originally an initiation rite before marriage; it also initiated a male into the life of the tribe. It is likely that the custom had a similar origin in Israel (cf. Gen 34; Exod 4:24-26, a very obscure episode). The link with marriage and tribal initiation would have been well in the background when the rite was carried out eight days after birth. The religious importance of the rite grew slowly. It is referred to in passing in the Pentateuch (Exod 12:44, 48; Lev 12:3; 19:23). During the exile, circumcision became the mark of the male who belonged to Israel and YHWH. In 167 B.C.E. the Seleucid king of Syria, Antiochus Epiphanes IV, forbade the practice in Palestine (1 Macc 1:14-15 [15-16]; 2:48 [51]). Fuller accounts of the history and practice of the rite are given by de Vaux (1961:46–48) and Sasson (1966).

15. SARAI, SARAH. Sarai preserves an old form; Sarah, with the common feminine ending, means "princess."

8. The Three Guests, Abraham, and the Promise (18:1-16)

¹Now YHWH appeared to him by the oak(s) of Mamre while he was sitting at the entrance to the tent in the heat of the day. ²He raised his eyes and looked about and there were three men standing in front of him; when he saw them he ran from the entrance to the tent to meet them and bowed low to the ground ³and said: My lord, if I have found favor in your eyes, please do not pass by your servant. ⁴Let a little water be brought and wash your feet and rest yourselves under the tree, ⁵and let me bring a little bread that you may sustain yourselves, then you may pass on—for why else have you passed your servant's way! And they said: Do as you say. ⁶So Abraham hurried to the tent to Sarah and said: Hurry! three measures of fine flour, knead it and make cakes. ⁷Then Abraham ran to the cattle and took a nice tender calf and gave it to the servant who hurried to prepare it. ⁸Then he took yoghurt and milk and the calf that he had prepared and set it before them, and he himself waited on them under the tree while they ate. ⁹Then they asked him: Where is Sarah, your wife? He said: Here, in the tent. ¹⁰Then he said: I assure you I will come back to you at this time next year when Sarah your wife will have a son. Now Sarah was listening at the entrance to the tent which was behind him. ¹¹Now Abraham and Sarah were old, advanced in years, and Sarah no longer experienced the cycle of women. ¹²So Sarah laughed to herself and said: Now that I am used up, shall I have pleasure? and my husband is old! ¹³Then YHWH said to Abraham: Why did Sarah laugh

and say: Am I really to bear a child now that I am old? [14]Is anything too difficult for YHWH? At the appointed time, at this time next year, I will come back to you and Sarah will have a son. [15]Now Sarah lied when she said: I did not laugh, because she was afraid. But he said: No, you did laugh. [16]Then the men rose and left and they looked down over Sodom and Abraham went with them to send them on their way.

Comment

The episode of the three visitors to Abraham's tent is, in the Abraham cycle, part of a larger complex of events and theological reflections which cover one day. The three men come to Abraham in "the heat of the day" (18:1). After rest and refreshment they set out for Sodom (18:16). There is divine soliloquy or reflection (18:17-21) after which the journey to Sodom is resumed (18:22a) while a dialogue takes place between YHWH and Abraham on the fate of the righteous and the wicked (18:23-33). The two messengers arrive at Sodom in the evening (19:1a). At dawn the next day they urge Lot and his family to leave the city (19:15). The fire and the brimstone rain down (19:24) and "early in the morning" Abraham comes to the place where he had had a dialogue with YHWH to view the devastated cities (19:27-28). The episode of Lot's daughters, their concern to continue the family line, and the consequent account of the origin of the Moabites and the Ammonites, follows as an appendix (19:30-38). The journey from Hebron, about nine hundred meters (3000 feet) above sea level, along a difficult winding road, takes two days. The distance between the two cities is some sixty kilometers (forty miles) as the crow flies. That the messengers leave Hebron in the afternoon and arrive at Sodom in the evening is not a problem in story.

At the beginning of chapter 18 there are three men. One of the men (or YHWH, v. 3 and *Notes*), "they" (v. 9) and YHWH (vv. 10-15) dialogue with Abraham and Sarah. "The men" set out for Sodom (vv. 16, 22). "Two messengers" (19:1) arrive in Sodom. They are "the men" (vv. 5, 8, 10, 12), "the messengers" (v. 15), and "the men" (vv. 16-17). Lot addresses "my L(l)ord (v. 18). This addressee, singular, replies to Lot (vv. 21-22).

Chapters 18–19 comprise a variety of literary types: a visit by strangers, an account of the announcement of a birth, a soliloquy on the theology of history, a theological dialogue, a report of an episode, all of which have been combined into the more or less loose unity that lies before us, and which have their origins in different eras and different stages of editing. The biblical complex of the chapters is meant to be read as a unit.

18:1-16 has its own unity within the broader complex. The visitors arrive at Abraham's tent (vv. 1-2), enjoy hospitality, deliver their message, and leave (v. 16). Many exegetes look instinctively for two separate narratives or themes, e.g., "two narratives have overlapped and been fused into one" (Westermann 1985:274), or there is "a conflation of two quite distinct themes" (Blenkinsopp 1982:119). The two narratives or themes are the announcement of the birth of a son to a childless couple (vv. 1a, 10-14) and the visit of divine messengers (vv. 1b-9). Van Seters (1975:207) extends the birth story to 13:18; 18:1a, 10-14; 21:2, 6-7. This may well be. But the attention here will be on the unit as it lies before us. The goal of the narrative is not just the assurance of *a* son, Isaac; it is the birth of a people's ancestor.

The first part of the story (vv. 1-8) is a fine study in contrast. We look on the quiet scene of the patriarch sitting under the oak in front of his tent in the heat of the day (v. 1); without more ado three travellers are there (v. 2); Abraham responds with the offer of hospitality (vv. 3-5); there is a bustle of activity to prepare the meal (vv. 6-8a); "hurry," Hebrew *māhār,* occurs three times in verses 6-7; then there is quiet again as Abraham serves the guests in the shade of the tree (v. 8b).

A dialogue follows the calm and refreshment. The interlocked themes of the Abraham cycle, Sarah's barrenness and the promise of a son and heir, recur (vv. 9-11). "Sarah your wife will have a son" (v. 10) recalls 15:4 and 17:16, 19; Sarah's age and barrenness (v. 11) recall 11:30; 15:2; 16:1. Sarah's laughter (vv. 12-15) takes up Abraham's laughter (17:17) and the name of the heir to come, Isaac (*yiṣḥaq*). The Lord is master of the situation: "is anything too difficult for YHWH?" (v. 14). His solemn assurance (vv. 10a, 14b) is enough, despite Sarah's doubt (vv. 12-15). Abraham encounters the Lord, YHWH, in his visitors. YHWH appeared to Abraham (v. 1a); Abraham saw three men standing in front of him (v. 2a); Abraham addressed them (one of them): My l(L)ord (v. 3a). The possessive personal pronoun in verse 3b, "your," is singular; in verses 4-5 it is plural; the subject of the verbs "wash," "rest," "sustain," "pass on," is plural; it is plural again at the end of verse 5, "they said." After the meal "they" asked Abraham (v. 9), who replied; then "he" (YHWH) said (v. 10). After Sarah had laughed (v. 12), "YHWH said" (v. 13). The "I" of verse 14 is YHWH, as is the subject of verse 15b, "But he said." Whatever the confusion or conflation of sources in the biblical text, Abraham meets YHWH in the visitors. The episode stands under the heading "now YHWH appeared to him . . . " (*yērā' YHWH*, v. 1a), just as does the divine address in chapter 17. "YHWH appeared to Abram" (v. 1a). Abraham encountered YHWH in the three visitors. Now that they have finished their task they rise and set their faces toward their next place of call, Sodom (v. 16). The theme of the wickedness of Sodom has already been sounded (13:13); it dominates the rest of the complex to the end of chapter 19. In chapter 17, "when God had finished speaking with him, he went up from Abraham" (v. 22). In chapter 18, "YHWH went when he had finished speaking with Abraham" (v. 33). In this way the editor or storyteller(s) binds together the passages in which YHWH communicates with Abraham.

Notes

1. YHWH APPEARED TO HIM. Many commentators since Gunkel (1901; 1910) refer to stories from Greek literature in which gods in disguise visit humans, e.g., Homer's *Odyssey* 17:485–87: "For the gods do take on all sorts of transformations, appearing as strangers from elsewhere, and thus they range at large through the cities, watching to see which men keep the laws, which are violent" (Richmond Lattimore).

3. MY LORD. The radicals *'dny* form the word "(my) lord"; when written *'ǎdonî*, the meaning is "my lord'; *'ǎdonay* means "my lords"; *'ǎdonāy* with the long "a" in the final syllable means "my Lord" and is reserved for the divinity. The MT of 18:3 and 19:18 reads *'ǎdonāy*, my Lord (YHWH); BHS proposes *'ǎdonî*, "my lord," in both cases.

9. The Justice of YHWH
(18:17-33)

¹⁷YHWH said: Shall I hide from Abraham what I am going to do, ¹⁸seeing that Abraham is to become a great and powerful people and all the peoples of the earth shall find blessing through him? ¹⁹Indeed, I have chosen him out so that he may charge his children and his house after him to observe the way of YHWH by doing what is just and

right, so that YHWH may bring on Abraham what he spoke to him.
²⁰Then YHWH said: Great indeed is the outcry against Sodom and
Gomorrah and grave indeed is their sin. ²¹Let me go down and see
if what they have done accords with the outcry against them that comes
to me; and if not, I will know.

²²So the men turned from there and went toward Sodom, while
Abraham remained standing before YHWH. ²³Then Abraham approached YHWH and said: Will you really sweep away the just with
the wicked? ²⁴Perhaps there are fifty just in the city—will you really
sweep away and not pardon the place for the sake of fifty just who
are in it? ²⁵Far be it from you to do such a thing, to kill the just with
the wicked, to treat the just like the wicked; far be it from you, the
judge of all the earth not to do what is proper. ²⁶YHWH said: If I
find fifty just in the city of Sodom, I will pardon the whole place for
their sake. ²⁷Abraham replied: May I presume to speak to my Lord,
I who am dust and ashes? ²⁸Perhaps there are five lacking to the fifty
just—will you destroy the whole city because of the five? And he said:
I will not destroy it if I find forty-five there. ²⁹And he spoke to him
again and said: Perhaps forty may be found there. And he said: I
will not destroy it for the sake of forty. ³⁰And he said: Please do not
be angry my Lord if I continue to speak—perhaps thirty may be found
there. And he said: I will not do it if I find thirty there. ³¹And he
said: May I presume to speak with my Lord—perhaps twenty may
be found there. And he said: I will not destroy it for the sake of twenty.
³²And he said: Please do not be angry if I continue to speak just
once—perhaps ten may be found there. And he said: I will not destroy it for the sake of ten. ³³YHWH went when he had finished speaking to Abraham, while Abraham returned to his place.

Comment

The order of the Hebrew words at the beginning of verse 17 are
a sign of a new beginning, though verses 17-19 presume what precedes and what follows whatever the era of their composition. The
passage is a later theological reflection. One of the traditions about
Abraham is that he is a prophet (20:7, 17). And, following a late
reflection in Amos 3:7: "Surely the Lord God does nothing without
revealing his secret to his servants the prophets." Abraham has a
place in God's saving plan (vv. 18-19). The language of verse 18 is
mainly that of 12:3 (see *Notes;* cf. 28:14; 22:18; 26:4) with "nations"
instead of "clans"; the perspective has widened. Abraham is to
charge his household to follow the covenant stipulations, "to do what
is just and right" (v. 19b). The consequence is that the promises will

be fulfilled (v. 19c; cf. 22:15-17, where the blessings will follow because of Abraham's obedience). "To do what is just and right," i.e., to do *ṣedeq-ṣĕdāqâ* and *mišpāṭ*, is to follow "the way of YHWH." *ṣedeq-ṣĕdaqâ* is often used in co-ordination with *mišpaṭ* (order, ordinance, judgment, a regular way of doing something). The combination is in essence a hendiadys (the expression of a complex idea by two words connected with "and") describing that proper order in the life of the people that is put there and willed by God (see my article, "Righteousness [*ṣedeq-ṣĕdāqâ*] in the Old Testament" in the *Anchor Bible Dictionary*), and is very frequent in the exilic and post-exilic writings, though by no means missing in the earlier literature.

Sodom and Gomorrah are a byword for wickedness in the Old Testament (Amos 4:11; Isa 1:9, 10; 13:19; Jer 23:14; 49:18; 50:40; Zeph 2:8; Adamah and Zeboim are added in Hos 11:8; cf. Gen 14:2, 8, 11). God will go and see for himself, experience, whether or not the reputation is deserved. With "Let me go down and see" we hear echoes of Genesis 11:7.

After the interlude of the divine soliloquy (vv. 17-21), "the men turned from there and went toward Sodom, while Abraham remained standing before YHWH" (v. 22), resuming "the men rose up and left and they looked down over Sodom and Abraham went with them to send them on their way" (v. 16). The second part of verse 22 anticipates 19:27 where Abraham returns early next morning after the destruction of the cities to the place where he had stood before YHWH. The men who come to Sodom are two (19:1), not three, as in 18:2. YHWH, whom Abraham encountered in the three, stays behind.

The writer of 18:17-33 has received the tradition that Sodom was destroyed and all its inhabitants perished except Lot and his wife (temporarily) and his two daughters, and in this context he discusses the problem of the fate of the just with the wicked.

God has chosen Abraham to charge his descendants to do what is just (v. 19). But is God himself just? Surely there are innocent people in Sodom, yet God has decided to destroy all (v. 17). The discussion is not theoretical; its occasion is experience. Surely innocent people were taken up in the destruction of the northern kingdom and Jerusalem. Verses 23-32 have a definite beginning: "Will you really sweep away the just with the wicked?" (v. 23b), and an end: "I will not destroy it for the sake of ten" (v. 32b). The word "sweep away" (*sāpah*, vv. 23, 24) is taken up by the messengers when they press Lot to leave the city (19:15, 17). The Old Testament was well aware of the solidarity of the community in guilt (Gen 20:9; Exod 34:7; Josh 7; Deut 21:1-9) just as it was aware of individual responsibility (Deut 24:16; Jer 31:29-30; Ezek 18). But the problem of the guiltless remained. Abraham knows that God has decided to destroy Sodom. He cannot alter the decision. Abraham does not intercede on behalf of the city; he does not "pray for Sodom" so that God may divert his wrath; he does not bargain or haggle with God (one finds "typical oriental haggling" in ch. 23, not here). All this is to misunderstand the passage. It is a question of the justice of "the judge of all the earth" (v. 25b). God insists that the innocent, if there are any, are not to perish. It is not that fifty or forty or twenty or ten are making atonement for the rest. This is neither stated nor implied. It is merely the fact of the just that will avert destruction. But why stop at ten? It has been suggested that it is the smallest unit that can constitute a group within the city (Blenkinsopp 1982:23; Westermann 1985:292). Lot is saved, and his wife (temporarily), and his two daughters, not so much as a group—Lot is not told to take his family—but as individuals who are specified. Further, it appears that there were no "just" in Sodom (19:4) even allowing for the rhetoric.

The dialogue is a theological discussion, or better, a theodicy or justification of God in the strict sense. But the problem of the justice of God is not solved entirely. God gives an assurance (v. 32b), the dialogue is finished, and YHWH and Abraham each goes his own way.

Notes

19. I HAVE CHOSEN HIM OUT. Literally, "I have known him."

22. According to the later Rabbis (in the C.E.), the scribes (*sopherim*) of the Great Synagogue, between Ezra (active in Jerusalem 458 B.C.E. and after, or 398 B.C.E. and after) and the death of Alexander the Great (323 B.C.E.), made eighteen changes to the text of the Bible in places which appeared offensive or showed lack of respect for God. These are called *tiqunim* of the *sopherim,* emendations of the scribes (usually abbreviated *tiq soph*). This passage is one of them. The *sopherim,* said the Rabbis, altered the original text which said that YHWH remained standing before Abraham. Did they make the alteration in 19:27 as well?

10. The Destruction of Sodom
(19:1-29)

¹When the two messengers arrived in Sodom in the evening, Lot was sitting at the gate of Sodom. ²When Lot saw them, he rose to meet them and bowed low to the ground and said: Please my lords, I pray you, turn aside to your servant's house and stay the night and wash your feet; then you can rise early in the morning and go your way. But they said: No, we will stay the night in the street. ³But he pressed them strongly; so they turned aside and went into his house, and he prepared a meal for them and baked bread and they ate. ⁴Before they lay down, the men of the city, the men of Sodom, young and old alike, all the people to the very last, surrounded the house ⁵and cried out to Lot: Where are the men who came to you tonight? Bring them out that we may have knowledge of them. ⁶Lot went out to them in front of the door and shut it behind him, ⁷and said: Please, my brothers, do nothing wicked. ⁸Look, I have two daughters who have not had knowledge of a man; let me bring them out to you and you do with them as you please; but as for these men, do nothing to them because they have come under the shelter of my roof. ⁹But they said: Out of the way! This one has come as a sojourner, they said, and now he will play the judge! Now we will deal worse with you than with them. And they surged forward against the man Lot to break down the door. ¹⁰But the men stretched out their hands and pulled Lot toward them into the house and shut the door. ¹¹And they struck the men at the door of the house, small and great alike, with a blinding light, so that they became exhausted trying to find the door. ¹²Then the men said to Lot: Is there anyone else who belongs to you here? [sons-in-law], your sons and your daughters and anyone who belongs to you in the city—bring them out of the place. ¹³We are going to destroy the place because the outcry is great before YHWH and YHWH has sent us to destroy it. ¹⁴So Lot went and spoke to his sons-in-law who were to marry his daughters and said: Up, get out of this place because YHWH is going to destroy the city. But he seemed to his sons-in-law to be joking.

¹⁵When dawn broke the messengers pressed Lot saying: Up, take your wife and your two daughters here lest you be swept away in the punishment of the city. ¹⁶But he lingered; so the men took hold of him and his wife and his daughters by the hand, as YHWH wanted to spare them, and led them away outside the city. ¹⁷When they had led them away outside, they said: Flee for your life! Don't look behind you and don't stop anywhere in the valley; flee to the mountains lest you be swept away! ¹⁸But Lot said to them: No, no, my

L(l)ord(s). [19]Look, your servant has found favor in your eyes and you have shown great grace to me in saving my life; but I, I cannot flee to the mountains lest misfortune strike me and I die. [20]Now, look, that city there is near enough to flee to. Yes, it is only small; let me flee there, small as it is, and save my life. [21]He said to him: I grant this request too; I will not overthrow the city you speak of. [22]Hurry, flee there; I can do nothing until you arrive there. So the city was named Zoar. [23]The sun had just risen over the land when Lot arrived in Zoar. [24]Then YHWH rained on Sodom and Gomorrah brimstone and fire from YHWH in the heavens, [25]and he destroyed these cities and the whole valley and all the inhabitants of the city and the produce of the ground. [26]But his wife looked behind her and became a pillar of salt. [27]Now Abraham rose early in the morning and went to the place where he had stood before YHWH. [28]And he looked down over Sodom and Gomorrah and over the whole valley, and there the smoke from the land had risen like the smoke of a furnace. [29]So when God destroyed the cities of the valley, he remembered Abraham and he delivered Lot from the midst of the destruction when he destroyed the cities in which Lot lived.

Comment

Sodom was a byword in Israel for the sinful city that was destroyed by God through a direct intervention (Deut 29:23; Isa 1:9; 13:19; Jer 30:40; 49:18; Ezek 16:46; Hos 11:8; Amos 4:11; Zeph 2:9; Ps 11:6; Lam 4:6). Gomorrah is always associated with it and at times Adamah and Zeboim (Gen 14:1-2). Whatever their disparate origins, the discussions and traditions about Sodom are brought together as a unity (18:17-21; 22-33; 19:1-29). On the eve of the destruction, "Abraham remained standing before YHWH" (18:22); on the following morning, after the destruction, "Abraham rose early in the morning and went to the place where he had stood before YHWH" (19:27). The first verse of chapter 19 continues 18:22a. The men, now messengers, arrive at Sodom. The contrast between Abraham and Lot is clear and deliberate. Abraham was sitting under a tree in front of his tent in the heat of the day; Lot is sitting at the city gate in the cool of the evening in the city in which he had a house. He offers hospitality, but the messengers would go on because they had not come to visit Lot, as they had to visit Abraham, but to destroy the city. There are many similarities in the language of 18:1-8 and 19:1-3. Lot, though a sojourner (or alien or migrant, 19:9), can sit at the gate with the elders of the city and address the men of the city on equal terms, "my brothers." The complete corruption of the city, and so the justification of its destruction, is implied in verse 4. Neither the citizens of Sodom nor Lot's sons-in-law (vv. 12-14) are able to hear God's message. Lot is bound strictly by the law of hospitality (v. 8b), but cuts a sorry figure when he offers to expose his betrothed daughters to degradation at the hands of the mob (v. 8a), and then a comic figure when he arouses the mob's anger and is yanked back into the house by the messengers whom he is protecting (v. 9). YHWH intervenes through the messengers to protect Lot. YHWH wants to spare even the not so just Lot, but Lot will dillydally (vv. 16-23); the messengers yank him again (v. 16), this time with his wife and daughters, and "dump" them all outside the city. Lot continues to dillydally (v. 20), and YHWH allows him to escape to Zoar, a small city nearby.

With sunrise and the flight of Lot's family, the fire and brimstone rain from heaven (vv. 23-24). The messengers had said, "don't look behind you" (v. 17). Lot's wife looked behind and became an instant stalagmite that continues to survey the Dead Sea forever and a day (v. 27). Abraham now returns to the place where he had discussed the question of the destruction of the just with the wicked (18:22-33) to view YHWH's work (vv. 27-28). He can only stand and ponder. A concluding verse (v. 29), usually attributed to the priestly writer (or editor), "is an example of scholastic succinctness at its best" (Speiser 1964:143). God remembered Abraham, just as he had remembered Noah (8:1), and rescued Lot because of his family tie with Abraham.

The story of the destruction of the cities of the valley is thought generally to be an etiology, i.e., a story to explain the peculiar geological formation of the area, its barrenness, the sea in which no fish can live, and the mineral deposits around the southern section of the Dead Sea. That it is a story is clear. The Lot tradition presumes that the area where Sodom lay was at one time rich and fertile (13:10). But the valley rift, the deposits of asphalt, sulphur, and the minerals were there millennia before Lot. Yet, there may have been some material happening that gave rise to the story of Lot at Sodom. The account of the "transformation" of Lot's wife (v. 26) is often said to be etiological, i.e., an explanation of a more than lifesize formation, vaguely resembling a human form, looking over the sea. But it is much more likely a motif that occurs from time to time in popular story (*Notes*).

Notes

1. Sodom. The "lowest" place on earth, some eight hundred meters (1350 feet) below sea level at the southern end of the Dead Sea, known to the Arabs today as Jebel Sdum or Usdum and in Israel as Sedom.

at the gate. Business and judgment were conducted in the area inside the city gate, probably a large fortified gate where the men of the city gathered in the evening.

5–8. For a similar incident, cf. Judges 19, the sin of Gibeah.

11. a blinding light. *sanwērîm:* "a loan word based on Akkadian *šunwurum,* an adjectival form with superlative or 'elative' force: 'having extraordinary brightness' " (Speiser 1964:1139–40). The only other occurrence of the word in the Old Testament is in 2 Kings 6:18.

18. my L(l)ord(s). The MT has *'ădonāy* with the long final "a," used when addressing the divinity. It is usually proposed to read *'ădonî,* "my lord."

20. only small. *mi-ṣ'ār,* a word play on *ṣā'ir,* small, and the name of the city *ṣo'ār.*

26. a pillar of salt. The motif of people or animals or things turned to stone occurs in Homer. The ship of the Phaiakians was returning to Scheria after conveying Odysseus back to Ithaka: "and the sea-going ship came close in, lightly pursuing her way and the Earthshaker came close up to her and turned her into stone and rooted her there to the bottom with a flat stroke of his hand" (*Odyssey,* 13:159–64; Richmond Lattimore). Again, the serpent that had devoured the sparrow and its brood, "the son of devious devising Kronos turned to stone" (*Iliad,* 2:319); and there was no one there to bury the children of Niobe "for the son of Kronos made stones out of the people" (*Iliad,* 24:611). And Niobe herself was turned into a stone which shed tears every summer (Ovid, *Metamorphoses* 6, 182ff., 301ff.). The motif occurs in other Greek writers and cultures.

11. The Daughters of Lot
(19:30-38)

[30]Now Lot went up from Zoar and dwelt in the mountain range with his two daughters because he was afraid to dwell in Zoar so he

dwelt in a certain cave with his two daughters. [31]Then the elder said to the younger: Our father is old and there is not a man in the land to come to us according to the custom of the world. [32]Come, let us make our father drunk with wine and lie with him and so continue the life of our descendants through our father.[33]And so they made their father drunk with wine that night and the elder went and lay with him but he knew nothing of her lying and rising. [34]On the following morning the elder said to the younger: I lay with my father last evening. Let us make him drunk again with wine tonight and you go and lie with him and so continue the life of our descendants through our father. [35]So they made their father drunk with wine again that night and the younger went and lay with him but he knew nothing of her lying and rising. [36]So the two daughters of Lot became pregnant by their father. [37]The elder gave birth to a son and called him Moab; he is the father of the Moabites to this day. [38]The younger also gave birth to a son and called him Ben-Ammi; he is the father of the Ammonites to this day.

Comment

The story of the early travels of Abraham mentions Lot merely as a relative of Abraham and a member of his caravan (11:27, 31; 12:4; 13:1). When the herdsmen of Abraham and Lot contend with each other over pasture lands, Abraham, the head of the caravan, offers Lot an amicable solution and Lot chooses the fertile Jordan valley in the region of Sodom and Gomorrah (13:5-12). Lot becomes a city dweller (19:1-2). He shows himself an ambivalent and uncertain character in the story. He is willing to protect his guests, but at the expense of his daughters whom he is ready to expose to degradation. He hesitates to leave Sodom (19:16); he does not want to accept the offer of refuge in the hills, but asks for the little city of Zoar (19:18-22). Now he is afraid to live in Zoar and flees to a cave in the hills (19:30). This, and the episode that follows, is the last that we hear of Lot. His story is linked closely with the Abraham cycle.

Lot's daughters want to continue the family line. Their husbands-to-be have perished in the destruction of Sodom (19:14b), and "there is not a man in the land" with whom the line of Lot can be continued (19:31b). In the ancient Near East, marriage or the continuation of the line was possible only within the group. Lot and his daughters are the only survivors of the group, so that the group can only survive through them. Hence the action, unsavory as it is both to Israel and to us (19:31-35). It is not a "new creation" story nor, originally, a gibe at the origin of the Moabites and the Ammonites, though it may well have been used later in this latter sense. Moab is the equivalent of *mē'ab,* "from father," *Ben 'Ammi,* the equivalent of "son of my kin" (children of Ammon).

12. The Ancestress and the Promise in Danger.
Abraham and Abimelech
(20:1-18)

¹Abraham journeyed from there to the region of the Negeb and settled between Kadesh and Shur. While Abraham was living as a sojourner in Gerar, ²he said of Sarah his wife: She is my sister. So Abimelech, king of Gerar, sent and took Sarah. ³Then God came to Abimelech in a dream by night and said to him: You are a dead man because of the woman you have taken; she is a married woman. ⁴But Abimelech had not approached her and he said: Lord, will you kill a people that is really innocent? ⁵Did not he himself say to me, she is my sister, and she too say, he is my brother. In the integrity of my heart and the innocence of my hands I have done this. ⁶Then God said to him in a dream: Yes, I know that you have done this in the integrity of your heart, but it was I too who withheld you from sinning against me and for that reason I did not allow you to touch her. ⁷Now give back the man's wife; because he is a prophet, he will pray for you that you remain alive; but if you do not give her back, know that you and all yours must die.

⁸So Abimelech rose early in the morning and summoned all his servants and told them all these things and the men were very frightened. ⁹Then Abimelech summoned Abraham and said to him: What have you done to us? How have I sinned against you so that you brought a great sin upon me and my kingdom? You have done to me what should not be done. ¹⁰And Abimelech said to Abraham: What did you have in mind that you did such a thing? ¹¹And Abraham said: Because I saw that there is no fear of God at all in this place and they will kill me because of my wife. ¹²And in fact she is my sister, the daughter of my father but not the daughter of my mother, and so she became my wife. ¹³And so when God called me to migrate from my father's house, I said to her: This is the loyalty you must show to me everywhere we go; say on my behalf that I am your brother. ¹⁴So Abimelech took sheep and oxen, male and female servants, and presented them to Abraham and gave back Sarah his wife to him. ¹⁵And Abimelech said: See, my land is before you, settle where you

please. [16]And to Sarah he said: See, I am giving your brother a thousand pieces of silver; this is a public justification of you before all of yours—you are entirely vindicated. [17]Then Abraham prayed to God and God healed Abimelech and his wife and his maid servants and they had children. [18]For YHWH had closed every womb of Abimelech's household because of Sarah, Abraham's wife.

Comment

The promise is in danger again. God has promised Abraham and Sarah that they will have a son within the year (18:1-15). The messengers who bear God's promise move on to their mission in Sodom while Abraham takes up the question of God's justice (18:22-33). Sodom and its inhabitants perish (19:1-29). In the biblical context Abraham moves on "from there" (20:1). There is no way of knowing where "there" is; it is a stereotyped formula. Sarah is now pregnant. Just as Sarah is put in danger in 12:10-20 after the broad promises of 12:1-3, so now she is put in danger after the specific promise of a son. That Sarah is old and is to have a son within the year are factors that do not impinge on the story.

There has been much discussion among exegetes about the relationship between the three episodes 12:10-20; 20:1-18; 26:1-16. Are they separate traditions of the same event? Do they belong to the alleged separate documentary sources of the Pentateuch? The position adopted here is that which has been well argued by Van Seters (1975:171–75) and Westermann (1985:318–29), namely that the author of 20:1-18 knew the well honed and brief narrative of 12:10-20 and elaborated on it to his own purpose. Both episodes are in the biblical context of Abraham "on the way" (12:9-10 and 13:1; 20:1); the "sister" theme is introduced at the beginning of each (12:13; 20:2); both Pharaoh and Abimelech "took" (12:15; 20:2) Sarah simply because they were the potentates of the region and could exercise power arbitrarily; hence Van Seters' remark, "It is not clear why the king (Abimelech) should suddenly have taken Sarah as his wife" (1975:171) is not necessary. Abraham asked Sarah to say she was his sister "that it may go well with me because of you" (12:13), and "to say on my behalf that I am your brother" (20:13b); each time it is to be to Abraham's advantage. And in the second story Abraham says that the continual deceit is a matter of loyalty: "this loyalty (*hesed*) you must show to me everywhere we go" (20:13). It does go well at once with Abraham before Pharaoh (12:16); but before Abimelech, only after the subterfuge has been uncovered (20:14). Both Pharaoh and Abimelech take a married woman, though each is unaware of her status; hence each is technically, though not subjectively, guilty of a "great sin" (20:9b), namely adultery. Punishment follows automatically in each case (12:17; 20:17b-18). Each potentate reacts with the same standard formula of reproach (12:18; 20:9-10; 26:10; cf. Gen 3:9-13; 4:9-11; 29:25). But the final solution of each is different: Pharaoh has Abraham and his household escorted to the border of his territory and expelled (12:20); Abimelech allows Abraham to settle in his territory wherever he pleases (20:13). There are new elements in the second story: (1) Abraham is a prophet who prays for Abimelech (20:7, 17); (2) Abraham does what he does because he "saw that there was no fear of God in this place" (20:11); (3) the public vindication of Sarah (20:16). The Abimelech story is not a narrative. It consists mainly of two long dialogues:

vv. 1-2   the journey into Abimelech's territory; he takes Sarah.
vv. 3-7   the dialogue between Abimelech and God.
vv. 8-13   the dialogue between Abimelech and Abraham.
vv. 14-16 the settlement between Abimelech and Abraham.
vv. 17-18 the conclusion.

The geographical details in verses 1-2 are confusing. Abraham was settled at Hebron/Mamre (13:18; 18:1). Kadesh is some ninety-five kilometers (fifty-seven miles) south of Beersheba, and Shur is on the Egyptian border (16:7). The location of Gerar is uncertain, but it is west of Beersheba. It has been identified with Tell-Jammeh, fourteen kilometers (eight miles) south of Gaza, or with Tell-Abu-Hureireh twenty-five kilometers (fifteen and one-half miles) southeast of Gaza, a long way north of the Kadesh-Shur line.

The dream is but a vesture to clothe the dialogue between Abimelech and God on the question of the innocent sufferer which is conducted in the form of accusation and defense. Abimelech's objective sin is that the woman was married. His defense is that he acted in "the integrity of my heart and the innocence of my hands" (v. 5b), words in which we hear echoes of the prayer of the innocent one who approaches the gates of the Temple (Ps 24:4). But even though Abimelech is subjectively without guilt in the matter of adultery, there has been a dislocation of the objective order which must be redressed. Hence, he must restore Sarah to her legitimate husband; otherwise the death penalty for a capital offense, *môt tāmût*, "you shall indeed die," heard so often in the laws of the Pentateuch, must follow. God has prevented a "great sin" (vv. 6b, 9). God described Abraham as a prophet, *nābî'*, that is, one who is called by God. He fulfills his role of intercessor or "one who prays" in verse 17. YHWH struck Pharaoh and his household with a disease, and this was the reason why Pharaoh summoned Abraham (12:17). YHWH closed the womb of the household of Abimelech, but this is mentioned only after the dialogue (unless it is implied in v. 7) in the context of Abraham's intercession (20:18). Elohim is the name used for God in 20:1-17.

Notes

4. LORD. Abimelech addresses God as *'ădonāy,* the form of address reserved in the Old Testament for the God of Israel.

8. PROPHET. *nābî'.* Akkadian *nabā'um* "to call" one who is called to hold an important post. Prophet in the present context is one who has been called by God for a purpose.

11. I SAW THAT THERE IS NO FEAR OF GOD AT ALL. Dahood (1980:90–91) has suggested, "Indeed, I have beheld (*'āmartî*) worthlessness (*raq*); there is no fear. . . ."

13. GOD CALLED ME TO MIGRATE. One of the very few places in the MT where the word for God, *'ĕlohîm* (plural form) is the subject of a plural verb.

LOYALTY. *ḥesed:* To translate by "kindness" or "favor" deprives the word of its force.

16. JUSTIFICATION . . . VINDICATED. Literally, "a covering of eyes before all of yours"; thus, Sarah is "vindicated," *nokaḥat,* passive.

13. The Birth of Isaac
(21:1-7)

¹Now YHWH visited Sarah as he had said and YHWH did to Sarah as he had spoken. ²So Sarah became pregnant and bore Abraham a son in his old age at the time of which God had spoken to him. ³Abraham called the son born to him, whom Sarah bore to him, Isaac. ⁴And Abraham circumcised his son when he was eight days old as God had ordered him. ⁵Abraham was a hundred years old when Isaac his son was born to him. ⁶And Sarah said: God has made laugh-

ter over me; everyone who hears will laugh over me. ⁷And she said: Who would have announced to Abraham, Sarah will suckle children, since I have born a son to his old age.

Comment

One can argue well that verses 3-5 are a fill-in by a priestly writer. Verse 1 takes up in two parallel sentences YHWH's "visitation" of Sarah promised in 18:10-15, and verses 2, 6-7 spell out the effects, with verses 6-7 harking back to the laughter theme of 17:17, 19 and 18:12-15. God is designated by the proper name YHWH in verse 1 (two times), and by *'ĕlohîm* in verses 2, 4.

14. The Expulsion of Hagar
(21:8-21)

⁸Now the child grew and was weaned and Abraham made a great feast on the occasion of Isaac's weaning. ⁹When Sarah saw the son of Hagar the Egyptian, whom she had born to Abraham, playing [with Isaac her son], ¹⁰she said to Abraham: Drive out this slave woman and her son because the son of this slave woman shall not be heir with my son Isaac. ¹¹But this troubled Abraham very much because of his son. ¹²So God said to Abraham: Do not be troubled because of the boy and your slave woman; whatever Sarah says to you, do it! Because your descendants shall be called after Isaac. ¹³And more, I will make the son of the slave woman a [great] nation because he is your descendant. ¹⁴So Abraham rose early in the morning, took bread and a skin of water and gave them to Hagar and put them on her shoulder and set her on her way with the child; she went and wandered in the desert of Beersheba. ¹⁵Now when the water in the skin was finished, she placed the child under one of the bushes, ¹⁶and went and sat down over against him, about a bow's shot distance, saying: Let me not look upon the death of the boy. So she sat over against him and raised her voice and wept. ¹⁷God heard the voice of the boy, and the messenger of God called to Hagar from heaven and said: What is the matter, Hagar? Do not be afraid, because God has heard the voice of the boy there where he is. ¹⁸Get up, lift up the boy, take him firmly by your hand, for I will make him into a great nation. ¹⁹Then God opened her eyes and she saw a well of water; so she went and filled the skin and gave the boy a drink, ²⁰God was with the boy, and he grew up and lived in the desert and became a bowman. ²¹And he lived in the desert of Paran, and his mother took a wife for him from the land of Egypt.

Comment

The Abraham cycle could well end with the birth of the son of the promise. But another episode is added. Verse 8 is a link with what precedes; verse 9 prepares the stage for what follows. There are two separate scenes: (1) Sarah makes her demand, Abraham is troubled, receives assurance from God, and sets Hagar and the boy on their way (vv. 10-11); (2) Hagar and the boy face death in the desert, Hagar receives assurance from God, Hagar and the boy are saved (vv. 15-19). Then there are two closing verses that take up God's concern for Ishmael (v. 20) and sketch his future. The name, Ishmael, is not used throughout the passage; he is *yeled,* child (vv. 14, 15, 16) or *na'ar,* boy or youth (vv. 12, 17 [two times], 18, 19, 20).

The present episode is not a variant of the episode of chapter 16. The stories are different. In chapter 16 the story tells of a childless couple who take the means normal in their culture to have an heir in the household. The mistress of the house reacts harshly to the secondary wife who has become presumptuous because she is pregnant. There is flight into the desert where YHWH, through his messenger, gives assurance to the secondary wife who reflects on her encounter and gives voice to her reaction with her name for the place. She returns to the household so that her son can live there as heir. The episode in chapter 21 tells a different story. By the biblical chronology, the son of the secondary wife is now fifteen (16:16; 17:17; 21:5). The son of the promise has supplanted him as primary heir. The mistress of the house, perhaps fearing for her future, does not want the son of the secondary wife to share in the inheritance, so she has her driven out of the household. Abraham is troubled by this, but God relieves his distress: "your descendants shall be called after Isaac . . . I will make the son of the slave woman a great nation because he is your descendant" (vv. 12b-13). Isaac is the channel through which the promises are to pass to Jacob (26:3, 5, 24; 28:3-5), but Ishmael and his descendants are to be blessed too. The secondary wife and her son now face death in the desert. But God intervenes and saves mother and son. Both stories underscore God's, and Abraham's, concern for the son of the secondary wife (16:10-11; 21:11-13, 17). The well has a different function in each story: in chapter 16 it is the place where God appears in his messenger; in chapter 21 it is the place to which God directs the secondary wife to provide water for the boy. The boy's future takes a different direction in each story (16:12; 21:20-2). The messenger of YHWH (16:7-12) and the messenger of *'ĕlohîm* (21:17-19) function differently. In the latter, the movement is from God to the messenger and back to God again. The details about Hagar, "When Sarah saw the son of Hagar, the Egyptian, whom she had borne to Abraham, playing" (21:9), refer back to chapter 16 and presume knowledge of it. The text shows all the signs of a literary creation and cannot be constricted within any literary genre, though it can justly be called a narrative because it is an account of an event as it moves through tension to climax and resolution.

One should note that the Pauline interpretation of this passage follows a rather harsh rabbinic line, and so too the interpretation of many Christian exegetes until recent decades. Paul writes: "But as at that time he who was born according to the flesh persecuted him who was born according to the Spirit, so it is now" (Gal 4:29). One can in no way interpret the Hebrew *mesahēq*, playing with, laughing with (21:9), in the sense of persecuting or molesting. The Midrash Rabbah interprets *mesahēq* in a very pejorative sense: "ravishing maidens, practicing idolatry, shooting arrows at Isaac"; so too Rashi.

Notes

8. ISAAC'S WEANING. At the age of two–three years.

9. PLAYING [WITH ISAAC HER SON]. *mesahēq*, echoing again the continued play on the name of Isaac which began in 17:17, 19. The words in square brackets are not in the MT but are supplied from the LXX.

10. SLAVE WOMAN. The word used in chapter 21 is *'amāh*; in chapter 16 it is *šiphāh*. It is difficult to make a clear distinction between the two.

14. WITH THE CHILD. Abraham would not put a fifteen-year old on Hagar's shoulders. The syntax is awkward and the translation above is a little rough with it, though no rougher than attempts to rearrange the order of the Hebrew words.

16. RAISED HER VOICE AND WEPT. Hagar is the subject of both verbs in the Hebrew text of the last words of verse 16; verse 17 reads: "God heard the voice of the boy." Hence, "the boy" is often made the subject of verse 16d. The LXX of verse 16d reads literally: "and the boy wept a cry."

15. The Treaty Between Abraham and Abimelech. The Well and Beersheba (21:22-34)

²²Now at that time Abimelech and Phicol the chief of his army said to Abraham: God is with you in all that you do. ²³Now then swear to me by God that you will not deal falsely with me or my children or my children's children, but as I have shown myself loyal to you, so do you to me and my land as long as you live as a sojourner in it. ²⁴So Abraham said: I swear. ²⁵Now Abraham remonstrated with Abimelech about a well of water that the servants of Abimelech had seized. ²⁶But Abimelech said: I do not know who has done this; you have said nothing about it to me and more, I have heard nothing about it until today. ²⁷So Abraham took sheep and cattle and gave them to Abimelech and the two of them made a treaty. ²⁸So Abraham set seven ewes apart. ²⁹Then Abimelech said to Abraham: What is the meaning of these ewes that you have set apart? ³⁰The seven ewes you must accept from me that they may be witness that I have dug this well. ³¹For this reason the place is called Beersheba because the two swore to each other. ³²So they made a treaty at Beersheba. Then Abimelech and Phicol departed and returned to the land of the Philistines. ³³Now Abraham planted a tamarisk at Beersheba and called on the name of YHWH, God Eternal. ³⁴And Abraham lived a long time as a sojourner in the land of the Philistines.

Comment

Toward the end of chapter 20 (vv. 15-17) Abimelech of Gerar had allowed Abraham to live in his territory wherever he pleased. Abimelech's words to Abraham (v. 22; see his words, virtually the same, to Isaac, 26:28) presuppose Abraham's prosperity. His request that Abraham "will not deal falsely" with him and his posterity and that Abraham will act with loyalty (*kăḥesed*) to him as he has to Abraham (v. 23) presumes 20:14-16. Abimelech had indeed responded to the divine visitation and loaded Abraham with gifts, but out of fear of the consequences (20:7b). This is good evidence that the passage follows on from 20:1-17 (18). Abimelech reminds Abraham that he is but a sojourner (v. 23b; cf. 20:1b). So Abraham, still dwelling among the Philistines, promises to swear (*'iššabea'*, I will swear) loyal conduct toward Abimelech (v. 24), and the two make a treaty (*kārat běrît*, v. 27). And Abraham continues his long sojourn among the Philistines (v. 34) with a reference back to Gerar (20:1b) which is in the land of the Philistines. A tradition about a dispute over a well and the origin of the name Beersheba forms a supplement (vv. 25-26, 32, 33). It presumes the other passage (vv. 22-24, 27, 34) which is interwoven with it. When Abraham remonstrates with Abimelech over a well seized by Abimelech's servants, an event about which Abimelech protests his ignorance (vv. 25-26), this is scarcely the beginning of an independent episode. The two make a treaty (*kārat běrît,* v. 32, cf. v. 27) at the well (*bě'ēr*); Abraham makes Abimelech acknowledge his (Abraham's) ownership of the well by making him (Abimelech) accept the seven ewes (vv. 28-30). There is a play on the words seven (*šeba'*, vv. 28, 29, 30) and oath (*šaba'*, v. 31b), giving a double origin of the name Beersheba, the well of the seven and the well of the oath. The whole action centers around Beersheba (vv. 30, 31, 33) and its name (vv. 28, 29, 30, 31b). Abimelech and his commander leave Beersheba and return to the land of the Philistines (v. 32). Gerar is about thirty-seven kilometers (twenty-three miles) west of Beersheba. Abraham remains at Beersheba in this tradition. He does not build an altar to YHWH there as he did formerly (12:7, 8; 13:18, and as do Isaac, 26:25, and Jacob, 35:7), but plants a tamarisk tree and calls on the name of YHWH (12:8; Isaac, 26:25) who is described further as God (the) Eternal (*'ēl 'olām*). Many scholars understand this action as the foundation of a place of worship (de Vaux 1961: 279, 293). But this is contested. When Abraham calls on the name of YHWH, it does not mean "that he is practicing a cult as understood in the sedentary period, but that he sees that station as a place where he called on his God" (Westermann 1985:350). The tree is a lasting landmark. Tradition associates Isaac with Beersheba where YHWH appeared to him and where he made an altar there and offered sacrifice (46:1-3). When the traditions were arranged into the biblical text, Abraham was given the place of honor as the first of the patriarchs to worship there.

Notes

33. GOD ETERNAL. *'ēl 'olām.* This is the only place where this descriptive title occurs in full. According to Cross (1973:47-49), it may be read as "the God Olam" or "the God of eternity." For "Olam" as a proper name for God, see Excursus: The Religion of the Patriarchs.

16. The Testing of Abraham
(22:1-19)

¹It was after these events that God tested Abraham when he said to him: Abraham! And he said: Here I am. ²And he said: Take your son, your only son, whom you love, Isaac, and go your way to the land of Moriah and there offer him as a burnt offering on one of the mountains which I will tell you. ³So Abraham rose early in the morning, saddled his ass and took his two servants and his son Isaac with him. He had split the wood for the burnt offering, and so he set out and went to the place that God had told him. ⁴On the third day Abraham raised his eyes and saw the place from a distance. ⁵And Abraham said to his servants: You stay here with the ass while I and the boy go there to worship; then we will come back to you. ⁶So Abraham took the wood for the burnt offering and laid it upon his son Isaac and he took the fire(-flint) and the knife. And the two of them went on together. ⁷Then Isaac said to his father Abraham: My father! And he said: Here I am, my son! And he said: Look, the fire(-flint) and the wood are here; but where is the lamb for the burnt offering? ⁸And Abraham said: God will provide the lamb for a burnt offering. And the two of them went on together. ⁹When they came to the place that God had told them, Abraham built the altar there and arranged the wood; then he bound Isaac his son and put him on the altar on top of the wood. ¹⁰And Abraham stretched out his hand and took the knife to slay his son. ¹¹But the messenger of YHWH called to him from heaven and said: Abraham! Abraham! And he said: Here I am! ¹²And he said: Do not stretch out your hand against the boy or do anything to him. For now I know that you are one who fears God because you have not refused me your son, your only son. ¹³And Abraham raised his eyes and looked—there was a ram caught by its horns in the thicket. So Abraham went and took the ram and offered it as a burnt offering in place of his son. ¹⁴And Abraham called the place "YHWH will provide," of which [event] it is said today: On the [this] mountain YHWH appears.

¹⁵Then the messenger of YHWH called to Abraham a second time from heaven. ¹⁶He said: I swear by myself, an oracle of YHWH, because you have done this and have not refused me your son, your only son, ¹⁷I will indeed bless you and will multiply your descendants like the stars of heaven and the sand which is on the shore of the sea and your descendants shall possess the gates of their enemies. ¹⁸And all the nations of the earth shall find blessing through your descendants because you have obeyed me.

¹⁹Then Abraham went back to his servants and they set out and went together to Beersheba and Abraham dwelt in Beersheba.

Comment

Three other stories about Abraham are added in chapters 22–24 before the cycle closes, the theme of each being sounded at the beginning: "God tested Abraham" (22:1); "Sarah died at Kiriarharba" (23:2), so a burial place had to be found for her; "I adjure you . . . go . . . to my own land and kinsmen to take a wife for my son Isaac" (24:3-4), so that the promise may be handed on. The story of the testing of Abraham is tied loosely to what precedes by the formula "It was after these events." But the words are not merely a formula. They imply: the son and the heir of the promise has been given; what now? The story stands under the heading "God tested Abraham" which determines the whole narrative, right through to verse 14 and through the subsequent reflection (vv. 15-18). God had given the promised heir as a free gift to Abraham; can Abraham go on believing and trusting in God when God asks him to renounce the promise? The story is a well-knit unity. "Your son, your only son" (vv. 2, 12) forms a frame; several themes run through the whole: "his son" (3, 4, 7 [my son], 9, 13), "a burnt offering" (*'olah,* 2, 3, 6, 7, 8, 13); "the place" (vv. 3, 4, 9, 14) which God has chosen (vv. [2], 2, 9); "one of the mountains" (v. 2) and "the mountain" (v. 14); "the wood" (vv. 6, 9); "the knife" (vv. 6, 10); "God (YHWH) will provide" (*yir'eh,* vv. 8, 14); and there are further plays on *rā'āh* (see, provide, appear): *wayyar',* "and he saw" (v. 13); *yērā'eh,* "he appears" (v 14); and the echo in *yērē' 'ĕlohîm,* one who fears God" (v. 12b). The reader/listener knows that it is a story and that Isaac has a future history; but Abraham of the story does not know this. Is God's word in verse 2 his last word? Does Abraham show a spark of hope when he says to his servants, "then we will come back to you" (v. 5b), and to Isaac, "God will provide the lamb for a burnt offering" (v. 8)? To suggest that Abraham is prevaricating is to distort the whole. Abraham is under the test right up to the denouement (vv. 11-13). He has come through it internally even though externally, and at the last moment, he does not in fact lose the promised heir.

None have described the literary movement, the tension, and the harrowing experience of the narrative better than von Rad (1972:238–45) and Auerbach (1968:3–23). Abraham is to take "your son, your only son, whom you love, Isaac." No comment is adequate. The writer delays on each detail of the preparation to set Abraham on his way "to the place that God had told him" (v. 3).

Abraham has three days to reflect (v. 4). The writer slows down the tempo as Abraham approaches the mountain. He pauses to watch Abraham distribute the instruments of sacrifice between himself and his son; "and the two of them went on together" (v. 6b). Isaac breaks the silence. The exchange is full of tension: "My father," "My son" (v. 7a). "God will provide" (v. 8a) gives a glimmer of hope and anticipates "YHWH will provide" (v. 14a); "And the two of them went on together." Again, no comment is adequate. (To say, with Kilian [1970:23-24], that the dialogue of verses 6-8 is of no importance for the movement of the narrative is to display less than the finest sensitivity to narrative technique.) The writer slows the tempo again as father and son come "to the place that God had told them" (v. 9a). He pauses to watch Abraham move through the six steps leading to the sacrifice (vv. 9b-10). As Abraham's arm with the knife in his hand is stretched out (vv. 10, 12b), YHWH's voice comes from the heavens through the messenger. Abraham has passed the test. He "fears God," i.e., his awe and reverence for God has issued into obedience; "your son, your only son" (vv. 2a, 12b) is to carry on the promise. Abraham's quiet prayer of praise, "YHWH will provide" (v. 14a), takes up his assurance to Isaac, "God will provide" (v. 8a). "On [this] mountain God appears" (v. 14b). It is on Moriah (v. 2), later identified as the place on which Solomon built the temple (2 Chr 3:1a), that YHWH appears. In this story, "Moriah" and "God will provide" are "story" names and not "real" names of identifiable places. The writer commemorates an event, not a place. And the event is under the direction of God from beginning to end. The story narrates that Abraham was tested by God, came through the test, was blessed by God, and praised God with "God will provide." Nothing remains but for Abraham and Isaac to go back to the place where they left the servants (vv. 5, 19a) and then return to Beersheba (v. 19b; 21:31-33).

But before Abraham departs from the mountain, the messenger of YHWH calls to him a second time. Some authors consider the passage (vv. 15-18) to be a "later addition," i.e., the story (vv. 1-14) was there at hand and the verses were added to it when it was edited into the final biblical text. Others (e.g., Van Seters 1975:238) attribute the four verses to the author of the story who uses the promise traditions with their dtn-dtr leaning to form an appendix to the story proper. The author of the appendix, whether he is the author of the story or not, and the promises have a different history in the tradition from the story, takes up from the story "the messenger of

YHWH'' and the key words "you have not refused me your son, your only son" (vv. 15-16). YHWH speaks through his messenger and confirms by oath (v. 16) the promise of descendants, inheritance (v. 17b), and blessing for the nations. The oath is taken up in the Isaac tradition (26:3b), while the promise of the land by oath runs right through the Book of Deuteronomy (Deut 1:8, 15; 6:10, 18, 23; 7:8, 13; 8:1; 9:5; 10:11; 11:9, 21; 19:8; 26:3, 15; 28:11; 30:20; 31:7, 20, 21; 34:4). The reason for the promise on oath is that Abraham "did not refuse me your son, your only son" (v. 16b; cf. vv. 2, 12b) and "because you obeyed my voice" (v. 18b). The call to obedience, on which the fulfillment of the promises rests, permeates the Book of Deuteronomy and the dtr history. The similes that belong to the promise tradition recur: I will multiply your descendants like "the stars of heaven" (v. 17; 15:3), like "the sand on the shore of the sea" (v. 17; 32:13 [12]); and the theme of blessing on the nations is distributed through both cycles of stories (v. 18; 12:3; 18:18; 26:4; 28:14). That "your descendants shall possess the gates of their enemies" (v. 17b) is taken up in 24:60. The Isaac tradition (26:2, 5, 24) takes up the theme that the promises are confirmed and handed on because Abraham obeyed (vv. 16, 18b).

A story (vv. 1-14, 19) and a collection of promises with a definite theological leaning (vv. 15-18) are brought together and linked. Each has a different history in the course of the tradition. The theological leaning points to an exilic or post-exilic period as the time when they were brought together.

It is fitting that the reader hear von Rad's moving reflection on the story:

> It has to do with the road out into Godforsakenness, a road on which Abraham does not know that God is only testing him. There is thus considerable religious experience behind these nineteen verses: that Yahweh often seems to contradict himself, that he appears to want to remove the salvation begun by himself from history. But in this way Yahweh tests faith and obedience! One further thing may be mentioned: in this test God confronts Abraham with the question whether he could give up God's gift of promise. He had to be able (and he was able), for it is not a good that may be retained by virtue of any legal title or with the help of a human demand. God therefore poses before Abraham the question whether he really understands the gift of promise as a pure gift (cf. the incomparable disputing of a legal claim 48:8-14). Finally, when Israel read and related this story in later times it could only see itself represented by Isaac, i.e., laid

on Yahweh's altar, given back to him, then given life again by him alone. That is to say, it could base its existence in history not on its own legal titles as other nations did, but only on the will of him who in the freedom of his will in history permitted Isaac to live. Is it too much to expect that the one who could tell such a story did not also make rather lofty demands on the thought of his hearers? (1972: 244-45).

Notes

2. OFFER HIM AS A BURNT OFFERING. Whether or not there was an older story that lay behind the biblical story, having its origin in a practice of child sacrifice and concluding with a prohibition of the sacrifice of a particular child, we do not know (Coats 1973:396). There is attestation for child sacrifice in the ancient Near East, but the extent should not be exaggerated (de Vaux 1964:54–90). De Vaux writes that the theory that animal victims were substituted for human victims and that human sacrifices came before animal sacrifices can no longer be defended: "Human sacrifice is attested most clearly in some societies which are relatively evolved and prosperous materially while morally decadent, as were Phoenicia and Carthage" (1964:52; Stager and Wolff 1984).

Evidence for human sacrifice is very dubious in pre-Islamic Arabia and the practice was condemned at the beginning of Islam. There is some evidence for the practice in seventh century B.C.E. Assyria. The king of Moab sacrificed his son on the wall of his city; the Israelites were convinced of the efficacy of the sacrifice and fled (2 Kgs 3:27). One can say in general, however, that human sacrifice was exceptional among the early semites outside Phoenicia. There are a number of biblical texts which speak of children being made to pass through fire (Lev 18:21; 20:20; Deut 12:31; 18:10; 2 Kgs 16:3; 17:17; 21:6; 23:10; Jer 2:13; 7:31; 19:5; Ezek 16:10; 20:26; 23:37; Mic 6:7). Do these texts attest the practice in Israel, or do they refer to the dedication of children to the service of Molech, as Weinfeld proposes? (1972).

MORIAH. cf. 2 Chronicles 3:1a. The suggestion that the original reading was *'el ('elohim) yir'eh* instead of Moriah *(moriyyah)*, and that verses 11, 14a originally read *'el* or *'elohim* for YHWH, and that the "later redactor" responsible for verses 15-18 substituted *'elohim* or YHWH for both, is but conjecture, based on very dubious premises (e.g., that of the existence of an Elohistic [E] strand or document), as is the proposal that verses 6-8 did not belong to the "original" (Kilian 1970) hypothetically constructed account which allegedly came down to "E" and then was supposedly "revised" by "J."

14. YHWH APPEARS. Literally, "shows himself"; LXX reads *en toi horei kurios ōphthē,* "on the mountain the Lord has appeared."

17. The Genealogy of Nahor, Abraham's Brother (22:20-24)

²⁰Now after these events it was reported to Abraham: Milcah too has borne children to your brother Nahor. ²¹Uz, his first-born, Buz, his brother, and Kemuel the father of Aram, ²²Chesed, Hazo, Pildash, Jidlaph, and Bethuel. ²³Now Bethuel begot Rebekah. These eight Milcah bore to Nahor, Abraham's brother. ²⁴And his secondary wife, whose name was Reumah, bore Tebah, Gaham, Tahash, and Maacah.

Comment

Verse 20a is here no more than a formula linking the genealogy of Abraham's brother loosely with verses 1-19. Sarah and Milcah are named together in 11:29. Sarah has borne a child at last (21:1-7); now Milcah's children are named. There are twelve sons in all, eight of the principal wife and four of the secondary wife, just as Ishmael (25:13-15) and Jacob (35:23-26) are each the father of twelve. This genealogy and those in 25:1-18 would seem to close the Abraham cycle after 21:1-7. But they have been separated by the stories of 21:8-21; 22:22-34, and the three freestanding stories of chapters 22-24.

Notes

21. UZ AND BUZ. These are the only names that are place names, Uz (Job 1:1; Jer 25:20), Buz (Jer 25:23), as well as personal names; probably to be located in the region of Edom and North Arabia.

23. BETHUEL. The father of Rebekah (24:24).

24. SECONDARY WIFE. *pilegeš:* a non-semitic word which appears in Greek (*pallakē*) and Latin (*pellex*); its origin is uncertain.

18. The Cave at Machpelah
(23:1-20)

¹Sarah lived a hundred and twenty-seven years. ²She died at Kiriath-arba, that is Hebron, in the land of Canaan; and Abraham went to mourn and weep for Sarah. ³Then Abraham rose from before his dead and said to the Hittites: ⁴I am an alien and sojourner among you; give me a burial plot among you so that I may bury my dead properly. ⁵The Hittites replied to Abraham: ⁶Listen to us, my lord. You are a great chief among us. Bury your dead in the best of our burial places. None of us will refuse you his burial place nor hinder you from burying your dead. ⁷Then Abraham stood and bowed down before the people of the land, the Hittites, ⁸and said to them: If it is your will that I bury my dead properly, then listen to me. Intercede for me with Ephron, the son of Zohar ⁹that he may give me the cave of Machpelah which he owns and which is at the end of his field; let him give it to me at the full current price in your presence as a burial plot. ¹⁰Now Ephron was sitting among the Hittites. Ephron the Hittite answered Abraham in the hearing of the Hittites, of all coming in at the city gate: ¹¹But my lord, listen to me; the field—I give it to you; together with the cave in it I give it to you; in the presence of my people I give it to you; bury your dead. ¹²Then Abraham bowed down before the people of the land. ¹³He spoke to Ephron the Hittite, in the hearing of the people of the land: But please, if you will listen to me. I give you the price of the field; take it from me and let me bring my dead there. ¹⁴So Ephron answered Abraham: ¹⁵My lord, listen to me. Four hundred shekels of silver—what is that between you and me? Now bury your dead. ¹⁶Abraham came to an agreement with Ephron. Abraham weighed out to Ephron the silver which he named in the hearing of the Hittites, four hundred shekels of silver at the current merchants' rate. ¹⁷So Ephron's field at Machpelah, to the east of Mamre, the field, the cave that was in it, and all the trees in the field and the whole area surrounding it, was made over ¹⁸to Abraham's possession in the presence of the Hittites, of all coming in at the city gate. ¹⁹After this, Abraham buried his wife Sarah in the cave of the field of Machpelah, to the east of Mamre, that is Hebron, in the land of Canaan. ²⁰So the field and the cave that was in it was made over to Abraham by the Hittites as a burial plot.

Comment

This story is another separate and independent tradition. It is framed by the notes recording Sarah's death (vv. 1-2) and burial (v. 19). Abraham is a resident alien (v. 4a) who has no land rights. He must buy land to bury his dead (v. 4b). Abraham addresses the Hittites three times (vv. 4, 8, 13) and the Hittites reply three times (vv. 5, 11, 15). The deal is clinched (vv. 16-18) and Abraham buries Sarah (v. 19). A summary verse records that Abraham has made a successful purchase and has achieved his aim; he now owns a burial plot.

The story is about "burying the dead" and a "burial plot" (vv. 4, 5, 8, 9, 11, 13, 15) and the negotiations are about the purchase of land for this purpose. The parties are the Hittites (lit., "the sons of Heth," vv. 3, 5, 7, 10, 16, 18, 20) who are in possession and Abraham, the resident alien, who is not. The formalities are typical of oriental bargaining: Abraham bows twice to "the people of the land," the Hittites (vv. 7, 12); they address him courteously as a "great leader" (or "chief" or "prince") and make a generous offer. The exaggerations are part of the procedure. Abraham asks them to be mediators with Ephron the owner of the cave that he wants (vv. 8-9). The word "give" (*nātan*) recurs. Abraham asks that Ephron "give" him the cave, but at the full price (v. 9). Ephron's three times repeated "I give it to you" (v. 11) means simply that he is ready to negotiate. Ephron uses his position to advantage. Abraham wants to buy the cave. Ephron owns the cave and the field in which it lies. So he proposes to sell both to Abraham who is not well placed to argue. (All this is part of the negotiating ritual in the Middle East today. The prospective buyer, after a period of haggling, turns to walk out of the shop; the merchant raises his voice and hands: "I give it to you." He has seen that the buyer is serious and that a deal can now be made satisfactory to both parties. I have gone through a dialogue similar to the Abraham-Hittite-Ephron dialogue many times in the suks of Damascus and Jerusalem, even to the words "I give it to you" as I turned to leave.) Abraham asks Ephron to let him pay for the field, thus asking him to name his price (v. 13). Ephron names four hundred shekels, a trivial price between a "great leader" (v. 4) and a prominent citizen of the land (v. 14), particularly when one compares Abraham's present landless status with what he can do after the purchase. Abraham really has no option. He has the price ready and weighs out the silver shekels (coinage was not yet in use). The word "listen" (*šāmaʿ*, vv. 6, 8, 11, 13, 15) belongs to the thrust and counterthrust of the negotiations. Abraham finally "listened to," came to an agreement with, Ephron (v. 16). The negotiations take place before witnesses: "in the hearing of the Hittites" (v. 10), "of the people of the land" (vv. 11, 13), "in the presence of the Hittites, of all coming in at the city gate" (vv. 10, 18). Negotiators conducted business in the space inside the city gate, and those coming in at the gate were those who had citizen's rights. Abraham is now owner of "the field, the cave that was in it, and all the trees in the field and the whole area surrounding it. . . . " (v. 17). His aim is achieved.

It has often been remarked that the story is "purely secular" and that God does not play a part in it (the name *'elohim* occurs only in the phrase "a great leader" [v. 6, or chief or prince, see *Notes*]). But one may ask if any of the actions of the patriarchs are "purely secular." What is the purpose of the story? I think that it is simple. Abraham is an alien who does not own land; he wants land for a burial plot; he must negotiate with the local inhabitants; he does so successfully in typical oriental fashion. Gunkel (1910:273–74) had noted that so many of the sites that the Israelites took over from the Canaanites were religious sites or sanctuaries. It may well have been that the cave of Machpelah was one such and that it was thought that the spirit of the place (the *numen*) or a god or hero lay buried there. Some Israelites may have thought that Sarah had taken the place of the spirit or deity. Cultic rites linked with the dead were practiced in Israel (Isa 65:4; exilic or post-exilic text). To avoid any abuse of this kind, the writer of chapter 23 disassociated Machpelah from any religious rites and presented it in secular wise simply as the place where the ancestors of the patriarchal period were buried and honored (25:9; 35:27-29; 49:30; 50:13). A burial plot where all were buried would forestall the cult of the individual. Van Seters (1975:295) has supported this explanation. One can say no more than that it is a possible explanation with no foundation in the text. Von Rad's explanation too goes far beyond the text (1972:250). The patriarchs were forever sojourners living "in the land of (their, my) sojournings" (*'eres měgurîm,* 17:8; 28:4; 36:7; 37:1; 47:9). "In death they were heirs and no longer strangers"; they were buried in their own land, "a very small part of the promised land," but not in Hittite earth. Westermann (1985:461) understands the burial in the overall context of chapters 17; 23; 28:1-5, namely the important family rites of birth, marriage within one's own clan, and death. It is a family story. This may well be part of the explanation.

Abraham was a hundred years old when Isaac was born (21:4; cf. 17:17 where Abraham is a hundred and Sarah ninety). Sarah dies at a hundred and twenty-seven (v. 1), Abraham being then a hundred and thirty-seven. Abraham dies at a hundred and seventy-five (25:7).

Notes

2. KIRIATH-ARBA. An old name for Hebron (Josh 14:15) the name of which is recorded in Numbers 13:22 (foundation c. 1700 B.C.E.). It means literally "the city of four." In Joshua 15:13 the second part of the name, *'arba'* (four) is taken as a proper name, "Arba was the father of Anak."

HEBRON. About thirty-two kilometers (twenty miles) south of Jerusalem. It is not known how ancient the tradition is that associates it with the burial of the patriarchs. The great mosque of el-Haram el Ibrahimi el-Khalil is built over a cave which is said to be that of Machpelah of the Old Testament. Only Moslems are permitted to enter it.

TO MOURN AND TO WEEP. A hendiadys which describes the funeral rites.

3. HITTITES. The writer introduces an antiquarian note with the Hittites. Genesis does not distinguish clearly between the Hittites, the Amorites, and the Canaanites among the earlier inhabitants of Palestine. The Hittites, whose language was non-semitic, were a powerful and dominating influence in Asia Minor in the second millennium B.C.E. They may be distinguished in the following way, after H. A. Hoffner:

(1) *Hattians:* the people whom the immigrant Indo-Europeans found inhabiting the central plateau of Asia Minor when they arrived about 2000 B.C.E. They were completely assimilated to the immigrants in the course of time;

(2) the Indo-European group which settled in Asia Minor about 2000 B.C.E. and rose to hegemony over the plateau's scattered centers about 1700. They adopted the name "men of Hatti" to identify themselves after they had established their capital on the site of the old Hattian city of Hattus (Boghaz-koy) about 1650 B.C.E.;

(3) the Hittite centers in southwest Anatolia and the Syro-Hittite states of the period 1100–500 B.C.E.;

(4) probably a term used in the annals of Sargon II of Assyria to designate the anti-Assyrian rebels from all kingdoms from the Euphrates to the border of Egypt. An ethnic component did exist in Palestine to justify Ezekiel's statement that Jerusalem's parentage was Amorite and Hittite (Ezek 16:3);

We do not encounter the Hittites of (1) and (2) above in the Bible. See further O. R. Gurney (1966), J. Lehmann (1977), de Vaux (1978:134–36). M. R. Lehmann (1953) has sought to interpret chapter 23 in the light of laws found in the Hittite legal codes (ANET 191:39, 46, 47). The reason why Ephron offered Abraham the field as well as the cave was, according to Lehmann, to unburden himself of certain obligations tied to the land and lay them on Abraham. According to these laws "if a person bequeathed or sold certain types of land in their entirety, the taxes or duties connected with them became the responsibility of the new owner. If he conveyed only a small part of the land, the taxes remained his own responsibility" (Hoffner 1969:33). But, as Hoffner notes, the Hittite laws are concerned with fields under feudal tenure involving rent or some service held as an "inheritance" and given, not sold, to another, and with fields of a craftsman which are bought by another. These conditions apply neither to Ephron nor Abraham.

Van Seters (1975:98–100, 293–95) and de Vaux (1978:255–56), among others, have looked to Neo-Babylonian "dialogue documents" for parallels to the sale of the field and its cave. Van Seters claims that "the story in Genesis 23 follows this model completely"; it is a "straightforward report of a transaction having to do with the formal transfer of a piece of land." The dialogue documents begin with a title, "tablet of"; the offer made by the solicitor follows in the form of direct discourse: "A went to B and spoke as follows." There is no further bargaining. The reply of the second party is recorded in the third person in stylized form. But in Genesis 23 there is a protracted dialogue and the only legal formula is "the current merchants' rate" (v. 16) and the only legal procedure is the mention of witnesses (vv. 17-18). The parallel is weak. Let the story stand as it is—a well told story with some similarities to the story of David's purchase of the threshing floor of Araunah the Jebusite (2 Sam 24:18-25). One cannot date it by analogies. The dialogue could have occurred at any time in the Middle East between 2000 B.C.E. and 2000 C.E.

4. AN ALIEN AND SOJOURNER. *gēr wĕtôšāb.* A resident alien, "an outsider with a 'permanent resident visa' " (Vawter 1977:261).

6. A GREAT LEADER. *nĕśî' 'ĕlohîm. 'ĕlohîm* is very probably used as a superlative adjective, cf. Genesis 1:2 and *Notes.* There may be overtones in the phrase: "elect of God."

16. THE CURRENT MERCHANTS' RATE. This is the equivalent of a very ancient Akkadian phrase *mahīrat illaku* = "the rate that is current." Omri bought "the hill of Samaria" for 6000 shekels (1 Kgs 16:24), and Jeremiah bought his field for seventeen shekels (Jer 32:9). The price that Abraham paid seems very high; but he did not have much option.

17. THE TREES. The mention of trees may be coincidental, though the Hittite documents mention trees in a property. They served as a landmark or boundary. The Hittite documents even note the number of trees in or surrounding a field.

19. A Wife for Isaac
(24:1-67)

¹Abraham was now old and advanced in years and YHWH had blessed him in everything. ²So Abraham said to his servant, the oldest of his house, who administered all that he had: Put your hand under my thigh: ³I adjure you by YHWH, God of the heavens and God of the earth, that you do not take a wife for my son from the daughters of the Canaanites among whom I live. ⁴Go rather to my own land and kinsmen to take a wife for my son Isaac. ⁵But the servant said to him: Perhaps the woman will not want to follow me to this land. Shall I then bring your son back to the land from where you came? ⁶But Abraham said to him: Take care not to bring my son back there. ⁷YHWH, God of the heavens, who took me from the house of my father and my kinsmen, who spoke to me and who swore to me: To your descendants will I give this land—he will send his messenger before you so that you will take a wife for my son from there. ⁸But if the woman does not want to follow you, you are free from this oath to me; only do not bring my son back there. ⁹Then the servant put his hand under the thigh of Abraham, his master, and swore to him accordingly.

¹⁰So the servant took ten of his master's camels and all sorts of gifts from his master and set out and went to Aram Naharaim, to the city of Nahor. ¹¹He made the camels kneel down at the well outside the city at evening at the time when the women come out to draw water. ¹²He said: YHWH, God of my master Abraham, grant me success here today and show loyalty to my master Abraham. ¹³Here I am standing at the well and the daughters of the inhabitants of the city are coming out to draw water. ¹⁴And let it be thus: the girl to whom I say: Please lower your jar that I may drink, and who an-

swers: Drink, and I will water your camels too! Let her be the one you have destined for your servant Isaac. And by this I will know that you have shown loyalty to my master. ¹⁵Now he had scarcely finished speaking when Rebekah came out; she was the daughter of Bethuel, son of Milcah, wife of Nahor, Abraham's brother; she was carrying her jar on her shoulder. ¹⁶She was a very beautiful girl, a virgin, whom no man had known. She went down to the well, filled her jar, and came up. ¹⁷The servant ran to meet her and said: Please give me a little sip of water from your jar. ¹⁸She said: Drink, sir! And she quickly lowered her jar to her hand and gave him a drink. ¹⁹When she had given him enough to drink she said: Your camels too—I will draw water that they may have enough to drink. ²⁰So she quickly emptied her jar into the water trough and ran again to the well to draw water and watered all his camels. ²¹But the man stood gazing at her in silence to know whether YHWH had made his journey successful or not. ²²Now when the camels had finished drinking, the man took a golden nose ring, half a shekel in weight [and put it on her face] and two bracelets for her arms, each ten gold shekels in weight. ²³And he said to her: Tell me please, whose daughter are you? Is there room in your father's house for us to stay the night? ²⁴She replied: I am the daughter of Bethuel, son of Milcah, whom she bore to Nahor. ²⁵And she added: And there is plenty of straw and fodder and room to stay the night with us. ²⁶Then the man bowed down low before YHWH ²⁷and said: Blessed be YHWH, God of my master Abraham, who has not withdrawn his loyalty and fidelity from my master. I— YHWH has led me safely on the way to the house of the kinsmen of my master.

²⁸Then the girl ran and told her mother's household all that had happened. ²⁹Now Rebekah had a brother whose name was Laban. ³⁰When he saw the nose ring and the bracelets on the arms of his sister, and heard what his sister Rebekah had to say—the man spoke thus to me—he ran outside to him at the well and found him standing there by his camels. ³¹He said: Come in, blessed of YHWH. Why do you remain standing outside? I have prepared the house and there is room for the camels. ³²So the man came into the house and he [Laban] unloaded the camels and gave them straw and fodder, and the man and his men water to wash their feet. ³³Then he laid food before him; but he said: I will not eat before I have said what I have to say. He said: Say it! ³⁴He said: I am the servant of Abraham. ³⁵It is YHWH who has blessed my master very much so that he has become great and has given him sheep and cattle, silver and gold, servants and maidservants, camels and asses. ³⁶Now Sarah, my master's wife, bore my master a son in her old age, and to him he has given all that he has. ³⁷My master made me swear saying: You are not to

take a wife for my son from the daughters of the Canaanites in whose land I live. ³⁸Rather go to my father's house and my clan and take a wife for my son. ³⁹I replied: Perhaps the woman will not follow me. ⁴⁰He said to me: YHWH before whose face I have walked will send his messenger with you and will make your journey successful so that you will bring back a wife for my son from my clan and my father's house. ⁴¹Then you will be free from the oath to me; if you go to my clan and they do not give her to you, you are free from the oath to me. ⁴²When I came to the well today, I said: YHWH, God of my master Abraham, if you are really making the journey that I undertake successful—⁴³see, I am standing by the well; when a young girl comes out to draw water and I say to her: Please give me a little water to drink from your jar, ⁴⁴and she says to me: Yes, drink, and for your camels too I will draw water—let her be the wife whom YHWH has destined for the son of my master. ⁴⁵Now I had scarcely finished my silent prayer when Rebekah came out with her jar on her shoulder and went down to the well to draw water. I said to her: Please give me a drink. ⁴⁶And she quickly lowered her jar and said: Drink, and your camels too, I will water them. So I drank, and she watered the camels too. ⁴⁷Then I asked her: Whose daughter are you? She replied: The daughter of Bethuel, son of Nahor, whom Milcah bore to him. So I put the nose ring on her face and the bracelets on her arms. ⁴⁸Then I bowed before YHWH and blessed YHWH, God of my master Abraham, who led me safely and faithfully on the way to take the daughter of the brother of my master for his son. ⁴⁹Now if you are ready to deal loyally and faithfully with my master, tell me; and if not, tell me, so that I know where I stand. ⁵⁰Then Laban and Bethuel answered: This event is from YHWH; there is nothing we can say one way or another. ⁵¹Here is Rebekah—take her and go, that she may be the wife of your master's son. ⁵²When Abraham's servant heard their words he bowed low to the ground before YHWH. ⁵³The servant brought out ornaments of silver and gold and garments and gave them to Rebekah and costly gifts to her brother and her mother. ⁵⁴Then he and the men with him ate and drank and stayed the night. When they rose in the morning he said: Let me go back to my master. ⁵⁵But her brother and her mother said: Let the girl stay with us some days, ten days, then she can go. ⁵⁶But he said to them: Do not detain me. YHWH has made my journey successful; let me go back to my master. ⁵⁷So they said: Let us call the girl herself and ask her. ⁵⁸So they called Rebekah and said to her: Will you go with this man? She said: I will go. ⁵⁹So they let Rebekah their sister and her nurse go with Abraham's servant and his men. ⁶⁰Then they blessed Rebekah and said to her: You, our sister, increase to tens of thousands; may your descendants increase to tens of thousands. ⁶¹So Rebekah and her maids went and mounted the camels and followed the man. And the servant took Rebekah and went.

⁶²Now Isaac had come from being in Beer-la-hai-Roi and was living in the Negeb. ⁶³Isaac has gone out into the field one evening to take some air. He looked up and saw camels coming. ⁶⁴When Rebekah looked up and saw Isaac she dismounted from the camel ⁶⁵and said to the servant: Who is the man there coming across the field to meet us? The servant said: He is my master. So she took her veil and covered herself. ⁶⁶Then the servant narrated to Isaac all that he had done. ⁶⁷Isaac then led Rebekah to the tent, to Sarah his mother, and he took Rebekah as his wife and loved her. Then Isaac was consoled after [the death of] his mother.

Comment

Genesis 24 is a carefully composed story about the quest for a wife for the son of the promise so that the promise may be handed on through him. Abraham, now an old man and facing death, has his faithful servant (v. 2a) swear to find a wife for Isaac amongst his own people (vv. 3-4). This theme, "a wife for Isaac from Abraham's clan," continues through verses 5-9 and impresses itself on the whole sixty-seven verses (vv. 14, 27, 36-41, 44, 48, 51, 58-61, 64-67), as does the presentation of gifts to Rebekah, her mother, and brother (vv. 22, 30, 47, 53). The theme of "God's providential guidance" is woven together with the "wife for Isaac" theme. God's messenger (vv. 7b, 40) guides the servant: "YHWH has led me safely on the way" (vv. 27b, 48); YHWH shows his loyalty and fidelity (*ḥesed, 'emet,* vv. 12b, 14b, 27a, 49a) throughout the journey and the negotiations; YHWH makes the journey successful (vv. 21, 40, 42, 56); Laban recognizes God's guiding hand: "This event is from YHWH; there is nothing we can say one way or another" (v. 50). YHWH's blessing has been effective in Abraham's life (v. 1). The servant takes up the theme: "It is YHWH who has blessed my master very much so that he has become great and has given him sheep and cattle, silver and gold, servants and maid servants, camels and asses" (v. 35), and taking up the stories of chapters 18 and 21 (v. 36). To the son of his old age, Abraham "has given all that he has" (v. 36b; cf. 25:5). And the son of the promise is to prosper just as Abraham did (26:12b, 13, 28).

The story, "a wife for Isaac from Abraham's clan," moves, without tension, climax, and resolution, through four acts:

Act one:
vv. 1-9   Abraham and the servant
vv. 10   The journey

Act two:
vv.11-27   The servant and Rebekah
vv. 28-31   The excitement in the house

Act three:
vv. 32-60   The servant in Laban's house; the "betrothal"
vv. 61   The return journey

Act four:
vv. 62-67   Isaac and Rebekah. The marriage

At the beginning of act one, the writer recalls that YHWH's blessing has been effective throughout Abraham's life (v. 1). Abraham
puts his servant under oath, making him swear by the source of life
where the dynamism to reproduce lies, "under my thigh" (v. 2b,
9). Abraham refers back to YHWH's oath (22:16; see comment
there: land, oath, and Deuteronomy; cf. 12:7; 15:18). The son of
the promise is to marry among his own clan. But there is to be no
going back, no return to Aram Naharaim, between the rivers (v. 10).
The son of the promise must remain in the land of the promise. The
journey to "the city of Nahor" (v. 10) takes about a month. But
the servant is already there (v. 10). The storyteller is not concerned
with travel and its details but with "a wife for Isaac" from Abraham's clan.

Act two opens at the well (*bě'ēr,* v. 11; it is a "spring," *'ayin,*
in vv. 30, 42, 43, 45). The servant prays (v. 12). His prayer is answered (vv. 15-25). He bows before YHWH in reverent thanksgiv-
ing (vv. 26-27, cf. vv. 42-44,48; esp. v. 52, the servant's reaction
to the success of his enterprise). His silent prayer and God's guiding
hand go together. God has shown loyalty (*ḥesed,* steadfast love, vv.
12, 14, 27) and fidelity (*'emet,* v. 27) to Abraham, his master.

The reader/listener knows that the young girl who comes to the
well is Rebekah. The servant has yet to learn this. She is the daughter of Bethuel (vv. 15, 24, 47). The servant asks about "her father's
house" (v. 23), but she runs back to "her mother's house" (v. 28).
The only place where Bethuel appears in the story is when he answers with Laban that the whole event is from the Lord (v. 50). But
the mother, not the father, takes part with Laban, her son, in the
negotiations (vv. 53-60). Some scholars suggest that in v. 50 *bêtô*
(*btw,* his household) be read for *bětu'el* (*btw'l*), i.e., Laban and his

household answered. Had Bethuel been alive he would have been the principal negotiator on Rebekah's behalf. Laban shows himself to be in the same mold as the Laban of chapters 29–31 (v. 31, "when he saw the ring and the bracelets"; v. 55, "let the girl stay with me some days").

Acts two and three are linked by the servant's account of the events at the well. He postpones the food of hospitality until he has rehearsed all (v. 33). So the episode of the well is told three times: in anticipation (vv. 11-14), in fact (vv. 15-24), in retrospect (vv. 42-49). There are two accounts of Abraham's commission to the servant: in fact (vv. 3-9), in retrospect (vv. 37-41). Repetition is a sign neither that the passage is early nor late. It is common literary usage in Mesopotamian literature, e.g., the Gilgamesh epic, and particularly in Homer (e.g., *Iliad* 2:23-34 and 60-70; 3:68-72 and 88-91; 9:122-57 and 264-99; 24:147-59 and 175-87). Nowhere does the servant mention Abraham's injunction not to bring Isaac to Aram Naharaim under any circumstances. This would have been offensive to the hosts. When the servant has finished his recital, the betrothal takes place (vv. 50-51), further gifts are given to Rebekah, and gifts to her brother and mother (v. 53), and the meal follows (v. 54a). The servant wants to return at once (v. 54b). But this would be contrary to the custom of the place. So there is question of a stay of ten days. The mother and the brother of Rebekah direct the formalities (vv. 55-60). They bless Rebekah and send her on her way together with the nurse who had looked after her from babyhood (v. 59, *mêneqet*). The month long return is dispatched in a verse (v. 61), as was the first journey (v. 10).

The stage is now set for act four, the meeting and marriage of Isaac and Rebekah (vv. 62-67). When Isaac approaches and is identified, Rebekah, who has dismounted from the camel, covers herself with her veil as part of the ceremony of marriage. Isaac takes her to his tent, to his mother, for the marriage. It seems that Abraham, who sent the servant on his mission, is now dead. He does not appear in this act in which the servant speaks of Isaac as "my master." The death of Abraham is told only in 25:7-11. Isaac loves Rebekah and she is his consolation when the mother dies. The story has reached its goal. But the final verse is not at all clear (see *Notes*). The story does not take up any ancient traditions. The writer is aware of the previous history of Abraham (vv. 1-9) and of the subsequent history of Isaac (v. 67), and knows that the promise has been handed on through Isaac. But the story is of his own making and is cut from whole cloth. The story is generally regarded as late, not because of the discursive repetitions, but for the following reasons: (1) the late designation for God: "God of the heavens and God of the earth (vv. 3, 7); (2) the word *gāmā'* in the Hiph'il (only here), "give me a little to sip" (v. 17), and the rare Hiph'il *mištā'eh* (from the root *š'h*), "stood gazing at"; (3) the mixed marriage problem which arose in an acute form in the post-exilic period; one is not justified in leaving the land even to contact a legitimate marriage; (4) the detailed prayer of the servant proceeds through stages that are familiar from Daniel, Tobit, and Jubilees. These arguments together would set the composition of the story in the post-exilic period. The story is one of three about a meeting at a well that ends in marriage, the other two are about Jacob and Rachel (29:1-14), and Moses and Zipporah (Exod 2:15b-22).

Notes

Speiser is of the opinion that "what we have here is virtually a restatement, in suitable literary form . . . of a sistership document," a *tuppi ahātūti,* a Hurrian marriage contract in which the brother acts in place of the father. This sort of contract involves (1) the principals in the case, (2) the nature of the transaction, (3) details of payment, (4) the girl's declaration of consent, (5) a penalty clause. But first, it is the brother of the mother who is powerful in fratriarchal society. Then, taking each point in order: (1) the principals are Rebekah's brother Laban *and* her mother, the father being dead (vv. 22, 53-57), and Abraham, through his servant; (2) there is scarcely a transaction; Laban and his mother respond to a request and see the event as guided by God (vv. 49, 50); (3) a bridal price was fixed; the gifts are predominently ornaments and garments (v. 51); (4) the marriage is settled without Rebekah's consent (vv. 50-51); when she says "I will go" (v. 58), she is assenting to a speedy departure; (e) there is no penalty clause. So there is no real parallel between the "sisterhood documents" and Rebekah's marriage. See Thompson (1974:248–52) and Van Seters (1975:76–78).

63. TO TAKE SOME AIR. The verb is *śuaḥ,* which occurs only here. The versions suggest "chat, pray, meditate, take a walk"; but this is no more than a guess.

67. [THE DEATH OF]. The words are not in the Hebrew text. It is often suggested that "to Sarah his mother" (v. 67a) is an insertion

and is grammatically impossible, and that the words in square brackets in the last part of the verse "after [the death of] his father," originally there, were removed "after [the death of] his father" (1) because Sarah is not mentioned elsewhere in this chapter and has died in 23:1-2, and (2) the change was made because Abraham is still alive in 25:1.

20. The Conclusion of the Abraham Story (25:1-18)

¹Abraham took another wife whose name was Keturah. ²She bore him Zimran, Jokshan, Medan, Midian, Ishbak, and Shuah. ³Jokshan begot Sheba and Dedan. The sons of Dedan were Asshurim, Letushim, and Leummim. ⁴The sons of Midian were Ephah, Epher, Hanoch, Abida, Eldaah. All these are the descendants of Keturah. ⁵Now Abraham gave all that he had to Isaac. ⁶But to the sons of his concubines he gave gifts and, while he was still alive, sent them away from his son Isaac eastward to the eastern country.

⁷This was Abraham's life span: he lived a hundred and seventy-five years. ⁸Abraham breathed his last and died ripe in age, old, and fulfilled in life, and was gathered to his people. ⁹Isaac and Ishmael his sons buried him in the cave of Machpelah, in the field of Ephron the son of Zophar the Hittite, east of Mamre, ¹⁰the field that Abraham bought from the Hittites. There Abraham was buried with his wife Sarah. ¹¹After the death of Abraham, God blessed Isaac his son and Isaac lived at Beer-la-hai-roi.

¹²These are the descendants of Ishmael, the son of Abraham, whom Hagar, the Egyptian, Sarah's maidservant, bore to Abraham. ¹³These are the sons of Ishmael in the order of their birth: Nebaioth, the first-born of Ishmael, then Kedar, Adbeel, Mibsam, ¹⁴Mishma, Dumah, Massa, ¹⁵Hadad, Tema, Jetur, Naphish, and Kedemah. ¹⁶These are the sons of Ishmael and these are their names after which their settlements and encampments were named: twelve chiefs according to their tribal groupings. ¹⁷This was Ishmael's life span, a hundred and thirty-seven years; he breathed his last and was gathered to his people. ¹⁸They dwelt from Havilah to Shur, which is east of Egypt on the way to Assyria; each made forays against his brothers.

Comment

The Abraham story concludes with an account of his death in typical genealogical form (vv. 6, 8, 10b), with reference back to the purchase of the burial plot (vv. 9-10a), framed by two genealogies (vv. 1-6, 12-18), which list the secondary lines that stem from the patriarch. The first genealogy has no link with what has preceded. Abraham may have married Keturah, mentioned here for the first time, after Sarah's death, or the passage may be a separate piece of tradition (cf. 1 Chr 1:32). The tribal names in the list in verse 2 are from south Palestine and northwest Arabia, the most important of which are the Midianites who are often mentioned in connection with the Israelites (Exod 2:25-26; 3:1; 18:1; Judg 6;8). The names of the sons of Dedan carry the normal Hebrew *-im* plural ending (v. 3), and the names of the sons of Midian are north Arabian. The two narrative verses (vv. 4-5) record that Abraham gave all that he had to Isaac (cf. 24:36b) and that he gave gifts to the sons of his concubines, mentioned only here, and sent them eastward, presumably to protect the full rights of Isaac as heir.

Abraham died at a hundred and seventy-five (v. 7). Sarah had died at a hundred and twenty-seven (23:1). Abraham was ten years older than she (17:17). He lived a hundred years in Canaan (12:4b) and survived Sarah by thirty-eight years. Abraham lived a full life and fulfilled God's plan for him (v. 8) and his sons, Isaac and Ishmael, buried him in peace (v. 9) with his wife in the burial plot that he had purchased from the Hittites, just as Jacob and Esau bury Isaac in peace later (35:29). The last verse of this section (v. 11) could well have been the conclusion of chapter 24, forming a nice inclusion: "YHWH had blessed Abraham in everything" (24:1) and "After the death of Abraham, God blessed Isaac his son" (25:11).

The *"tôlĕdôt"* formula (cf. 2:4a) occurs again (v. 12). The twelve tribes mentioned as descendants of Ishmael can all be identified as Arab tribes who are partly nomadic, partly sedentary (v. 16). Nebaioth and Kedar (v. 13) are mentioned in Assyrian documents (cf. Isa 60:7). Mishnah, Dumah, and Mossa are associated with Tema (v. 14), a city in northwest Arabia which may have been a center of worship for the Ishmaelites. Tema is mentioned in an Assyrian inscription of Tigleth-Pileser III (744–727 B.C.E.; ANET 283), and was the place to which Narbonidus, the last of the Babylonian line (555–539 B.C.E.), withdrew for some years (ANET 306, 313). The purpose of the genealogies is to link the descendants of Abraham with groups of Arab tribes.

Notes

6. HE GAVE GIFTS AND, WHILE HE WAS STILL ALIVE, SENT THEM AWAY. A useful, though remote, background is a law in the code of Lipit-Ishtar (1900-1850 B.C.E., Sumerian): "If a man married a wife (and) she bore children and those children are living, and a slave also bore children for her master (but) the father granted freedom to the slave and her children, the children of the slave shall not divide the estate with the children of their (former) master" (ANET 160:25).

16. SETTLEMENTS AND ENCAMPMENTS. These are temporary settlements of "semi-nomads," at times protected by a wall (Num 30:10).

18. FROM HAVILAH TO SHUR. Better, Havilah by Shur. There are several places known as Havilah (cf. 2:11); Shur (16:7).

EACH MADE FORAYS. "he settled over against all his people" (RSV). *nāpal,* the last word of the verse, is in the singular; it means "to fall, to camp"; *'al pĕnê* is used in an adversative sense.

3

The Jacob Cycle
(25:19—36:43)

Just as the dominant theme of the Abraham cycle, "Now Sarai was barren, she had no child" (11:30), was sounded at the beginning, so too is a dominant theme of the Jacob cycle, namely conflict, sounded, though mutedly (25:23-26). The conflict between Jacob and Esau is set in motion by the deception (ch. 27), then left suspended when Jacob flees to Paddan-aram (28:1-9). Then a second conflict arises, this time between Jacob and Laban (chs. 29–31). Within the Jacob-Laban conflict, there is a third, between Rachel and Leah: "When Rachel saw that she bore Jacob no children, she became jealous of her sister" (30:1). The conflict between the two sisters continues in the episode of the mandrakes (30:14-16). The conflicts are resolved in the reverse order: (1) God remembers Rachel so that she gives birth to Joseph (30:22-24), and the sisters become aware that Laban their father has withheld and misused their inheritance (31:14-16); (2) Jacob and Laban settle their differences peacefully with the treaties at Gilead (31:43-54); (3) Jacob and Esau come together in peace after twenty years of separation (ch. 33).

The theme of blessing runs through the cycle as it does through the Abraham cycle (the patriarchal "signature tune"). The narrative of the deception is filled with the noun bless and the verb bless, twenty-two times in all (ch. 27). Isaac wishes the blessing of God, *El šadday,* on Jacob when he sends him to Paddan-aram (28:3-4); Esau takes note of the blessing (28:6); blessing passes on through Jacob (28:14). Laban acknowledges that God's blessing works to his own advantage through Jacob (30:27) and Jacob takes up the theme (30:30). Jacob too acknowledges the effect of God's blessing

(31:4-13, 41-42). Jacob couches his prayer for protection against Esau in the framework of God's promise: "I will prosper you" (32:10, 13 [9, 12]). Jacob sends an offering or gift to Esau out of the fruits of God's blessing (32:14-17 [13-16]). The nightly attacker blesses Jacob (32:27, 30 [26, 29]). Finally, Jacob can give back to Esau something of the blessing stolen, "my blessing" (33:11) out of the abundance of God's blessing (33:4-11). The promise "to be with you" accompanies the blessing (28:14; 31:3; the divine presence is also assured to Isaac [26:2]).

The theme of return to the land also runs through the Jacob cycle. When Rebekah tells Jacob to flee, she says that he can return at a suitable time (27:45). Isaac blesses Jacob so that he may possess the land of Abraham (28:3-4). God gives Jacob the land with the blessing at Bethel and assures him that he will bring him back (28:13-15). Jacob takes up this theme in his vow (28:21). God instructs Jacob in Paddan-aram: "Return to the land of your fathers" (31:13), and "Now rise up, go from this land and return to the land of your kinsmen" (31:13). Jacob comes to the city of Shechem (33:18) and, after the episode there, returns to Bethel at God's command (35:1-15). He finally returns to his father Isaac at Mamre (35:27). Jacob then settles in the land of his fathers' sojournings, in the land of Canaan (37:1).

On leaving the land of Canaan and on returning to it twenty years later, Jacob has two profound experiences of God (28:10-20; 32:23-33 [22-32]). He goes from each of these in the strength of God, from the first on his journey to Paddan-aram, from the second to meet his brother Esau, left twenty years ago breathing murder (27:41). The writer brings Jacob back to Bethel, the holy place of his first experience, and reworks the Bethel episode (35:9-15). Jacob has other meetings with (31:3; 32:2-3 [1-2]) or communications from God (31:11-13; 35:1, 9-13).

Traditions, linking Jacob with regions, cities, and sanctuaries are many and varied. The Edom (Esau, Seir) tradition appears very early in the cycle (25:23-26; 29:24) and is taken up in the account of the deception (27:39-40). Jacob is linked with Gilead in the border treaty with Laban (31:43-54). The episodes in chapters 32–33 take place in Transjordan, north of Edomite territory (Seir, 32:4 [3]; 33:14-16). The Edomite tradition closes with a long list of Esau's grandchildren and a catalogue of early Edomite "kings" (ch. 36). A Transjordan tradition has Jacob and his household spending some time in what appears to be a sedentary lifestyle at Succoth where he builds

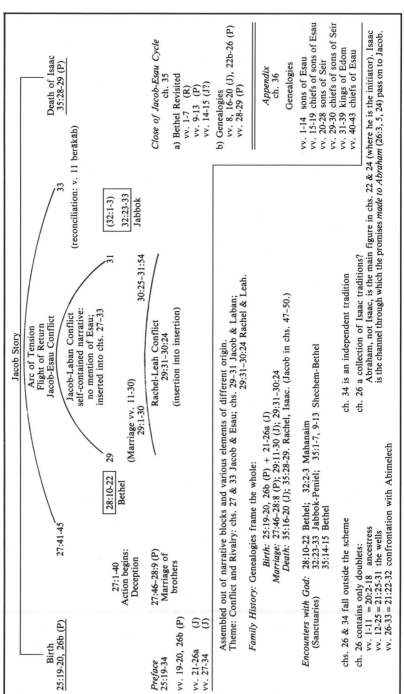

The Jacob-Esau Cycle

Genesis 25.19-36:43

Jacob Story

Death of Isaac
35:28-29 (P)

Arc of Tension
Flight of Return
Jacob-Esau Conflict

(reconciliation: v. 11 berakah)

33

Jacob-Laban Conflict
self-contained narrative:
no mention of Esau;
inserted into chs. 27-33

31

Rachel-Leah Conflict
29:31-30:24

(insertion into insertion)

30:25-31:54

(32:1-3)
32:23-33
Jabbok

29

(Marriage vv. 11-30)
29:1-30

28:10-22
Bethel

27:41-45

27:1-40
Action begins:
Deception

27:46-28:9 (P)
Marriage of
brothers

Birth
25:19-20, 26b (P)

Preface
25:19-34

vv. 19-20, 26b (P)
vv. 21-26a   (J)
vv. 27-34   (J)

Close of Jacob-Esau Cycle
ch. 35

a) Bethel Revisited
vv. 1-7   (R)
vv. 9-13   (P)
vv. 14-15 (J?)

b) Genealogies
vv. 8, 16-20 (J), 22b-26 (P)
vv. 28-29 (P)

Appendix
ch. 36
Genealogies

vv. 1-14   sons of Esau
vv. 15-19   chiefs of sons of Esau
vv. 20-28   sons of Seir
vv. 29-30   chiefs of sons of Seir
vv. 31-39   kings of Edom
vv. 40-43   chiefs of Esau

Assembled out of narrative blocks and various elements of different origin.
Theme: Conflict and Rivalry: chs. 27 & 33 Jacob & Esau; chs. 29-31 Jacob & Laban;
        29:31-30:24 Rachel & Leah.

Family History: Genealogies frame the whole:
    Birth: 25:19-20, 26b (P) + 21-26a (J)
    Marriage: 27:46-28:8 (P); 29:11-30 (J); 29:31-30:24
    Death: 35:16-20 (J); 35:28-29. Rachel, Isaac. (Jacob in chs. 47-50.)

Encounters with God: 28:10-22 Bethel; 32:2-3 Mahanaim
    (Sanctuaries)   32:23-33 Jabbok-Peniel; 35:1-7, 9-13 Shechem-Bethel
                        35:14-15 Bethel

chs. 26 & 34 fall outside the scheme   ch. 34 is an independent tradition
ch. 26 contains only doublets: ch. 26 a collection of Isaac traditions?
    vv. 1-11 = 20:2-18 ancestress   Abraham, not Isaac, is the main figure in chs. 22 & 24 (where he is the initiator). Isaac
    vv. 12-25 = 21:25-31 the wells   is the channel through which the promises *made to Abraham* (26:3, 5, 24) pass on to Jacob.
    vv. 26-33 = 21:22-32 confrontation with Abimelech

Figure 3

a house (*bayît*) for himself and sheds (*sukkôt*) for his cattle (33:17). And Jacob dwells some time in Shechem (33:19; 34). Bethel (see *Comment,* 28:10-22) was an important sanctuary in northern Israel and the attention given to it indicates a strong northern influence. The link with Paddan-aram (northern Mesopotamia) and with Laban the Aramean is mentioned early in the cycle (25:20) and Paddan-aram recurs throughout (25:20; 28:2, 5, 6, 7; 31:18; 33:18; 35:9, 26; cf. 46:15, an enumeration of Jacob's children born there). For all that the Jacob-Laban story may have been independent originally, it is anticipated in these passages and in 27:43-44; 28:1-5. The name for God, *El šadday* (see 17:1), occurs in two important passages in the cycle (28:3; 35:11) as well as in the conclusion of the Jacob story (48:3; see *Comment,* 35:9-15). These many Jacob traditions are brought together, theologized, and laid out on the promise themes which are formulated in the same regular pattern, with the same language, and the same similes as in the Abraham cycle, indicating a common editing of the two cycles.

Isaac is a lesser figure. There is a collection of traditions about him in chapter 26, but all that is narrated about him there has already been narrated about Abraham: the ancestress in danger (26:1-16–20:2-18); the wells (26:15-25 = 21:25-31); the confrontation with Abimelek (26:26-33 = 21:22-32). Isaac, whose birth is the goal of the Abraham story, is simply the channel through whom the promises made to Abraham pass on to Jacob (26:3, 5, 24; 28:3-4). The old, dim-eyed Isaac, deceived by Rachel and Jacob in chapter 27, can still impart blessings, though not as he had intended. And he can send Jacob on his way to Paddan-aram invoking on him the blessing of *El šadday* (28:3).

1. Birth of Jacob and Esau.
The Conflict Begins
(25:19-34)

[19]These are the descendants of Isaac, the son of Abraham. Abraham begot Isaac. [20]Now Isaac was forty years old when he took his wife Rebekah, the daughter of Bethuel the Aramean of Paddan-aram, the sister of Laban the Aramean. [21]Isaac prayed to YHWH on behalf of his wife because she was barren, and YHWH granted his prayer so that Rebekah his wife became pregnant. [22]When the children were crushing each other within her, she said: If this is so, why do I [live]?

So she went to inquire of YHWH. ²³YHWH said to her:
Two nations are in your womb,
two peoples are dividing themselves [even] within you;
one people shall be stronger than the other,
the elder shall serve the younger.
²⁴When the time came for her to give birth, there were indeed twins
in her womb. ²⁵The first came out ruddy, like a hairy mantle all over,
and he was named Esau. ²⁶Then his brother came out, his hand grasping Esau's heel, and he was named Jacob. Now Isaac was sixty years
old when they were born.

²⁷The boys grew up and Esau became a skillful hunter, a man of the
field, while Jacob was a quiet man, staying among the tents. ²⁸Isaac
preferred Esau because he ate from the hunt; Rebekah preferred
Jacob.

²⁹One day when Jacob was boiling broth, Esau came in from the field
and he was exhausted. ³⁰Esau said to Jacob: Let me gulp down some
of that red [stuff], that red [broth] there; I'm exhausted; and so he
is named Red (Edom). ³¹But Jacob said: First sell me your birthright.
³²And Esau said: Look—I'm dying! What use is my birthright to me?
³³Jacob said: First swear to me. So he swore to him and sold his birthright to Jacob. ³⁴Then Jacob gave Esau bread and lentil broth. He
ate and drank and rose up and went. Thus Esau disdained the birthright.

Comment

The story of Isaac is the story of his sons, Esau and Jacob. Though
Isaac's wife Rebekah is barren (25:21) like Sarah (11:30), her barrenness does not play the same important and pervading role that
it plays in the Abraham cycle. One of the main themes of the cycle,
conflict, is sounded at once in three stages: (1) the birth (vv. 19-26):
the twins are in conflict in their mother's womb: "they were crushing each other" (v. 22); they are in conflict in the birth itself as Jacob
comes from the womb grasping Esau's heel (*'aqēb*); (2) parental
preference (vv. 27-28): this lays the groundwork for conflict; (3) the
birthright (vv. 29-34): Jacob usurps Esau's place by compulsion.
There is conflict, or the basis for conflict, in each of the three stages:
in the birth, in the process of growing up, in youthful maturity. The
conflict between the two brothers foreshadows the conflict between
the two nations, Edom/Seir and Israel (v. 23; Mal 1:2-5; Rom
9:10-12), that stem from them. The subjugation of Edom by David
and Solomon (2 Sam 8:13-14; 1 Kgs 11:14-15) and the continual

struggle between Edom and Israel (1 Kgs 11:17-22; 22:47-48; 2 Kgs 3:8-12; 8:20-2; 14:7-10, 22; 16:6; Isa 63:1-2; Jer 49:7-11; Ezek 25:12-14; 35:1-15; 36:5; Amos 1:111-12; Obad) are projected back into the patriarchal period. The first of the twins, Esau, is *'admônî,* ruddy (v. 25). Esau, exhausted from his hunting in the field, gasps for a mouthful of "that red (*hā'ādom*) [broth] there . . . and so he is named Red (*'ēdôm*)" (v. 30). The writer sketches the character of the twins, notes the parental preferences (vv. 27-28), and repeats the word birthright (*běkorâ*); with this very last word in chapter 25 ringing in the ears of the listener/reader, the stage is set for the deception and conflict of chapter 27, where the lost *běkorâ* is taken up again; Jacob had not only taken Esau's *běkorâ,* but also his *běrākâ,* blessing (27:36b).

Notes

20. PADDAN-ARAM. The name (Gen 25:20; 28:2, 5-7; 31:18; 33:18; 35:9, 36; 46:15; 48:7 [Paddan]) designates a region in northwest Mesopotamia. The origin of the word Paddan is unknown. Aram is the territory of the Arameans. It is also known as Aram Naharaim (Gen 24:10), i.e., Aram of (between) the two rivers (Tigris and Euphrates).

22. TO INQUIRE OF YHWH. A reference to an institution known during the period of the monarchy as the "YHWH oracle."

26. JACOB. The noun *'āqēb* means "heel, footprint"; the verb *'āqab* means "follow at the heel, circumvent, supplant (Hos 12:4 [3])." Hence the adjective *'āqob* (Jer 17:60) means "deceitful." As the second of the twins came from Rebekah's womb, his hand was grasping his brother's heel (*'āqēb*). In 27:36, Esau exclaims: "Is he not rightly named *ya'āqob* (Jacob, "he supplants or circumvents"), for he has supplanted me (*ya'qěběnî*) twice." Thompson (1974:37-39) disagrees with Freedman's proposal to read an "original" form of the man in Jacob-Eĺ of Deuteronomy 33:28 which understands *'el* as the name for God and not as the preposition. Thompson (43-50) also discusses the name Jacob in detail "as it is one of the most common West Semitic names of the ancient Near East" (43).

30. EDOM. The region south-southeast of the Dead Sea toward the gulf of Aqabah.

31. BIRTHRIGHT. Esau sells his right as the firstborn for Jacob's red lentil soup. The rights of the firstborn are codified in Deuteronomy 21:17-21 and Numbers 27:1-11: (1) only sons have a right to inherit, unless there is no male issue (cf. Num 36:6-9); (2) the eldest son is to receive a double share. It seems that in patriarchal society the eldest son had precedence, but that the patriarch could change the order of precedence. Jacob demoted Reuben, Simeon, and Levi for misdemeanors (Gen 49:3-7; cf. Gen 35:22; 34:25-31), and Judah succeeded to the rights of the firstborn. Jacob also gave precedence to Ephraim over his elder brother Manasseh (Gen 48:8-20). Documents from Nuzi (cf. 12:10-20, *Notes*) have been alleged as providing parallels to the biblical situation. But in one of these documents the two parties who contract for a "double portion" and a "single portion" are not natural brothers and the contract concerns the distribution of an inheritance, not a right of a firstborn; in the other one, Tuphitilla yields to his brother Kurpa-zah his right to inherit an orchard in exchange for three sheep. But again, it is not a case of the right of a firstborn. It is a fictitious adoption contract in which one party has adopted the other as his "brother" so as to legalize the transfer of property which could not be transferred legally outside the family (Thompson 1974:280-84; Van Seters 1975:87-95; de Vaux 1978:250-51, 253-54).

2. The Ancestress and the Promise in Danger.
Isaac and Abimelech
(26:1-33)

¹Now there was a famine in the land besides the earlier famine in the time of Abraham; so Isaac went to Gerar, to Abimelech; king of the Philistines. ²Then YHWH appeared to him and said: Do not go down to Egypt; stay in the land which I will tell you. ³Sojourn in this land and I will be with you and I will bless you, for I will give all these lands to you and your descendants and so I will fulfill the oath that I swore to Abraham your father. ⁴I will multiply your descendants like the stars of the heavens and I will give all these lands to your descendants so that all the nations of the earth shall find blessing through your descendants, ⁵because Abraham obeyed me and kept my charge, my commandments, my statutes, and my law. ⁶So Isaac dwelt in Gerar. ⁷When the men of the place asked about his wife he said: She is my sister, because he was afraid to say: she is my wife, [thinking] lest the men of the place kill me because of Rebekah; for

she was beautiful. [8]Now when he had been there quite some time, Abimelech king of the Philistines, looking down through his window, saw Isaac caressing Rebekah his wife. [9]So Abimelech summoned Isaac and said: Well then, she is your wife! How could you say: She is my sister! Isaac said to him: Because I thought I would die because of her. [10]And Abimelech said: What is this that you have done to me! One of the people might have lain with your wife and so would have brought guilt upon us. [11]So Abimelech issued a command to the whole people: Whoever touches this man or his wife shall be put to death.

[12]Now Isaac sowed in that land and in that same year he reaped a hundredfold; and YHWH blessed him [13]so that the man became wealthier and wealthier until he was very wealthy indeed. [14]He came to own flocks and herds and a large household so that the Philistines were envious of him. ([15]Now the Philistines had blocked up and filled with earth all the wells which his father's servants had dug in the time of his father Abraham.) [16]So Abimelech said to Isaac: Go away from us because you have become far too powerful for us. [17]So Isaac left the place and encamped in the valley of Gerar and stayed there. ([18]Isaac dug again the wells which they had dug in the time of his father Abraham and which the Philistines had blocked up after Abraham's death and he named them following the names that his father had given them.) [19]When Isaac's servants dug in the valley and found a spring of running water, [20]the herdsmen of Gerar contested the claim of Isaac's servants saying: The water is ours. So he named the spring Esek because they had disputed with him. [21]When they dug another well they again contested it, so he named it Sitnah. [22]He moved on from there and dug another well, but they did not contest it, so he named it Rehoboth, saying: Now YHWH has made space for us so that we can be fruitful in the land. [23]Then he went up from there to Beersheba.

[24]YHWH appeared to him that night and said: I am the God of Abraham your father, Do not fear for I am with you and I will bless you and I will multiply your descendants because of Abraham my servant. [25]So he built an altar there and called on the name of YHWH and pitched his tent there; and Isaac's servants dug a well there.

[26]Now Abimelech came to him from Gerar with his adviser Ahuzzah and his army chief Phicol. [27]But Isaac said to them: Why have you come to me? You are my enemies; you have sent me away from you. [28]But they said: We see clearly that YHWH is with you so we thought: We should put each other on oath, we and you, and make a treaty with you [29]that you will do us no harm just as we have not attacked you and have done you only good and let you go in peace. Now you have been blessed by YHWH. [30]So he prepared a meal for them and they ate and drank. [31]They rose early in the morning and

exchanged oaths, and Isaac sent them on their way and they departed from him in peace. [32]That same day Isaac's servants came and told him about a well they had dug. They said to him: We have found water. [33]He named it Shibah; and so the city is known by the name Beersheba to this day.

Comment

The story of Jacob and Esau is interrupted by a chapter which brings together into a literary unity a group of traditions about Isaac. Abraham has already been the subject of similar stories: the wife-sister and Abimelech (ch. 20), a confrontation with Abimelech and a treaty with him (21:22-24, 27, 34), a dispute over wells, and the origin of the name of Beersheba (21:25-26, 32, 33). Tradition associates all three patriarchs with Beersheba, Abraham (21:31-32; 22:19), Isaac (26:32-33), and Jacob (46:1-5). Isaac is regarded as the channel through whom the promises made to Abraham (26:3, 5, 24; 28:4) are passed on to Jacob.

The author of chapter 26 is aware of the stories about Abraham, Sarah, and the Pharaoh/Abimelech (12:10-20; 20:1-18). This famine that drove Isaac southward was another famine besides the one that drove Abraham down to Egypt (v. 1). Isaac, like Abraham, settled in Gerar where Abimelech was king (20:1-2; 26:1). But the story is interrupted. YHWH appears to Isaac and repeats the promises (vv. 2-5). There is nothing corresponding to this in 12:10-20 and 20:1-18. YHWH is introduced by the standard formula *wayyērā' YHWH ('elohim)* (12:7; 17:1; 18:1; 26:2, 24; 35:9). There are five points of contact between the divine addresses in 26:2-5 and 22:16-18: (1) the oath (26:3 and 22:16); (2) "I will multiply your descendants" (26:3-4 and 22:17); (3) "like the stars of the heavens" (26:4a and 22:17); (4) "all the peoples of the earth shall find blessing (*hitbārăkû*) through your descendants" (26:4b and 22:18a); (5) because of Abraham's obedience (26:5 and 22:16). The themes and formulas of 26:2-5 are taken up again in 28:4: "I will be (am) with you" (26:3a), "I will bless you . . . and I will multiply your descendants" (26:3a, 4), because of Abraham (26:5a). These formulas are characteristic of the deuteronomic-deuteronomistic theology, in particular the combination of the oath and the land (26:3), the obedience (22:16; 26:5, 24), and "my charge, my commandments, my statutes, and my law" (26:5).

The account of Isaac's journey southwards continues in verse 6. The wife-sister theme is resumed, as well as the reason for the subterfuge, namely the fear that the patriarch will be killed if it is known that the woman is his wife (12:2; 20:11; 26:9). The formula of accusation: "What is this that you have done to us?" is virtually the same in each case (12:18; 20:9; 26:10). Once again the ancestress and the promise are in danger. But this time they are saved, not by a divine intervention, but by simple observation (v. 8). Even though Isaac and Rebekah have been quite some time in Abimelech's jurisdiction, Rebekah has not been taken into the harem. No one has touched her, no one shall touch her (v. 11), but "one of the people may have lain with your wife and so would have brought guilt on us" (v. 8).

In verses 12-13 the writer has brought together several themes and stories. The blessing of YHWH works itself out in Isaac's prosperity (vv. 12-14), and this leads to a double confrontation with Abimelech (vv. 16 and 26-29). Isaac is told to leave the region in the immediate vicinity of Abimelech (v. 16). When Isaac goes to the valley of Gerar (v. 17) and his servants dig there (v. 19), disputes arise over wells with the local inhabitants (vv. 19-21). When the disputes are settled, Isaac goes up to Beersheba (v. 23) where YHWH appears to him again and repeats the promises to him (v. 24). Isaac responds to the reassurance by building an altar and calling on YHWH (v. 25; cf. 12:7, 8; 13:18; 21:33; 33:10; 35:7). Isaac continues to prosper under YHWH's blessing (vv. 28a, 29b) so that Abimelech initiates dialogue which Isaac at first sees as a confrontation (vv. 26-27). However, the problem is resolved peacefully (vv. 30-31).

Verses 15 and 18 each break the thread of the narrative (but see Rendtorff 1977:32–34). They are antiquarian references which link the wells in the area with Abraham who had lived for a time in Gerar (20:1). The problem of water and wells (vv. 19-22, 25b, 32-33) was a major issue for "semi-nomads." The treaty of peace (v. 30-31, *bĕ šālôm*) is important for both Isaac, who continues to prosper under the divine blessing, and Abimelech, who acknowledges that Isaac's prosperity is due to YHWH. The author makes a Philistine acknowledge YHWH. Abimelech and Isaac exchange oaths (vv. 28, 31), as had Abimelech and Abraham (21:31). Abimelech, when proposing the treaty, alleges as a reason that he and his people "have done you only good and let you go in peace" (v. 29). He is somewhat disingenuous as he had dismissed Isaac (v. 16) and Isaac was at first suspicious when he approached (v. 27). A meal seals the treaty (v. 30). The episode ends with yet another explanation of the name

Beersheba (vv. 32-33; cf. 21:29-31). The well (*bĕ'ēr*) that Jacob's servants discovered is named Shibah (*šib'â*); hence the name of the city, Beersheba (*šebû'â*, oath). The last two verses (vv. 34-35) have their continuation in 27:46-28:9.

Notes

20-22. ESEK, SITNAH, REHOBOT. Esek (*'ēśeq*) is from a verb meaning "contest, dispute," used only here; Sitnah (*śitnah*) is derived from *śāṭān*, adversary; Rehobot means "spaces," because YHWH has made space (*hirḥîb*).

3. Jacob Deceives His Father
(27:1-45)

[1]When Isaac was old and his eyes were so dim that he could not see, he called his elder son Esau and said to him: My son! And he answered: Here I am! [2]And he said: Listen now. I am old and I do not know when I shall die. [3]Now then, take your weapons, your quiver and your bow, and go out into the field and hunt me some game, [4]and make me a tasty dish, such as I like, and bring it to me so that I may eat; and so I may bless you before I die. [5]Now Rebekah was listening when Isaac spoke to his son Esau. When Esau had gone into the field to hunt game and bring it in, [6]Rebekah said to her son Jacob: I heard your father speaking to your brother Esau; he said: [7]Bring me game and make me a tasty dish so that I may eat; and so I may bless you in the presence of YHWH before I die. [8]Now obey me my son and do as I order you. [9]Go to the flock and get me two fine young goats so that I may make them into a tasty dish such as your father likes. [10]Then bring it to your father so that he may eat and so bless you before he dies. [11]But Jacob said to his mother Rebekah: Look, Esau is a hairy man but I, I am a smooth man. [12]Perhaps my father may feel me and I will seem to be mocking him and I will bring a curse, not a blessing, upon me. [13]Upon me be your curse, my son! Now obey me; go, get [the goats] for me. [14]So he went and got them and brought them to his mother and she made a tasty dish such as his father liked. [15]Then Rebekah took her elder son Esau's best clothes which she had with her in the house and she put them on Jacob her younger son. [16]And she put the goat skins on his hands and on the smooth part of his neck. [17]Then she gave her son Jacob the tasty dish and the bread that she had made. [18]So he went to his father and said: My father! And he said: Here I am; who are you, my son? [19]Jacob

said to his father: I am Esau your firstborn. I have done as you told me; come now, sit up, and eat of my game so that you may bless me. ²⁰But Isaac said to his son: How is it that you have found it so quickly my son? He said: YHWH your God put it in my way. ²¹Isaac said to Jacob: Come close that I may touch you my son and see if you are really my son Esau or not. ²²When Jacob came close to his father Isaac, he felt him and said: The voice is the voice of Jacob but the hands are the hands of Esau. ²³But he did not recognize him because his hands were hairy like the hands of his brother Esau. And so he blessed him. ²⁴He said: Are you really my son Esau? He answered: I am. ²⁵Then he said: Bring it to me so that I may eat of my son's game and so bless you. Then he brought it to him and he ate; and he brought him wine and he drank. ²⁶Then his father Isaac said to him: Come close my son and kiss me. ²⁷So he came close and kissed him. When he smelled the smell of his clothes he blessed him and said: See, the smell of my son is like the smell of a field that YHWH has blessed:

> ²⁸May God give you of the dew of the heavens and of the richness of the earth, and plenty of grain and wine.
> ²⁹May peoples serve you and nations bow before you.
> Be master over your brothers, and may your mother's sons bow before you.
> May those who curse you be cursed, and those who bless you be blessed.

³⁰Just as Isaac had finished blessing Jacob and Jacob had scarcely left the presence of his father Isaac, Esau his brother came in from the hunt. ³¹He too had prepared a tasty dish and brought it to his father and said: Let my father rise up and eat of his son's game so that you may bless me. ³²His father said to him: Who are you? He said: I am your son, your firstborn, Esau. ³³Then Isaac trembled violently all over and said: Who was it then who hunted game and brought it to me? I have already eaten it all before you came and so have blessed him, and he shall remain blessed. ³⁴When Esau heard his father's words he gave a loud and bitter cry and said to his father: Bless me, me too, my father. ³⁵But he said: Your brother came deceitfully and took your blessing. ³⁶And he said: Yes, is he not rightly called Jacob (*ya'ăqob*)! He has supplanted me (*ya'qĕbēnî*) twice! He took my birthright and now he has taken my blessing! Have you not kept a blessing for me? ³⁷Isaac answered Esau: See, I have made him master over you and have given him all his brothers as servants and have provided him with grain and wine; what is left for you, my son? ³⁸Esau said to his father: Have you just one blessing, my father? Bless me, me too, father! Then Esau cried out and wept. ³⁹His father Isaac answered him:

Far from the richness of the earth shall be your dwelling,
   far from the dew of the heavens above.
⁴⁰By your sword you shall live, your brother you shall serve.
But the time shall come when you shake yourself free,
   and tear his yoke from your neck.

⁴¹So Esau bore animosity against his brother Jacob because of the blessing that his father bestowed on him and he said to himself: The time for mourning my father is close and then I will kill my brother Jacob. ⁴²When Rebekah was told what her older son Esau was saying, she sent for her younger son Jacob and said to him: See, your brother Esau is harboring thoughts against you so as to kill you. ⁴³Now my son, obey me. Up and flee to my brother Laban in Haran, ⁴⁴and stay with him some time until your brother's fury abates, ⁴⁵until your brother's anger turns away from you and he forgets what you have done to him. Then I will send for you and bring you back. Why should I lose the two of you in one day?

Comment

Chapter 27 is about blessing and deception. The structure is well defined: (1) Isaac wants to pass on his blessing (vv. 1-4); (2) the deception is in two parts: (a) the preparation (vv. 5-7); (b) the execution (vv. 18-19); (3) the deception exposed (vv. 30-40); (4) the consequences (vv. 41-45). The verb "bless" (*bārak,* sixteen times) and the noun "blessing" (*běrākâ,* six times) occur twenty-two times in all in the chapter. Isaac, now an old man (v. 2), wants to pass on his blessing, that is, he wants to confirm Esau his firstborn (*běkor,* vv. 19, [24], 32) as heir with the conventional rights of the firstborn. In the biblical sequence, Esau has already sold his birthright (*běkorâ,* 25:29-34), and the story in chapter 27 is aware of this: "He (Jacob) took my birthright (*běkorâ*) and now he has taken away my blessing (*běrākâ*)" (v. 36), thus taking up the four times repeated *běkorâ* of 25:29-34. Isaac wants to eat his favorite food so as to be in good spirits to pass on the blessing. This sequence, eat and so bless, is repeated several times with variations of the prepositions of purpose: the son is to bring game (*ṣayid*) from the hunt (*ṣud,* vv. 5, 7, 25, 31, 33) so as to prepare the tasty dish (*maṭ'ammîm,* vv. 4, 7, 9, 14, 17, 31) that Isaac likes so that, nicely satisfied, he may pronounce the blessing: the "so that" is expressed by *ba'ăbûr* (vv. 4, 19, 31), *ba'ăbur 'ăšer* (v. 10), *lěma'an* (v. 25), and the *waw* consequential (vv. 7, 33). On four occasions the subject of "bless" is "soul" (*nepeš,*

vv. 4, 19, 25, 31), "my soul" or "your soul." That the meaning is any more than "I" or perhaps, "with all my being," is very dubious; cf. Pss 103:1, 2, 22; 104:1, 35: "Bless YHWH, my soul," i.e., my whole being, "praise YHWH." It is to read much into the text to see in verses 18-29 some sort of pre-cultic rite: the (solemn) approach (vv. 18-19), the identification (vv. 21-24), the eating of the meal (vv. 25-26), the embrace and kiss (v. 27a), the blessing (vv. 27b-29). The whole forty-five verses are dominated by blessing and deceit.

The roles of the four actors in the drama are important. Isaac senses that death is near. He likes his favorite food; it will dispose him well to give the blessing. When he discovers that he has been deceived, he is terrified. He tells Esau: "I have eaten it all and so have blessed him before you came, and he shall remain blessed" (v. 33). The blessing has been given and cannot (?), or at least shall not, be revoked. Why? Certainly not because something of the patriarch's "being" or "soul" (*nepeš*) has passed on to Jacob, but simply because a solemn, deathbed action has been performed. He probably regards the blessing given to Jacob as God's disposition and choice; and he has made Jacob "master over your brothers" (v. 29). Isaac was forty years old when he married Rebekah (25:20). There was a period during which Rebekah was barren. The twins would have been at some stage of maturity when Isaac sensed that he was to die soon and so must give his blessing (27:1-4). There were the twenty years when Jacob was away in Paddan-aram. Isaac was one hundred and eighty years old when he died after Jacob's return, and Jacob and Esau buried him (35:28-29). The final author has brought disparate traditions together. Rebekah directs the whole action of deception. Her preference for Jacob has been noted (25:28). She was listening when Isaac sent Esau to hunt and so make preparations for the blessing (vv. 5-7). "Obey me and carry out my orders" (v. 8; cf. v. 43). She is prepared to take the consequences upon herself (v. 13). She has access to Esau's "best clothes" (v. 15). When she realizes that the consequences of what she has done threaten disaster, she again directs the action (vv. 41-45). After Jacob departs for Paddan-aram, Rebekah plays no further role in the Jacob cycle. She is mentioned in passing (28:5; 29:12; 35:8) and her death and burial place are noted (49:31).

Jacob is the pliant, acquiescent instrument in Rebekah's hands. At his birth, he is grasping Esau's heel (*'āqeb*). So his name is "he who grasps the heel," or "Heeler." He has already taken advantage of Esau's stolid obtuseness (25:29-34). He is the usurper who has taken the birthright (*bĕkorâ*) and the supplanter who has stolen the blessing (*bĕrākâ,* v. 36). The shift in meaning from the noun "heel" (*'āqeb*) to the verb "follow at the heel," "supplant," "attack" (*'āqab*) allows the meaning "he has supplanted me twice" (v. 36; cf. *Notes,* 25:26).

Esau, stolid and thoughtless (25:29-34), is justly outraged (vv. 34-38) and murderously disposed (vv. 40-41). Twenty years later (ch. 33), he is much more mature and a different person.

The pronouncement of blessing on Jacob (vv. [27b]-29) is a composite piece in which the author brings together a number of standard formulas and traditional ways of speaking. Isaac acknowledges that it is YHWH who prospers the grain in the field and so gives it a healthy smell (v. 27b); the healthy smell of his son's (Esau's) clothes moves Isaac to pronounce his own blessing (v. 27a) on the usurper. An ancient tradition is brought into the next part of the blessing (v. 28). The dew (*ṭal*) of heaven and the richness (*šemen,* lit., fatness) of earth are very likely a pair that describes the water (dew and rain) that gives fertility (see *Notes*). The grain and wine are the produce of the fertile earth which God, not Canaanite Baal, effects. With the blessing of fertility, Isaac pronounces the blessing of dominion or rule. It is a blessing on Jacob (Israel) who (which) has become a state. The plural in verse 29b, "your brothers . . . your mother's sons" is not to be pressed literally. The curse and blessing in the last lines of verse 29 are a fixed formula found in Numbers 24:9b with the sequence "curse" and "blessing" reversed (cf. 12:3). The "non-blessing" upon Esau (vv. 39-40) takes up the "fatness and dew" theme of verse 28. It is not a curse but a pronouncement on the hard life of the desert-dweller who, as well as being far from the rain of fertility, is to live by the sword. The state, Israel (Jacob), has conquered Edom (Esau); but Edom will at some time break free (v. 40; 2 Kgs 8:20-22; cf. *Comment* on 25:29-34). It is prophecy after the event.

Notes

27-29. DEW, RICHNESS, GRAIN, WINE. The word pair "dew and richness" (*ṭal, šemen*) is an ancient Canaanite combination. In a text from Ugarit, the Maiden Anath "pours the fatness of [de]w in bowl" so as to wash her hands. She draws water and bathes; the water is

"Sky-[d]ew, fatness of earth, Spray of the Rider of the Clouds; Dew that the heavens shed, [Spray] that is shed by the stars" (ANET 136B:30–38). The fatness of dew (richness, Gen 27:28, 39) would be the rain which, with the dew on the Palestinian mountain range, gives fertility to the earth. Grain (*dāgān*) and wine (*tîrôš*) are a well established combination which appears as a pair twenty-nine times in the Old Testament (i.e., Deut 7:13; 11:24; 12:17; 14:43; 18:4; 28:51; 33:28), and a number of times as a pair with, or separately with, oil (*yiṣhār,* Miller, P. D. 1980b).

4. Esau's Wives and Jacob's Departure (26:34-35; 27:46-28:9)

[34]When Esau was forty years old he took as wife Judith the daughter of Beeri the Hittite and Basemath the daughter of Elon the Hittite. [35]But they were a source of bitterness to Isaac and Rebekah.

[46]So Rebekah said to Isaac: I loathe life because of the Hittite women. If Jacob takes a wife like these from the Hittite women of the land, what's life worth for me?

28:1 So Jacob called Isaac and blessed him and charged him: Do not take a wife from the women of Canaan. [2]Up, go to Paddan-aram to the house of Bethuel your mother's father; take a wife there from the daughters of Laban your mother's brother. [3]May El šadday bless you and increase and multiply you, and may you become an assembly of peoples. [4]May he give you and your descendants with you the blessing of Abraham so that you possess the land where you sojourn which God gave to Abraham. [5]So Isaac sent Jacob away and he went to Paddan-aram to Laban the son of Bethuel the Aramean, the brother of Rebekah, the mother of Jacob and Esau. [6]Now Esau saw that Isaac had blessed Jacob and sent him to Paddan-aram to take a wife there, and that as he blessed him he charged him: Do not take a wife from the women of Canaan, [7]and that Jacob obeyed his father and his mother and went to Paddan-aram. [8]When Esau saw that the Canaanite women did not please his father Isaac, [9]Esau went to Ishmael and took as wife Mahalath daughter of Ishmael, son of Abraham, sister of Nebaioth, besides the wives he had.

Comment

The problem of Esau's wives from the local population (for Hittites, cf. *Notes* ch. 23) emerges in 26:34-35 and is continued in 27:46.

Abraham had made his trusted servant swear that he would "not take a wife for my son from the daughters of the Canaanites among whom I live" (24:3). Isaac now lays the same injunction upon Jacob (28:1). Jacob is to take a wife from the patriarchal family in Paddan-aram (cf. 25:20). Isaac pronounces a blessing on Jacob and sends him on his way (vv. 3-4, 5). The formulas and content of these verses have much in common with 35:9-15 and 48:3-4: (1) God who blesses is *El šadday* (cf. 17:1); (2) the promise of descendants and land is made to Jacob; (3) Jacob is to become an assembly (*qahal*) of peoples/nations (cf. 17:4-5; 48:4). This all points to a common editing. When Esau learned of the blessing, injunction, and sending, he went to take a wife from the other branch of the family of Abraham, Ishmael. Esau also took wives from the Canaanites (36:2-5). So Esau's wives were:

Judith, daughter of Beeri the Hittite and
Basemath, daughter of Elon, the Hittite. (26:34)
Mahalath, daughter of Ishmael, sister of Nebaioth. (28:9)
Adah, daughter of Elon, the Hittite.
Oholibamah, daughter of Anah, son of Zibeon, the Hivite,
Basemath, daughter of Ishmael, sister of Nebaioth. (36:2-5)

The whole passage indicates a post-exilic reworking of material when the "mixed marriage" problem has become acute. It is saying that there is no reason at all to marry outside one's family, clan, or people. Look at the example of the patriarchs. Esau now disappears from the scene to reappear twenty years later (32:4-9 [3-8], 14-21 [13-20]; 33; 36:29b). The conflict between the twins is left hanging in the air and unresolved.

5. Jacob at Bethel
(28:10-22)

[10]Jacob set out from Beersheba and went on his way to Haran. [11]Now he chanced on a certain place and spent the night there because the sun had set. He took one of the stones of the place and put it at his head and lay down to sleep in that place. [12]He dreamt that there was a stairway set earthwards with its top reaching heavenwards, and that there were heavenly beings going up and coming down on it. [13]And YHWH stood before him and said: I am YHWH the God of Abraham your father and the God of Isaac; the land on which

you are lying I am giving to you and your descendants. ¹⁴Your descendants shall be like the dust of the earth and shall spread to the west and to the east and to the north and to the south, and all the clans of the earth shall find blessing through you and your descendants. ¹⁵I will be with you and will protect you wherever you go and I will bring you back to this land; I will not leave you until I have done all that I have told you. ¹⁶When Jacob awoke from his sleep he said: Truly YHWH is in this place and I did not know. ¹⁷He was afraid and said: How awesome is this place; it is none other than the house of God and the gate of heaven. ¹⁸Then Jacob rose early next morning; he took the stone which he had put at his head and set it as a pillar and poured oil on top of it. ¹⁹He named that place Bethel; but earlier the name of the city was Luz.

²⁰Then Jacob made a vow and said: If God is with me and protects me on this journey which I am making and gives me bread to eat and clothes to wear, ²¹and I return safely to my father's house, then YHWH shall be my God, ²²and this stone which I have set up as a pillar shall be the house of God; and of all that you give me I will give a tenth to you.

Comment

The passage divides itself readily: there is the itinerary note (v. 10; a continuation of 26:23?); Jacob's arrival at "the place," his preparations to spend the night there, and his dream (vv. 11-13a); the divine address in the form of promise (vv. 13a -15); Jacob's reaction to the dream (vv. 16-19b); Jacob's vow (vv. 20-33). As the divine address both resumes and anticipates so much material, it will be considered first. These verses presuppose the broader context of the story of the patriarchs. The presentation formula by which God identifies himself to Jacob: "I am YHWH the God of Abraham your father and the God of Isaac" (v. 13a, b) is found elsewhere with variations (15:7; 31:42; 32:10 [9]; 46:3). The promise of the land (v. 13b) to you and/or your descendants is all-pervading (12:7; 13:14-15; 15:7, 18; 17:8; 22:17; 26:2-3; 28:13, 15; 35:12). The land that is promised here is *hā 'āreṣ,* i.e., the land in its length and breadth, not just "the place" (v. 13b). The descendants are to be "like the dust of the earth" (v. 14a; 13:16) and are to spread to the four points of the compass (v. 14a; cf. 13:14), and "all the clans of the earth shall find blessing through you" (v. 14b, *kôl mispeḥôt hā'ădāmâ nibrĕkû,* exactly the same wording as in 12:3; in 18:18 the same form of the verb, Nipʻal, is used, but with *kôl gôyê hā 'āreṣ,* "all the nations of the earth [world]''; in 22:18 and 26:4, the formula is ''all the nations of the earth [world],'' but with the Hitpa'el form of the verb, *hitbārĕkû,* which has the same meaning). The assurance of divine presence, assistance, and guidance back to the land is characteristic of the Jacob cycle (26:3, 24; 28:15 [20]; 31:3; 32:10 [9]; 46:3; [48:15, 21; 50:24]). The verses 13a-15 extend far beyond the present episode at Bethel; they embrace the whole patriarchal story (and more).

The account of Jacob's experience at Bethel is a coherent independent piece (vv. 11-13a, 16-19a). Jacob came across, chanced upon, a certain place; *hā māqôm,* with the definite article, ''the place,'' could be understood as the ''sanctuary,'' though Jacob did not yet know that it was a sanctuary. He took a stone from the sanctuary and put it ''at his head,'' not ''under his head'' so as to use it for a pillow (it is the same phrase as used in 1 Sam 18:13, 16, where Michal put a pillow of goat's hair ''at the head'' of the bed, and in 1 Sam 26:7, where Saul's spear was stuck in the ground ''at his head''). This stone was to be some sort of protection. In his dream, Jacob saw, not a ladder, but an ascending ramp (*sullām*) or stairway, like the ascent to a ziggurat or temple, which joined heaven and earth. It was this that revealed to Jacob that he was in a holy place. ''Heavenly beings'' (v. 12, lit., ''messengers'' or ''angels of God,'' *mal'ăkê 'ĕlohîm*) were descending and ascending the ramp. These are not the messenger of YHWH (cf. 16:7-11; 22:11-12, 15). They are more like the ''sons of God'' (*bĕnê 'ĕlohîm,* divine beings) of Psalm 29:1; Job 1:6; 2:1. They underscore the link between heaven and earth and are a sign of the holiness of God. The phrase *mal'ăkê 'ĕlohîm* occurs only here and in 32:2 (1) where these ''angels of God'' or ''divine beings'' are a sign of God's power. Jacob wakes up and gives voice to his realization that YHWH dwells ''in this place and he is in awe before the overpowering majesty of God (vv. 16-17). The place is the house of God (*bêt 'ĕl,* the future name) and the gate of heaven, i.e., the place of access to God. Jacob had woken up with shock after his dream. It is now morning. He rises early, anoints the stone at his head (it is now formally a sacred stone), and calls ''that place,'' i.e., the whole area, the house of God, *bêt 'ĕl* (v. 19a). Bethel has been mentioned in 12:8 and 13:3 where the writer, describing events that are earlier in the biblical chronology, has no problem in using the later name of the place. A note adds that the former name of the place was Luz, ''almond tree.'' The account of Jacob's experience is now closed. Jacob leaves his land both as a fugitive from his brother and as suitor for a wife from his own clan. He has encountered God and can, in the biblical perspective which unites a sanctuary story (vv. 11-13a, 16-19a) with the promises (vv. 13a-15), continue his journey under God's protection.

Three verses (vv. 20-22) are added to complete the biblical account of the episode at Bethel. They are neither part of the promises (vv. 13a -15) nor part of the story (vv. 11-13a, 16-19a). God has already given assurance of protection and safe return (v. 15); but the conditions of the vow are "if God is with me . . . and I return safely" (vv. 20-21a). Jacob has already set up a stone and named the place the house of God (vv. 18-19a); but now he vows that the stone shall be the house of God (v. 22a). "Then YHWH shall be my God" (v. 21b) indicates that a place of worship of YHWH is to be set up; but this has been done already (vv. 18-19a). The payment of tithes (v. 22b) presupposes a sedentary society and regular worship. Jacob addresses God in the second person singular (the rest of vv. 20-22 is in the third person). Like the Melchizedek passage (14:20), it bases and legitimates tithing in the patriarchal period.

The biblical writer links a sanctuary in Israel with the patriarch Jacob. The house of Joseph took Bethel (Judg 1:22-25). Bethel was an important sanctuary and place of assembly in the period before the monarchy (Judg 20:18, 26; 21:2; 1 Sam 7:16). The prophets of the eighth century spoke out against the abuses in Bethel (Hos 10:1-8; Amos 5:5; 7:10-17). The sanctuary was linked with the beginnings of prophecy (2 Kgs 2:3, 23). It was razed to the ground as part of the centralizing reforms of Josiah (2 Kgs 23:15-20).

Tradition, and it is clearly an Israelite (northern) tradition, has associated the sanctuary at Bethel with the patriarch Jacob. Luz (v. 19b) was already a place of worship before the Israelite settlement. Whether there was a story of its original foundation retold at the place itself and later applied to Jacob is a matter of conjecture. To synthesize all: There was an independent, self-contained story (vv. 11-13a, 16-19) about the patriarch Jacob and the sanctuary at Bethel, a story which may possibly be based on an earlier story commemorating the foundation of the sanctuary; this story was joined to the broader patriarchal context by means of the promise material (vv. 13a -15). The whole is fitted into Jacob's journey to Haran by the itinerary verse (v. 10). The final verses (vv. 20-22), which have no intrinsic link with the story, legitimize the practice of vows and tithing by setting them in the patriarchal period. Jacob now continues his journey to Haran in the strength of God.

(*Comment* and *Notes* have been joined together for this passage.)

6. Jacob and Laban. Jacob's Marriage
(29:1-30)

¹Jacob then continued his journey and came to the land of the people of the east. ²He looked around and caught sight of a well in a field and three flocks of sheep lying beside it because the flocks were watered from that well. There was a large stone over the mouth of the well. ³When all the flocks had gathered there, they would roll the stone from the mouth of the well, water the sheep, and then put the stone back in its place over the mouth of the well. ⁴Jacob said to them: My brothers, where are you from? They said: We are from Haran. ⁵And he said to them: Do you know Laban, the son of Nahor? They said: We know him. ⁶He said to them: Is he well? They said: He is well. Look now, Rachel his daughter is coming with the sheep. ⁷He said to them: It is still full day; it is not yet time for the animals to be gathered together; why not water the sheep and go and pasture them? ⁸But they said: We cannot until all the flocks are gathered together; then the stone is rolled away from the mouth of the well and we water the sheep. ⁹While he was still speaking with them Rachel came with her father's sheep; she tended them. ¹⁰When Jacob saw Rachel, the daughter of Laban, his mother's brother, and the sheep of Laban, his mother's brother, Jacob went up and rolled the stone from the mouth of the well and watered the sheep of Laban his mother's brother. ¹¹Then Jacob kissed Rachel and raised his voice and wept. ¹²Then Jacob told Rachel that he was her father's kinsman, the son of Rebekah; so she ran and told her father. ¹³When Laban heard the news of Jacob his sister's son, he ran to meet him and embraced him and kissed him and brought him to his house. He told Laban all these things. ¹⁴Laban said to him: Indeed, you are my flesh and blood. And he stayed with him a month. ¹⁵Then Laban said to Jacob: Yes, indeed you are my kinsman; but should you work for me for nothing? Tell me what your wages should be. ¹⁶Now Laban had two daughters, the elder named Leah and the younger Rachel. ¹⁷Leah's eyes were without lustre, but Rachel was beautiful and graceful. ¹⁸Jacob loved Rachel, so he said: I will work for you for seven years for Rachel your younger daughter. ¹⁹Laban said: Better to give her to you than to anyone else; stay with me. ²⁰So Jacob worked seven years for Rachel and they seemed but a few days, so much did he love her. ²¹Then Jacob said to Laban: The time is up. Give me my wife that I may go to her. ²²So Laban invited all the men of the place and gave a feast. ²³Now in the evening he took his daughter Leah and brought her to him and he went to her. ²⁴(Laban gave his maid Zilpah to his daughter Leah to be her maid.) ²⁵But in the morning—it is Leah! He said to Laban: What is this that you have done to me? Was it not for Rachel that

I worked for you? Why have you deceived me? ²⁶Laban said: It is not the custom here to give the younger before the elder. ²⁷Complete these seven days and then we will give you the other as well for another seven years of working for me. ²⁸And Jacob did so; he completed these seven days. Then Laban gave him his daughter as wife. ²⁹(Laban gave his maid Bilhah to his daughter Rachel to be her maid.) ³⁰So Jacob went to Rachel as well. He loved Rachel more than Leah and worked another seven years for Laban for Rachel.

Comment

Jacob is now in Paddan-aram (28:2), in Aramean country (28:4; 31:20, 24), looking for the household of his mother's brother Laban, who is both a second cousin by blood and uncle to Jacob (ch. 24; 27:43; 28:2). Jacob left Beersheba in the south of Canaan for Haran (28:10). He was still on Canaanite soil, "the land of my sojournings" (47:9), when he encountered God at Bethel. Just as in the case of Abraham's servant (24:10), there is not a word about the month-long journey from Canaan to Paddan-aram. Both Jacob and the servant are simply there, a characteristic of popular narrative technique. Abraham had sent his servant "to my own land and kinsmen to take a wife for my son Isaac" (24:4). Now Isaac has sent Jacob "to Paddan-aram to the house of Bethuel your mother's father; take a wife there from the daughters of Laban your mother's brother" (28:2). The laconic dialogue with the Aramean herdsmen at the well is purely functional. They assure Jacob that he is where he should be, note that Rachel is approaching, finish off the dialogue as she comes, and take no further part in the story. The well, a quiet meeting place, now becomes a center of bustling activity. Just as Rachel had run to tell the household of the arrival of a kinsman (24:28), so now does Rachel again (29:12). Laban, then as a prospective brother-in-law, now as a prospective father-in-law, extends the welcome of the household (24:31; 29:13). Jacob now knows that he has reached his goal (29:14).

Jacob had come as one sent by his father, but also, in the biblical context, as a fugitive (27:43-45). Hence, he does not come bringing gifts as had Abraham's servant (24:10). Jacob has no option but to accept when Laban proposes that he work for him (29:15). This verse joins together the two parts of the narrative unit (vv. 1-30), the second part being introduced by adapting the standard formula of the storyteller: "A certain man had two sons (daughters), the one . . . ,

the other . . . ." Jacob loved and wanted as wife Rachel the younger. Laban is ready to have her marry a member of the clan so as
to have a good worker in the household for the next seven years (vv.
18-19). So the conflict between Jacob and Laban, the second in the
cycle, begins. Jacob, the deceiver, is now himself deceived. Jacob,
stunned by the deception—"but in the morning—it is Leah!" (v.
25)—retorts with the traditional formula of accusation: "What is
this that you have done to me?" (v. 25; cf. 3:13; 4:10; 12:18; 20:9).
Laban rides the deception easily by referring blandly to the local custom of marrying off the eldest daughter first (v. 26). The week's
wedding festivities have begun. Jacob must complete them. He really
has no option, for he cannot offend the guests (v. 28). But he is tied
to another seven years of work for Laban as payment for Laban's
concession in giving him Rachel as well as Leah.

Notes

1. PEOPLE OF THE EAST. Literally, "sons of the east," i.e., the tribes
beyond the Jordan, east and northeast of Canaan.

2. RACHEL HIS DAUGHTER. In this culture, young women worked
as shepherdesses together with their male counterparts.

14. YOU ARE MY FLESH AND BLOOD. Literally, "my bone and my
flesh." The formula is a traditional expression of lasting relationship (Gen 2:23; Judg 9:2; 2 Sam 5:2; 19:13, 14 [12, 13]).

7. Jacob's Children
(29:31–30:24)

³¹When YHWH saw that Leah was less loved he opened her womb;
but Rachel remained barren. ³²Then Leah became pregnant and bore
a son and named him Reuben. She said: Because YHWH has looked
on my distress, surely my husband will love me now. ³³She became
pregnant again and bore a son. So she said: YHWH has heard that
I am less loved, so he has given me this son too. She named him
Simeon. ³⁴She became pregnant again and bore a son. So she said:
Now this time my husband will be united with me because I have borne
him three sons. Therefore she named him Levi. ³⁵She became pregnant again and bore a son. So she said: This time I will praise YHWH.
Therefore she named him Judah. Then she stopped bearing.

30:1 When Rachel saw that she bore Jacob no children, she became jealous of her sister and said to Jacob: Give me children, else I shall die. ²Jacob became angry with Rachel and said: Am I in the place of God who denied you the fruit of the womb? ³She said: Here is my maidservant Bilhah; go to her that she may bear upon my knees so that I too may be built up from her. ⁴So she gave him her maidservant Bilhah as wife and Jacob went to her. ⁵Bilhah became pregnant and bore Jacob a son. ⁶So Rachel said: God has given me judgment for me; he has listened to me too and has given me a son. So she named him Dan. ⁷Bilhah, Rachel's maidservant, became pregnant again and bore Jacob a second son. ⁸So Rachel said: I have struggled mightily with my sister and have prevailed. She named him Naphtali. ⁹When Leah saw that she had stopped bearing, she took Zilpah her maidservant and gave her to Jacob as wife. ¹⁰Then Zilpah Leah's maidservant bore Jacob a son. ¹¹So Leah said: What good fortune! So she named him Gad. ¹²Then Zilpah, Leah's maidservant, bore Jacob a second son. ¹³So Leah said: How happy I am! Yes, young women will call me happy. So she named him Asher.

¹⁴At the time of the wheat harvest Reuben went and found mandrakes in the field and brought them to his mother Leah. Then Rachel said to Leah: Come, give me some of your son's mandrakes. ¹⁵But she said to her: Is it a small matter that you have taken my husband? Will you take my son's mandrakes as well? Rachel said: Well then, let him lie with you tonight in exchange for your son's mandrakes. ¹⁶When Jacob came in from the field in the evening, Leah went to meet him and said: It is to me you are to come because I have hired you with my son's mandrakes. So he lay with her that night. ¹⁷Then God listened to Leah and she became pregnant and bore Jacob a fifth son. ¹⁸Leah said: God has given me my reward because I gave my maidservant to my husband. So she named him Issachar. ¹⁹Leah became pregnant again and bore Jacob a sixth son. ²⁰Leah said: God has endowed me with a fine dowry; now at last my husband will honor me because I have borne him six sons. She named him Zebulon. ²¹After that she bore a daughter and named her Dinah. ²²Then God remembered Rachel and God listened to her and opened her womb. ²³She became pregnant and bore a son. She said: God has taken away my humiliation. ²⁴So she named him Joseph, saying: May YHWH add to me another son.

Comment

The passage has been fashioned into a unity out of a formulaic account of the birth of Jacob's children and narrative material. Even so, the passage as a whole can lay claim to a narrative unity. The narrative tension is introduced in the first verse: "When YHWH saw that Leah was less loved he opened her womb, but Rachel remained barren" (29:31). The writer resumes here the theme of Jacob's preferential love for Rachel over Leah. The way to conflict is open. Leah bears four sons while Rachel remains childless. The tension heightens with the exchange between Rachel and Jacob (30:1-2), which gives vent to the frustration of both and jars the harmony between them (29:18, 20, 30), and is maintained with the episode of the mandrakes (30:14-16) and Leah bearing two more sons. The tension is finally resolved when Rachel gives birth to Joseph (30:22-24). So the arch of tension extends from 29:31 to 30:24. Within the narrative span in which the short, stylized, birth formulas hide the course of many years, Leah bears four sons (29:31-35), Bilhah bears two on behalf of Rachel (30:1-8), Zilpah bears two on behalf of Leah (30:9-13), Leah bears two more sons (30:17-20) as well as a daughter (30:21), and finally Rachel bears a son and prays for a second son (30:22-24). The accounts of the birth of each of the eleven sons (plus the birth of Benjamin, 35:16-19), follow a fixed pattern and use a fixed set of formulas with very little variation. The formulaic presentation of the birth of Jacob's eleven sons is set into a narrative framework within which a long series of events move through tension to climax and resolution. The writer's theological perspective is that God directs pregnancy and birth (29:31a, 32b, 35a; 30:2b, 6a, 17a, 18a, 20, 22, 23b, 24b; cf. 16:2, 11; 18:10-14; 20:18). The names of the twelve sons of Jacob (add Benjamin from 35:16-20) were known to the writer who constructed brief notes or events about each birth to explain the names. The names do not derive from popular etymology. These twelve names are personal names in the present context and occur in Genesis as personal or tribal names in 35:22-28; 46:8-25; 49:1-17.

Notes

29:32. REUBEN. There is no explanation of the name in the text. It could mean "see, a son," *rā'û bēn.*

33. SIMEON. Could be explained as "(YHWH) has heard my distress," *šāma' 'onî.*

34. LEVI. Linked with the verb *lwh,* to join oneself to.

35. JUDAH. *hôdāh,* praise YHWH, cf. 49:8, "Judah, your brothers shall praise you."

30:6. DAN. *dānanni,* "God has given judgment for me," *dān,* to judge.

8. NAPHTALI. *ptl,* to twist. The text reads literally: "(with) mighty twistings I have twisted myself," *naptûlê 'ĕlohîm niptaltî.*

10. GAD. *bā gād,* "with (the help of) Gad," or understanding the preposition *bĕ* as *beth essentiae,* i.e., emphatic, "what good fortune." Gad is a divinity of good fortune (Isa 65:11); it is the equivalent of the Greek *tychē,* and is well attested in the Phoenician and Palmyrean inscriptions of Syria in Hellenistic times (Cooke 1903:269; Donner-Röllig 1964:90-91, 145, 303; Jean-Hoftijzer 1865: 57).

13. ASHER. Linked with the noun *'ešer* or *'āšār,* which is used only in the plural construct *'ašrê,* "the happiness of."

14-16. MANDRAKES. These are mandragora or "love apples," reddish in color with a soft, tomato-like center, thought to be an aphrodisiac.

18. ISSACHAR. The verb *śākār* means to hire; the noun is the price of hire, the wage, or the reward. Leah hired Jacob for the night with her son's mandrakes (v. 16b). She now exclaims that God has given her a reward or wage. The reason for the name is the event that has taken place (vv. 16-17).

20. ZEBULUN. *zĕbādân . . . zĕbed ṭôb:* "God has endowed me with a fine endowment." *yizbĕlēnî,* "will honor me." This is the only occurrence of the verb *zbl.* The meaning is derived from the context and the noun *zĕbul,* elevation, height.

21. DINAH. There is no explanation of the name. Dinah is the center of the episode in chapter 34.

23. JOSEPH. There is a play on two words, *'āsap,* to take away, and *yāsap,* to add to. "God has taken away (*'āsap*) my humiliation . . . may YHWH add to me another son."

8. Jacob Outwits Laban
(30:25-43)

²⁵After Rachel had borne Joseph, Jacob said to Laban: Let me go so that I may return to my own home and land. ²⁶Give me my wives and my children for whom I have worked for you so that I may go. You know how I have worked for you. ²⁷Laban said to him: Please, allow me to say so—I know by divination that YHWH has blessed me because of you. ²⁸Tick off your wage, he said, and I will give it to you. ²⁹He said to him: You know well how I have worked for you and what has become of your flocks because of me. ³⁰You had very little before I came; now they have increased abundantly and it is high time that I attended to my own household as well. ³¹He said: What shall I give you? But Jacob said: You shall give me nothing. If you do for me what I tell you, I shall again feed and take care of your flock. ³²I shall go through all your flocks today and pick out (the spotted and speckled sheep) all the black lambs among the sheep and all the speckled and spotted among the goats; these shall be my wages. ³³My fair dealing shall answer for me later when you come to check my wages. Every goat that is not spotted or speckled, every sheep that is not black, shall be accounted stolen by me. ³⁴Laban said: Agreed, let it be as you have said. ³⁵So on the same day he [Laban] picked out the striped and speckled he-goats and all the spotted and speckled she-goats, all that had white on them, and all the black lambs, and gave them to his sons to look after. ³⁶Then he put three days journey between himself and Jacob, while Jacob tended what remained of Laban's flock.

³⁷Then Jacob took fresh sticks of poplar, almond, and plane tree and peeled strips from them so as to lay bare the white on the rods. ³⁸Then he stood the sticks which he had peeled upright, facing the flocks, in the water-troughs where the flocks came to drink; the flocks bred when they came to drink. ³⁹The flocks went to heat in front of the sticks and the females gave birth to striped and spotted and speckled young. ⁴⁰Then Jacob picked out the lambs and turned them facing toward the striped and the black of Laban's flock. And so he set aside flocks for himself which he did not add to Laban's flock. ⁴¹When the stronger were in heat, Jacob put the sticks in the troughs in front of them so that they might breed among the sticks. ⁴²But when the flock showed itself to be weak he did not put [the sticks in front of them]; so the weak were for Laban, the strong for Jacob. ⁴³So the man became more and more wealthy and had abundant flocks, female and male servants, camels, and asses.

Comment

Jacob wants to return to his own country. But Laban, it seems, still has some claim on him (vv. 25-26). When Jacob says that he has worked hard for Laban (v. 26b), Laban acknowledges this and grants that the blessing that has been his has come from YHWH, Jacob's God, because of Jacob (v. 27). Jacob acknowledges this too (v. 30a). Jacob first refused any wage (v. 31a), but then suggests one (v. 32b). In the ancient Near East, goats were generally black and sheep white. Jacob proposes that he remove the striped-spotted-speckled-mottled goats and black sheep from Laban's flocks and keep them as his wages (v. 33). But Laban removes these striped-spotted-speckled-mottled goats and black sheep, puts them in the care of his sons, and sends them off on a three-day journey (vv. 35-36). Jacob is then left with the rest of Laban's flocks (v. 36b). By a curious and cunning device, beyond the ken of the modern herdsman, he proceeds to breed striped-spotted-speckled-mottled goats from black goats and black sheep from white sheep (vv. 37-41). He uses only the stronger of both for this purpose so that his flocks are ultimately better than those of Laban (v. 42). So Jacob's shrewdness makes him a wealthy man with a wealth honestly, though cunningly, acquired (vv. 33a, 43). Jacob knew what he was going to do (v. 33) before Laban anticipated him and cheated him by removing the motley members of his flocks (vv. 35-36). God's blessing is again with Jacob. It is very likely that an old herdsman's tale has been incorporated into the Jacob cycle and applied to Jacob. The multiplication and repetition of the words striped-spotted-speckled-mottled create some problems in the text.

Notes

27. BY DIVINATION. The verb *niḥēš,* to divine, is an intensive, Pi'el, form and is used only as such. It has the same three radicals as *nāḥāš,* serpent.

9. Jacob Departs. Treaty with Laban (31:1–32:1 [Eng 31:55])

¹When Jacob heard Laban's sons saying: Jacob has taken all that was our father's and all this wealth of his he has made from what was our father's, ²he saw that Laban's attitude to him was not as it

was before. ³So YHWH said to Jacob: Return to the land of your
fathers and your kinsmen and I will be with you. ⁴Then Jacob sent
for Rachel and Leah and called them to the field where his flocks
were. ⁵He said to them: I see that your father's attitude to me is not
as it was before. But the God of my father has been with me. ⁶You
yourselves know that I have worked for your father with all my
strength. ⁷Yet your father has cheated me and has changed my wages
ten times; but God has not allowed me to suffer harm. ⁸If he said
the spotted ones shall be your wages, all the flocks bore spotted; but
if he said the striped shall be your wages, all the flocks bore striped.
⁹So God has taken away your father's cattle and given them to me.
¹⁰Now, at the mating season I lifted up my eyes and saw in a dream—
the he-goats mounting the flocks were striped, spotted, and mottled.
¹¹Then the messenger of God said to me in a dream: Jacob. I said:
Here I am. ¹²He said: Lift up your eyes and look—all the he-goats
mounting the flocks are striped, spotted, and mottled for I have seen
all that Laban has been doing to you. ¹³I am the God [who appeared
to you at] Bethel where you anointed a pillar and made a vow to me.
Now rise up, go from this land and return to the land of your kinsmen. ¹⁴Then Rachel and Leah answered him: Is there any share of
the inheritance of our father's house still left to us? ¹⁵Are we not
regarded by him as foreigners? Indeed, he has sold us and has consumed the money given for us. ¹⁶All the wealth that God has taken
away from our father belongs to us and our children. So now, do
all that God has told you. ¹⁷So Jacob put his children and his wives
on camels, ¹⁸and drove all his livestock and all the possessions he had
acquired, livestock and flocks, in Paddan-aram so as to go to his father in the land of Canaan. ¹⁹Now Laban had gone to shear his sheep,
so Rachel stole her father's household gods. ²⁰Jacob had lulled the
heart of Laban the Aramean by not telling him that he was fleeing.
²¹He fled with all that he had; he set out for and crossed the river
and made in the direction of the mountains of Gilead. ²²When Laban
was told on the third day that Jacob had fled, ²³he took his kinsmen
with him and pursued him for seven days and caught up with him
in the mountains of Gilead. ²⁴But God came to Laban the Aramean
in a dream by night and said to him: Take care to say nothing at all
to Jacob.

²⁵When Laban overtook Jacob—Jacob had pitched his tent on the
mountain, and Laban had pitched his with his kinsmen on the mountains of Gilead—²⁶Laban said to Jacob: What have you done, lulling
my heart and carrying off my daughters like prisoners of the sword.
²⁷Why did you flee secretly and deceive me and say nothing to me?
I would have sent you on your way with joy and songs, with tambou-

rine and zither; ²⁸you did not allow me to kiss my grandchildren and daughters. Ah! you have acted foolishly! ²⁹I had it within my power to do you harm, but the God of your father spoke to me yesterday and said: Take care to say nothing at all to Jacob. ³⁰But now, you have gone away because you have longed so much for your father's house; [but] why have you stolen my gods? ³¹Jacob answered Laban: Because I was afraid; I thought that you would take your daughters from me by force. ³²Whosoever you find has your gods shall not live. In the presence of our kinsmen point out what is yours here and take it. Jacob did not know that Rachel had taken them. ³³So Laban went to Jacob's tent, to Leah's tent, and to the tent of the two maidservants, but found nothing. Then he went from Leah's to Rachel's tent. ³⁴Now Rachel had taken the household gods and put them in the camel's saddle and was sitting on them. Laban searched the whole tent but found nothing. ³⁵Then she said to her father: Do not be angry with me, my Lord, for I am not able to rise in your presence because the lot of women is upon me. He searched, but he did not find the household gods. ³⁶Then Jacob became angry and took Laban to task; he retorted to Laban: What wrong have I done? What is my offense that you have pursued me? ³⁷Even though you have felt through all my goods, what have you found of all your household goods? Set it here before my kin and your kin, and they may decide between us two. ³⁸I have been with you twenty years now and your ewes and the she-goats have not miscarried, nor have I eaten the rams of your flocks. ³⁹A carcass torn by wild beasts I have never brought you; I have borne the loss myself. You demanded of me what was stolen whether by day or by night. ⁴⁰This is how I lived: the heat consumed me by day, the cold by night, and sleep fled from my eyes. ⁴¹These twenty years I have worked for you in your household, fourteen years for your two daughters and six years for your flocks, and you have changed my wages ten times. ⁴²If the God of my father, the God of Abraham and the Fear of Isaac, has not been with me, you would have sent me away empty-handed. But God saw my affliction and the labor of my hands and warned you last night. ⁴³Then Laban replied to Jacob: The daughters are my daughters and the children my children and the flocks my flocks and all that you see is mine. But as for my daughters and the children whom they have borne, what shall I do for them now?

⁴⁴Come now, let us make a treaty you and I; [let us make a cairn] and it shall be a witness between you and me. ⁴⁵So Jacob took a stone and set it up as a pillar. ⁴⁶Then Jacob said to his kinsmen: Gather stones. So they took the stones and made a cairn and ate there beside the cairn. ⁴⁷Laban called it Jegar-sahadutha, and Jacob called it Galeed. ⁴⁸And Laban said: This cairn is a witness today between you

and me and so it is named Galeed, ⁴⁹that is, the watch tower (Miz-pah), of which he said: May YHWH watch between you and me when one is out of sight of the other. ⁵⁰If you ill-treat my daughters and if you take wives other than my daughters when no one from among us is there to see, then God is witness between you and me. ⁵¹Then Laban said to Jacob: See this cairn and this pillar that I have erected between you and me; ⁵²this cairn is a witness, so too this pillar, that I will not pass beyond this cairn to your side and you will not pass beyond this cairn and this pillar to my side to do harm. ⁵³Let the God of Abraham and the God of Nahor (the God of their fathers) judge between us. And Jacob swore by the Fear of Isaac his father. ⁵⁴Then Jacob offered sacrifice on the mountain and called his kinsmen to eat bread; so they ate bread and passed the night on the mountain.

32:1 [Eng 55]Laban rose early in the morning, kissed his grandchil-dren and daughters, and blessed them. Then Laban set out on his re-turn home.

Comment

Chapter 31 is to be understood in the context of what has gone before and what follows. There are many cross references to chap-ter 30 and within the chapter itself. Jacob reminds his wives "that I have worked for your father with all my strength" (v. 6) and coun-ters Laban's case with a convincing reminder of all that he has done for him (vv. 38-41), recalling his own words to Laban in their previ-ous dialogue (30:26, 29-30). His account of the mating of the striped, spotted, mottled sheep and goats (vv. 8-12) presumes the devices of 30:37-43. The theme of Jacob's address to Rachel and Leah is that God is with him and has prospered him (vv. 5b, 7b, 9, 11, 13). This follows YHWH's assurance that "I will be with you" (v. 3b). The theme "return to the land of your fathers and your kinsmen" (vv. 3, 13) frames the address as an *inclusio,* and recurs in verses 18b, 30. The verse "I am the God [who appeared to you at] Bethel" (v. 13) is central and shows familiarity with the traditions of 28:10-20. The God who sent Jacob on his way and assured him that he would be with him and bring him back (28:15), now reaffirms that he will continue to be with him and guide him back to his own land (v. 3). The theme of Laban as a cheat recurs (vv. 6-7, 14-16, 42). It is this, together of course with the birth of Joseph to Rachel (30:22-24), that resolves the conflict between Rachel and Leah who realize only now that they have been cheated by their father. Another recurrent theme is that of Laban's superior power by which he can restrict Jacob (vv. 29, 31, 42b). But Laban is warned that might is not right: "Take care to say nothing at all to Jacob" (vv. 24, 29). "Jacob had lulled the heart of Laban the Aramean by not telling him that he was fleeing" (v. 20), and Laban asks angrily: "What have you done, lulling my heart?" (v. 26). Laban complains that he has not been allowed to kiss his grandchildren and daughters farewell (v. 28a). After the treaty has been enacted (vv. 43-54) he kisses and blesses them (32:1 [Eng 31:55]). The theme of Laban's concern for his grandchildren and daughters recurs four times (vv. 26, 28, 43, 32:1a [Eng 55]). In the final sentence of the statement of his case to Laban, Jacob says: "but God saw my affliction and the labor of my hands and warned you last night" (v. 42b), thus taking up the divine address: "for I have seen all that Laban has been doing to you" (v. 12b). The theme of the stolen household gods (*teraphim*) is sounded in verse 19b and resumed in vv. 30b, 32-35 (and resolved in 35:2-4?). The complexities of the account(s) of the treaty will be explained below.

There may well have been an original, simple narrative of Jacob's departure, Laban's pursuit of him, their reconciliation, and their definitive parting. And verses 4-13 and verses 43-54 may well be later expansions. But the text before us has been knitted together skillfully with many cross references and recurrent themes. The main theological thrust is in verse 3 and verses 4-13. God is with Jacob (v. 3), has guided him on his way to Paddan-aram (v. 13), has been with him during his twenty-year sojourn there (vv. 4-13), and will guide him back to his own land (vv. 3, 13). Laban and Jacob state their cases against each other like litigants before a tribunal (vv. 25-43) where the main issues are raised, to the decisive advantage of Jacob. The climax of the narrative comes in verse 42 where Jacob can state as proven from the history of twenty years that God is with him. The Jacob-Laban conflict is resolved by the treaty (vv. 43-54); each makes a solemn promise and goes his own way, and Laban makes his exit from the patriarchal scene.

Verses 10-13 present a problem. Verse 10 begins with an indication of time: "Now at the mating season." Jacob then lifted up his eyes and "saw in a dream—the he-goats mounting the flocks were striped, spotted, and mottled." Then immediately in verse 11 "the messengers of God said to me in a dream," and the passage about the multicolored he-goats is repeated (v. 12). There seem to be two accounts of a revelation which have been fused together. Westermann (1985:491–92) has proposed two original accounts. The first is:

10a   Now at the mating season
11   The messenger of God said to me in a dream:
       Jacob. I said: Here I am.
12a   He said: Lift up your eyes and look—
       all the he-goats mounting the flocks
       are striped, spotted, and mottled.
10a, b And I lifted up my eyes and saw in a dream—
       the he-goats mounting the flocks
       were striped, spotted, and mottled.

The second, repeating verse 11, is:

11   Then the messenger of God said to me in a dream:
       Jacob. I said: Here I am.
13a   And he said: I am the God [who appeared to you at]
       Bethel where you anointed a pillar and made a vow to me.
12b   I have seen all that Laban has been doing to you.
13b   Now rise up, go from this land and
       return to the land of your kinsmen.

The words in square brackets in verse 13a are supplied from the LXX
and the two Targums. Verse 13b is not a mere doublet of verse 3.
In the present text the two verses form the beginning and the end
of the passage.

The two wives, Rachel and Leah, are reconciled fully when they
realize that they have been cheated of their inheritance by their father (vv. 14-16). The process of reconciliation had begun with the
birth of Rachel's child Joseph (30:22-24).

While Laban is away at the shearing festival (v. 19a), Jacob takes
the opportunity to depart without notice (vv. 17-24) and Rachel ap-
propriates the "household gods" (*teraphim*, v. 19b). In the present
context these are images of family gods which are passed on from
father to son (or adopted son) conferring leadership in the family.
To possess them does not confer the right of inheritance or property (see *Notes*). Laban was very upset that they had been taken (vv.
30-35). They could not have been very big as Rachel was able to hide
them under the camel-kār, a sort of palanquin attached to the saddle
on the camel. The brief episode, all important to Laban, makes a
mockery of the gods (referred to as *'ĕlohîm* in vv. 30, 32) as a woman
in an alleged state of ritual and legal uncleanness, "the lot of women
is upon me" (v. 32b), is sitting upon them.

The treaty that seals the reconciliation between Jacob and Laban
is complex (vv. 43-54). It consists of an agreement about the treatment of Laban's daughters and a non-aggression pact, or at least

a definition of territorial limits (vv. 51-53). The whole action in verses 43-54 is under the heading: "Come now, let us make a treaty you and I" (*nikrĕtāh bĕrît*, v. 44a). This gives unity to the final text which in the course of the history of its parts seems to have two endings (vv. 50 + 53b and v. 54). The whole action *is* the treaty. Nothing is put in writing. As the treaty ("it," v. 44b) cannot be a witness, some scholars supply the words "let us make a cairn" *before* verse 44b. The Greek adds "no one is with us, see God is witness between you and me" *after* verse 44b. The following verse (v. 45) does not have a context. Jacob accepts Laban's proposal of verse 44, has his kinsmen gather stones, and erects a cairn (vv. 46-47). Two explanations of the name of the cairn are given, one in Aramaic and one in Hebrew (v. 47). The Hebrew name, *gal 'ēd* (vv. 47, 48), means the cairn (or heap) is witness, and the additional name Mizpah (v. 49) derives from the Hebrew verb *ṣāpāh,* to watch over. YHWH will watch over the cairn and treaty. The treaty is enclosed between two expressions of concern by Laban for his daughters (vv. 43, 50). It is a treaty of reconciliation guaranteeing the welfare of Laban's family.

The treaty of verses 51-53a defines borders. It is broader than the family treaty of verses 43-50. Laban had proposed the treaty for the protection of his daughters in verses 43-44. He takes the initiative again in verse 51. Jacob had already erected a pillar (v. 45). Laban now points to the cairn and pillar that he himself had erected (v. 51). Both cairn and pillar establish the border limits between Aram and Canaan. Neither is to cross the border with aggressive intent (v. 52). Each swears by, and so is to be punished by, his own God if he transgresses. The phrase in round brackets, "the God of their fathers," is an explanatory note in the text. It is not certain whether the half-verse, "and Jacob swore by the Fear of Isaac his father" (v. 53b), refers to this or the previous treaty. The oath takes up the divine appellation of verse 42. The treaty is sealed by a sacrifice and a meal over which Jacob presides (v. 54). The final verse (32:1 [Eng v. 55]) takes up the theme that encloses the first treaty (vv. 43, 50), resuming Laban's concern for his grandchildren and daughters which he had sounded in his confrontation with Jacob (vv. 26, 28). Again, the action is the treaty. The Jacob-Laban story concludes with 32:1 (Eng v. 55).

It should be noted that in this treaty passage there are (1) the subject matter of two treaties (vv. 50 and 52); (2) two signs of each treaty, a pillar (vv. 45 and 52) and a cairn (vv. 46-47 and 52); (3) two meals

(vv. 46b and 54). Both verses 48 and 52 begin: "This cairn is a witness," verse 52 adding "so too this pillar."

It seems that there was an ancient piece of tradition telling of a border treaty between the Patriarch Jacob and the Aramean Laban fixing some place in the mountain range of Gilead (Galeed) as the boundary. This tradition has come down to the narrator of the Jacob-Laban story who has worked it into his account of the treaty of reconciliation between Jacob and Laban.

Notes

13. I AM THE GOD [WHO APPEARED TO YOU AT] BETHEL. The words in brackets are supplied from the Greek and the Targums. The Hebrew text has only *'ānokî hā 'ēl bêt 'ēl,* which could be understood as "I am God himself, (the God of) Bethel." God introduces himself to Jacob in a similar way later, on the way down to Egypt: *'ānokî hā 'ēl 'ĕlohê 'abîkā,* "I am God himself, the God of your father" (46:3). In each case *'ēl* is preceded by the definite article *hā.* Deutero-Isaiah writes "thus says *hā 'ēl* YHWH" (Isa 42:5), "God himself, YHWH."

15. HE HAS SOLD ME. The bridal price that Jacob paid for Rachel and Leah was twenty years hard work. They received nothing of it.

19A. NOW LABAN HAD GONE TO SHEAR HIS SHEEP. The sheep shearing was a festival (cf. 38:12-19).

19B. HOUSEHOLD GODS. *tĕrāphîm.* The word most probably derives from the Hittite-Hurrian *tarpiš.* It occurs fifteen times in the Old Testament, always with the plural ending *-îm* but in one context clearly with a singular meaning (1 Sam 19:13,16). Michal took a *tĕrāphîm,* laid it on the bed, put a pillow of goat's hair at its head, and covered it with clothes so as to allow David to escape from Saul's henchmen. It must have been life-size. In Judges 17, a *tĕrāphîm* is a molten image. The *tĕrāphîm* are classed with idols in Hosea 3:4; 2 Kings 23:24. The *tĕrāphîm* utters nonsense in Zechariah 10:2. In the present passage they are images of gods (vv. 30, 32) that can be concealed easily under the structure attached to the camel's saddle. It has been proposed that possession of the household gods could, in Hurrian law and custom, confer a legal title to an estate. The documents from Nuzi, mentioned in the note on 15:2, have been alleged in support. This sale-adoption of the title-holder is to take the gods of Nashwi (the one in whose name the contract is drawn up [ANET 219 (2)]). But no link is made between possession of the gods and inheritance of the estate. Possession of the gods indicates rather the leadership of the family or clan (Hoffner 1968; 1969; 1973:217; Seybold 1976; de Vaux 1978:251–53).

24, 29. NOTHING AT ALL. Literally, "from good to bad." This is a *merism,* i.e., the naming of two extremes to embrace the whole.

25-43. There is nothing in the whole Jacob-Laban story to indicate that Laban had adopted Jacob or that Jacob was in any way in a state of slavery or servitude to Laban. Laban, as the property owner and father of Jacob's wives, held a decided advantage over Jacob who had come to him as a fugitive. There are laws about the conditions of employment of shepherds and their assistants by owners of large herds and flocks in the Code of Hammurapi (ANET 177:261–68) which provide a useful general background to verses 38–40. Further, verse 43 is important for understanding Laban's position. He does not want to lose a group of good cattle hands (for contracts about hiring shepherds, cf. Finkelstein 1968).

42, 53b. THE FEAR OF ISAAC. *paḥad yiṣḥaq.* The word *paḥad* has been rendered by kinsman or parent (de Vaux 1978:271), fear (Hillers 1972; Puech 1984), thigh (Malul 1985), refuge (Kopf 1958), and has been linked with the deity Haddad (Lemaire 1985). The three times repeated *paḥad* YHWH, "terror of YHWH," in Isaiah 2:10, 19, 21, would favor "fear."

44. LET US MAKE A CAIRN. These words are not in the Hebrew text.

47, 49. JEGAR-SAHADUTHA, GALEED, MIZPAH. The first is an Aramaic name, "heap of the testimony," the equivalent of the Hebrew *galʿēd,* meaning the same. Mizpah (v. 49) is derived from *ṣāpāh,* to watch over. The verse reads: "that is, the watchtower (*miṣpāh,* with the definite article *ha*) of which he said (or, it is said) may YHWH watch (*yiṣep*) you and me when one is out of sight of the other." The heap of stones or cairn, *galʿēd,* is the boundary between Aram and Canaan. It lies on the mountain range of Gilead, *gilʿēd,* east of the Jordan, at about the same latitude as the middle point of Lake Gennesereth.

10. Jacob Prepares to Meet Esau
(32:2-22 [Eng 32:1-21])

(In this and the following passage, the numbering of the Hebrew verses is one in advance of the English. Only the Hebrew numbering is given. Subtract one digit to find the English.)

²Jacob set out on his way and heavenly beings met him. ³When he saw them, Jacob said: This is a company of God. And he called the place Mahanaim.

⁴Then Jacob sent messengers on ahead of him to his brother Esau in the land of Seir in the territory of Edom. ⁵He ordered them: You are to say this to my lord Esau: Your servant Jacob says: I have been sojourning with Laban up to now. ⁶I have cattle, asses, and sheep, male and female servants, and I have sent to tell my lord so as to find favor in your eyes. ⁷When Jacob's messengers returned to him they said: We came upon your brother Esau, but he is already on his way to meet you with four hundred men. ⁸Jacob was very afraid and disturbed, so he divided the people with him, the sheep and the cattle and the camels into two companies. ⁹He thought: If Esau comes upon one company and strikes it, then the remaining company will survive.

¹⁰Then Jacob said: God of my father Abraham and God of my father Isaac, YHWH, who said to me: Return to your land and your kinsmen and I will prosper you. ¹¹I have fallen short of all the acts of steadfast love and the fidelity that you have shown to your servant. With my staff only I crossed the Jordan; here and now I have grown to two companies. ¹²Deliver me, I pray, from the power of my brother, from the power of Esau, for I am afraid of him lest he come and strike me and the mothers with the children. ¹³But it was you who yourself said: I will indeed prosper you and I will make your descendants like the sand of the sea which cannot be counted for numbers. ¹⁴So he passed the night there.

Then he took an offering for his brother Esau from what he had acquired, ¹⁵two hundred she-goats and twenty he-goats, two hundred ewes and twenty rams, ¹⁶thirty milch camels with their young, forty cows and ten bulls, twenty she-asses and ten he-asses. ¹⁷He put each herd separately under the care of a servant and said to them: Go on ahead of me and put a space between the separate herds. ¹⁸He gave orders to the first: When Esau my brother approaches you and asks: To whom do you belong? Where are you going? To whom do these ahead of you belong? ¹⁹Then say to him: To your servant Jacob. They are an offering to my lord Esau and he himself is coming after us.

²⁰He gave the same orders to the second and to the third and to all who went in charge of the herds. Thus you are to speak to Esau when you meet him. ²¹And say further: Your servant Jacob is coming after us. [Jacob] thought: I will appease him with the offering that precedes me; only then will I see him in person; perhaps he will receive me favorably. ²²So Jacob's offering went on ahead of him, while he himself spent the night in the camp.

Comment

Jacob sets out on his way back to Canaan and encounters immediately the "heavenly beings," "messengers of God" (*mal'ăkê 'ĕlo-hîm*, vv. 2-3 [Eng 1-2]). He had seen them at Bethel (28:12). There, they were going up and coming down the ramp that reached from the earth heavenward. They were a sign of God's holiness and majesty to which Jacob responded: "Truly YHWH is in this place and I did not know . . . how awesome is this place" (28:16-17). Here, they are a sign of God's power. They are a company, *mahăneh,* so Jacob calls the place *mahănāyîm* (two companies, dual). Jacob can now go on in the strength of God. Mahanaim is located on the King's Highway in east Jordan, south of Gilead.

Esau had left the scene twenty years ago when he went to Ishmael to take a wife from that branch of the Abraham clan in addition to his Hittite wives (28:6-9), and had not been mentioned in the meantime. Now, with no previous introduction, he is coming to meet Jacob as Jacob returns to Canaan (32:4 [3]). Jacob sends two embassies to meet him (vv. 4-8a + 8b-9 [3-7a + 7b-8] and vv. 14-22 [13-21]). The messengers are to let Esau know that God has prospered Jacob during his years with Laban (v. 6 [5]). But Jacob is afraid when the messengers return and tell him of Esau's large retinue (vv. 7b-8a [6b-7a]). So he divides his large household, his flocks, herds, and camels into two groups for safety's sake (vv. 8b-9 [7b-8]). Jacob tells the messengers a second time to insist that God's blessing has been with him (vv. 14-22 [13-21]) and, conscious that he had usurped Esau's blessing twenty years before, sends an offering or gift (*minhâ,* vv. 14, 19, 21, 22 [13, 18, 20, 21]) from the fruits of God's blessing (14b [13b]) to appease him.

Jacob prays to be delivered from Esau (v. 12 [11]). He invokes the "God of my father Abraham and God of my father Isaac, YHWH," (v. 10 [9]), the God who had said to him at Bethel: "I am YHWH, the God of Abraham and the God of Isaac" (28:13). The prayer is elaborated with promise material already familiar, and set between the two embassies to Esau. The God of Bethel had promised: "I will be with you and will protect you wherever you go, and bring you back to this land" (28:15). Jacob now calls on "YHWH, who said to me, return to your land and your kinsmen, and I will prosper you" (v. 10 [9]); cf. 31:3, 13. Jacob further recalls the promise of "descendants like the sand of the sea which cannot be counted for numbers" (v. 13 [12]) made to Abraham after his supreme act of obedience (22:17). The three key promises of the Jacob cycle are brought together: (1) "will be with you"; (2) "return to the land of your kinsmen"; (3) "I will prosper you." Jacob asks God's protection in the name of his promises, conscious of "all the acts of steadfast love (*ḥāsādîm*) and fidelity (*'emet*) that you have shown to your servant" (v. 11 [10]). The narrator has framed all with the assurance "I will prosper you" (vv. 10b, 13a [9a, 12a]). But Jacob must undergo one more experience before he meets Esau.

11. Jacob Wrestles with "a Man"
(32:23-33 [Eng 32:22-32])

²³That night he arose and took his two wives and his two maidservants and his eleven children and crossed the ford of the Jabbok. ²⁴He took them and sent them across the wadi with all that he had, ²⁵so that Jacob was left alone. Then a man wrestled with him until daybreak. ²⁶When he [the man] saw he was unable to prevail over him, he struck his thigh so that Jacob's thigh joint was dislocated as he wrestled with him. ²⁷Then he said to him: Let me go! Day has broken. But he said: I will not let you go until you have blessed me. ²⁸Then he said: What is your name? And he said: Jacob. ²⁹He said: No longer shall your name be Jacob but Israel, because you have acted as a prince with God and with men and have endured. ³⁰Then Jacob asked him: Now tell me your name. But he said: Why do you ask my name? Then he blessed him there. ³¹So Jacob named the place Penuel: Yes, I have seen God face to face, yet my life has been spared. ³²The sun rose on him as he passed by Penuel; but he was limping because of his thigh. ³³That is the reason why even to this day the people of Israel do not eat the sinew of the nerve along the thigh joint because he had struck the sinew of the nerve along Jacob's thigh joint.

Comment

Jacob is on his journey southward to meet Esau who is journeying northward from Edom/Seir. The normal procedure on an itinerary is to camp the night, then rise early in the morning and continue on the way. The sequence in the present itinerary would be: Jacob "spent the night in the camp" (v. 22b), [rose early and] took his two wives . . . and crossed the ford of the Jabboq" (v. 23b). Then he lifted up his eyes and saw Esau coming to him with four hundred men" (33:1). But the writer must have Jacob alone for the night encounter. So although preparations have been made to camp the night on the northern side of the wadi Jabboq (v. 22b), Jacob has the whole caravan transported across the wadi that night. Verse 24 is a seam (or link) which attaches the story of the encounter to the itinerary. To cross a steep ravine (v. 23b) and then to recross it in the same night (v. 24a, "he . . . sent them across") is no problem in story. Jacob is now alone (v. 25a) so that the biblical story of the encounter can proceed (vv. 25b-32). "A man" (*'îš,* no definite article) wrestled with Jacob until daybreak. The Hebrew word play throughout the story is obvious: the name of the wadi is *Yabboq;* "he wrestled" is *yē'ābēq;* Jacob's name is *ya'ăqob.* This "man" is the attacker and the active party. Jacob resists and holds off the attacker but is brought almost to submission by a blow on the thigh. Even so, Jacob wants to separate from him in peace. The contest is a draw. The storyteller and the reader or listener know that the attacker is, in however mysterious form, God. Jacob of the story does not know and will not know until verse 31. The irony is that Jacob is asking God's blessing, but does not know it. The attacker asks Jacob his name so that he can exercise power over him (v. 28). With that power, he changes Jacob's name. Jacob (*ya'ăqob*) is no longer "he supplants," but Israel (*yiśrā'ēl*), "God rules" (lit., acts as a prince, *śrr,* see *Notes*). God, and no one else, is to rule Jacob-Israel from now on, "because you have acted as a prince (a ruler) with God and with men, and have endured" (v. 29 [28]). I suggest that "with God and with men" is a merism, the statement of two extremes to express totality. Jacob has won the birthright, the blessing (both instituted by God in the patriarchs' eyes) and ultimately the conflict with Laban. He has endured through all, and now he endures with God. Jacob, though he does not know it, asks power over God by asking the attacker's name. The attacker refuses the request and blesses Jacob (v. 30 [29]). But in fact it is God who blesses him. So God sends Jacob on his way with a blessing. Only in the dawn after the night long struggle does Jacob realize that the encounter has been with God (v. 31 [30]). Jacob has seen God "face to face" (*pānîm 'el pānîm*), so that he calls the place *Peni'el,* the face of God. But

God whom he has "seen" does not take away his life. Jacob limps his way past *Penu'el* as the sun rises. (Jacob is still on the northern side of the wadi.) This is the end of the story. Jacob has struggled with God, has been graced by God, and carries the mark of the struggle, at least temporarily, in his limp. The final verse (v. 33 [32]) notes a food taboo not known elsewhere in the Old Testament. It is very likely a later taboo that has grown up in Israel to which a (or, the) writer wanted to give a biblical basis. "The sinew of the nerve along the thigh joint" is taboo because it belongs to the reproductive organs, the source of life. Jacob, blessed by God, can now go on to meet Esau.

The story has been considered so far only in its biblical context. Scholars are virtually unanimous that the background to the story is animistic. There was widespread belief that demons or spirits or varieties of *numina* (awesome spiritual powers) resided in streams, stones, and trees and often resisted any approach to the material objects that they inhabited. A mysterious demon would have lived in the wadi Jabboq and a story of his fearsome attacks on travellers who attempted to cross it has been applied to Jacob. Jacob then is attacked by a malevolent demon who would prevent him crossing. There are many suggestions about the content of the "original" story. Westermann, for example, writes: "The text narrates only the beginning and the end of the contest, and all that follows is the naming of the place. . . . The basis then is a (detailed) narrative, a local story, which explained the name Penuel (or Jabboq), but did not yet contain the name Jacob. It is taken up into an itinerary in the form of an abbreviated report (like vv. 2-3) dealing with Jacob's return" (1985:514-15).

Scholars are further agreed that the "original" story has undergone a process of growth. The following account of this alleged process, which remains hypothetical, is from G. Hentschel (1977). It is modern and clear and reflects, at least in its broad lines, much recent thinking and methodology. There are six stages in the process of growth:

(1) A local pre-Israelite story narrates that the hero is attacked by a nocturnal demon and wrestles with him till dawn. The attacker is overcome and asks the hero to let him go before daybreak. The hero agrees on condition that he receives a blessing: "A man wrestled with him until daybreak (v. 25b [24b]). Then he said to him: Let me go! Day has broken. But he said: I will not let you go until

you have blessed me (v. 27 [26]). Then he blessed him there (v. 30b [29b]). The sun rose on him as he passed by Penuel" (v. 32a [31a]).

(2) The roles of the contestants are reversed: "When he [the man] saw that he was unable to prevail over him, he struck his thigh so that his thigh joint was dislocated as he wrestled with him (v. 26 [25]). Then he asked him: Now tell me your name. But he said: Why do you ask my name?" (v. 30a [29a]).

(3) The contest was transferred to a spectacle before God when the YHWH religion became dominant: "So he named the place Peniel: Yes, I have seen God face to face, yet my life has been spared" (v. 31 [30]).

(4) Still later, the story acquired the Jacob motif: "Then he said: What is your name? And he said: Jacob. He said: No longer shall your name be Jacob but Israel, because you have acted as a prince with God and with men and have prevailed" (vv. 28-29 [27-28]).

(5) The Yahwist fits the story into the Jacob cycle by means of glosses: "The same night he arose . . . and crossed the ford of the Jabbok (v. 23 [22]) . . . He took them . . . and Jacob was left alone" (vv. 24-25a [23-24a]).

(6) Later glosses: "but he was limping because of his thigh" (v. 32b [31b]). "That is the reason . . . " (v. 33 [32]).

Something like this may well have happened. But any such reconstruction must remain more or less intelligent conjecture.

The story of Jacob at the Jabbok certainly supplied matter for further reflection in Israel. The prophet Hosea knows the story in some form and elaborates:

> The Lord has an indictment against Judah
> and will punish Jacob according to his ways,
> and requite him according to his deeds.
> In the womb he took his brother by the heel,
> and in his manhood he strove with God.
> He strove with the angel and prevailed,
> he wept and sought his favor (Hos 12:3-5 [2-4]).

The "man" of Genesis has now become "the angel," and Jacob has "prevailed"; Hosea adds that Jacob "wept and sought his favor." G. Vermes (1975:12–14) has pursued the angel further in Jewish tradition, and what follows is indebted entirely to his research. The Targum Neofiti (discovered in the Vatican Library only in the 1950s by Diaz Macho and published by him) identifies Jacob's adversary as the angel Sariel who appears "in the likeness of man." Sariel is a prince in charge of the heavenly choirs. When the adversary Sariel says to Jacob: "Let me go," the reason is that "the time has come for the angels on high to praise and I am the chief of those who praise." When the adversary changes Jacob's name to Israel, he, Sariel, says: "For you have conducted yourself as a prince with angels from before the Lord, and have prevailed against them." Vermes notes further that in the War Rule (9:12-15), one of the Dead Sea Scrolls, Sariel is one of the four archangels who protects the four battle formations. He is thus able to make the following enlightening equation: a man (Genesis) = Sariel (Targum Neofiti) = one of the four angels (Qumran). Vermes notes finally that the Targum Neofiti explains the name Israel from the Hebrew *śrr,* to rule, to act as a prince. (W. T. Miller [1984:97–117] has given an extensive discussion of the Jabbok story in Jewish tradition.)

In the biblical context, Jacob can now go on to meet Esau. When Jacob was leaving Canaan, he encountered God at Bethel and went on to Paddan-aram with the assurance that God was with him and would bring him back safely (28:10-20). Now, as he returns to Canaan with a wife from his own clan, he encounters God again and proceeds in the strength of God's blessing to meet his brother.

Notes

23. JABBOK. Nahr-ez-Zerqa (the blue river) flows into the Jordan on the eastern side about forty kilometers (twenty-five miles) north of the Dead Sea. Together with the Yarmuk, just below the lake of Galilee, it is the main tributary of the Jordan. The Jabbok is a very steep ravine which becomes a raging torrent after heavy rain.

27. THE DAY HAS BROKEN. Spirits or ghosts roam at night. The ghost of Hamlet's father "faded on the crowing of the cock," "was about to speak when the cock crew"; "but even then the morning cock grew loud, and at its sound it shrunk in haste away." The ghost itself said: "But, soft! methinks I scent the morning air; brief let me be!" (Hamlet Act 1, Scenes 1, 2, 5). Many other examples could be cited.

29. ISRAEL. The first part of the name, *yśr,* has been derived from *śrh,* to persist or contend; *śrh,* to fight; *śr',* to rule; *yšr,* to be straight or upright; *šrr,* to be strong. The derivation favored here is from *śrr,* to rule or act as a prince, following Vermes and the Targum Neofiti. Hence, the meaning "God rules," or "may God rule."

31, 32. Peni'el, Penu'el. Both mean "the face of God." The former is chosen for assonance with *panîm* (v. 31 [30]).

12. Jacob and Esau Reconciled (33:1-20)

¹When Jacob lifted up his eyes and saw Esau approaching and four hundred men with him, he divided the children between Leah, Rachel and the two maidservants. ²He put the maidservants and their children in front, then Leah and her children, and Rachel and Joseph last. ³He himself went in front of them. He bowed to the ground seven times as he drew near to his brother. ⁴But Esau ran to meet him and embraced him and fell on his neck and they kissed each other. ⁵When he lifted up his eyes and saw the women and the children he said: Who are these with you? And he said: The children with whom God has graced your servant. ⁶Then the maidservants and their children drew near and bowed down. ⁷Then Leah and her children drew near and bowed down; and last Joseph and Rachel drew near and bowed down. ⁸And he said: What do you intend with all this company that I meet? He said: To find favor in the eyes of my lord. ⁹Then Esau said: I have plenty, my brother. Let what is yours be yours. ¹⁰Jacob said: No, I pray you. If I have found favor in your eyes, accept this offering from me. For seeing your face is for me like seeing the face of God; you have received me favorably. ¹¹Accept, I pray you, my blessing brought to you because God has graced me and I have enough. He pressed him and he accepted it.

¹²Then he [Esau] said: Let us go on our way and I will go ahead of you. ¹³But he said to him: My lord knows that the children are frail and the flock and herds giving suck are a concern to me and if they are overdriven for a day the whole flock will die. ¹⁴Let my lord go on ahead of his servant and I will lead them on quietly according to the pace of the caravan and the children until I come to my lord at Seir. ¹⁵Then Esau said: Let me leave with you some of those with me. But he said: Why so? Let me only find favor in the eyes of my lord. ¹⁶So Esau returned that day to Seir. ¹⁷Jacob set out for Succoth and built himself a house and made sheds for his cattle. And so he named the place Succoth.

¹⁸Then Jacob came to Salem, the city of Shechem, in the land of Canaan on his return from Paddan-aram, and he camped before the city. ¹⁹Then he bought the piece of land where he had pitched his tent from the sons of Hamor, the father of Shechem for a hundred pieces. ²⁰There he set up an altar and named it El-Elohê-Israel.

Comment

Jacob now resumes his journey after the episode at the Jabbok during the night. He is on the southern side of the ravine. He looks up and sees Esau and his entourage approaching. The reconciliation of the brothers is the conclusion of the Jacob-Esau story, though Esau appears again briefly to bury his father (35:29). This last of the three conflicts in the cycle, which has been left hanging in the air for twenty years, is now resolved. The chapter divides itself easily into the mutual greeting (vv. 1-11), the leave taking (vv. 12-17), and some further itinerary notes (vv. 18-20). The writer notes again (v. 1) that Esau is approaching with four hundred men (32:7 [6]). Jacob himself leads his family to meet his brother after arranging his wives and their children in ascending order of honor. Jacob's ceremonial procession is in contrast to Esau's spontaneous approach (vv. 3-4), and the solemnity is enhanced by the repetitions in verses 6-7. His ceremonial greeting derives from the protocol of the ancient oriental courts. For example, a Canaanite king writing to the Egyptian Pharaoh, Amen-hotep III (fourteenth century B.C.E.): "At the feet of the king, my lord, and my Sun-god, seven times and seven times I fall" (Amarna Letters, ANET 483–89; a regular court formula in the letters from p. 485ff.) Esau harbors no resentment from the deception of twenty years earlier and his warmth leads to the brothers' embrace (v. 4). Jacob's large family and his flocks and herds are a sign that God's blessing is with him (vv. 5-10). Because of God's blessing, Jacob can give back to Esau something of his father's blessing which he had taken by deception: "Accept, I pray you, my blessing *(bĕrākâ)* brought to you because God has graced me . . . " (v. 11). The offering or gift *(minḥâ,* 32:14, 19, 21, 22 [13, 18, 20, 21]; 33:10) is now "my *bĕrākâ. "* Esau understands and accepts, and the reconciliation is completed (v. 11b). Jacob has seen God "face to face" (32:30 [29]). He can now see "the face of God" in Esau coming to meet him so graciously (33:10).

The brothers now have different life-styles and goals. Jacob has no intention of joining Esau in Seir (v. 14b). Esau again understands, and the polite exchange in verse 15 allows each to go his own way (vv. 16-17). Jacob returns to Succoth, near Penuel, where he builds a house for himself and "sheds" *(sukkot)* for his cattle. He becomes a sedentary for a time.

The scene now moves to the western side of the Jordan, before the city of Salem, where Jacob buys land from the sons of Hamor, father of Shechem, thus preparing for the story in chapter 34. Jacob erects an altar and names it *El-Elohê-Israel* (v. 20). Attention has already been drawn to this patriarchal practice (12:7, 8; 13:18; [21:33]; 26:35; 33:20; 35:7). El is the proper name of the ancient supreme god of Canaan. For the patriarchs, El is simply God, the supreme one. Here, Jacob erects an altar to El (the supreme one), the God of (the patriarch) Israel.

Notes

11. BĔRĀKÂ. Several scholars have noted that Jacob gives back something of the stolen blessing to Esau: Alonso (1985:100); Fishbane (1975:28); Fokkelmann (1975:226–27); Westermann (1985:526).

17. SUCCOTH. The word means simply "sheds." This Transjordan tradition about Jacob has him leading a sedentary life there for a time. The name appears again in Joshua 13:27; Judges 8:3. It is located about two kilometers north of the Jabbok, near Penuel. There is another Succoth mentioned in Exodus 12:37; 13:10; Numbers 33:5-6.

18. SALEM. Modern exegesis generally understands the word *šālēm* as an adverb, "safely." Hence the RSV renders: And Jacob came safely to the city of Shechem." Shechem then is the name of a city. But the alleged adverb is awkwardly placed. In the translation above, Shechem is the name of a person, anticipating verse 19 and chapter 34. The name, of course, is used of both a city and a person. Dhorme (1956) renders *šālēm* as place name, the modern Salim. The Gospel of John mentions that John the Baptist was baptizing at "Aenon near Salim, because there was much water there" (3:23). Albright (1954:247) writes that "the near-by sources of Wadi Far'ah are extremely well provided with water." The place name is attested earlier than the New Testament period, and sherds (ceramic pieces) from the area go back some centuries beyond. Sheikh Salim is about six kilometers (four miles) southeast of Shechem (modern Tell Balata, on the outskirts of Nablus). The LXX and the Syriac understand the word as a place name.

19. A HUNDRED PIECES. The Hebrew word rendered "pieces" is *qĕšîtâ* (Josh 24:32; Job 42:11). Dhorme notes that it really means "lamb." Hence his translation *pécune*, money, itself derived from the Latin *pecus*, a flock. There was no minted coinage in the patriarchal period (cf. 23:16).

13. The Rape of Dinah
(34:1-31)

¹Now Dinah, the daughter whom Leah had borne to Jacob, went out to visit the women of the region. ²When Shechem the son of Hamor the Hivite, chief of the region, saw her, he took her, slept with her, and humiliated her. ³But with his very being he clung to Dinah Jacob's daughter; he loved the girl and spoke feelingly to her. ⁴Then Shechem said to Hamor his father: Take this girl for me for wife. ⁵When Jacob heard that he had defiled his daughter Dinah, his sons were with his herds in the field; so Jacob kept silent until their return. ⁶Then Hamor the father of Shechem went to Jacob to speak with him. ⁷When Jacob's sons came in from the field and heard of it, the men were indignant and very angry because he had committed an outrage against Israel by sleeping with Jacob's daughter; such ought not be done. ⁸But Hamor spoke with them. He said: Shechem my son—he is full of passion for your daughter; give her to him as wife, I beg you. ⁹Intermarry with us; give your daughters to us, and take our daughters for yourselves. ¹⁰You shall live with us; and the land shall be open to you; settle and move about freely in it, and acquire property in it. ¹¹And Shechem said to her father and her brothers: Let me find favor in your eyes and whatever you ask of me I will give. ¹²Set as high a brideprice and gift as you will, and I will give it; only give me the girl as wife. ¹³Jacob's sons answered Shechem and Hamor his father deceitfully and spoke to him who had defiled Dinah their sister. ¹⁴They said to them: We cannot do such a thing as to give our sister to one who is uncircumcised; that would be a disgrace to us. ¹⁵Only on this condition will we come to terms with you, that all your males be circumcised like us. ¹⁶Then we will give you our daughters and take yours and will settle with you and become one people. ¹⁷But if you do not listen to us and be circumcised, then we will take our daughter and go. ¹⁸What they said pleased Hamor and Shechem the son of Hamor. ¹⁹So the young man made no delay in doing this because he was enraptured with Jacob's daughter; and he was held in the highest esteem in his father's house.

²⁰So Hamor and Shechem his son went to the gate of their city and addressed the men of their city: ²¹These men are well disposed toward us. Let them settle in the land and move about freely in it. The land is broad enough for them. Let us take their daughters for wives and let us give them ours. ²²But only on this condition will the men come to terms to settle with us and become one people— that all our males be circumcised as they are. ²³Their herds, their property, their cattle— will they not be ours! Only let us come to terms with them so that they will settle with us. ²⁴So all who went in and out at the city gate

agreed with Hamor and Shechem his son, and all males were circumcised, all who went in and out at his city gate. ²⁵Now on the third day, when they were still in pain, Jacob's two sons Simeon and Levi, brothers of Dinah, took their swords, entered the city in security, and killed every male. ²⁶Hamor and Shechem his son too they killed with the blade of the sword, and they took Dinah from Shechem's house and went. ²⁷Jacob's sons came in over the slain and plundered the city which had defiled their sister; ²⁸and they took their flocks, their cattle, their asses, and all that was in the city and in the field, ²⁹and all their possessions and children and wives, and plundered everything that was in their houses. ³⁰Then Jacob said to Simeon and Levi: You have stirred up trouble for me by making me stink among the inhabitants of the land, the Canaanites and Perizzites. But I, I am few in number; if they unite against me they will strike me down and I will be destroyed together with my household. ³¹But they said: Is he to treat our sister like a whore?

Comment

Jacob, and of course his sons (certainly not the "frail" children of 33:13), has now settled at Salem, the city of Shechem. Dinah (30:21), the figure about whom the action revolves, is introduced at once (v. 1). She remains completely passive throughout. She is the daughter of Leah; the sons of Leah, Simeon and Levi, speak the final words in the story: "Is he to treat our sister as a whore?" (v. 31). The story is about violence and defilement done to Dinah the daughter of Leah, the less preferred wife of Jacob, and the reaction of her full brothers. Dinah is the constant point of reference throughout the story. She is: "the daughter whom Leah had borne to Jacob" (v. 1), "Jacob's daughter" (v. 3), "his daughter Dinah" (v. 5), "Jacob's daughter . . . your daughter" (v. 8), "their sister" (v. 13), "our sister" (v. 14), "our daughter" (v. 17), "Jacob's daughter" (v. 19); "Simeon and Levi brothers of Dinah . . . took Dinah" (vv. 25-26), and rejected indignantly the violence done to her: "Is he to treat our sister like a whore?" (v. 31). The injury done to the family is to the fore, and the repeated "Jacob's daughter" underscores the duty of the head of the family to react. Two words are prominent through the story: *lāqaḥ,* "take," used with a variety of nuances from "take with violence" to "accept" (vv. 2, 4, 9, 16, 17, 21, 25, 26, 28), and *ṭimmē',* "defile" (ritually), placed at three key points (vv. 5, 13, 27). The course of the narrative may be set out thus:

vv. 1-2	Dinah is introduced. Shechem seizes and humiliates her
vv. 3-4	Shechem's passion for Dinah
vv. 5	Jacob remains silent at Dinah's defilement
vv. 6	Hamor goes to Jacob to request Dinah for Shechem
vv. 7	Jacob's sons are angry at Dinah's defilement
vv. 8	Hamor tells Jacob's sons of Shechem's passion for Dinah
	vv. 9-10 Hamor speaks:
	intermarriage, settlement, property
vv. 11-12	Shechem tells Jacob's sons of his passion for Dinah
	vv. 13-17 Jacob's sons speak:
	circumcision, intermarriage,
	settlement, one people, Dinah
vv. 18-19	Hamor and Shechem react favorably
	vv. 20-23 Hamor and Shechem address the citizens
	circumcision, intermarriage,
	settlement, one people, advantage to Hivites
vv. 24	Hivites circumcised
vv. 25-26	Simeon and Levi slaughter the Hivites and take Dinah
vv. 27-29	Jacob's sons plunder the city of the Hivites
vv. 30	Jacob's reaction and fear
vv. 31	Simeon and Levi defend their vengeance on Dinah's behalf

The action of the story is set in motion by an act of violence done to Dinah as she is visiting the women of the region. Jacob and his sons have been near the city for some time and the visit is a sign of a certain harmony. Shechem becomes infatuated with Dinah, and the theme of his passion recurs three times (vv. 3-4, 11-12, 19). Shechem holds a trump card because Dinah is in his possession (vv. 17, 26). Is Jacob's silence indifference or masterly inactivity? (v. 5). The repeated ''Jacob's daughter'' calls for reaction on his part. But he would be helpless without the assistance of his sons. The arrival and reaction of the sons (v. 7) is put between Hamor's two speeches, one to Jacob, unrecorded, (v. 6), and the other to Jacob's sons (v. 8). Did Hamor and Jacob's sons arrive at the same time? Hamor proposes intermarriage, settlement, and common property (vv. 9-10). Shechem speaks of his passion for Dinah, who is in his possession (vv. 11-12). Jacob's sons take up all these themes, adding the non-negotiable condition of circumcision, and the prospect of becoming one people with the Hivites. The ritual of circumcision is foremost in their speech. It is the marriage of their sister to an uncircumcised that is a disgrace. There is only an oblique reference to the rape in verse 17b (vv. 13-17). The writer arouses the reader's indignation at Shechem's act of violence, then mitigates it slightly with Shechem's passion for Dinah and his readiness to marry her. The reader is left puzzled at Jacob's silence, but is in empathy with Jacob's sons. The sons answer deceitfully (v. 13) because they know that Hamor and Shechem are negotiating from a position of strength with Dinah in their possession. But the reader does not yet know what is behind the deceit. Hamor and Shechem take up the themes of circumcision, intermarriage, settlement, and one people in their address to the Hivites (vv. 20-23), but they look only to the advantage to the Hivites (v. 23a). They mention neither the rape of Dinah nor Shechem's passion for her, the very reasons for the whole action of the drama.

The writer has aroused sympathy for Jacob's brothers, but has introduced a note of unease when they answer "deceitfully" (v. 13). Simeon and Levi, Dinah's full brothers, react with gross excess. The slaughter reaches far beyond any reasonable retaliation. They take Dinah (v. 26), thus fulfilling their threat (v. 17), even though their condition has been fulfilled. Jacob's sons plunder the city "which had defiled their sister" (v. 28). The city shares in the guilt of Shechem. The sons of Israel show themselves no better than their neighbors or any other people of the ancient Near East. Jacob's reaction is fear for his family. This is not mere selfishness. He has the right to be concerned. He admonishes Simeon and Levi. Their reply, though defiant, also shows concern for the family: "Is he to treat our sister like a whore?" (v. 31). Jacob and his caravan must continue their journey to Hebron (35:27) after their lengthy stay near the city of Shechem. But there is more to be done in the biblical story, before they leave Shechem definitively (35:1-4). A terror from God (or a mighty terror) restrains the surrounding cities from taking vengeance on them for the slaughter of the Hivites.

The writer leaves the reader or listener ambiguous. He arouses righteous indignation at the rape of Dinah. He allows a certain sympathy at Shechem's readiness to set right the situation, but lets the reader know that, with Dinah in their house, Hamor and Shechem negotiate from strength. He leaves us puzzled over Jacob's silence. He introduces an ominous note with the deceitful reply of Jacob's sons, though this is a counterbalance to the advantage held by the Hivites. He revolts us with the wholesale slaughter and plunder of the city and leaves us with Jacob's genuine concern for his family and the defiant justification of family honor and vengeance by Simeon and Levi. Finally, he sees the protective hand of God that wards off counter-vengeance from the sons of Israel (35:5).

Westermann (1985:535–37), following an insight of Wellhausen, understands chapter 34 as an amalgamation of two stories together with a substantial contribution of an editor in the process of amalgamation. One story would be a family story of the rape of Dinah (vv. 1-2) followed by vengeance taken by her brothers (vv. 25-26). The other would be "an account of the peaceful settlement of an Israelite group in the region of a Canaanite city." The substance of this second story is found in the negotiations in verses 9-10, 13-17, 21-23. The whole would have been reworked by an editor in accordance with the requirements of Israelite practice and the prescription of Deuteronomy:

> When the Lord your God brings you into the land which you are entering to take possession of it, and clears away many nations before you, the Hittites, the Girgashites, the Amorites, the Canaanites, the Perizzites, the Hivites, and the Jebusites, seven nations greater and mightier than yourselves, and when the Lord your God gives them over to you and you defeat them; then you must utterly destroy them; you shall make no covenant with them, and show no mercy to them. You shall not make marriages with them, giving your daughters to their sons or taking their daughters for your sons (Deut 7:1-3).

One can argue well for such a process, though Westermann's arguments for doublets, inconsistencies, clumsiness in structure, strange changes in locale, and so on, are far from convincing. One must exegete the biblical passage as it lies before us with all its dramatic impact, due regard being had for its possible or probable process of formation (Westermann in the long run does this). The chapter would have received its final form in the Deuteronomic period, late seventh or early sixth century, or even, because of the strong emphasis on circumcision, in the post-exilic period.

Notes

12. BRIDEPRICE AND GIFT. The word "brideprice," *mohar,* occurs three times in the Old Testament: Genesis 34:12; Exodus 22:16; 1 Samuel 18:25. The brideprice was, in origin, very probably regarded as an economic recompense for the loss of a worker within the household, as young girls of marriageable age contributed by taking care of flocks and herds, reaping, weaving, and so on.

14. Bethel Revisited. Return to Hebron
(35:1-29)

¹Now God said to Jacob: Arise, go up to Bethel and stay there, and build an altar there to El who appeared to you when you were fleeing from your brother Esau. ²So Jacob said to his household and to all who were with him: Put away the foreign gods that are with you, purify yourselves, and change your clothes. ³Then let us arise and go up to Bethel where I will build an altar to El who has answered me on the day of my distress and has been with me along the way that I have gone. ⁴So they handed over to Jacob all the foreign gods that they had with them and the rings that were on their ears, and Jacob burned them under the terebinth near Shechem. ⁵As they journeyed a terror from God came upon the surrounding cities so that they did not pursue the sons of Jacob. ⁶Then Jacob and all the people with him went to Luz, that is, Bethel, in the land of Canaan. ⁷He built an altar there and named the place El-Bethel because God had appeared to him there when he was fleeing from his brother. ⁸Deborah, Rebekah's nurse, died and was buried under the oak below Bethel, and he named it the oak of weeping.

⁹God appeared again to Jacob when he left Paddan-aram and blessed him. ¹⁰God said to him: Your name is Jacob; no longer shall your name be called Jacob, but Israel shall be your name; so he named him Israel. ¹¹Then God said to him: I am El šadday; increase and multiply. A nation, yes an assembly of nations shall come from you, and kings shall come forth from your body. ¹²The land that I gave to Abraham and to Isaac I give to you and I give the land to your descendants after you. ¹³Then God went up from him at the place where he had spoken with him. ¹⁴Then Jacob set up a pillar at the place where he had spoken with him, a pillar of stone, and poured a drink offering on it and poured oil on it. ¹⁵So Jacob named the place where God had spoken with him Bethel.

¹⁶They journeyed then from Bethel, and when there was still some distance to go to Ephrath, Rachel was in labor and her birth pains were severe. ¹⁷In the midst of her severe pains the midwife said to her: Do not be afraid, you will have another son. ¹⁸As life left her, for she was dying, she named him Ben-oni, but his father named him Benjamin. ¹⁹Rachel died and was buried on the way to Ephrath, that is, Bethlehem. ²⁰So Jacob set up a pillar over her grave, and it is known to this day as the pillar of Rachel's grave. ²¹Israel journeyed on and pitched his tent beyond Migdal-Eder.

²²ᵃWhile Israel was dwelling in that region Reuben went and lay with his father's concubine Bilhah. But Israel heard of it. ²²ᵇThere were twelve sons of Jacob:
²³the sons of Leah: Reuben (Jacob's firstborn), Simeon, Levi, Judah, Issachar, and Zebulun;
²⁴the sons of Rachel: Joseph and Benjamin;
²⁵the sons of Bilhah, Rachel's maid: Dan and Naphtali;
²⁶the sons of Zilpah, Leah's maid: Gad and Asher.
These are the sons who were borne to him in Paddan-aram.
²⁷Then Jacob came to his father Isaac at Mamre, Kiriath-arba—that is Hebron—where Abraham and Isaac had sojourned. ²⁸Now Isaac was a hundred and eighty years old. ²⁹Isaac breathed his last and died, and was gathered to his people, old and fulfilled in life; his sons Esau and Jacob buried him.

Comment

This chapter brings to a close the account of Jacob's return from Paddan-aram and his definitive resettlement in Canaan. Jacob is still in the region of the city of Shechem. God orders Jacob to go up to Bethel (v. 1) and Jacob carries out the order (v. 7). A brief report records the death of Deborah, Rebekah's nurse (v. 8). God appears again to Jacob at Bethel (vv. 9-15). Then there is a self-contained episode of Rachel's death when giving birth to Benjamin (vv. 16-20). The writer notes Reuben's misbehavior (v. 22a). There follows a complete list of the sons of Jacob (vv. 22b-26). Jacob finally returns to Hebron and his father Isaac. Isaac dies, and Jacob and Esau bury him "old and fulfilled in life" (vv. 27-29). All these divine communications, deaths, and episodes are set into the framework of the final stage of the itinerary. Jacob journeys from the city of Shechem to Bethel (vv. 1, 3, 6). He buries Deborah near Bethel. Rachel dies and is buried on the way south from Bethel to Hebron (vv. 16, 19). Jacob journeys on beyond Migdal-Eder (v. 21). He then arrives at Mamre (Hebron), the goal of the itinerary (v. 27). The themes of death and birth run through the whole (vv. 8, 16-18, 19-20, 22b-26, 28-29).

The first episode is carefully constructed (vv. 1-7). It is not said how God gave Jacob the command. The order: "Arise, go up to Bethel and stay there, and build an altar there to El who appeared to you when you were fleeing from your brother Esau" (v. 1) is balanced by the execution of the order: "He built an altar there and named the place El-Bethel because God had appeared to him there when he was fleeing from his brother" (v. 7). In between, Jacob has communicated God's order to the people (vv. 2-3), the people have carried out the order (v. 4) and, with Jacob, have set out (v. 5) and arrived at Bethel (v. 6). The burial of the "foreign gods" and the assorted trinkets are a sign of a religious reorientation and acceptance of the supreme God, El, the God of Abraham, Isaac, and Jacob (v. 4). Among the "foreign gods" would be the *teraphim* that Rebekah had stolen from Laban (31:19, 30-35). This episode points the way to Joshua 24:3, 23: "Your fathers lived of old beyond the Euphrates, Terah, the father of Abraham and of Nahor, and served other gods," and to Judges 10:10-16; 1 Samuel 7:3-5. Westermann (1985:543, 551), with other exegetes, is convinced that verse 5 is a sequel to 34:25-26 and follows immediately on 34:29a. This may be. But after the slaughter and plunder (34:35-39), Jacob and his household are still in the region and, in the biblical context, receive there the order to go on to Bethel. A terror from God (or, a mighty terror), the result of 34:25-29 and 35:1-4, restrains the surrounding cities from attacking the caravan to take vengeance. The episode of verses 1-7 had nothing to do with 28:20-22. It is not the fulfillment of the vow made there. Neither vow nor tithes are mentioned.

Rachel's nurse (v. 8) was mentioned in 24:59. We now know that her name was Deborah. The name of her burial place is *'allôn bākû,* the oak of weeping.

God's blessing continues at work in Jacob as he moves toward the goal of his journey from Paddan-aram. The standard formula for a divine appearance, *wayyērā' 'ĕlohîm (YHWH),* is used (v. 9; 17:1). The beginning and end of this passage are very like the corresponding verses of chapter 17 (vv. 1, 22), "then God went up from him at the place where he had spoken with him" (v. 13). The change of name from Jacob to Israel is repeated with no reason or explanation of the change given (v. 10; 32:29 [28]). God who blesses introduces himself as *El šadday* (17:1; 28:3) and the blessing is pronounced in formulas and themes already familiar and to be repeated:

35:11-12	28:2-3	48:3-6
I am *El šadday*	May *El šadday* bless you	*El šadday* appeared to me in the land of Canaan and blessed me and said to me

35:11-12	28:2-3	48:3-6
increase and multiply	increase and multiply	I will increase you and multiply you
A nation, yes an assembly of nations shall come from you. The land that I gave to Abraham and to Isaac I give to you and your descendants after you.	and may you become an assembly of peoples. May he give to you and your descendants with you the blessing of Abraham so that you possess the land where you sojourn which God has given to Abraham.	and I will make you an assembly of peoples. and I will give this land to you and your descendants after you as an everlasting possession.

These three passages show every sign of common editorial work. The divine name *El šadday,* the theme and formula "increase and multiply," the assurance of land to the patriarch and his descendants, and the unusual "assembly (*qāhāl*) of nations (*goyyîm*) or peoples (*'ammîm*)" favor this. Further, there is an obvious link between 35:11 and the accumulation of promises in chapter 17:

35:11	17:6b
A nation, yes an assembly of nations, shall come from you, and kings shall come forth from your body.	I will make nations of you

17:16b
I shall bless her and she shall issue into nations; kings of peoples shall come from her.

In the earlier account of the episode at Bethel, Jacob "took the stone which he had put at his head and set it up as a pillar and poured oil on it. He named that place Bethel" (28:18-19a). In the present passage Jacob "set up a pillar at the place where he had spoken with him, a pillar of stone, and poured a drink offering on it and poured oil on it. So Jacob named the place where he had spoken to him Bethel" (vv. 14-15). And the promise of the land is common to the divine addresses in both Bethel accounts (35:12; 28:13). But there are differences. The setting up of the pillar in the first story evolves out of the story itself (28:11b, 18), as does the name Bethel, when

Jacob realizes that the place is "the house of God and the gate of heaven" (28:17b) and applies the description "the house of God" literally to the place as its new name (22:19b). In chapter 35, there is no such natural evolution in the account (vv. 14-15). God dwells in Bethel (28:16b), but in the later account "God went up at the place where he had spoken with him" (v. 13). Jacob put the stone at his head as a protection (28:11b); but later, he puts it up "at the place where he had spoken with him" (v. 14b) and, as well as anointing the stone, he pours a libation offering over it (v. 14b). It is very likely that the present account is a reworking of the earlier account in chapter 28. Neither in verses 1-7 nor in verses 9-15 is there any sign of the fulfillment of the vow made in 28:20.

Jacob continues on his itinerary from Bethel to Hebron (v. 16a) and as his caravan approaches Ephrath, about fourteen kilometers (ten miles) south of Bethel, Rachel, who is pregnant, has a very difficult birth. As she is dying, she names the son *Ben-'ônî*, "son of my sorrow"; but Jacob changes the name to *Ben-yamin*, "son of the right hand" or "son of the south." He is Jacob's twelfth son. The traditional tomb of Rachel, and hence Ephrath, is located about seven kilometers (four miles) north of Jerusalem. Jacob sets up a pillar over her grave. Verses 16 and 19 are repeated almost word for word in Jacob's deathbed address (48:7).

Jacob (Israel) continues his itinerary (v. 21a). After noting Reuben's misdeed (v. 2a; 49:4), the writer gives a systematic list of the sons (tribes) of Jacob according to their mothers. He includes Benjamin among those born in Paddan-aram (vv. 24, 26), but he does not mention Dinah. Jacob finally reaches Hebron (Mamre), the place of the sojournings of Abraham and Isaac. The writer introduces a note of reconciliation and peace as Jacob and Esau bury their father in the cave of Machpelah (v. 29; cf. 49:31), just as had the writer earlier when Isaac and Ishmael buried Abraham there (25:9).

Notes

16. EPHRATH. Located somewhere on the border between Ephraim and Benjamin about seven kilometers (four miles) north of Jerusalem (cf. 1 Sam 10:2; Jer 31:15), Ephrathah is linked with Bethlehem (Ruth 4:11; Micah 5:1 [2]) and in parallelism with "the fields of Jaar" (Ps 132:6). This may be due to a later tradition locating Rachel's tomb at Bethlehem.

21. MIDGAL-EDER. "The tower of Eder." Location unknown, though obviously between Ephrath and Hebron.

27. PADDAN-ARAM. See *Notes* on 25:20.

29. ISAAC WAS A HUNDRED AND EIGHTY YEARS OLD. See *Comment* on chapter 27. Isaac would have lived on for some time after Jacob's return.

15. The Descendants of Esau (The Edomites)
(36:1-43)

¹These are the descendants of Esau, that is Edom. ²Esau took his wives from the daughters of Canaan: Adah the daughter of Elon the Hittite, Oholibamah the daughter of Anah the son of Zibeon the Hivite, ³and Basemath, the daughter of Ishmael and sister of Nebaioth. ⁴Adah bore to Esau Eliphaz; Basemath bore Reuel; ⁵Oholibamah bore Jeush, Jalam, and Korah. These are the sons of Esau who were born to him in Canaan. ⁶Then Esau took his wives, his sons, his daughters, and all the members of his household, his cattle, all his beasts, and all his property that he had acquired in the land of Canaan and went into a land away from his brother Jacob, ⁷for their possessions were too great for them to dwell together and the land of their sojournings was not able to support them because of their cattle. ⁸So Esau dwelt in the hill country of Seir. Esau is Edom.

⁹These are the descendants of Esau, the father of Edom, in the hill country of Seir.

¹⁰These are the names of the sons of Esau: ¹¹The sons of Eliphaz were Teman, Omar, Zepho, Gatam, and Kenaz. ¹²(Timna was a concubine of Eliphaz, Esau's son; she bore Amalek to Eliphaz.) These are the sons of Adah, Esau's wife. ¹³These are the sons of Reuel: Nahath, Zerah, Shammah, and Mizzah. These are the sons of Basemath, Esau's wife. ¹⁴These are the sons of Oholibamah the daughter of Anah the son of Zibeon, Esau's wife; she bore to Esau Jeush, Jalam, and Korah.

¹⁵These are the chiefs of the sons of Esau. The sons of Eliphaz the firstborn of Esau: the chiefs Teman, Omar, Zepho, Kenaz, ¹⁶Korah, Gatam, and Amalek; these are the chiefs of Eliphaz in the land of Edom; they are the sons of Adah. ¹⁷These are the sons of Reuel, Esau's son: the chiefs Nahath, Zerah, Shammah, and Mizzah; these are the chiefs of Reuel in the land of Edom; they are the sons of Basemath, Esau's wife. ¹⁸These are the sons of Oholibamah, Esau's wife: the

chiefs Jeush, Jalam, and Korah; these are the chiefs born of Oholibamah the daughter of Anah, Esau's wife. [19]These are the sons of Esau (that is, Edom) and these are their chiefs.

[20]These are the sons of Seir the Horite, the inhabitants of the land: Lotan, Shobal, Zibeon, Anah, [21]Dishon, Ezer, and Dishan; these are the chiefs of the Horites, the sons of Seir in the land of Edom. [22]The sons of Lotan were Hori and Heman; and Lotan's sister was Timna. [23]These are the sons of Shobal: Alvan, Manahath, Ebal, Shepho, and Onam. [24]These are the sons of Zibeon: Aiah and Anah; he is the Anah who found the hot springs in the wilderness while he was pasturing the asses of Zibeon his father. [25]These are the children of Anah: Dishon and Oholibamah the daughter of Anah. [26]These are the sons of Dishon: Hemdan, Eshban, Ithran, and Cheran. [27]These are the sons of Ezer: Bilhan, Zaavan, and Akan. [28]These are the sons of Dishan: Uz and Aran. [29]These are the chiefs of the Horites: the chiefs Lotan, Shobal, Zibeon, Anah, [30]Dishon, Ezer, and Dishan; these are the chiefs of the Horites, according to their clans in the land of Seir.

[31]These are the kings who reigned in the land of Edom, before any king reigned over the Israelites. [32]Bela the son of Beor reigned in Edom, the name of his city was Dinhabah. [33]Bela died, and Jobab the son of Zerah of Bozrah reigned in his place. [34]Jobab died, and Husham of the land of the Temanites reigned in his place. [35]Husham died, and Hadad the son of Bedad, who defeated Midian in the land of Moab, reigned in his place, the name of his city was Avith. [36]Hadad died, and Samlah of Masrekah reigned in his place. [37]Samlah died, and Shaul of Rehoboth on the Euphrates reigned in his place. [38]Shaul died, and Baalhanan the son of Achbor reigned in his place. [39]Baalhanan the son of Achbor died, and Hadar reigned in his place, the name of his city was Pau; the name of his wife was Mehetabel, the daughter of Matred, daughter of Mezahab.

[40]These are the names of the chiefs of Esau according to their families and their dwelling places, by their names: the chiefs Timna, Alvah, Jetheth, [41]Oholibamah, Elah, Pinon, [42]Kenaz, Teman, Mibzar, [43]Magdiel, and Iram; these are the chiefs of Edom (that is, Esau, the father of Edom) according to their dwelling places in the land of their possession.

Comment

Just as the descendants of Ishmael, blessed by God (17:20; 21:13, 18), were listed at the end of the Abraham cycle (25:12-18), so too the descendants of Esau (Edom), a sharer in Jacob's blessing (33:11), are listed at the end of the Jacob cycle (though the end of the Jacob story is interwoven with the end of the Joseph story [chs. 46–50]). These links of kinship are underscored in the Book of Deuteronomy where the Israelites are warned: "You shall not abhor an Edomite, for he is your brother" (Deut 23:8 [7]). Chapter 36, a redactional unity, divides itself easily: the wives and sons of Esau (vv. 1-8); the sons of Esau (vv. 9-14); the chiefs of the sons of Esau (vv. 15-19, identical with the sons); the sons of Seir (vv. 20-28); the chiefs of the sons of Seir (vv. 29-30, identical with the sons); the kings of Edom (vv. 31-39); the chiefs of Esau (an appendix). These names are repeated in 1 Chronicles 1:35-54. The names of Esau's wives have been arranged schematically under section 4. Esau's Wives and Jacob's Departure (26:34-35; 27:46-28:9). The names Judith and Mahalath (26:34; 28:9) have dropped out of the list of Canaanite wives (36:2-4). Adah has replaced Basemath as the daughter of Elon, and Basemath has taken the place of Mahalath as the daughter of Ishmael and the sister of Nebaioth. Oholibamah appears as a third wife. Their sons and grandsons, all true Edomites, are:

Adah: Eliphaz: Teman, Omar, Zepho, Gatam, Kenaz, [Amalek].
Oholibamah: Jeush, Jalam, Korah.
Basemath: Reuel: Nahath, Zera, Shamnah, Mizzah.

The five grandsons of Adah, the three sons of Oholibamah, and the four grandsons of Basemath, twelve in all, are the chiefs of the sons of Esau (vv. 15-19). But add to these Amalek (vv. 12, 15), son of the concubine (*pilegeš*, v. 12, cf. *Notes* on 22:24). The sons of Ishmael too were "twelve chiefs according to their tribal groupings" (25:16).

The sons of Seir, the Horite, are seven in all (vv. 20-28). Together with their sons they make up eighteen. The seven are the chiefs of the Horites (vv. 29-30). There is a note in the list which mentions that Anah found (hot) springs in the desert while pasturing asses (the "hot" comes from the Vulgate *aquae callidae*).

The next section (vv. 31-38 = 1 Chr 1:43-50) lists eight kings of Edom. The writer notes that these kings "reigned in the land of Edom before any king reigned over the sons of Israel" (v. 31). If the Edomite kings reigned in direct succession, then the beginnings of monarchy in Edom would be some time in the thirteenth century B.C.E. But, as de Vaux (1978:516-17) notes, the list may not be chronological. Each king comes from a different city and we may have no more than a list of small Edomite "kingdoms" like the Canaanite city states in the land to which Israel came. The "kings" may have been no more than leaders of nomadic groups. In verses 32, 33, 35, 38, the father of the new king had not reigned before. De Vaux notes further that the form of the list of the Edomite kings resembles in essentials the form of the list of the minor judges (Judg 3:31; 10:1-5; 12:8-15). The pattern in the Edomite list is: he reigned, the name of the king's city, he died, X reigned in his place. A unique addition in the list is that "Hadad . . . defeated Midian in the land of Moab" (v. 35). Edom was conquered by David (2 Sam 8:13b-14) and Hadad, king of Edom, rose up against Solomon (1 Kgs 11:14-22). E. A. Knauf (1985b) has argued recently that " 'the Edomite list' Genesis 36, 31-39, derives most probably from the end of the sixth or the beginning of the fifth century B.C."

In the appendix (vv. 40-43), the names Kenaz and Teman are as they were before (v. 15). Timna is a concubine in verse 12, a Horite in verse 22, and a clan name in verse 40. Oholibamah, daughter of Anah (vv. 2, 5, 24, 18, 25) is a clan name in verse 41. In addition, there are eight new names.

There are in all more than two hundred names in chapter 36, eighty of which are not repeated. About half of them are unknown to us. Most of the names are semitic and most of the unknown names are in the Horite list (vv. 20-28). But de Vaux (1978:137) has cautioned that attempts to explain them as Hurrian are not convincing. Westermann notes finally the importance of chapter 36 for the history of political development from family (vv. 105, 106-08, 120-28), through tribal society (vv. 15-19, 28-29, 40-43), to monarchy (vv. 31-39).

Notes

(Westermann discusses the names in detail [1985:566–67]).

1. EDOM. The hill country southeast of the Dead Sea.

2. HITTITE, HIVITE. For Hittite, see *Notes* chapter 23. In the eighteen lists in the Old Testament, the Hivites are mentioned sixteen times as early inhabitants of Palestine west of the Jordan. They inhabited the hill country with the Amorites and the Jebusites. But "it is simply not possible to give any ethnic importance to the name 'Hivite' or to ascertain its origin" (de Vaux 1978:137–39).

8. SEIR. East of the Arabah (32:4 [3]; 33:14; 36:8, 20). In Deuteronomy 1:2 it is west of the Arabah.

15, 19, 40. CHIEFS. *'allûp.* A political or military leader, probably deriving from *'lp,* a thousand.

20, 29. HORITES. Groups of Hurrians moved south into Palestine, the evidence showing that they were there in the fifteenth–fourteenth century. The Israelites encountered descendants of these Hurrians when they entered Palestine. The Old Testament spoke of them as Horites. They lived exclusively in Edomite territory (14:6; 36:20).

4

Excursus 1
The Patriarchs and History

In 1871 Julius Wellhausen wrote in his *Prolegomena:* "It is true that here (i.e., in the sources J E P) we attain to no historical knowledge of the Patriarchs but only of the period when the stories about them arose among the Israelite people; this later age is here unconsciously projected in its inner and outward features into remote antiquity where it is reflected like a transfigured mirage [*ein verklärtes Luftbild*]" (ed. 1957: 318-19).

Thomas L. Thompson (1974:7) refers to this passage from Wellhausen as making "good methodological sense," and continues: "The validity of this principle that the historical knowledge about the patriarchs is commensurate with the antiquity of the traditions about them is implicitly borne out even by the most vociferous critics of Wellhausen. . . . "

Thompson's very thorough study of the patriarchs in the Bible leads him to the conclusion that "no aspect of the patriarchal stories . . . can clearly and exclusively be dated to a period earlier than the Iron Age. . . . " (325-26). Thompson's main concern is with the historical and archaeological data outside the Bible as evidence for the dating of the patriarchal stories; he finds that this data does not provide any evidence for setting the content and formation of these stories earlier than the late Iron Age period, 900 B.C.E. and after.

John Van Seters (1975:38) comes to similar conclusions. He writes that "There is nothing in this presentation of the 'nomadic' patriarchs which is inappropriate to the portrayal of pastoral life in the

253

period of the late Judaean monarchy or exilic periods, but there is much that speaks against the choice of an earlier period."

Van Seters argues that "the Yahwistic version of the (patriarchal) tradition dates to the exilic period," and that the priestly version "which is . . . a direct literary supplement to the earlier work, must be later and post-exilic in date. This dating of the Yahwist is based on the fact that while he consciously portrays a primitive age without the political structures of a later day he still gives frequent clues to his own time" (310).

Both Thompson and Van Seters reject as invalid the alleged parallels between certain social and legal practices in the patriarchal stories and similar practices attested in the Nuzi tablets, the Hittite laws and the various Mesopotamian legal codes. These writings are very useful as a general Middle Eastern background against which the patriarchal stories are told. But the parallels break down when pressed in detail. Thompson and Van Seters are not the first to query the parallels. The Hittite scholar H. A. Hoffner (1968) had already done so, and Roland de Vaux had shown extreme caution and doubt in his posthumously published history of Israel (1978:161–287).

In the century from Wellhausen to Thompson and Van Seters the wheel of scholarship has turned the full circle.

1. From Wellhausen to the 1970s and 1980s

Contemporary with Wellhausen, Franz Delitzsch (1872) presented his seven stages in God's saving action in Israel from Creation to Jesus Christ in which the patriarchs were the third stage. At the same time August Dillmann (1875³, 1892⁶, 1895) sought the historical basis of the Abraham-Isaac-Jacob-Joseph story in the constant movements of people from N-W Mesopotamia southwards towards Arabia, Canaan, and Egypt. The Hebrews in the strict sense (Israelites) belong to the latest layer here. Next come the "Panbabylonists" H. Winckler (1903) and A. Jeremias (1904, 1903⁴) who would derive everything in the Old Testament from Babylon. Winckler explained Abraham from astral mythology; Abraham was a representative of the moon god in human form. E. Meyer (1920, 1931²) explained the patriarchs as local Canaanite deities; the stories about them developed in three stages from myth to hero story to popular story, from gods to hero-giants to farmers or nomads. Another view, parallel to the previous one, saw the patriarchs as tribal eponyms. The names of the patriarchs and their wives are really the names of tribes, and the three great patriarchs are not to be understood as individuals but as symbols of three states of development in a process of migration and settlement extending over two hundred years. So A. Klostermann (1896), R. Kittel (1888, 1892), B. Stade (1881). Otto Eissfeldt (1923) explained the patriarchal stories as basically, though not in every text, tribal history and maintained right to the end that they were at least partially tribal history.

The basic principle of the work of Hermann Gunkel, announced in the first edition of his Genesis commentary in 1901, was "Die Genesis ist eine Sammlung von Sagen," "Genesis is a collection of popular stories." He put great emphasis on the oral stage that preceded the literary stage. The stories had their origin in particular life-settings. "They must have circulated for a long time as good stories and have had their origin purely in imagination and phantasy." Gunkel comments that they belong to the realm of pure story (*novellistisch*) or fairy-tale (*märchenhaft*). He looked for the smallest units as the most original.

The archaeological approach dominated patriarchal studies in the period 1925–1970 and was supported mainly by scholars from the United States and France. The best synthesis is presented by W. F. Albright (1957: ch. 4). Other prominent Americans of this school were Nelson Glueck, G. E. Wright (1957, 1962[2]), John Bright (1959, 1972[2], 1980[3]), and F. M. Cross (1973). This "biblical archaeology" movement aimed to restore historical credibility to the patriarchal figures and to confound all that was incorporated in Wellhausen and his followers. The thesis was that the most important Near Eastern material unearthed by archaeology confirms the substantial historicity of the patriarchs and the stories about them. This material comprises:

(1) personal names and place names in Genesis that correspond to names in Mesopotamia,

(2) legal practices and social customs that correspond to similar practices and customs in the Nuzi texts, the Code of Hammurapi, the Hittite laws,

(3) the migrations of the patriarchs in the context of the movements of peoples in the ancient Near East—Amorites, Aramaeans, Hyksos, Ḥab/piru,

(4) personal names in the patriarchal stories that correspond to names in the ancient Near East which give access to the essential characteristics of patriarchal religion.

Henri Cazelles (1966: 81–156) has given the classical presentation of the patriarchs and history in his masterly dictionary article. He maintains that the patriarchal story is historical in essence and that Genesis contains virtually a biography of Abraham.

After a century of scholarship then, we have come back to a truly Wellhausian position as expounded by Thompson and Van Seters. Now there is general agreement on two important matters: (1) it is not possible to locate the migrations of the patriarchs within the alleged great movements of peoples, semitic or otherwise, in the Near East in the second millennium B.C.E.; (2) the parallels between patriarchal legal practices and social customs and those found in the documents from the second millennium are not to be pressed. Nevertheless all are agreed that the archaeological finds provide a most useful background to the Old Testament.

The passages in Genesis 12-36 to which parallels have been alleged from the ancient Near East have been listed in the *Notes* on Genesis 12:10-13:4 and each has been considered in detail as it occurs in the text.

2. Patriarchal Society and Nomadism

In his long review of the books of Thompson and Van Seters, Albert de Pury (1978) considers, among many other matters, the social situation that the patriarchal stories reflect. It is a situation, he concludes, different from, and at least typologically anterior to, that found in the books of Judges and Samuel. He sums up the differences in five points:

(1) the patriarchal clans are mobile, on the move, and are not land proprietors;

(2) the cities in the Genesis stories are seen "from outside" (see esp. chs. 26; 34); they symbolize the inhabitants of the country; they represent the autochthonous population;

(3) the social structure of the patriarchal groups is that of practical autonomy where the power of the father or of the eldest brother is quasi-absolute (this, of course, is not exclusive to semi-nomads); in contrast to the Book of Judges, the clans act as small independent units;

(4) there is no "Yahwistic" warlike mentality. "God of the Father" is a title given by the clan to the "El" whom it venerates at its central place *māqôm,* not an independent God who would be "identified" secondarily with the El of the place; (5) the patriarchal clans are conscious of their extra-Palestinian provenance.

Thus de Pury concludes that the narratives, at least the Jacob stories, preserve in substance a tradition going back to "proto-Israelite" groups.

The patriarchs are usually described in a general way as semi-nomads. Their life-style, it is often said, reflects a semi-nomadic society of small cattle breeders and pastoralists. There has been much research in recent years into the phenomenon of nomadism in Central and Western Asia in the second millennium B.C.E. and the second millennium C.E. Western Asia is an area north of a line drawn from the southern tip of the Caspian Sea to the northern tip of the gulf of Aqabah. Michael B. Rowton of Chicago has addressed the question of nomadism in this area in a continuing series of articles, 1965-1982. Rowton introduces his studies by clearing the ground. The nineteenth century a priori presupposition that civilization progressed in a straight line from food-gathering through nomadism to agriculture must be abandoned. It does not conform to the facts. Then,

> In Western Asia the usual distinction between the realm of the nomad and that of the sedentary does not apply. In many areas the pastoral land was encircled by urban settlement, either partially or completely; the grazing lands visited by the nomads constituted enclaves partly or completely within the sedentary zone. This enclave-nomadism needs to be sharply distinguished from nomadism in the great open steppes of Central Asia, or the deserts and the arid steppes of Arabia (1974:1-2).

The nomadism of Central Asia and Arabia is best called "external nomadism." Outside these areas the nomads were "enclosed in blocks of desert, semi-desert, and highland country within the general sweep of civilization." Rowton calls this type of nomadism "enclosed nomadism." These tribes are not "semi-nomads," but full-time nomads; they are both nomadic and sedentary the whole year round. Enclosed nomadism "includes both village tribesmen who spend a few months of the year out in the steppes or in mountain fastness, as well as nomads who live the year round in camp" (1973:251). Enclosed nomadism is in very close contact with sedentary society. Hence, there is an inherent tendency to symbiosis (256). There are four basic elements to enclosed nomadism (257–58).

(1) *the town in nomadic territory:* the town acts as a link between the nomad and the state;

(2) *seasonal migration (transhumance):* the nomads migrate through or into regions inhabited by the sedentaries, and so there is close interaction between nomad and sedentary, between tribe and state;

(3) *symbiosis:* there is a natural tendency to symbiosis between nomad and sedentary because enclosed nomadism has its roots in regions where pastoral and agricultural land are closely interwoven;

(4) *continuous sedentarization:* the process is gradual.

Rowton describes the situation as "dimorphic social and political structure," or simply "dimorphic structure"; it consists of the double process of interaction between nomad and sedentary, between tribe and state (1973:202). This has been characteristic of life in Western Asia in varying degrees for thousands of years. "Tribal society and urban society remain linked in a state of somewhat precarious equilibrium" now one is dominant, now the other (1976:17). Rowton then points out that dimorphic structure was every bit as important a factor in the Syro-Palestinian region as it was in Mesopotamia (31). It is a type of social structure portrayed in the Mari documents, about 1830–1760 B.C.E., namely that of small cattle breeders (sheep and goats) with donkeys as transport animals.

When Rowton turns to the question of the patriarchs, he takes up at once the recent view that the traditions represent late literary speculation to be dated in the period of the monarchy or later. He concludes:

> The material discussed in these articles does not support this view. On the contrary, it points to a written or more probably oral, tradition rooted in close interaction between nomad and sedentary, between tribal society and urban society. But interaction of this kind, for which I am using the term dimorphic structure, was in Palestine characteristic of second and third millenia B.C., not of the period of the monarchy (1977:195).

Rowton does not want to argue that the patriarchal stories have historical content, that is, that they portray historical events as they actually happened. His proposal "is merely that the earliest oral tradition is rooted in fairly intimate knowledge of a social environment which has nothing to do with the period of the monarchy" (195). It is a type of nomadism "based on a close symbiosis between pastoralism and agriculture and is conditioned by a physical environment in which economic risk is a dominant factor" (196). The role of the patriarchal leader is that of the parasocial leader; he is a "link between tribal society and urban society, living, as he did, part of the time in tent with tribesmen, part of the time within urban society." This mode of life is well attested for all three patriarchs in Palestine: Abraham in Gerar and Egypt, Isaac in Gerar, Jacob in Shechem (196). And in Transjordan "we find Jacob negotiating a more or less formal modus vivendi with both groups (nomad and sedentaries) just as in Palestine Isaac negotiates in Gerar, Jacob in Shechem" (197).

Rowton is in broad agreement with Thomas L. Thompson and John Van Seters that there is no evidence for a migration of Semites from Mesopotamia to Palestine; but the Old Testament does not claim this. He also agrees with them that the Nuzi material cannot be used either to date the patriarchs or to provide precise social and legal parallels. But he is convinced that the Mesopotamian material, in particular the Mari material, has a great deal to tell us about the patriarchal period, as well as about the later period in the history of Israel (197).

To sum up Rowton's opinion: there is a definite layer of tradition in the patriarchal stories that can be explained only from the social phenomenon of enclosed nomadism of the second millenium B.C.E. in Western Asia, but not from the period of the Israelite monarchy.

Within this general structure of enclosed nomadism, patriarchal society is portrayed as essentially family society. It is the family, the extended family, of Abraham and Jacob that is always on the move; it is within the family that ordinary events take place. These families do not engage in war (ch. 14 remains an enigma and is out on a limb; ch. 34 is a tribal story), nor do they, as a body, confront political powers. They experience the ordinary family events of birth, marriage, and death. Abraham's family experiences the pain of no son, hence no heir and this runs like a thread through the Abraham story; in fact it constitutes the story. The story moves from no son, "Now Sarai was barren, she had no child," 11:30, to the birth of a son, 21:1-3. The absence of a son is the subject of several independent stories in between, chapters 15; 16; 18:1-15. After the birth of the son come the stories of the son in danger, chapter 22, the wooing of a wife for the son, chapter 24, the preparations for death, chapter 23; 24:1-2, and the death, 25:7-11. Without the theme of the son, there is no Abraham cycle. The Jacob cycle is essentially a family cycle. There is the birth, 25:19-26, followed by the intra-family deceptions, chapter 27; then come the marriage and the family and clan quarrels, chapters 29–31; next there is reconciliation within the family, chapter 33, death within the family, Deborah, Rebekah's nurse, 35:6, and Rachel, 35:16-20. Finally, the patriarch Jacob dies, 48:1-22; 49:28-33; the end of the Jacob cycle is fitted compactly into the Joseph story.

3. Concluding Reflections

The introductions to the Abraham (chs. 12–25) and Jacob (chs. 25–36) cycles, and we may add the very small Isaac "cycle" (ch. 26), together with the outlines which accompany them, show that they are collections of traditions about these three patriarchs. Each tradition has been given a certain unity and set into a chronological framework.

Common to the Abraham texts is that (1) Abraham always appears as "the father," (2) the texts look to the future in a son, (3) Abraham has a direct and personal relationship to God. But the Abraham reflected in the patriarchal story is a many faceted figure: he is the believer, 15:6; the one who walks before God, 17:1; the just man who raises the problem of justice with God, 18:16b-33; the God-fearing man who withstands the test, chapter 22; the man who trusts in the providence of God, chapter 24. The unmanageable chapter 14 presents him as a hero figure like Gideon in the Book of Judges. The figure of Abraham has a history and reflects different stages in the progression of the Abraham tradition.

None of the Abraham stories as such goes back to what we call the patriarchal period. But, as we have seen, there are certain structures in the society they reflect which do not belong to the post-occupation of the land period.

Chapter 26 has the appearance of a collection of Isaac traditions. It contains only doublets: the story of the ancestress in danger (vv. 1-11) has already been told twice of Abraham in chapters 12 and 20; the stories of the wells (vv. 12-15) and of the confrontation with Abimelech (vv. 26-33) have already appeared in the Abraham cycle, 21:25-32. Isaac is not portrayed as a figure of the stature of Abra-

ham or Jacob. He is rather presented as the channel through which
the promises made to Abraham (26:3, 5, 24; 28:3-4) are passed on.
The text of the Jacob-Esau cycle has a unity but, like the Abraham cycle, a unity given it by the careful assembling and joining
together of blocks of diverse narratives and by the strong theological thrust of the narratives of the divine encounters. Again, none
of the narratives formally as such would go back to the patriarchal
period. And by the patriarchal period I mean, at least for the present, a time before the settlement, and no more.

As we shall see in the excursus on the promises, the traditions about
the patriarchs have, as it were, been set out on a grid of promises.
We note but three examples: (1) the assurance of universal blessing
through the patriarchs, 12:3; 22:18 (through Abraham), 26:4 (through
Isaac), 28:14 (through Jacob), all with strikingly similar wording;
(2) the constant assurance of countless descendants (e.g., 13:15; 15:4;
17:2, 19; 26:16; 26:4; 35:11); (3) the assurance in the name of *El
šadday* (28:2-3; 35:11-12; 48:3-6). These examples, and more, are
certain signs of the heavy theological editing of the traditions.

The traditions about Abraham, Isaac and Jacob are not inventions; they were there at hand to the writers in the period of the
monarchy who handed them on, interpreted them, adapted them to
their own situation, and used them to justify social and cultic practices of their time. These writers were transmitters, contributors,
storytellers and theologians. Thus circumcision is traced back to the
patriarchs by the priestly writer in chapter 17; the payment of tithes
is rooted in the Melchizedek episode when Abraham gave a tenth
to the priest-king of Salem, 14:18-20, and in the foundation of the
sanctuary at Bethel, when Jacob vowed " . . . and of all that thou
givest me, I will give the tenth to thee," 28:22. This too is a justification of the practice of vows in later Israel. When God promises
Isaac, "I will multiply your descendants as the stars of heaven . . .
because Abraham obeyed my voice and kept my charge, my commandments, my statutes, and my laws," 26:4-6, we hear the voice
of Deuteronomy. It has been suggested that the theological discussion about the justice of God and the destruction of Sodom in
18:16b-33—and it is a theological discussion and neither an intercession on behalf of Sodom nor an attempt to beat God down—
reflects Israel as it faces, or after it has seen, its own destruction.

There is a massive period of formation behind the text of Genesis
11:27–36:43 as it lies before us. The chapters reflect various stages
in the progress of the traditions about the patriarchs until they

achieved the only form in which we have them. But are the patriarchs merely inventions? In such a tradition-bound society I scarcely think so. Though we have no biography of them, yet the traditions do reflect aspects of a society structure which do not belong to Palestine of the first millennium B.C. The writers were convinced that there was a pre-settlement period that had direct links with Israel.

5

Excursus 2
The God of the Patriarchs

Most studies of the religion of the patriarchs over the last five decades have taken as their point of departure Albrecht Alt's monograph, "The God of the Fathers" (1929) which appeared in English only in 1966. Alt started from the designations for God in the patriarchal texts. These names, which linked God with a person, the God of Abraham, the God of Isaac, the God of Jacob, were names given by nomadic groups on the edge of the desert to the divinity or divinities which they worshipped. Alt noted that many centuries later, from the third century B.C.E. to the third century C.E., similar nomadic groups which moved from the desert, the Nabataeans and the Palmyrenes, used similar designations for their gods. He, and those who took their lead from him, based their discussions almost exclusively on the designations for God, El, with some descriptive, appositional, or possessive title. They presupposed that a religion is virtually identical with its idea or understanding of God, an attitude, as Claus Westermann has pointed out, very like that of medieval theology which dealt first with the tract *De Deo Uno* (1980:98). "El" is the only name for God that occurs in the patriarchal stories; hence the religion is an "El" religion. For Alt, El or the Elim were at first local Canaanite numina. For a later writer, Frank M. Cross, El is the proper name of the head of the Canaanite pantheon; hence the religion of the patriarchs is a special form of the Canaanite religion. Cross is on firm ground here inasmuch as El has been shown to be the proper name of the highest of the gods in the fourteenth century Ugaritic texts.

The discussion that follows presupposes the reflections of de Pury (1978:610, 613–14) and the study of nomadism by Rowton (1965-82) outlined in EXCURSUS 1.

1. The Patriarchs Meet God

The religion of Genesis 12–50 is not a religion that is worked out theoretically. There is no dissertation or philosophical reflection on the nature of God. The stories portray what the patriarchs do normally and naturally. These acts of religion conform to the life-style of the patriarchs, to enclosed nomadism, and to family society. The patriarchs meet God on the way and build altars to him or erect stones at different places, 12:7, 8; 13:18; 26:25; 28:22; 35:7. They also meet God on the way without building altars, 15:1-7; 16:7-14; 18:1-14; 21:8-14, 15-18; 32:1-2; 46:1-3. The patriarch himself presides over the worship; he builds the altar, he prays, he receives the visit from God. There is no priest, no liturgical mediator. There is nothing that reflects the fixed place of worship, the temple, the priests and levites and liturgical system of the monarchy. God and patriarch meet naturally as the patriarch moves about. The encounter is personal. God speaks directly, holds dialogues, gives a name. God knows Abraham, 18:19, God tests him, 22:1, and God struggles with Jacob, 32:22-23. The religious actions of the patriarchs are not constricted by any system. They conform to the enclosed nomadism and the family society of a non-sedentary culture.

The God of the patriarchs is a nomadic deity; he is not tied to a sanctuary; he belongs to the patriarch and his extended family. He appears to Abraham at the place through which Abraham moves, at Shechem, 12:7, and where Abraham settles, at Mamre, 13:18 and 18:1. Abraham's servant invokes him in Upper Mesopotamia, chapter 24. The God of Jacob protects him wherever he goes, 28:15, 20; 35:3; he protects him against Laban's intrigues, 31:12, and against Esau, 32:12. The God of the patriarchs is involved with the person and the small group.

Alt has written that the patriarchs were "receivers of revelation" and "founders of cult." The former is a proper description; the latter is misleading. After their encounters with God at Mamre, Bethel, Beersheba and Bethel, the patriarchs did not 'institute" anything; nothing was carried on in the name of the so-called "institutor." Jacob set up a pillar at Bethel and poured oil on it, 28:18; 35:14;

on the second occasion he also poured out a drink offering, 35:14; he called the place *bêt-'ēl* (28:19), and the pillar that he set up was to be *bêt-'ēl,* 28:22; the place where God spoke to him later he called El-Bethel, 35:7, or simply *bêt-'ēl.* But there is no sign of an "institution" or a cult to be carried on. These were already holy places. The patriarchal stories may have been given their final form any time from the ninth to the sixth centuries B.C.E.; but they do not reflect the religious practices or actions of this period. A different religious tradition, a different comportment before God, is associated with the fathers. It is difficult to conceive that this tradition was invented more or less contemporaneously with the final form of the stories as they stand in the Hebrew Bible. Central to the religion of Yahweh in the period of the monarchy are the temple, the liturgy, the priesthood, the levitical system, organized and regular sacrifice at the one place. All this is missing from the story of the patriarchs in Genesis.

2. El—God

The stories tell us that the patriarchs met their God at different places. God appeared to Abraham at Haran, 11:32; 12:1-3, and later, after his migration, "on the way" at Shechem, near the oak of Moreh, 12:7, and at Bethel, 12:8; Abraham went on to the Negeb, 12:9; 13:3, where God spoke to him again, 13:14; then yet again at Hebron, by the oaks of Mamre, 13:18. It was at Mamre too that God gave the definitive promise of a son, 18:1-15. God dialogued with Abraham on the way to Sodom, 18:16ff., 22ff. Abraham prayed to God in Gerar, 20:17, and God dealt personally with him in the Hagar episode, 21:12-13; Abraham met God again in the great test in chapter 22. God met Hagar in the wilderness, 16:7-14; 21:15-21. There is no sign that Abraham founded a cult.

God appeared to Isaac at Gerar, 26:2-5; at a "certain place," which Jacob called Bethel, 28:10-20; in Aram Naharaim, 31:3, 11-13; at Mahanaim, 32:1-2; at the Jabbok, 32:23-33; at Shechem twice, 33:18-20; 31:5; at Bethel again, 35:9-15, and finally at Beersheba, 46:1-4. Again, there is no sign that Jacob founded a cult.

The God of the patriarchs can appear anywhere and can be met anywhere. He has no fixed dwelling; God is there wherever the patriarch happens to wander.

When one removes the proper name Yahweh, which was revealed first to Moses, and which has been projected back to the very beginnings, Genesis 4:27, then this God whom the patriarchs meet is known by the common semitic word, El. Alt considered El, or the Elim, to be local Canaanite numina. Frank M. Cross (1973:1–75) thinks that El of the patriarchal stories, the only name for God that occurs there, is the God El of Canaan, the head of the Ugaritic pantheon. Hence the religion of the patriarchs is a special form of the Canaanite El religion. I propose that El of the patriarchal stories is neither of these, but simply "God," the supreme being. El is for the most part an appellative of the deity in the Hebrew Bible; in a few rare cases, it may be the proper name of the deity El.

El is used in Genesis with a number of epithets or descriptive phrases: *'ēl 'elyon*, 14:18-20; *'ēl qōnê šāmayim wā'āreṣ*, 14:19; *ēl 'ōlām*, 21:33; *'ēl bêt'ēl*, 31:13; 35:7; *'ēl 'ĕlohê yiśra'ēl*, 33:20; *'ēl ro'i*, 16:13; *'ānōkî hā'ēl 'ĕlohê 'ābîkā*, 46:3; *'ēl šadday*, 17:1; 28:3; 35:11; 48:3; to these add 43:13; 49:25; *'ānî YHWH 'ĕlohê 'abrāhām 'ābîkā wē'lohê yiṣḥaq*, 28:13. The names are formed with *'ēl*, except the last (cf. *YHWH 'elohê haššāmayim* . . . 24:7).

El is equated with YHWH in the psalms. For example:

> YHWH is my crag, and my fortress, and my deliverer,
> El *('ēli)* is my rock in whom I take refuge. (Ps 18:3)

> The word of *YHWH* on the waters,
> *El,* the glorious (or God of glory) thunders. (Ps 29:3)

> Hear my prayer *YHWH,*
> give ear to my prayer *El.* (Ps 39:13)

The parallel occurs twice in the oracles of Balaam:

> How can I curse whom *El* has not cursed,
> How can I denounce whom *YHWH* has not denounced. (Num 23:8)

> *YHWH* their God (Elohim) is with them,
> and the shout of their king is amongst them;
> *El* brings them out of Egypt. . . . (Num 23:21b-22)

YHWH and El are also juxtaposed:

> Arise *YHWH, El* lift up your hand,
> and do not forget the afflicted. (Ps 10:12)

Into your hand I commend my life,
You have redeemed me *YHWH El;*
Truly I hate those who cultivate vain idols,
But I trust in *YHWH.* (Ps 31:6-7)

It has been suggested that *YHWH* and *El* form a double name, *YHWH-El,* which has been separated into its component parts (Dahood 1965; 1970). But there are scholars who do not agree (Freedman 1976:67).

The equation or combination of YHWH and El is easy if El is simply God, the supreme God, and not just the head of the Canaanite pantheon. It would present no difficulty to those who made the transition from or equation of El to YHWH. It is typical of the constant monotheizing tendency of the Hebrew writers.

The composite name, *'ēl 'elyôn* occurs in Psalm 78:35 where it is parallel to *'ĕlohîm;* in the same psalm, *'elyôn* is parallel to *'ēl* in verses 17-18, and to *'ĕlohîm;* in verse 56. Also, *'elyôn* is a regular epithet or substitute for God in the psalms. The following are typical of many examples:

How can *'El* know? Is there knowledge in *'Elyôn?* (73:11)

They defied the commands of *'El,*
They spurned the counsel of *'Elyôn.* (107:11)

'Elyôn is in parallelism with both *šadday* and YHWH in Psalm 91:1, 9. It occurs with vestiges of a polytheistic background in Psalm 97:9:

Indeed you (*YHWH*) are *'Elyôn* over all the whole earth,
You are lifted high above all *'ĕlohîm.*

The title is firmly fixed in the liturgical language of Israel (*'Elyôn* occurs in the liturgical tradition in Psalms 7:18; 9:3; 18:14; 46:5; 47:3; 50:14; 57:3; 73:11; 82:6; 83:19; 87:5; 91:1, 9; 92:2; 97:5, 9; 107:11 [Dahood 1970:xxxix; Lack 1962:44-64]).

The phrase which describes *'El 'Elyôn* in the Melchizedek passage in Genesis 14:18-20, *qoneh šāmayyîm wā 'āreṣ,* creator of heaven and earth, has a parallel outside Israel in the eighth century Karatepe inscription where *'ēl,* the creator of earth, *'l qn 'arṣ* is parallel to Baal of heaven, *B'l šmm.* The phrase has been found recently on a jar-handle from the eighth–seventh century in the excavations in the Jewish sector of Jerusalem, *qn 'arṣ* (Cross 1973:51, n. 25; Fitzmyer 1967:11–12, line 11; 37–38). A similar phrase, maker of heaven and earth, *'ośeh šāmayim wā 'āreṣ,* occurs as a refrain describing YHWH in Psalms 115:15; 121:2; 124:8; 134:5.

The writers who preserved the traditions of Exodus 3 and 6 knew, through the tradition, that the God of the patriarchs was a personal God: "I am the God of your father, the God of Abraham, the God of Isaac, and the God of Jacob," Exodus 3:6. The priestly tradition knew that the tetragram was revealed to Moses and that God had revealed himself to the fathers as *El šadday.* (A detailed discussion of *El šadday* is to be found in the *Notes* to Gen 17:1).

After Abraham concluded the treaty with Abimelech, he called on the name of *'el 'ōlām,* 21:33. According to Cross, *'el 'ōlām* may be read as "the god Olam" or "the God of eternity" ("the ancient god"). Why not "God, (the) eternal" (*'elohê 'ōlām* in Isa 40:28 is a construct chain)? Dahood has found the divine name, *'ōlām,* several times in the Psalms (1966: xxxvi, e.g., Pss 12:8; 24:7, 9; 31:2; 52:11; 71:1; 73:12; 75:10; 89:2-3; 119:111, 160. One can argue that the difficult text in Ps 110:4b, "you are a priest for ever . . . ," should be rendered, "you are a priest of the Eternal"). Though Cross (1973:48, n. 11) hesitates, noting, "had he found fewer instances his case would appear stronger," nevertheless virtually all the instances alleged by Dahood can be well argued. And so *'ōlām* too, as well as *'elyôn,* is fixed in the liturgical usage of Israel.

El who appeared at Bethel is a different case. In 35:7, Jacob called the place at Luz, where he built an altar, *'el bêt-'el.* The God who appeared to him in Aram introduced himself with the words, *'ānōkî hā'el bêt-'el,* 31:13; and the deity used a similar formula of introduction when Jacob was going down to Egypt *'ānōkî hā'el 'elohê 'ābîkā,* 46:3. Cross thinks that we should read "the God of Bethel" in the two earlier Jacob passages, and not "the God Bethel." But God introduces himself in both places with the formula, *'ānōkî hā'el,* that is *'el* with the definite article. In Deutero-Isaiah we read, "thus says *hā'el YHWH,* 42:5; and in Isaiah 43:12; 45:22; 46:9 we find *'ānî* or *'ānōkî 'el* without the article before *'el.* This El, with or without the article, designates the supreme being.

I would render *'el 'elohê yiśrā'el,* 33:20, as God, the God of Israel (the patriarch)—not very enterprising and perhaps tautological. *El ro'i,* 16:13, could be God, the one seeing me. We have seen that *El šadday* is very likely "God, the steppe one."

The priestly tradition used the name *El šadday* right up to the revelation of the tetragram in Exodus 6; Genesis 17:1; 28:3; 35:11; 48:3

are all P. *El šadday* was, in the priestly tradition, the name by which God revealed himself to the fathers. And it is an ancient Canaanite name appropriate to the nomads of the steppe. The name *šadday*, without *El*, is found six times in the psalms and prophets, twice in the oracle of Balaam, twice in Ruth, and thirty-one times in Job. In Psalm 91:1 it is in parallelism with Elyon:

> Let him who sits in the shelter of *'Elyôn*,
> who passes the night in the shade of *šadday*,
> say, O YHWH, my refuge and my crag,
> my God (*'ĕlohay*), in whom I trust.

In Genesis 49:25, the composite name *El šadday* is divided into its two parts, *El* and *šadday* (Wyatt 1977–78:101–02; Dahood 1970: xxxix-xli):

> By *'ĕl*, your father, may he help you,
> And by *šadday*, may he bless you.

And again in Numbers 24:16. Once more an ancient name for or title of God has become part of Israelite poetry and worship.

Frank M. Cross (1973:60) concludes his study of the patriarchal names for God with the paragraph:

> We have found that the epithets *'ĕl 'ôlām*, *'ĕl qōnê 'arṣ*, *'ĕl 'ĕlōhê yiśrā'ĕl*, and *'ĕl [ba'l?]* *bĕrît* are epithets of *'Ēl* preserved in Patriarchal tradition; *'ĕl 'elyōn* probably is added, along with *'ĕl bet-'ĕl*, and finally there is a good possibility that *'ĕl šadday* is an epithet of Canaanite or Amorite *'Ēl* (or both).

We find then that there are a number of ancient names for or epithets of God, used in the patriarchal stories, which have become part of Israelite worship and poetry. These names are not late creations. They occur in the earliest Hebrew poetry, the Song of Miriam, the Song of Deborah, the Oracles of Balaam, the Testament of Moses, The Song of Moses, the Testament of Jacob, and other early songs, laments and psalms, such as 1 Samuel 2; 2 Samuel 1; 2 Samuel 23; Psalms 18; 29; 68; 72; 89 (Freedman 1976). The names passed into Hebrew worship at an early stage and were readily equated with YHWH. Virtually all of them were linked with El. If El is simply God, the supreme God or being, then this would offer no difficulty.

This, of course, does not mean that a writer in the exilic or post-exilic period could not have used these names. Nevertheless, if the names could have been introduced in the later period, it does not mean that they must have been introduced then.

El then is God, and the patriarchal names may be rendered:

'*ēl 'elyôn*	God, he exalted (most high, supreme)
'*ēl qoneh*	God, the creator
'*ēl ro'i*	God, the (one) seeing me (?)
'*ēl 'ōlām*	God, the eternal
'*ēl bêt-'ēl*	God, (the one of) Bethel
'*ēl 'ĕlohê yiśrā'ēl*	God, the God of (the patriarch) Israel
'*anōkî hā'ēl*	I am God Himself, the god of your father . . .
'*ēl šadday*	God, the steppe one.

3. Conclusion

What then do we say in conclusion about the religion of the patriarchs?

(1) The individual stories about the patriarchs do not portray that which actually happened; they have undergone a long process of transmission, and were given their present form sometime in the period of the monarchy.

(2) The stories individually and as a cycle reflect a life-style that we call "enclosed nomadism" which is characteristic of Western Asia in the second millennium, not of Palestine in the first millennium, B.C.E. The form of society is that of the family or the extended family.

(3) There is no sign in the patriarchal stories of the religious practices of the monarchic period; there is no temple, no central cult, no liturgy with liturgical prescriptions, no priests or levites.

(4) The religious practices in the stories conform easily to the nomadic way of life.

(5) The God of the fathers is a personal God, who is met anywhere at any time. He is not restricted to place; he is there, "on the way." There is no question of monotheism or monolatry or polytheism. There is no competition or confrontation between god and god. The God of Abraham, the God of Isaac, the God of Jacob are not present simultaneously. The deity is just El, God, wherever he is met or appears, and because he is God, the supreme one, he is given unquestioning obedience.

If these elements of the religion of the patriarchal stories, which are not characteristic of the religion of the monarchy, are not a genuine part of the patriarchal tradition, then they must be a creation of writers in the period of the monarchy—an unlikely hypothesis in such a tradition-bound society.

We cannot write a rounded account of the history or of the religion of the patriarchs. We can only point to certain elements which the biblical texts preserve. When we remove the proper name, YHWH, and all characteristics of Yahwism, we are left with a personal God who is the God of the father of the clan (the extended family) and of the clan itself; he has no name; he is just El, God, the high God, the eternal one, the God of this father of this group, the God who appeared at this place. The father worships this God; he prays and presides at the worship; there is no mediator at the place of worship. This God preserves the group through a son, and guides the group "on the way." It is a simple, uncomplicated religion where God comes directly to the person, and the person goes directly to God with no more ado.

6

Excursus 3
The Promises

The promises are in essence divine addresses (or quotations from or references to them) expressing for the era of their origin or use a confidence that God is with his people, guiding them, increasing them, and giving them secure living space. They are projected back into the patriarchal period with the conviction of the period when they were written that as God was with the patriarchs, so will he be with his people. The patriarchal traditions are laid out on this grid of promises which gives them coherence. But the grid was not made at one casting. It was the result of a process of continual recasting until it reached the form which it has now taken in the definitive Hebrew text.

The promises are often described as secondary to the patriarchal narratives. This is correct inasmuch as the original patriarchal narratives or traditions carried only the promise of a son (Abraham tradition) and, it can be argued, the promise of guidance, presence, or assistance (some form of "I am with you," Jacob tradition). They are not "secondary" in the sense of "additions" to an already established text. Martin Noth (1972; German 1948) had maintained that the promises are not the theme of the patriarchal narrative. But David J. A. Clines (1978:29) has argued well that "the theme of the Pentateuch is the partial fulfillment—which implies also the partial non-fulfillment—of the promise to or blessing of the patriarchs."

The promises as they lie before us tell of something that happens between God and the patriarchs, and so are part of patriarchal religion. Most of the divine addresses in chapters 12–36 (add 46:2-4) are promises. God makes the promises directly, without a mediator. Promises are constitutive of narratives (16:1-14; 18:1-16a); narratives are constructed for the promises (15:1-6, 7-21); the promises are brought together so as to form an address by God (17:1-22); they form an independent scene (13:14-17) or episode (12:7; 26:24-25), or are introduced into or linked with narratives (15:13-16; 22:15-18; 26:2-5; 28:2-3; 28:13b-15; 35:9-13; 46:2-4); there is a blessing with promise at the beginning of the Abraham (12:2-3), Isaac (26:2-5), and Jacob (28:13b-15).

There are broadly speaking four promises: of a son, of guidance or assistance or presence, of land, of descendants. The blessing and the covenant are not really promises, but must be considered in the context of the promises.

1. Blessing

Blessing permeates the promises. It activates the powers already given to *hā'ādām,* male and female, in creation so as to issue into myriads of descendants and so Abraham himself "will be a blessing . . . and so all the clans of the earth shall find blessing through you" (12:3; cf. 28:14b). The formulation is somewhat different, but the same sense is there, when Abraham (22:18) and Isaac (26:4) are each assured "that all the nations of the earth shall find blessing through your descendants." The assurance that the blessing on each of the patriarchs is to be universal is given at the beginning of the stories about each (12:3; 26:4; 28:14). In 12:3 and 28:14b the nip'al form of the verb *bārak,* bless, is used (see 12:3, *Notes*) together with the word *mišpĕḥot,* clans, families; in 22:18 and 26:4 it is the hitpa'el form of *bārak* (12:3, *Notes*) with the word *goyyîm,* nations. The variations would indicate different layers of editing. The position of each of these assurances of universal blessing at the beginning of each cycle is a sign that blessing is the "signature tune" of the patriarchal narrative (cf. further P. D. Miller [1984:475], quotation given under *Comment* on 11:27-12:9). Blessing is not an independent promise theme but, as we have noted, is all-pervading. It always occurs in conjunction with other themes, and especially with the theme of increase or countless descendants (Rendtorff 1977:49; Westermann 1980). The blessing works itself out in the Jacob story in the success that Jacob has with cattle breeding, a success which affects Laban as well (30:25-43; 32:10-13 [9-12]; 33:10-11). Abraham (13:2-3, 6) and Isaac (26:12-14) are under God's blessing as breeders of cattle.

2. Covenant

The covenant is best understood as a solemn assurance by God that he has bound himself to his people and that he will be their God (17:7-8; *Comment* on chapters 15; 17; see further *Comment* on Genesis 6:18; 9:8-17).

3. A Son

As we have seen in the introduction to and commentary on the Abraham cycle, the promise of a son is confined to this section. The absence of a son is noted at the very beginning (11:30) and a son is promised implicitly immediately afterwards in the blessing of 12:1-3. This promise is linked with descendants (15:1-6; 16:11) and blessing (17:6); it occurs alone in 18:1-16a. After the long literary delay from 18:16b through to the end of chapter 20, not to mention the years of waiting by Abraham (15:1-6; 17:17-19, 21; 20:5) and Sarah (16:2; 17:15-16; 18:9-15), the promise is fulfilled (21:1-7). But Ishmael too, though not the son of promise, shares in the blessing that comes to the human race through Abraham (17:20; 21:13, 18b). The promise of a son so permeates the Abraham cycle that the story is unintelligible without it. One can argue then that this promise belongs to the oldest form of the Abraham tradition.

4. Guidance-Assistance-Presence

This promise belongs to the Jacob cycle only in the Book of Genesis, but is not limited to Genesis. It runs right through the Old Testament. It occurs in various forms in the Jacob story: "I will be with you" (26:3, Isaac; 31:3; 46:3-4), "I am with you" (26:24, Isaac; 28:15), "the God of my fathers has been with me" (31:5 [cf. 28:20]; 31:42; 35:3), "God will be with you" (48:21). It is usually found together with the promises of increase (46:3-4), increase and blessing (26:24-25), increase, blessing, and land. It occurs by itself only in 31:3. The promise is linked closely with Jacob's journeys and so may well go back to the earliest traditions of Jacob the wanderer. The theme of Jacob on the move from and back to Canaan has been considered in the introduction to the Jacob cycle and in the *Comment* on chapters 31 and 32. The Jacob cycle is framed by the guidance theme (28:15; 31:3, 13; 46:2-4). The theme of guidance is implicit in the Abraham story where Abraham is told to go "to the land that I will show you" (12:3).

5. Land

Several authors, in particular Westermann (1980) and Rendtorff (1977:42-48), have pointed out the long and varied tradition history of the promises of the land and of numerous descendants. The promise of the land alone is made to Abraham (12:7; 15:7-21; [24:7]); it is also made together with the promise of descendants (13:14-17; 35:11-13; [48:3-4]), and with the promise of descendants in the context of blessing (26:2-6; [28:3-4]; 28:13b-15). The land is promised to Abraham: "I will give this land (it) to *you and your descendants* I give (I will give, I have given) the (this) land (it)" (13:15; 17:8; 26:3; [28:4]; 28:13b; 35:12); to his descendants: "I (will) give this land (all these lands) to your descendants" (12:7; 15:18; [24:7]; 26:4; [48:4]). The references in square brackets are to recollections of one of the patriarchs, not to direct divine addresses. In each case the word "descendants" in the plural renders the Hebrew singular word *zera'*, seed. On three occasions there is reference to the oath which God swore to give the land to Abraham and/or to multiply his descendants (22:16; 24:7; 26:3). The promise of the land on oath runs right through the Book of Deuteronomy (1:8, 15; 6:10, 18, 23; 7:8, 13; 8:1; 9:5; 10:11; 11:9, 21; 19:8; 26:3, 15; 28:11; 30:20; 31:7, 20, 21; 34:4). The conclusions about the promise of the land are: (1) "to you," "to you and your descendants," "to your descendants," together with the different collocations of these phrases in the sentence both in relation to the verb and to each other (cf. Rendtorff 1977:42) are signs of variation in the process of the history of tradition of this promise; (2) the promise of the land, all dominant in the Book of Deuteronomy, and the oath indicate that this theological-historical thinking stems from those circles responsible for the theology found in that book. As the traditions in Deuteronomy did not appear suddenly, neither did the promise of the land to the patriarchs. The promise in Deuteronomy is the promise of a settled land. V. Maag (1958) has proposed that the forerunner of the promise of the land may have been the promise of newer or better pastures (transhumance) in the pre-settlement or nomadic period. Hence the promise in an inchoate form may go back to the nomadic period.

6. Descandants (zera', seed)

This promise is not found alone, but together with the promise of a son (above), of land and blessing (13:14-17; 26:2-5; 28:3-4; 28:13b-15; 35:11-13; 48:3-4, 16, 19); of guidance-assistance-presence (22:17-18; 26:2-5; 26:24-25; 46:3-4); of blessing (18:18-19; 22:15-18). There are fixed formulas to express the multitude of descendants: "I will multiply . . . (and/or) . . . I will make fruitful" so that they will be as "the stars in the sky" (15:5; 22:17; 26:4); "as the dust of the earth" (13:16; 28:14); "as the sand by the sea" (22:17; 32:13 [12]).

God will make Abraham (12:2) and Jacob (46:3) "a great nation"; Abraham will become "a great and powerful nation" (18:18); God will make Ishmael "a (great) nation" (21:13, 18; 17:20b). In chapter 17, there is a heaping up of the promise of descendants:

vv. 4, 5   Abraham will be "the father of a great number of nations"
v. 6   "I will make nations of you and kings shall come from you"
v. 16   "she (Sarah) shall issue into nations and kings shall come from her"
v. 20   "He (Ishmael) shall beget twelve princes and I will make him a great nation"

Isaac prays that Jacob may give rise to an assembly (*qāhal*) of peoples (28:3); God blesses Jacob to become an assembly (*qāhal*) of nations (35:11); and Jacob recalls this blessing (48:4).

Though there are standard formulas, similes, and metaphors, these are not used mechanically but vary at different stages of the tradition. This promise is pronounced retrospectively; it speaks from the standpoint of the greatest expansion of Israel from the river of Egypt to the great river, the Euphrates.

7. Conclusion

Blessing is not a promise but is all pervading throughout the patriarchal period. The promise of a son is part of the earliest Abraham tradition. The promise of guidance-assistance-presence may well go back to the earliest traditions about Jacob as a wandering Aramean. It is peculiar to the Jacob cycle in the patriarchal story and it flows over into the Moses traditions up to the promised land. It is there in the prophetic tradition. The promises of the land and of descendants each has its own independent history and each has undergone its own variety of formulations and adaptations in the process leading to the final biblical text.

The Joseph Story
(37–50)

THE HISTORY OF EXEGESIS: A BRIEF NOTE

(a) *Julius Wellhausen*. Most commentators on the Joseph story quote Julius Wellhausen's reflection on Genesis 37–50:

> The main source for this last section of Genesis is also JE. One suspects that this work, here as elsewhere, is a synthesis of J and E; our earlier results impose this solution and would be profoundly affected were it not demonstrable. I maintain that to begin by wanting to break up this fluent narrative about Joseph into sources is not an error, but as necessary as the breaking down of Genesis throughout (1899; repr. 1963:52).

Wellhausen was of the opinion that if source criticism ran aground on the Joseph story, then it ran aground throughout the Book of Genesis as a whole. He explained the Joseph story by means of his own finely developed documentary theory of source criticism according to which the Joseph story is a combination of the two already existing, independent, self-contained stories written by J and E.

(b) *Hermann Gunkel, Hugo Gressmann and Gerhard von Rad*. Hermann Gunkel (1910; 1922) recognized an essential unity in the Joseph story but remained bound by the classical source division into J and E. He did not consider J and E to be dependent on each other, nor either of them to be the real shaper of the Joseph tradition. Each found a great artistic composition at hand, the composer of which had made use of traditional story motifs such as one good and several bad brothers, the spurned woman, the poor person, stranger, or

278

foreigner who is called in to solve a problem which has baffled the local experts and who is rewarded, and of stories/tales already in existence. A great artist creates a continuous story out of individual pieces. He molds the material into an artistic unity. For Gunkel, the following narratives, in their basic content, form a continuous story, a clear unity: chapter 37, Joseph taken to Egypt; chapter 42, the first meeting of the brothers with Joseph; chapter 43, the second meeting; chapter 45, Joseph reveals himself to his brothers; chapter 46, Jacob journeys to Egypt; chapters 48; 49:29-33, Jacob's last will and death; chapter 50, Jacob's burial and Joseph's death. Chapters 39–41, Joseph's rise, fall, and elevation in Egypt, and 47:13-26, Joseph's economic measures, have their own independent traditions; but the present story is unintelligible without chapters 39–41. Chapter 38, the story of Judah and Tamar, and 49:2-27, the blessings of Jacob, do not belong originally to the Joseph story. Yet Gunkel, despite his basic and correct insight, wants to cling in some way to J and E versions. He never reconciled his dilemma of unity and diversity.

Gunkel's student, collaborator, and friend, Hugo Gressmann (1923) gave a similar explanation of the Joseph story. "The Joseph story as handed down to us forms, almost in its entire compass, a self-contained literary unity" (1923:2). And Gressmann continues that because it is not possible to distinguish J and E throughout, source criticism often comes to different conclusions. Nevertheless Gressmann, correct in his basic insight into the story's unity, as was Gunkel, still adhered to the division into sources. For example, of the E and J versions of the two meetings of the brothers with Joseph (chs. 42–43), only half of each is preserved; E is the first, and knows nothing of Benjamin. Throughout several pages, Gressmann analyzes the text into sources, additions, unevennesses, variants and writes that "the three original forms of the story, reconstructed here, proceed from the same presupposition: to fulfill the ideal demand of justice, Joseph had to punish his brothers for what they had done to him" (1923:40). The text before us is a *Novelle,* the life-history of Joseph according to a definite plan. These two great scholars grasped the essential unity of the story, but remained handicapped by the presuppositions of source division. They saw an artistic whole, yet saw it composed from two different versions.

Von Rad too (1949; 1976, tenth ed.) wants both a unity and sources. "The Joseph story is not a 'cycle of stories' (*Sagenkranz*) woven together out of originally independent and self-contained narrative units, but it is from beginning to end an organically coherent narrative; it is not a *Sage* but a *Novelle"* (1976:356). Writing of the Joseph story in the narrower sense (chs. 37; 39–47; 50) von Rad says: "the text of these chapters, prescinding from a very few parts from the priestly source, is an artistic composition out of the presentations of the sources J and E. Both documents clearly contained a Joseph story. The redactor bound them together in such a way as to insert extensive parts of the parallel Elohistic version into the Yahwistic Joseph story and so create a still richer narrative. In any case, the advantage gained from this inter-mingling of sources is incomparably greater than the disadvantage" (1976:284). Once more, the Joseph story is "an organically coherent narrative," "an artistic composition," but the result of putting together two already existing compositions. So neither J nor E is the artist, but an anonymous redactor helped, it seems, by the already existing contributions of J and E.

(c) *More recent source division.* Three recent discussions of the Joseph story, L. Ruppert (1965; 1985), H.-C. Schmitt (1980; 1985), and L. Schmidt (1986), are all bound completely to source division. "Everyone," they note, agrees on those editorial snippets which belong to the priestly editor. So these scholars subtract the "agreed" priestly pieces and analyze what is left. According to Ruppert, J used material or a story already available. E arose, or was redacted, with a knowledge of J. The parallelism between J and E is not due to an imagined common source, G (*Grundlage*). The Jehovist, (R^JE), less a redactor than a composer of genius, put together J and E. He was a creative reworker and as such an author. He was responsible for the relatively self-contained matter to which P added his editorial touches. One of Ruppert's main conclusions (1985:48) is that we must adhere to the "three classical narrative pentateuchal sources" as "self-contained documents" in the proper sense, as well as to the usual dating of them. Schmidt proposes that there was an original Joseph story (a Judah-Israel layer) which underwent an "Elohistic" reworking (a Reuben-Jacob layer). There followed a late, many-layered, "Yahwistic" reworking of the "Elohistic" work. Schmitt gives the usual reasons, alleged "doublets," variations in the name Jacob/Israel, why there must have been two Joseph stories which have been joined together. First there was the Yahwist's Joseph story, then the Elohist's Joseph story which used the Yahwist's story; the priestly Joseph story was very fragmented; the Jehovist (R^JE) joined J and E together with some glue of his own. Then came the end redaction and additions. All three authors spend a great amount of time diagnosing what is certainly or probably or possibly J or E. The surgery represents a very limited and esoteric intramural aspect of German "exegesis" which opens and advances the discussion not at all. All that is said by them has been said already a thousand times ten thousand during the last hundred years and more.

(d) *More recent unity*. Many exegetes in recent years consider the Joseph story to be a unity. Frank Crüsemann (1978) is of the opinion that the Joseph story is older than J who took it over as a self-contained unity, an original unity, not composed out of two sources. The tensions in the text arise from reworking, commenting, and glossing in the course of the process of tradition. According to Herbert Donner (1976:24), "the text of the Joseph story as handed down cannot be distributed among the narrative works of the Yahwist and the Elohist with the compelling certainty that can be achieved elsewhere in the Pentateuch. Criteria for pentateuchal source division fail in Genesis 37–50." In the third volume of his monumental commentary on Genesis, Claus Westermann (1986) supports the essential unity of the Joseph story in the stricter sense (chs. 37; 39–45; parts of chs. 46–50). Other recent writers who support a unity in the story are R. N. Whybray (1968), W. Brueggemann (1972), G. W. Coats (1976), I. Willi-Plein (1979).

A READING OF THE JOSEPH STORY

There emerges from a reading of the Joseph story a certain sense of unity, a series of cross-references, theological clamps, somewhat rough transitions, narrative arcs of tension which cross, intersect, finish within the story, and extend from beginning to end. Despite the sense of unity, it is obvious, to use what has now become a common metaphor in biblical circles, that the story was not cast from one mold at one pouring. It is also obvious that Jacob plays an important role in chapters 37–50 and that from chapter 46 onwards, the end of the Jacob story is interwoven with the end of the Joseph story. With the notable exceptions of Westermann (1986) and Luis Alonso Schökel (1985), exegetes have not given sufficient attention to the important role of Jacob.

THE JOSEPH STORY

Chapters 37–50 are commonly, and correctly, known as the Joseph story. The figure of Joseph binds them together. He is central in 37:2b, "Joseph was seventeen years old; he was guarding sheep.

282

The Joseph Story
Genesis 37–50
[based on C. Westermann, *Genesis 37–50*, 1986]

P-Frame		P-Frame
37:1-2		50:12-14

39–45   46–50

37;

Joseph story in narrower sense   Conclusion of Jacob (and patriarchal) story woven with
                                        conclusion of Joseph story + additions. (All further P
                                        passages are in chs. 46–50.)

Family story: 46   healing of breach

37   breach in family
(expansion of patriarchal story,
directed to death of Jacob;
37:35; 42:38; 43:27-28; 44:22, 29, 31;
45:9, 13, 28; 46:30)

39–41   political story

42–45   family & political motifs
        prolonged into two return journeys

38 ———— belong to conclusion of Jacob story ———— 49

God in act: 39:2, 3, 5, 21, 23; 40:8;   Theological statements   45:5-8   50:17-21
41:16, 25, 32, 38, 39; 42:28; 44:16

46-50

Conclusion of:

Joseph story	Jacob story (P)	Additions
1. *Reunion:* 46:5b, 28-30	1. *Emigration to Egypt:* 46:6-7	1. (to P)
5b Jacob's departure (follows 45:24-28)		46:8-27 list of names
28-30 Arrival in Goshen		47:13-27 Joseph's economic measures
		50:15-21 reconciliation confirmed
2. *Provision for family: Settlement in Egypt:* 46:31-34; 47	2. *Jacob blesses Pharoah:* 47:7-10	2.
46:31-34 Brothers prepare for audience	47:11, 27b In Egypt (Ramses)	46:1-5a conclusion to Joseph story begins
47:1-6 Audience with Pharoah	They settle, multiply	
47:11, 12, 27a Settlement	Verse 28 Jacob's age	48:13-22 before death
		49:1b-28a
3. *Jacob's Legacy, Death, Burial:* 47:29-31; 48-50	3. *Jacob's Legacy, Death, Burial:* 48-50	50:22-26 after burial
Legacy: 47:29-31 Request for burial in Canaan	*Legacy:* 48:3-6 (7) Jacob adopts	(all three additions contain promise of Exodus, 46:4; 48:21; 50:24-25)
48:1-2, 8-12 Jacob blesses Joseph's sons	49:1a, 28b Jacob blesses	
Death 49:28b-33 Jacob's death	49:29-32 Jacob's request	
& 50:1 Joseph's laments	*Death* 49:33 Death	
Burial 50:-2-3 Embalmment; 70 days mourning	&	
50:4-14 (omit 12-13) Burial in Canaan	*Burial* 50:12-13 Burial	
50:14 Joseph returns to Egypt		

Figure 4

283

. . . "; in 50:26, "Joseph died at the age of a hundred and ten." The peace of Jacob's family is shattered at the beginning of the story as a consequence of Jacob's preferential love for Joseph: "When the brothers saw that their father loved him more than them, they hated him and could not so much as greet him in peace *(šālôm)*" (37:4). This peace is restored when Joseph makes himself known to his brothers in Egypt: "Then he kissed all his brothers and wept over them. Only then did his brothers speak to him" (45:15); and the peace is confirmed after Jacob's death when "Joseph wept at their words to him" (50:18) and "said to them: Do not be afraid" (50:19, 21). When Joseph tells his brothers his first dream, he says: "my sheaf rose and stood upright while your sheaves gathered round and bowed down (verb, *šḥh,* see *Notes)* to mine" (37:7); then, in the second dream, "the sun and the moon and the eleven stars were bowing down (*šḥh*) to me" (37:9). Jacob asks him: "Am I and your mother and your brothers to bow down (*šḥh*) to the ground before you?" (37:10) When the brothers come down to Egypt, they do indeed bow down to Joseph, not knowing who he is (42:6; 43:26, 29), and the same verb is used. When Joseph's silver goblet is found in Benjamin's pack, the brothers return to Joseph: "They fell (*nāpal*) to the ground before him" (44:14). Finally, after Jacob's death, still conscious of their guilt, "they went in and fell down (*nāpal*) before him. . . . " (50:18). The brothers had asked Joseph indignantly: "Are you going to be king (*mālok timlok*) over us or ruler (*māšôl timšol*) over us?" (37:8). Later, Joseph will say to his brothers: "he (God) appointed me a father to Pharaoh and lord over his household and ruler (*mošēl)* in the whole land of Egypt" (45:8), and the brothers will take up the words and say to Jacob: "Joseph is still alive and it is he who is ruler (*mošēl*) in the land of Egypt" (45:26). Joseph says to his brothers: "Tell my father of the dignity (*kābôd,* glory) that is mine in Egypt. . . . " (45:13). So the dreams are fulfilled and Joseph's "glory" shines forth. The brothers all have a share in the savage act of injustice when they sell their own brother into slavery, despite the interventions of Reuben (37:22, 29) and Judah (37:26-27) to mitigate his fate. The narrator keeps this card in his hand and plays it so many years later: "We are certainly guilty with regard to our brother; we saw his anguish of soul when he begged mercy from us; but we did not listen. . . . " (42:21-23). He underscores the irony because Joseph understands all, though the brothers do not know it. When the goblet is found in Benjamin's pack, Judah exclaims in the presence of Joseph: "God has found out the sin of your servants" (44:16). And their guilt returns after their father's death: "What if Joseph should bear a grudge against us for all the evil we have dealt him?" (50:15).

The story of Joseph's rise, fall, and elevation in Egypt (chs. 39–41), whatever its origin, is, in the Joseph story as it lies before us, necessary so that Joseph may be in a position to help his family in time of famine and at the same time heal the breach in the family. God is with Joseph throughout this period (39:2, 3, 5, 21, 25), and Joseph is well aware that it is God who interprets dreams (40:8; 41:16, 25, 32, 38, 39). Joseph sees the action of God in the whole drama from beginning to end (45:5-8; 50:17-21). The brothers have no need to fear or be distressed: "Now do not be distressed or reproach yourselves . . . because God sent me ahead of you to save lives . . . but God sent me ahead of you to preserve you. . . . " (45:5, 7). "God planned good so as to preserve the lives of many people" (50:20). Joseph touches on, but does not dwell on, the brothers' guilt: " . . . because you sold me . . . " (45:5), and "you planned evil against me" (50:20a). The brothers have been taken up into a great action of God and so are to have no fear. Joseph will not play God (50:19). The brothers are the servants (slaves) of God, not of Joseph; the narrator plays on the word *'ebed,* slave/servant. Let us note too the consistent portrayal of Joseph's emotions; he wept on six occasions (42:24; 43:30; 45:1-2, 15; 46:29; 50:17).

The brothers make two journeys down to Egypt and have two audiences (better, three, adding 44:14-34) with Joseph, the second of which is unintelligible without the first. There is no question of doublets here. Each journey, each audience, advances the action towards its climax.

The cross-references, resumptions, repetitions of motifs, arcs of tension, resolutions, all argue for a unified Joseph narrative in the text as it lies before us, whatever fragments, stories finished or unfinished, or themes the author may have used. The narrator is in charge throughout. It is a storyteller with all the advantages that a storyteller enjoys, not an "historian," who is speaking.

THE JACOB STORY

Jacob plays an important role in Genesis 37–50. An extended story of his life has been presented under the heading "The Jacob Cycle" (25:19–36:43). Jacob returned to Canaan after his twenty years in Paddan-Aram and "came to his father Isaac at Mamre, Kiriath-arba—that is Hebron—where Abraham and Isaac had sojourned"

(35:27). "Now Jacob settled in the land where his father had sojourned, in the land of Canaan" (37:1). The writer continues: "This is the story (*tôlĕdôt*) of Jacob" (37:2a). It can, of course, only be the story of Jacob's later life and of his family. Jacob has a preferential love for Joseph which he shows by having the sleeved tunic made for him. This arouses the hatred of his brothers. Whereas the brothers hate Joseph more and more (37:4, 5, 8) because of the position that he assumes through his dreams, Jacob simply rebukes his preferred son and ponders over the matter (37:11). When the brothers deceive their father and let him conclude that Joseph is dead—their main concern is to have Joseph out of the way, dead or alive—Jacob laments: "I will go down to the realm of the dead (*šĕ'olâ*) mourning my sons" (37:35). The lament echoes through the story all the time that Jacob is separated from Joseph (42:38; [43:14]; 44:29, 31), and with it echoes too the theme that Jacob knows that he himself is moving along the path to death, *"šĕ'ol-wards"* (37:35b; 42:38; 44:22, 28-29, 31; 45:28; 47:9; 48:1; 49:1, 28b-33).

Jacob is completely out of the picture during the years of Joseph's rise-fall-elevation in Egypt. However, it is Jacob who takes the iniative when the famine comes (42:1-2; 43:1). He plays his part when the brothers return (42:29-38) and takes up again his lament of going down in sorrow to the realm of the dead (37:35b; 42:28). When Judah finally persuades Jacob to allow Benjamin to go down into Egypt (43:1-14), Jacob continues his lament: "But I—if I am bereaved, I am bereaved" (43:14b). Judah makes much of the strong bond between Jacob and Benjamin in his long speech to Joseph (44:16-34) which moves to a climax with "I could not go back to my father if the boy were not with me; I could not look upon the sorrow that would fall upon my father" (44:34). It is the old father and his suffering that brings Joseph to breaking point. Joseph's message to Jacob is: "Come down to me, do not delay" (45:9b). And Jacob, stunned and disbelieving, yields to the facts: "Enough. Joseph my son is still alive; I will go down and see him before I die" (45:28). Jacob goes down to Egypt, assured by a typical patriarchal encounter with God (46:2-4): "Do not be afraid to go down to Egypt . . . I will go down with you into Egypt and I will bring you up again. . . . " So Jacob sets out from Beersheba (45:5). Joseph meets him in Goshen, and Jacob pronounces his *Nunc Dimittis:* "Now let me die; I have seen your face again and you are alive" (46:30). Joseph presents Jacob to Pharaoh and at Pharaoh's behest settles him in the land of Goshen (47:6, 11). "So Israel settled in the land of

Goshen. . . . '' (47:27a). And Jacob lives out the rest of his days there (47:28). The time draws near for Israel/Jacob to die, so he bequeaths his legacy and pronounces his last words (47:29–48:22 + 49:29-33). Jacob dies (49:33) and is buried in the cave at Machpelah in Canaan (50:12-13), the burial place of the patriarchs (Gen 23; 49:29-32).

From 45:28 onwards there is a solemn buildup towards the conclusion of the patriarchal period (45:28; 46:2-4; 47:7-9; 47:29-31; 48:1-22; 49:1, 29-33; 50:13). Jacob puts Joseph under oath to bury him in the grave of the patriarchs: "When I lie with my fathers, bring me out of Egypt and bury me in their grave" (47:30). With his very last words, Jacob recalls solemnly the burial of Abraham and Sarah, Isaac and Rebekah, and his own wife Leah in the cave in the field of Machpelah which "Abraham acquired from Ephron the Hittite as a burial plot" (49:29-32; for the burial of Rachel, cf. 35:16-20; 48:7). He is then "gathered to his people" (49:33b). Finally, "his sons brought him to the land of Canaan and buried him in the cave of the field of Machpelah, the field which Abraham acquired as a burial plot from Ephron the Hittite east of Mamre" (50:13). The sons of Jacob bury their father, just as the sons of Abraham (25:9) and the sons of Isaac (35:29) had buried their fathers. The era of the patriarchs has ended. They rest in peace together at Machpelah in Canaan.

The conclusion is: the Joseph story in the stricter sense is a unity; the story of Jacob's old age is coherent and continuous. From chapter 46 onwards, the end of the Joseph story and the end of the Jacob story have been woven together, a solemn ending to the patriarchal story being built into the latter. The narrator or an editor links the patriarchal period with the future of the "sons of Israel" (50:25) in Joseph's last words (50:24-25). There is also what is commonly known as "additional" material, the list of Israelites who went down into Egypt (46:8-27), the account of Joseph's economic measures in Egypt (47:13-26), and the "blessings of Jacob" (49:2-27).

The individual roles of Reuben and Judah should be noted. Reuben, as the eldest of the brothers and so with a responsibility for the young Joseph, does not want Joseph to suffer any bodily harm; he plans to restore him to his father (37:21-22, 29); he takes this up again when, years later, the brothers are made very conscious of their crime (42:21-22); then he rashly offers his own two sons as "sacrifice" to guarantee Benjamin's safety (42:37). Judah intervenes to prevent bloodshed, but is content to sell Joseph into slavery

(37:25-27). He plays a prominent role in chapters 43–44; first, he goes guarantee for Benjamin and persuades Joseph to allow Benjamin to go down to Egypt with his brothers (43:8-10); he pleads eloquently with Joseph, playing on the bond between Jacob and Benjamin and on his father's grief. It is Judah whom Jacob sends on ahead to meet Joseph. This has led D. B. Redford (1970) to postulate an original "Reuben version" of the Joseph story which was combined with a later "Judah version," and worked over by a redactor, both versions having their origin in the period 650–550 B.C.E. H.-C. Schmitt (1980) reverses the order; the Judah version from the period of the early monarchy is the original version, while the Reuben version comes from the exilic or post-exilic period. H. Seebass (1978) is impressed by the prominence given to Judah in the text which lies before us. He notes further that Judah exercises the function of a judge in the Tamar story (38:24-26), and that Judah is set over Joseph in the blessings of Jacob (49:8-12 as against 49:22-26). He concludes that 49:2-28 is no mere "insertion" from a later hand, but an indispensable part of the patriarchal narrative which began in 12:1-3. Certainly, the prominence given to Judah indicates a period of writing and composition when the tribe of Judah was prominent. This, of course, covers some centuries of the monarchy.

THE JOSEPH STORY AND WISDOM

In a very influential essay, Gerhard von Rad (Germ. 1953; Eng. 1966) linked the Joseph story with the wisdom tradition of the royal court. He concluded that "the Joseph narrative is a didactic wisdom-story which leans heavily upon influences emanating from Egypt, not only with regard to its conception of an educational ideal, but also in its fundamental theological ideas" (1966:300). Von Rad developed the wisdom theme in the later editions of his commentary on Genesis. He saw the portrait of Joseph as that of a young man, well educated and conscientious, trusting and trustworthy, just as the wisdom teachers taught. Joseph was an official at court (1976 [tenth ed.]:358). But there are limitations to von Rad's portrait of Joseph as a wisdom figure. The wisdom elements are restricted to chapters 40–41 where a number of the qualities of Joseph elaborated by von Rad do appear. Joseph suggests that Pharaoh look about for "a wise and intelligent man" (41:33, *nābôn wĕ ḥākām*) to supervise the administration of the land. Pharaoh takes up these words and applies them to Joseph (41:39). But one cannot sustain the court-wisdom origin of other elements in the story. The wife of Potiphar in chapter 39 (see *Comment*) is the spurned woman rather than the seductress against whom the Book of Proverbs warns (Prov 2:16-19; 5:1-23; 6:20-25). The key theological passages (45:5-8; 50:17-21) are less "man proposes but God disposes" (cf. Prov 16:9; 19:21; the Wisdom of Amenemopet xix:16 "One thing are the words which men say, another is that which the god does" [ANET 423]) than the overarching action of God into which the brothers are taken up (see *Comment*).

THE JOSEPH STORY AND EGYPT

There is no parallel to the Joseph story as a whole in extra-biblical literature. But some sections, covered in more detail in the commentary, have an Egyptian background, near or remote: the attempted seduction by Potiphar's wife, the interpretation of dreams, the tradition of seven lean years, the viceroy of Egypt (all in chs. 39–41). There is a general knowledge of court protocol (41:37-45), of dining customs (43:32), of divination (44:4-5). But there is no interest in the great buildings or the general culture of Egypt. One can scarcely allege Joseph's words to his brothers: "Tell my father of the dignity that is mine in Egypt and of all that you have seen. . . ." (45:13), in favor of an interest in things Egyptian. J. Vergote (1958) has argued that the Joseph story reflects much ancient Egyptian regal, social, and economic life. But D. B. Redford (1970) takes up twenty-three elements used to support ancient Egyptian influence and argues that they need only reflect practices of the middle of the first millennium B.C.E. The truth is probably a mingling of these two views. Practices first attested in writings or reliefs in the middle of the first millennium would have had a long history. They would not have appeared suddenly on the stage of ancient Near East without previous and lengthy rehearsal. Palestine had been trading with Egypt since at least 2000 B.C.E.; the remains of temples at Byblos show a marked Egyptian influence and date from the nineteenth century; and the Tell-el-Amarna correspondence of the fourteenth century between the "king of 'Jerusalem' " and the Egyptian Pharaoh reveals details of the small Canaanite dependencies. It should be no surprise that Egyptian influence has left its mark.

THE LITERARY FORM OF THE JOSEPH STORY

Gressmann described the Joseph story as a *Novelle,* a description taken up by von Rad (cf. 1.(a) above), and by many commentators since. It is in order to use modern European literary terms to describe the literature of the ancient Near East which grew out of a very different civilization 2500–4000 years ago, provided that one is aware of the limitations under which one is working. The modern terms can be used only analogously, and even so only with severe limitations. One cannot force ancient writings into modern categories.

The terms *novelle* (old French), *novela* (Spanish), *novella* (Italian), and later *Novelle* (German), have their origin in the Renaissance period; they describe certain "romances," longer or shorter, which tell of the exploits of heroes. The English term "novel," and its European equivalent, Roman, are not suitable to describe the Joseph story which is neither long enough nor broad enough to come under this category. One has only to consult Benno von Wiese's *Novelle* (eighth ed., 1982), with its twenty pages of bibliography, and the contributions on "Novelle" in the J. B. Metzler *Deutsche Literaturgeschichte. Von den Anfängen bis zur Gegenwart* (1984 second ed.:164–66) and the *Metzler Literatur Lexikon* (1984:308–10) to realize how difficult it is to agree about what precisely the term covers. The term "short-story" can be reasonably applied to chapters 39–41 of the Joseph story—Joseph's rise-fall-elevation in Egypt. But it is a short-story within a short-story as this term can describe chapters 37; 39-41; 42-45, as well, though they cover a period of some twenty-two years; Joseph is seventeen years old at the beginning (37:2b); he is thirty when he enters Pharaoh's service (41:46); there have been seven years of plenty and two years of famine when Joseph makes himself known to his brothers (45:6). But time does not always matter that much to the storyteller.

It is misleading to describe "The Joseph Story" as a *Novelle*, without further precision, as happens at times, giving the impression perhaps that the term covers chapters 37–50. Let us be content with what we have—a short-story, chapters 37; 39–45, which contains within it what could be an independent short-story as indicated above, chapters 39–41, but which itself in the present context is essential to chapters 37; 39–45. We have already seen that in chapters 46–50 the conclusions of both the Jacob story and the patriarchal story as a whole are woven together with the conclusion of the Joseph story (50:17-21 + 50:22-26 [edited]), to which has been "added" (by whom?) an enumeration (46:8-27), a report of economic measures undertaken by Joseph (47:13-26), and a series of tribal sayings/blessings (49:2-28a).

THE DATE OF THE JOSEPH STORY

We have noted that J. Vergote (1958) has argued that the Joseph story reflects much ancient Egyptian regal, social, and economic history and that D. B. Redford (1970) has undertaken to explain these Egyptian traits from Egyptian writings and monuments of the middle of the first millennium B.C.E. Redford has also proposed that the alleged Reuben and Judah versions of the story had their origin and were joined together at this period. Gressmann (1923:16) maintained that the tribal motifs were so strong that the nucleus of the story must be older than 1000 B.C.E. Von Rad (1966; 1972–76) and Westermann (1986:29) favor the Solomonic period for the origin of the story and the Egyptian influence. And T.N.D. Mettinger in his work on Solomonic state officials concludes: "Thus I take the Joseph narrative to be a literary unit of didactic character, its setting being the wisdom court in Jerusalem in the Solomonic-post-Solomonic period. In this setting a narrative with such a strong Egyptian flavor is wholly comprehensible" (1971:154). Thus there is a strong, but by no means universal, opinion which dates the origin and formation of the Joseph story in the early period of the monarchy. The opinion of Frank Crüsemann (1978:143–54) should be noted here. The story, he maintains, comes out of the davidic-solomonic period and, with its image of a wise one, is a typical representative of "solomonic enlightenment." It is concerned with nothing less than the attempt to legitimize royal taxation by arguing from the internal politics of provision for the future. The goal of the story is reconciliation (ch. 50). This is achieved on the basis of Joseph's particular role of dominion. At the beginning (37:5-11) this role is rejected; at the end it is accepted (50:15-21) and acknowledged in its divine origin. The story is a model for divided Israel: internal reconciliation between lord and dependents: an acknowledgement of power that maintains life and that taxes and provides for the future, and that recognizes that the subjects are not the lord's slaves but God's servants.

1. Joseph Sold into Egypt
(37:1-36 + 39:1)

37:1 Now Jacob settled in the land where his father had sojourned in the land of Canaan. ²This is the story of Jacob. Joseph was seventeen years old; he was guarding sheep, an (attendant) boy to the sons of his father's wives Bilhah and Zilpah, and he brought a bad report of them to their father.

³Israel loved Joseph more than his brothers because he was the son of his old age; he made him a sleeved tunic. ⁴When his brothers saw that their father loved him more than them, they hated him and could not so much as greet him in peace.
⁵Now Joseph had a dream, and when he told it to his brothers they hated him even more. ⁶He said to them: Listen to this dream which I have had. ⁷We were out in the field binding sheaves when my sheaf rose and stood upright while your sheaves gathered round and bowed down to mine. ⁸His brothers said to him: Are you going to be king over us or ruler over us? And they hated him still more because of his dream and what he said. ⁹And he had yet another dream which he told to his brothers. He said: I have had another dream: the sun and the moon and eleven stars were bowing down to me. ¹⁰When he told his father and his brothers, his father rebuked him and said to him: What is this dream that you have had? Am I and your mother and your brothers to bow down to the ground before you? ¹¹So his brothers were jealous of him, but his father pondered the matter.
¹²His brothers had gone to pasture his father's sheep at Shechem. ¹³Israel said to Joseph: Your brothers are pasturing the sheep at Shechem. Come, I will send you to them. He said: I am ready. ¹⁴Go then, he said to him, and see if it is well with your brothers and well with the sheep and bring me back word. So he sent him from the valley of Hebron and he came to Shechem. ¹⁵A man met him as he was wandering in the fields and asked him: What are you looking for? ¹⁶I am looking for my brothers. Could you tell me where they are pasturing the sheep? ¹⁷The man said to him: They have moved from here. In fact I heard them saying: Let us go on to Dothan. So Joseph went after his brothers and found them at Dothan. ¹⁸When they saw him in the distance, and before he drew near to them, they plotted to kill him. ¹⁹They said to each other: Look, the master-dreamer, here he comes. ²⁰Now is our chance to kill him and throw him into one of the pits and say that a wild animal has eaten him. Then we shall see what his dreams are worth. ²¹When Reuben heard this he tried to save him from their hands and said: Let us not take his life. ²²So Reuben said to them: Don't shed blood. Throw him into this pit in the wilderness, but do him no harm. He wanted to save him from them and bring him back to his father. ²³When Joseph came up to his brothers, they stripped off his tunic, the sleeved tunic that he was wearing. ²⁴They took hold of him and threw him into the pit; the pit was empty; there was no water in it.
²⁵ᵃThey sat down to eat.
²⁵ᵇWhen they looked up, they saw a caravan of Ishmaelites coming from Gilead on their way down to Egypt with their camels carrying gum, balm, and resin.

²⁶Judah said to his brothers: What is to be gained by killing our brother and covering up his blood? ²⁷Come, let us sell him to the Ishmaelites and let us not lay our hands on him; he is our brother, our own flesh. His brothers agreed.

²⁸ᵃMeanwhile some Midianite merchants who were passing by drew Joseph up out of the pit,

²⁸ᵇand sold Joseph to the Ishmaelites for twenty silver pieces and they brought Joseph down to Egypt.

²⁹When Reuben returned to the pit, Joseph was not there; he tore his garments.

³⁰He returned to his brothers and said: The boy is not there—and I—where do I turn?

³¹Then they took Joseph's tunic, slaughtered a goat, and dipped it in the blood. ³²Then they tore the tunic and brought it to their father and said: This is what we have found; do you recognize your son's tunic; is this it, or not? ³³He recognized it and said: My son's tunic; a wild animal has eaten him. ³⁴Then Jacob tore his garments, put sackcloth about his loins, and mourned his son for many days. ³⁵All his sons and daughters came up to console him, but he would not be consoled. And he said: I will go down to the realm of the dead mourning my son. Thus his father wept for him. ³⁶Meanwhile the Midianites sold him to Egypt, to Potiphar, an official of Pharaoh, chief of the guard.

39:1 Now Joseph had been brought down to Egypt, and Potiphar, an official of Pharaoh, chief of the guard, an Egyptian, acquired him from the Ishmaelites who had brought him down there.

Comment

Jacob had returned from Paddan-aram after twenty years and had settled in Hebron where Abraham and Isaac had lived. He and Esau buried Isaac (35:27-29). The story of Jacob is resumed in 37:1 after the long list of the descendants of Esau in chapter 36. The word *tôledôt* in 37:2a can only refer to Jacob and his family and the last years of Jacob's life.

Chapter 37 is well constructed: verse 2b introduces Joseph as a seventeen year old youth; verses 3-4 and verses 5-11 give the two grounds for the brothers' hatred of Joseph; verses 12-17 describe a quiet scene in which Joseph, all alone, is exposed to the brothers' hate; verses 18-24, 25-30 see the brothers plotting; verses 31-35 describe their deceit of their father; verses 25b, 28, 36 provide the account of the sale into slavery.

Joseph is an "attendant boy" (v. 2) to the sons of Bilhah and Zilpah, that is to Dan and Naphtali, Gad and Asher. He brought "a bad report" about them to Jacob. The Hebrew word for "bad report" is *dibbâ;* specifically, it is a (true) report of something bad. It is the word used of the report which the scouts brought back of the promised land (Num 13:32; 14:36, 37). To speak of Joseph as a "bearer of malicious tales" or as indulging in "tale bearing," as do some commentators (e.g., Humphreys 1988:86, 100; 34, 35) is to go beyond the text and to distort the presentation of Joseph. In any case, one should not be surprised that these four brothers may have misbehaved, though there is no indication of what they may have done. A glance at the "form book" shows that Simeon and Levi wreaked wholesale slaughter on the Shechemites (ch. 34), and that "Reuben went and lay with his father's concubine Bilhah" (35:22a). And Judah's conduct to be described in chapter 38 is less than commendable. If the four brothers of 37:2a were guilty of misconduct, they would be running true to the form of the sons of Jacob.

Verses 3-4 are not an immediate narrative continuation of verse 2a; the narrative particle with the appropriate verb form is missing. The verses are a statement of one of the reasons for the brothers' hatred. Throughout the narrative, the reader/listener is in the hands of the storyteller who now sounds themes that are to be taken up later. First, the family peace is broken: "his brothers . . . could not so much as greet him in peace (*šālôm*)" (v. 4). The storyteller heightens the effect of the brothers' hate by repeating the word "hate" three times (vv. 4, 5, 8); their hate culminates in jealousy (v. 11) and is to explode in their plot to get rid of Joseph (vv. 18-30). When Joseph tells his brothers through his dreams that they are to bow before him (*šḥh,* vv. 7, 9, 10), their hate boils over (vv. 5, 8); but later, they do bow before him (*šḥh*, 42:6; 43:26,29) and fall down before him (44:14; 50:18). They ask indignantly if he is to be ruler (*mošēl,* v. 8) over them. He does become ruler (45:8), and they themselves take up the word *mošēl* in their message to Jacob (45:26). Are the sun, moon, and stars in their splendor to do obeisance to him (v. 9)? Yes, they (his father and brothers) are to see his "glory" (*kābôd*) in Egypt (45:13).

It is misguided, contributes in no way to exegesis, and distorts the story to continually designate the young Joseph as does Humphreys (1988) in his recent book: "spoiled brat" (23), "spoiled and boastful brat" (25), "spoiled youth" and "spoiled brat" (87), "spoiled young man" (92), "a boastful, if insensitive self-inflation" (102), "the boasts of a spoiled youth" (108), "boastful, self-centered, and spoiled" (109), "a spoiled youth" (130), "spoiled and pampered" (184)—this is just a selection of passages. Very little of this can be justified from the text, and much of it reads more like popular journalism than sober exegesis. The preferential love of an old father for a young son, a sleeved tunic, and a certain naiveté on Joseph's part, do not justify a long litany of disparagement.

The quiet interlude of verses 12-17 prepares for the outrage that follows. When the brothers, and all are involved, see the "master-dreamer" (v. 19) coming, they call to kill (vv. 18, 20). Only Reuben, the eldest, and so responsible for Joseph to his father (vv. 21-22, 29-30), shows any sense of restraint and propriety. Judah's less bloodthirsty counsel prevails: "What is to be gained by killing our brother and covering up his blood?" (v. 26); but a brother's blood cannot be covered up: "your brother's blood that has been shed is crying out to me from the ground" (Gen 4:10). Judah, however, is quite ready to sell Joseph into slavery, and the brothers agree (v. 27). The brothers strip the sleeved tunic, the symbol of the father's love, from Joseph, dip it in goat's blood, tear it, present it to their father, and let him draw the conclusion (vv. 23, 31-35). The whole extended family, "all his sons and daughters" (v. 35), join in the formal lament. The brothers are mentioned no more, and Jacob's lament: "I will go down to the realm of the dead mourning my son" (v. 35), echoes over the next twenty-two years, to be taken up again in the storyteller's good time in 42:38 (cf. 44:29, 31). There are two incongruities in the chapter. First, Jacob's rebuke to Joseph after he tells the second dream: "Am I and your mother and your brothers to bow down to the ground before you?" (v. 10b) gives the impression that Sarah, whose death is reported in 35:16-20, is still alive, and that Benjamin, the youngest ("eleven stars," v. 9b) is there. But the tradition of 37:5-11 may have grown up independently, or the verses may be part of the license of the storyteller, that is, he is saying that the whole family is to acknowledge Joseph's superior position. Second, there appear to be two traditions of the way in which Joseph was sold into Egypt. The brothers had thrown Joseph into a pit (v. 24). Some Midianite merchants who were passing by drew Joseph out of the pit (v. 28a). The brothers had seen a caravan of Ishmaelites on its way down into Egypt (v. 25b), and at Judah's suggestion decided to sell Joseph to them (vv. 26-27). But the Midianites who had taken Joseph out of the pit sold him to the Ishmaelites (v. 28b) who brought Joseph down to Egypt. When the story of Joseph is taken up again in 39:1, "Potiphar . . . acquired him from the Ishmaelites who had brought him down there." It is said three times that the Ishmaelites brought Joseph down to Egypt (37:28b; 39:1a [implicitly]; 39:1b). It is said that the Midianites sold Joseph "to the Ishmaelites" (37:28b) and "to (*'al,* towards, the place for which he was destined) Egypt" (37:36a). There is no account of the sale of Joseph by the brothers to the Ishmaelites, but only of Judah's proposal (37:26-27). But Reuben, it seems, was not aware of the proposal (37:29-30). There seems to be a mingling of two traditions of the way in which Joseph was disposed of: Ishmaelites, 37:25b, 26-27, 28b; 39:1; Midianites, 37:28a, 28b, 36. One could, of course, explain 37:36 in this way: the Midianites sold Joseph so that he went down to Egypt and ended up as the property of Potiphar. This could be the case, but the exercise arouses the suspicion of "concordism" and does not quite account for the Reuben problem (37:21-22, 29-30).

Notes

1. WHERE HIS FATHER HAD SOJOURNED. Literally, "the land of the sojournings of his father." The word *mĕgûrîm,* sojournings, is an abstract plural formation from the verb *gûr,* to dwell as an alien; it is found in Genesis 17:8; 28:4; 36:7; 37:1; 47:9 (two times); Exodus 6:4; Ezekiel 20:38; Psalm 119:54; Job 18:19; Lamentations 2:22; add Sirach 16:8. It is usually in the combination, "land of sojournings"; in Genesis 47:9, Jacob speaks of "the years of" and "the days of my sojournings"; cf. Ezekiel 20:38.

3. SLEEVED TUNIC. *kĕtonet passîm.* Not a workman's tunic which would have either short sleeves or no sleeves at all, but a tunic of one at leisure.

4. IN PEACE. *šālôm.* In verse 14, Jacob sends Joseph to see if all is well (*šālôm*) with his brothers and the flocks.

5-11. BOW DOWN. The verb is usually derived from the root *šḥh.* Much more likely it is an old *šaf'el* causative form with an in-fixed -t, from the root *ḥwy* (R. Meyer 1969:162-63).

19. MASTER-DREAMER. A reasonable rendering of *ba'al haḥlomôt,* "master of dreams."

28B. TWENTY SILVER PIECES. Cf. Leviticus 27:5, the valuation of a male slave between five years old and twenty. The brothers paid with and were repaid in *kesep,* silver. There was no coined money in Egypt or Palestine before the close of the sixth century B.C.E.

32-33. YOUR SON'S TUNIC. Cf. Exodus 22:13; evidence before the court.

2. Judah and Tamar
(38:1-30)

¹At that time Judah left his brothers and pitched his tent with an Adullamite named Hirah. ²And there Judah saw the daughter of a Canaanite named Shua; he married her and went to her. ³She became pregnant and bore a son and called him Er. ⁴She became pregnant again and bore a son and called him Onan. ⁵She became pregnant yet again and bore a son and called him Shelah. ⁶Judah took a wife for Er, his first-born, whose name was Tamar. ⁷But Er, Judah's first-born, was wicked in the eyes of YHWH so that YHWH killed him. ⁸So Judah said to Onan: Go to your brother's wife and do a brother-in-law's duty and raise up descendants to your brother. ⁹But Onan knew that the descendants would not be his; and so whenever he went to his brother's wife he spilled his seed on the ground so as not to give descendants to his brother. ¹⁰But what he did was wicked in the eyes of YHWH who killed him also. ¹¹Then Judah said to Tamar, his daughter-in-law: Go back to your father's house as a widow until Shelah, my son, has grown up; because he was afraid that he too would die like his brothers. So Tamar went and lived in her father's house.

¹²In the course of time Shua's daughter, Judah's wife, died. After Judah had mourned her, he and his associate, the Adullamite, went up to the sheep-shearers at Timnah. ¹³When Tamar was told, your father-in-law is going up to Timnah to shear his sheep, ¹⁴she took off her widow's clothes, veiled herself, draped herself, and sat at the gate to Enaim which is on the way to Timnah because she knew that Shelah had grown up and that she had not been given to him as wife. ¹⁵When Judah saw her, he thought that she was a prostitute because she had veiled her face. ¹⁶He turned to her where she sat by the roadside and said: Come, let me go with you! He did not know that she was his daughter-in-law. She said: what will you give me so as to come to me? ¹⁷He said: I will send you a kid from the flock. She said: But give me a pledge until you send it. ¹⁸He said: What pledge will I give you? She said: Your signet ring, your cord, and the staff that you carry. He gave them to her; then he went to her and she became pregnant by him. ¹⁹Then she rose up and went home. She took off her veil and put on her widow's clothes again. ²⁰When Judah sent the kid

by his associate the Adullamite to recover the pledge from the woman, he could not find her. ²¹He asked the men of the place: Where is the temple-prostitute (who used to sit) by the roadside at Enaim? But they said: There was no temple-prostitute here. ²²So he went back to Judah and said: I did not find her; and the men of the place said: There was no temple-prostitute here. ²³So Judah said: Let her keep it lest we be mocked. Yes, I did send a kid, but you did not find her.

²⁴Some three months later Judah was told: Tamar, your daughter-in-law has played the prostitute and is pregnant because of her conduct. Judah said: Bring her out and let her be burnt. ²⁵As she was being brought out, she sent to her father-in-law and said: I am pregnant by the man to whom these belong. See if you recognize whose these are—the signet ring, the cord, and the staff. ²⁶Judah recognized them and said: Justice is with her, not with me. Why did I not give her to my son, Shelah. He did not have intercourse with her again.

²⁷When the time of her bearing came, there were twins in her womb. ²⁸While she was giving birth, one of them put out a hand. The midwife took it and tied a scarlet thread on it saying: This one came out first. ²⁹As soon as he drew back his hand, his brother came out. She said: So you have made the breach! And she named him Perez. ³⁰Then his brother who had the scarlet thread on his hand came out; he was named Zerah.

Comment

The story of Judah is not part of the Joseph story, which it interrupts, as is clear from 39:1 which takes up 37:36 after the break in the narrative. But it is an aside in the conclusion of the Jacob story inasmuch as it narrates an episode in the life of one of Jacob's sons. There has already been one story about the sons Simeon and Levi (ch. 34) and a note about Reuben (35:22). The story is carefully constructed. Verses 1-11, very factual and prosaic, set the stage for the main action in verses 12-26, with the dramatic denouement in verses 24-26. There follows the account of the birth and naming of the twins in verses 27-30, as it were an epilogue, but not integral to the structure and purpose of the story as such.

The action of act one (vv. 1-11) takes place within a radius of about sixteen kilometers of Hebron where the "Jacob people" are living side-by-side with the Canaanites and a son of Jacob can freely marry a daughter of a Canaanite. This is an indication of the "early" (pre-1000 B.C.E.) origins of the story. The place names can be accounted for readily. Adullam, whence comes Judah's associate (v.

1), is about sixteen kilometers northwest of Hebron and is probably the modern site *esh-Sheik-Madkur* (Josh 15:35; 1 Sam 22:1; Micah 1:15). Chezib, mentioned only here in the Old Testament, is very likely the equivalent of Achzib (Josh 15:44; Micah 1:14) on the site of Tell-el-Beda, five kilometers south of Adullam. Enaim may be Enam (Josh 15:34) near Adullam (but see *Notes*). Timnah is more likely the Timnah of Joshua 15:37, in the region southeast of Hebron than that of Joshua 15:10; 19:45. J. A. Emerton (1975) discusses the geography fully.

No reason is given why Judah "left his brothers" (v. 1a), and the Joseph story proper (chs. 37; 39–45; parts of chs. 46–50) is not aware of this tradition, though Judah's sons, Er, Onan, and Shelah, as well as Perez and Zerah, are mentioned among the "sons of Israel" who went into Egypt (46:8, 12). The wife whom Judah took for his son Er, Tamar, was Canaanite (v. 6). Er's early death is attributed to some unknown misdeed simply because it was an early death (v. 7). Judah requires his second son, Onan, to carry out the levirate duty codified in Deuteronomy 25:5-10: when a husband had died leaving no son, his next brother was required to go to the widow and beget a son from her; this son was to be reckoned as a son of the deceased husband so as to perpetuate his name, and not as a son of the brother who fathered him. The brother of the deceased did not marry the widow, but simply begot a son in the name of his brother. Onan is unwilling to carry out this duty; his early death is seen as a punishment from YHWH (vv. 8-10). Judah, fearful of an early loss of his third son, Shelah, postpones the duty of giving him to Tamar to beget a son (v. 11). The first part of the story ends with Tamar, a widow, sent back to her father's house and deprived of her legal right. Judah has been the main actor in part one.

Tamar is the central figure in part two (vv. 12-26). These fifteen verses are narrative in the strict sense, that is, the account of an event as it moves through episodes to a climax and resolution. The storyteller passes no judgment on the conduct of Tamar or Judah. He allows the narrative to speak for itself: there are the preparatory events (vv. 12, 13-14) which underscore Tamar's sense of the injustice done to her (v. 14b), the business-like negotiations between "prostitute" and client and the equally business-like demand for a pledge on payment by the "prostitute" (vv. 16-18), Judah's attempt to redeem the pledge (vv. 20-22), and his genuine satisfaction that he has done his duty in this episode (v. 23). There is a pause in the action of the narrative (v. 24a). The tension rises with the report of Tamar's pregnancy (v. 24b); it reaches and is maintained at its climax as Judah pronounces judgment and Tamar is brought out to be burnt (vv. 24c, 25a); the resolution is left to the last moment (v. 25b); the pledges are produced and recognized (vv. 25b, 26a), and Judah acknowledges that the law is on Tamar's side (v. 26b). The narrative really ends here. The point at issue is not whether Tamar's action of presenting herself as a prostitute and deceiving Judah was right or wrong, though she was as close to the line as one could be, nor whether Judah was right or wrong in having intercourse with a (ritual?) prostitute; it is a matter of justice before a law/custom of the place and time by which both Judah and Tamar were bound.

Judah and his associate were going up to the sheep-shearing at Timnah. This was very likely a festival (Gen 31:19; 1 Sam 25:2-8; 2 Sam 13:23-29). Judah thought that Tamar was an ordinary prostitute (v. 15, *zonāh*). When the Adullamite went looking for her to redeem the pledge, he asked about a temple- or sacred-prostitute (vv. 21 [two times], 22, *qĕdēšâ*). It may be that Judah thought that commerce with a temple-prostitute would advance the fertility of the flocks. There are several warnings against ritual prostitution in the Old Testament (Deut 23:19 [18]; Hos 4:13-14; Prov 7:1-27). The pledges that the "prostitute" required from Judah, his signet-ring, his cord, and his staff, were of little material, but great personal value. When it is announced that Tamar is pregnant, Judah exercises the right of the head of the family, even though she is living with her own family (vv. 11b, 19a), and orders her to be burned (v. 24). He considers her bound to his family and under obligation to wait for the third son, Shelah, to carry out the levirate duty, even though he has denied and continues to deny her this right (v. 14b). Burning seems to have been an older form of punishment; Deuteronomy 22:21-24 prescribes stoning.

After the denouement, the twins whom Tamar is to bear are seen to be legitimate. Perez (the breach-maker) and Zerah are, with Tamar, in the line of Davidic ancestry (1 Chr 2:1-14), and all three are mentioned in the genealogy of Jesus (Matt 1:3). The list of Perez' descendants in Ruth 4:18-22 reaches its climax in David.

The story could well end with verse 26a where Judah acknowledges that Tamar has the law on her side. Verse 26b and verses 27-30 do not advance the story any further. Verse 26b states that Judah has acknowledged that Tamar is a member of the family and consequently intercourse with her is forbidden; verses 27-30 are in themselves irrelevant to the story, for which it does not matter whether

Tamar has conceived twins or not; all that matters for the story is that she has become pregnant. The presence of the verses may be due to the fact that the davidic line is traced from Judah (see references above).

As to the place and period when the story originated, one can say little with certainty. "Jacob people" and Canaanites are living side by side at peace and are intermarrying, and the area within which the events take place is around Hebron. One might put the story at about 1000 B.C.E., give or take one hundred years. Emerton (1979:414-15) looks to a period between the eleventh and eighth centuries B.C.E. G. A. Rendsburg (1986) has worked out a very intricate and tenuous parallel between names in the Judah-Tamar story, Judah-Hirah-(daughter of) Shua-Er-Onan-Shelah-Tamar and a series of names from the David story, David-Hiram-Bathsheba (deceased first-born of David and Bathsheba)-Amnon-Solomon-Tamar, and concludes that "the story was written in the 900s to inform its readership not so much about Judah and his family, but about David and his. The author's motive is clear: to poke fun at the royal family" (444). The author's motive may be clear, but Rendsburg is the first to see it.

Notes

6. TAMAR. The name means "palm tree." G.R.H. Wright (1982) is of the opinion that behind the story lies the mythical tradition of a king who greatly desired his own daughter or of a princess who greatly desired her father. The union took place at a festival or at harvest time as a result of some scheming. A child was conceived and the mother transformed into a tree. Joseph is buried under a tree at Shechem (Josh 24:32) and is likened to a tree in the blessings of Jacob (Gen 49:22). Joseph's birth is in the context of the fruit of the mandragora tree (Gen 30:14-24). The Tamar story, according to Wright, "is essentially non-historical and derives from the myth of the dying and returning savior begotten in incest and born in/by/from the tree" (529). Joseph "dies" and returns to his family. This is the rationale for the insertion of the Tamar story into the Joseph story.

7. GO TO YOUR BROTHER'S WIFE. The levirate marriage (Deut 25:5-10). The word "levirate" derives from the Latin *levir,* brother-in-law.

14. ENAIM. NEB reads: "where the road forks in two directions on the way to Timnath," and in verse 21: "where the road forks," cf. G. R. Driver (1958:72). Driver does not consider Enaim to be a place name, but links it with an Arabic noun *'ayum* meaning "eye" and a "tract of country."

3. Joseph in Egypt: His Rise, Fall, and Elevation (Chs. 39–41)

¹Now Joseph had been brought down to Egypt and Potiphar, an official of Pharaoh, chief of the guard, an Egyptian, bought him from the Ishmaelites who had brought him down there.

²YHWH was with Joseph so that he became a successful man; and Joseph lived in the house of his Egyptian master. ³When his master saw that YHWH was with him, and was giving him success in all that he did, ⁴Joseph found favor in his eyes; he put him in charge and entrusted him with his household and with all that he had. ⁵From the time that he entrusted him with his household and all that he had, YHWH blessed the house of the Egyptian because of Joseph, and the blessing of YHWH was upon all that he had both in house and in field. ⁶He left all that he had in Joseph's care and concerned himself with nothing but the food that he ate.

Now Joseph was handsome and of fine appearance. ⁷It was after these events that his master's wife set her eyes on Joseph. She said: Lie with me. ⁸But he refused and said to his master's wife: Think of my master; he does not know more than I about what goes on in the household; he has put everything that he has in my hands. ⁹He is not greater in this house than I; he has withheld nothing from me but you, inasmuch as you are his wife. How could I do so great a wrong as this and sin against God? ¹⁰She kept asking Joseph day after day, but he refused to lie with her or to be with her. ¹¹One day when he came to the house to do his work, none of the members of the household were there. ¹²She took hold of his cloak and said: Lie with me! But he left his cloak in her hand and fled and ran from the house. ¹³When she saw that he had left his cloak in her hand and fled outside, ¹⁴she called out to the men of the household and said to them: Look, my husband has brought a Hebrew to us to play with us; he came to be with me, but I cried out aloud. ¹⁵When he heard me raise my voice and cry out, he left his cloak by me and fled and ran outside. ¹⁶So she kept his cloak by her until his master came home. ¹⁷Then she told him her story; she said: The Hebrew slave whom you brought to us (came to) play with me. ¹⁸But when I raised my voice and cried

out, he left his cloak by me and fled outside. ¹⁹When his master heard
the story that his wife told him, saying this is what your slave did
to me, he was very angry. ²⁰Joseph's master took him and put him
into the place of detention where the king's prisoners were held; he
remained in the place of detention. ²¹But YHWH was with Joseph
and remained steadfast to him so that he found favor with the chief
of the place of detention. ²²So the chief of the place of detention put
all the detainees who were in the place of detention under Joseph's
care; and he was in charge of all their work. ²³He did not concern
himself with anything that he had put under Joseph's care, inasmuch
as YHWH was with him and was giving him success.

40:1 It was after these events that the cupbearer of the king of Egypt
and the baker offended their master the king of Egypt. ²Pharaoh was
angry with his two officials, the chief cupbearer and the chief baker.
³He put them in custody in the house of the chief of the guard, in
the place of detention where Joseph was held. ⁴The chief of the guard
appointed Joseph their overseer; they remained some time in custody.
⁵On the same night each of the two had a dream, each needing its
own interpretation, the cupbearer and the baker of the king of Egypt
who were held in the place of detention. ⁶When Joseph came to them
in the morning, he saw that they were troubled. ⁷So he asked Pharaoh's
officials who were in custody with him in the house of his master:
Why are your faces downcast today? ⁸They said to him: We have had
a dream and there is no one to interpret it. Joseph said to them: Do
not interpretations belong to God? Now tell them to me. ⁹The chief
cupbearer told Joseph his dream: In my dream there was a vine before me; ¹⁰there were three branches on the vine; it budded, it blos-
somed, and its clusters ripened into grapes. ¹¹Pharaoh's cup was in
my hand; I took the grapes and squeezed them into Pharaoh's cup
and put the cup in Pharaoh's hand. ¹²Then Joseph said to him: This
is its interpretation. The three branches are three days. ¹³Within three
days Pharaoh will raise your head and restore you to your post and
you will put the cup in Pharaoh's hand as you used to do when you
were his cupbearer. ¹⁴But remember me when things go well with you,
and please keep faith with me—remember me before Pharaoh and
get me out of this place. ¹⁵For I was abducted from the land of the
Hebrews and I have done nothing that I should be put in a dungeon.

¹⁶When the chief baker saw that the interpretation was favorable,
he said to Joseph: I too had a dream; there were three baskets of white
bread on my head. ¹⁷In the top basket there were all sorts of baked
goods for Pharaoh, but the birds were eating them from the basket
on my head. ¹⁸Joseph answered: This is its interpretation. The three
baskets are three days. ¹⁹Within three days Pharaoh will raise your

head from you and will hang you on a tree and the birds will eat your flesh from you. ²⁰The third day was Pharaoh's birthday and he gave a feast for all his courtiers, and he raised the head of the chief cup-bearer and the head of the chief baker in the presence of his court-iers. ²¹He restored the chief cupbearer to his position, and he put the cup in Pharaoh's hand. ²²But the chief baker he hanged as Joseph had interpreted to them. ²³But the chief cupbearer did not remember Joseph; he forgot him.

41:1 Some two years later Pharaoh had a dream. He was standing by the Nile ²when seven cows, sleek and fat, came up from the river and grazed among the reeds. ³Then seven more cows, gaunt and lean, came up from the river and stood by them on the bank of the Nile. ⁴The gaunt and lean cows ate the seven sleek and fat cows. Then Phar-aoh woke up. ⁵He went to sleep and had a second dream. Seven ears of grain, full and good, were growing on one stalk. ⁶Then seven ears, thin and shrivelled by the east wind, grew up after them. ⁷The thin ears swallowed the seven full and good ears. Then Pharaoh woke up. It was a dream. ⁸In the morning he was troubled in mind; he sent and summoned all the priestly diviners and sages of Egypt and told them his dream; but no one was able to interpret it for Pharaoh. ⁹Then the chief cupbearer spoke up to Pharaoh: Let me now remember my sin. ¹⁰Pharaoh was angry with his servants and put me in custody in the house of the chief of the guard, me and the chief baker. ¹¹Both of us, he and I, had a dream on the same night, each dream needing its own interpretation. ¹²There was a Hebrew attendant there with us, a slave of the chief of the guard; we told him our dreams and he in-terpreted each dream for us. ¹³And it turned out just as he interpreted them to us; me, he restored to my post, him, he hanged. ¹⁴So Phar-aoh sent and summoned Joseph. They hurried and brought him out of the dungeon; he shaved and changed his clothes and came into Pharaoh's presence. ¹⁵Pharaoh said to Joseph: I have had a dream and no one can interpret it. I have heard of you. It is said that when you hear a dream you can interpret it. ¹⁶Joseph answered Pharaoh: Not I, but God will answer for the well-being of Pharaoh. ¹⁷Then Phar-aoh said to Joseph: In my dream, I was standing by the bank of the Nile. ¹⁸Seven cows, sleek and fat, came up from the river and grazed among the reeds. ¹⁹Then seven more cows came up, gaunt, ugly, and lean. I have never seen such ugly cows in the whole of the land of Egypt. ²⁰Then the seven lean and ugly cows ate the first seven, the fat ones. ²¹And though they swallowed them, no one could tell that they were in their bellies; they looked as ugly as before. ²²Then I saw in my dream: seven ears of grain, full and good, were growing on one stalk; ²³then seven more ears, withered, thin, and shrivelled by the east wind, grew up after them. ²⁴The withered ears swallowed up the seven good ears. I spoke to the priestly diviners, but none could explain it to me.

²⁵Then Joseph said to Pharaoh: Pharaoh's dream is one dream. God has told Pharaoh what he is going to do. ²⁶The seven good cows are seven years and the seven good ears are seven years. This is all one dream. ²⁷The seven gaunt and lean cows that came up after them are seven years. And the seven withered ears, shrivelled by the east wind, are seven years of famine. ²⁸It is as I have said to Pharaoh: God has made known to Pharaoh what he is going to do. ²⁹Seven years are coming in which there will be abundance in the whole of Egypt. ³⁰Then there will come seven years of famine after them, and the abundance in the land of Egypt will be forgotten, and the famine will destroy the land. ³¹There will be no sign of the abundance in the land because of the famine which will be very severe. ³²That Pharaoh has dreamt twice means that God has decided and will soon bring it about.

³³Now Pharaoh should look about for a wise and intelligent man and put him in charge of the land of Egypt. ³⁴Pharaoh should appoint supervisors over the land and take one-fifth of the produce of the land of Egypt during the seven years of abundance. ³⁵They should collect all the produce of these good years that are coming and put the grain under Pharaoh's control in the cities, and guard it. ³⁶This grain will serve as a reserve for the land against the seven years of famine that will come in the land of Egypt. Thus the land will not be wiped out by the famine.

³⁷The plan pleased Pharaoh and his courtiers. ³⁸Pharaoh said to his courtiers: Can we find a man like this who has the spirit of God? ³⁹Then Pharaoh said to Joseph: Inasmuch as God has made known all this to you, there is no one as wise and intelligent as you. ⁴⁰You will be in charge of my household and all my people will obey you. Only the throne, I myself, will be above you. ⁴¹Then Pharaoh said to Joseph: I appoint you over the whole land of Egypt. ⁴²Pharaoh took his signet ring from his hand and put it on Joseph's; he dressed him in fine linen and put a chain of gold around his neck. ⁴³He had him ride in his second chariot and the cry went before him "Abrek." Thus he set him over the whole land of Egypt. ⁴⁴Pharaoh said to Joseph: I am Pharaoh. Without you, no one shall move hand or foot in the whole land of Egypt. ⁴⁵Pharaoh named Joseph Zephenath-paneah, and he gave him as wife Asenath, daughter of Potiphera, priest of On. Then Joseph went out over the land of Egypt. ⁴⁶Joseph was thirty years old when he entered the service of Pharaoh the king of Egypt. Then Joseph left Pharaoh's presence and traversed the land of Egypt.

⁴⁷The land produced an abundance of grain in the seven years of plenty. ⁴⁸He gathered all the grain of the seven years in the land of Egypt and brought it to the cities, storing in each the grain from the surrounding fields. ⁴⁹So Joseph stored up grain like the sand of the sea, such a huge quantity that he stopped measuring it; it could not be measured. ⁵⁰Two sons were born to Joseph before the years of famine came, born to him by Asenath, the daughter of Potiphera, priest of On. ⁵¹Joseph named the firstborn Manasseh because, he said, God has made me forget all my hardship and my father's house. ⁵²He named the second Ephraim because, he said, God has made me fruitful in the land of my hardship. ⁵³When the seven years of abundance came to an end in the land of Egypt, ⁵⁴seven years of famine began as Joseph had said; there was famine in all lands, but in the whole of the land of Egypt there was bread. ⁵⁵When the famine spread through Egypt, the people cried out to Pharaoh for bread. Pharaoh told all Egypt: Go to Joseph and do what he tells you. ⁵⁶The famine spread over the land. Joseph opened all the reserves of grain and sold it to the Egyptians, because the famine was severe in the land of Egypt. ⁵⁷The whole world came to Egypt to buy grain from Joseph, because the famine was severe everywhere.

Comment

The writer takes up the story of Joseph after the Judah-Tamar episode, resuming 37:25b, 26-27; 37:28b; 37:36, and repeating word for word the name and office of the Egyptian who acquired Joseph: " . . . Potiphar, an official of Pharaoh, chief of the guard . . . " (37:36b; 39:1b). Chapters 39–41 should be read and commented on as a unit, not because they have been cut anew from whole cloth, but because, whatever the previous history of their component parts, they have been arranged and edited and bound together so as to form a coherent story of Joseph's rise-fall-elevation in Egypt. The writer and his sources were familiar with the well-known folktale motifs of the rejected, adulterous woman and of the pauper/stranger/foreigner who is called in to solve a problem that has baffled the local experts and is rewarded for his service. The motif of the self-composed, educated, wise young man appears in chapters 40–41. It may be that there were three different stories available to the writer, of a rejected adulterous wife, of an explanation of prisoners' dreams, of a king's dreams and their solution. Be this as it may. All the material at hand has been joined together by the writer. 39:20-23 is fitted into 40:1-3; Joseph and Pharaoh's officials come together in "the place of detention" (39:20, 22; 40:3). Chapter 40 is, in the biblical context, a preparation for chapter 41, and is tied to it nicely by a specific formula. Joseph asks the cupbearer: "But remember me when things go well with you, and please keep faith with me— remember me before Pharaoh and get me out of this place" (40:14). "But the chief cupbearer did not remember Joseph; he forgot him" (40:23). Later, two years later, "the chief cupbearer spoke up to Pharaoh: Let me now remember my sin . . . " (41:9). All is over-layed by the theme that YHWH is with Joseph (39:2, 3, 5, 21, 23; YHWH, because the storyteller is speaking from his perspective), and that God is working in Joseph and is the interpreter of dreams (40:8; 41:16, 25, 32, 38, 39; add 39:9b; Joseph and Pharaoh [vv. 38, 39] each speak from his own perspective). Each of the three chap-ters/stories has its own arc of narrative tension, as Westermann (1986:60) has well pointed out.

Chapter 39. Joseph rises from a state of slavery (v. 1) to a posi-tion of authority and responsibility under the action of YHWH (vv. 2-6a). Verse 6b, "Now Joseph was handsome and of fine appear-ance," prepares the action in scene two: " . . . his master's wife set her eyes on Joseph . . . ." Joseph's rejection of the advances of his master's wife is based on trust confided to him and marital/so-cial justice, a breach of which is a "great wrong" and a "sin against God" (v. 9b). Her persistence meets with resistence which leaves evi-dence in her hands that triggers off her two outbursts (vv. 14-15, 17-18) to two different audiences; they are substantially the same; they are not a sign of "two sources" but part of the dramatic ef-fect. The master's reaction and the punishment are relatively mild, and Joseph is back where he began, in a state of captivity "in the place of detention where the king's detainees were held" (vv. 20, 22). But "YHWH was with Joseph (him)" (vv. 21, 23), so that the narrative arc arrives at a "bridge pylon" matching the one from which it began in verses 2-6a. God's *ḥesed,* steadfast love or faith-ful loyalty, is with Joseph. The action of the drama (vv. 6b-20) has ended and a quiet interlude follows.

Chapter 40. Joseph, though in detention, enjoys a position of trust and limited authority. It was simply "after these events" that two important officials of Pharaoh's household fell into disfavor. There is no indication of how long Joseph had been in custody. Whatever the origins of chapter 40, it is, in its position in the Joseph story, a preparation for Joseph's elevation in chapter 41. When Joseph comes to attend Pharaoh's officials "in the morning," and each men-

tions a dream as the cause of his worry, Joseph makes it clear to
them that he has no system for interpreting dreams but that interpretation belongs to God. Joseph interprets the dream easily and briefly.
The cupbearer is to be reinstated (v. 13). Joseph asks the cupbearer
to keep faith (*ḥesed*) with him and "get me out of this place" (v.
14b) because "I have done nothing that I should be put in a dungeon" (v. 15b; dungeon, Hebr. *bôr,* the same word as used for pit
in 37:20, 22, 24, 28a, 29). But it is two years before the cupbearer
"remembers" (v. 14b, 23; 41:9) Joseph. After the simple and immediate fulfillment of Joseph's interpretation of the dreams (vv.
20-22), there is another period of quiet (v. 23; 41:1a).

Chapter 41. The account of Pharaoh's dream may have been originally an independent narrative. In any case, it has been fitted into
the Joseph story, linked closely with the story of the dreams of the
court officials, elaborated, woven about with the traditional folk-
tale motif of the pauper/stranger/foreigner who solves a problem
and is rewarded, and so becomes an essential part of the story of
Joseph's elevation to the position of viceroy. The two accounts of
Pharaoh's dreams (vv. 1-8, 17-24a), one a report, the other a narration by Pharaoh himself, and of the failure of the priestly diviners
to interpret the dreams (vv. 8, 24b), are not signs of "sources" but
are part of the dramatic movement of the story. They are nicely separated by the cupbearer's sudden "remembering" of Joseph's skills
after a lapse of two years (vv. 9-13) and the summons of Joseph
to Pharaoh's presence. Joseph is brought out of the dungeon (*bôr,*
cf. 40:15b) from which he had asked the cupbearer to have him freed.
Joseph answers Pharaoh's request for an interpretation of his dreams
just as he had answered the cupbearer and baker (v. 16; 40:8b): the
interpretation of dreams belongs to God, not to any divining system, and God will look to Pharaoh's well-being (*šālôm,* v. 16).
Joseph interprets Pharaoh's dreams as quickly and as directly as he
had the dreams of the cupbearer and baker (vv. 25-32). He then goes
on to give Pharaoh advice (vv. 33-36). Joseph has conducted himself like "a wise and intelligent man" (*nābôn wĕ ḥākām*); he now
advises Pharaoh to look about for such a man to appoint as Egypt's
economic administrator (v. 33). Pharaoh perceives that Joseph is
such a man (v. 39) and that he does not interpret dreams according
to the system of the priestly diviners but from God, the god of Pharaoh and the God of Joseph (vv. 38-39). He appoints Joseph viceroy
and invests him with the symbols of office, the ring, the robe, the
gold chain, and puts the second chariot in the land at his disposal

(vv. 40-43). The story of the elevation of an imprisoned foreigner to the office of viceroy could end with verses 44-46. Thirteen years have elapsed since Joseph had narrated his dreams to his brothers (37:2b, Joseph is seventeen; 41:46, Joseph is thirty). Joseph now holds the highest office in Egypt under Pharaoh and has been given a wife (v. 45), daughter of a priest of Heliopolis, northeast of Cairo. So two of the tribes of Israel, Manasseh and Ephraim, are sons of an Egyptian mother, herself the daughter of an Egyptian priest (vv. 50-52). There is a description of Joseph's economic measures (vv. 47-49) and of his administration during the years of famine (vv. 53-57). With the spread of the "famine in all lands, but in the whole of the land of Egypt there was bread" (v. 54b), and the note that "the whole world came to Egypt to buy grain from Joseph, because the famine was severe everywhere" (v. 57), the stage is set for Joseph's family to enter (42:1-2), and Joseph is in a position to help them economically and to heal the breach in the family.

CHAPTERS 39-41 AND THE EGYPTIAN BACKGROUND

(1) *The adulterous wife.* Many exegetes regard the Egyptian story of the brothers Anubis and Bata (names of Egyptian gods) as a close parallel to Genesis 39:7-20; " . . . it must have been known to the narrator. It is incomprehensible that some exegetes contest this. . . . " (Westermann 1986:65). The Egyptian story from the nineteenth dynasty, closely dated to 1225 B.C.E., is translated in full in ANET 23-25 where it occupies almost four full columns. The two brothers, Anubis the elder, and Bata the younger, work harmoniously in the fields. The younger is described as a good man: "Why, the strength of a god was in him." There is a chronology of several days work. When seed runs short, the elder brothers sends the younger home to fetch more. The wife of the elder brother admires the strength of the younger, "and she wanted to know him as one knows a man . . . come, let's spend an hour sleeping together." She promises to make him fine clothes. The younger brother rejects her: "See here—you are like a mother to me, and your husband is like a father to me . . . what is this great crime you have said to me? Don't say it to me again. And I won't tell a single person. . . . " She becomes afraid, she takes fat and grease to make herself ill and does herself up as if she has been beaten. When her husband returns, she accuses the younger brother of molesting her, taking up his very words and saying that this is what *she* said to *him*. The elder brother

waits behind the cowshed door with a sharpened lance so as to kill the younger. The first two cows that enter the shed turn to the younger brother and warn him of the danger. He sees his brother's feet and the end of the lance under the door and runs. His brother chases him. The younger prays to the god Re-Har-akhti who puts a body of water full of crocodiles between the two. The younger finally persuades the elder of his innocence: " . . . you carried your lance on the word of a filthy whore!" He cuts off his own penis, throws it into the water, and flees to the valley of cedars. The elder brother returns home, kills his wife, throws her to the dogs, and sits mourning his younger brother.

The Egyptian story is summarized at length in order to show how little of it corresponds to Genesis 39:7-20. Certainly there is similarity in the dialogue, in the woman's approach and the younger brother's rejection of her. But adultery was known as the "great crime" or "great wrong" or "great sin" in the ancient Near East as W. L. Moran (1959:280–81) showed long ago, so that the author of Genesis 39 need not have picked up the phrase from the Egyptian story. He may well have been familiar with the story, or with a version of it. If so, he made limited use of it. Moran has drawn attention to four Egyptian marriage contracts in which adultery is referred to as a "great sin." The "great sin" is also to be found in the Akkadian documents of Ugarit (see further Gen 20:9; Exod 32:21, 30, 31; 2 Kgs 17:21).

(2) *Dreams*. There were systems for interpreting dreams in Egypt (ANET 495). The text is from the nineteenth dynasty (c. 1300 B.C.E.). The editor of the text cites evidence that the text may be as early as the twelfth dynasty (2000–1800). The pattern is set out thus:

"if a man sees himself in a dream:

white bread being given him	—Good:	it means things at which his face will light up
seeing a large cat	—Good:	it means a large harvest will come to him
looking into a deep well	—Bad:	putting him into prison."

There are about two hundred examples in the original text. Joseph does not use this system of the "priestly diviners." God interprets the dreams through him.

(3) *Seven lean years*. There is a text from the Ptolemaic period (second cent. B.C.E.; ANET 31), the setting of which is the reign of Djoser of the third dynasty (c. 2800), which gives the reasons why

a stretch of land on the Nile south of Elephantine has been dedicated to Khnum, god of Elephantine. It is a question whether it is a priestly forgery of some later period justifying a claim to territorial privileges, or whether it actually records a grant of land 2500 years earlier. The text is carved on a rock near the first cataract. The king is speaking: "I was in distress on the Great Throne, and those who were in the palace were in heart's affliction from a very great evil, since the Nile had not come in my time for a space of seven years. Grain was scant, fruits were dried up, and everything which they eat was cut short." Later, the god Khnum says: "I know the Nile. When he is introduced into the fields, his introduction gives life to every nostril, like the introduction (of life) to the fields . . . The Nile will pour forth for thee, without a year of cessation or laxness for any land." We can say no more than that Egypt had a tradition of seven lean years which, by a contractual arrangement between Pharaoh and a god, were to be followed by years of plenty.

(4) *The viceroy.* There are texts (ANET 212–13) relating to Rekhmi-Re, viceroy (or Vizier) in Upper Egypt under Thut-mose III (c. 1490–1436). Pharaoh, of course, was supreme. But he delegated. The most important official was the viceroy who was directly responsible to Pharaoh, and to whom most other officials were responsible. The three important symbols of his authority were the ring, the linen garment, and the gold chain around the neck. Scenes of investiture are well known in Egyptian art from the fifteenth century B.C.E. There are thirty-two examples from the reign of Thutmose IV (fifteenth century). Redford (1970:208–26) discusses the whole procedure in detail. He is of the opinion that " . . . the induction ceremony of Genesis 41 belongs to the realm of popular Märchen in vogue in the middle of the first millennium B.C." (225). This may be, but investiture had been going on for more than a thousand years before that time.

Notes

39:1. POTIPHAR, AN OFFICIAL. The name occurs only here and in 37:36. There is a variant of it in 41:45, 50. It means "he whom Re gives." The word translated by "official" is *sārîs,* literally, eunuch. "Castration of the human male was not practiced in Egypt, as far as is known, nor in Greece and Rome, except under Oriental influence . . . Since the Egyptians did not practice castration, it is improbable that the Egyptian royal servants and officers—Genesis 37:36; 39; 40:2, 7—were eunuchs. But the wording may have entered these passages when the stories were retold in a time when servants were usually castrated" (J. L. McKenzie 1965:252–53).

12. CLOAK. The word used in verses 12, 13, 15, 16, 18 is *beged.* It describes any kind of garment from the simplest to the noblest, from the filthy clothing of a leper to the robes of the high priest. When von Rad (1976:299) describes Joseph's garment as "a long close-fitting piece of clothing, girded at the waist," he causes difficulties. How did Joseph run away, leaving it in her hand? Did she tear it off him? It must have been some sort of readily detachable robe.

14, 17. TO PLAY WITH. *ṣāḥaq.* To laugh, play. Used in some sort of sexual sense in Genesis 26:8.

HEBREW. See *Comment* on Genesis 14:13. Used five times in the Joseph story: 39:14, 17; 41:12 (by foreigners); 40:15 (by Joseph before foreigners); 43:22 (by the narrator).

20. PLACE OF DETENTION. *bêt hassohar,* the place where those are kept who are awaiting some sort of trial.

40:3–4. IN CUSTODY. *mišmar;* describes a state rather than a place.

11. I TOOK THE GRAPES AND SQUEEZED THEM. The Egyptians pressed juice from grapes by mechanical means. Redford (1970:205) notes: "Yet in Ptolemaic times unfermented grape juice, squeezed by hand and mixed with water, is described by temple texts as a refreshing beverage to be drunk by the king." Certainly. This may well be the first recorded case of the practice, but this does not necessarily mean that the first time that it was done was in the Ptolemaic period.

16B. WHITE BREAD. *ḥorî.* Ebla, *lú-ḫari,* baker of white bread; products from white (Dahood 1980; 1981).

41:43. 'ABRĒK. According to Redford (1970:226–28) the form is an Egyptian imperative with a prothetic *aleph* from the Hebrew *brk* and means "do obeisance"; the word entered into Egypt in the period of the New Kingdom.

45. ZEPHENATH-PANEAH. The Egyptian name given to Joseph means very probably, "God speaks and he lives." It does not occur elsewhere.

ASENATH. Joseph's wife: "belonging to the goddess Neith."

51. MANASSEH. "God has made me forget."

52. EPHRAIM. "God has made me fruitful."

4. *Between Canaan and Egypt: The Reconciliation (Chs. 42–45)*

¹When Jacob saw that there was grain in Egypt, he said to his sons: Why are you looking at each other? ²He said: See, I have heard that there is grain in Egypt; go down and buy some for us that we may live and not die. ³So Joseph's brothers, ten of them, went down to buy grain in Egypt. ⁴But Jacob did not allow Benjamin, Joseph's brother, to go with his brothers for fear that some harm come to him.

⁵So the sons of Israel went down to buy grain with the others who were going down because there was a famine in the land of Canaan. ⁶Joseph was governor there and it was he who sold grain to all the people of the land. Joseph's brothers came and bowed down before him with their faces to the ground. ⁷When Joseph saw his brothers he recognized them but made as though not to know them and spoke harshly to them. ⁸He said to them: From where have you come? They said: From the land of Canaan to buy grain. ⁹Joseph recognized his brothers but they did not recognize him. ¹⁰Joseph remembered the dreams that he had had about them. He said to them: You are spies; you have come to look out the weakness of the land. ¹¹They said to him: No my lord; your servants have come to buy grain. We are all sons of one man; we are honest people; your servants are not spies. ¹²He said to them: No, you have come to look out the weakness of the land. ¹³They said: we your servants are twelve brothers, sons of one man in the land of Canaan; the youngest is with our father at present, and one is no more. ¹⁴Joseph said to them: As I said to you, you are spies. ¹⁵In this way you shall be tested; by the life of Pharaoh, you shall not leave this place unless your youngest brother comes here. ¹⁶Send one of you to bring your brother while you are detained here; your words shall be tested to see if you are truthful; if not, by the life of Pharaoh you are spies. ¹⁷So he detained them in custody for three days. ¹⁸Joseph said to them on the third day: Do this and you shall live; I am one who fears God. ¹⁹If you are honest people, then one of your brothers is to remain in custody where you are; but you, you go and bring grain to your hungry household. ²⁰But bring the youngest of your brothers to me and so confirm what you have said and not die; and they did so. ²¹Then they said to each other: We are certainly guilty with regard to our brother; we saw his anguish of soul when he begged mercy from us; but we did not listen; and

so this disaster has come upon us. ²²Then Reuben answered them: didn't I tell you, don't harm the boy, but you didn't listen; and now his blood—we must pay for it. ²³They did not know that Joseph understood because he used an interpreter. ²⁴He turned away from them and wept. Then he turned back and spoke to them: he took Simeon from among them and put him in custody before their eyes. ²⁵Joseph gave orders that their bags be filled with grain, that each one's silver be put back in his sack, and that provisions be given them for the journey. And this was done. ²⁶They loaded the grain on their asses and went. ²⁷When one of them opened his sack to give his ass fodder at the overnight stopping place, he saw his silver in his sack; it was there at the top of his pack. ²⁸He said to his brothers: My silver has been put back; look, it is in my pack; their heart sank; they turned to each other and said: What is this that God has done to us?

²⁹When they came to Jacob their father in the land of Canaan, they told him all that had happened to them. ³⁰The man, the lord of the land, spoke harshly to us; he alleged that we were spying on the land. ³¹We said to him: We are honest men, we are not spies. ³²We are twelve brothers, the sons of our one father; one is no more, and the youngest is at present with our father in the land of Canaan. ³³This man, the lord of the country, said to us: I shall know that you are honest men by this; leave one of your brothers with me, but take the grain that your hungry households need and go. ³⁴Bring your youngest brother to me and I shall know that you are not spies but honest men; I will give your brother to you and you can move around freely. ³⁵When they emptied their sacks, each found a bag with his silver in his sack. When they and their father saw their sacks of money, they were afraid. ³⁶Jacob, their father, said to them: You are making me childless; Joseph is no more, Simeon is no more, you are taking Benjamin from me; everything has fallen on me. ³⁷Then Reuben said to his father: Kill my two sons if I do not bring him back to you. Put him in my care; I will bring him back to you. ³⁸But he said: My son shall not go down with you; his brother is dead and he alone is left. Something could happen to him on the way as you go, and you will bring my grey hairs in grief to the realm of the dead.

43:1 The famine was still severe in the land. ²When they had used up the grain that they had brought from Egypt, their father said to them: Go back and buy us a little more grain. ³But Judah said to him: The man warned us specifically: You shall not see my face unless your brother is with you. ⁴If you allow our brother to go with us, we will go down and buy grain for you. ⁵But if you do not allow him, we will not go down, because the man said to us: You shall not see my face unless your brother is with you. ⁶Israel said: Why have you harmed me by telling the man that you had another brother. ⁷They said: The man asked expressly about ourselves and our family, saying, is your father still alive? have you a brother? We answered all these questions of his. How could we know that he would say, bring your brother down. ⁸Judah said to Israel his father: Let the boy go with me; let us be up and going and let us live and not die, we and you and our little ones. ⁹I myself will go surety for him; from my hand shall you require him; if I do not bring him back and restore him to you, I shall be guilty before you all my life. ¹⁰Had we not delayed, we had been there and back twice by now. ¹¹Then Israel their father said to them: If it must be, do this. Take some of the best products of the land in your baggage and bring them down to the man, a little balsam and honey, tragacanth gum, myrrh, pistachio nuts, and almonds. ¹²Take double the silver with you, the silver that was returned in your packs you must take back with you, perhaps it was a mistake. ¹³Take your brother, and up, go back to the man. ¹⁴May *El šadday* be merciful to you in the man's presence and may he send your other brother back and Benjamin. But I—if I am bereaved, I am bereaved.

¹⁵So the men took the gift and the double amount of silver and Benjamin with them; they set out and went down to Egypt and presented themselves to Joseph. ¹⁶When Joseph saw Benjamin with them, he said to his steward: Bring these men into the house; kill an animal and make ready for they are to eat with me at noon. ¹⁷The man did as Joseph told him and brought the men into Joseph's house. ¹⁸Now the men were afraid when they were brought into Joseph's house and they said: It is because of the silver that was returned in our sacks the first time that we have been brought here—he wants to make up a charge against us and overpower us and take us and make us slaves with our asses. ¹⁹So they approached Joseph's steward and spoke to him at the entrance to the house. ²⁰They said: Listen, my lord. We came down once before to buy grain. ²¹When we came to the overnight stopping place we opened our packs, each found his full weight of silver in the top of his pack; we have brought it back with us. ²²We have brought more silver with us to buy grain; we do not know who put the silver in our packs. ²³He said: All is well (*šālôm*); don't be afraid; your God, the God of your father has put a treasure in your packs; I received your silver; then he brought out Simeon to them. ²⁴The man brought the men into Joseph's house, gave them water to wash their feet and fodder for their asses. ²⁵They made ready the gift for Joseph's arrival at noon for they had heard that they were to eat there. ²⁶When Joseph arrived at the house they presented the gift which they had with them and bowed to the ground before him. ²⁷He asked if all was well with them; and then: Is all well with your father, the

old man of whom you spoke? Is he still alive? ²⁸They said: All is well with your servant, our father; he is still alive. They prostrated and bowed down. ²⁹When he raised his eyes and saw Benjamin his brother, the son of his mother, he said: Is this your youngest brother of whom you spoke to me? And he said: May God be gracious to you, my son. ³⁰Joseph hurried on because he was deeply moved at his brother and was on the verge of tears, and so he went to his private room and wept. ³¹Then he washed his face, came out, controlled himself, and said: Serve the meal. ³²They served him separately and them separately and the Egyptians eating with him separately, because the Egyptians cannot eat with the Hebrews; it is an abomination to them. ³³The brothers were seated before him in order from the eldest to the youngest. And they looked at each other in amazement. ³⁴Then he sent a portion of what was before him to them, but Benjamin's portion was five times larger than all the others. They drank and grew merry with him.

44:1 Then Joseph ordered his steward: Fill the packs of the men with as much grain as they can take and put each man's silver in the top of his pack. ²And my goblet, the silver goblet, put in the top of the pack of the youngest together with his silver for the grain. And he did as Joseph told him. ³In the morning, at first light, the men were sent on their way with their asses. ⁴They set out from the city. They had not gone far when Joseph said to his steward: Up and after the men, and when you have caught up with them say to them: Why have you repaid good with evil? ⁵Why have you stolen my silver goblet? Is it not the one from which my lord drinks and in which he practices divination? You have done wrong by doing this. ⁶When he caught up with them he repeated all this to them. ⁷But they said to him: How can my lord say things like this? Far be it from your servants to do anything like this. ⁸See, the silver that we found in the top of our packs we brought back to you from the land of Canaan, so how can we have stolen silver or gold from your lord's house? ⁹With whomsoever of your servants it is found, he shall die, and we shall be your master's slaves. ¹⁰He said: Well then, just as you say. With whomsoever it is found shall be my slave, but you shall go free. ¹¹Each quickly lifted his pack to the ground and opened it. ¹²He searched, beginning from the eldest down to the youngest. And the goblet was found in the pack of Benjamin. ¹³Then they tore their garments and each loaded his ass and they returned to the city. ¹⁴When Judah and his brothers arrived at Joseph's house, he was still there. They fell down to the ground before him. ¹⁵Joseph said to them: What is this that you have done? Did you not know that a man such as I practices divination? ¹⁶Then Judah said: What can we say to my lord? What answer can we make? How justify ourselves? God has found out the sin of your servants;

we, we are my lord's servants, both we and the one who was found to have your goblet. ¹⁷But he said: Far be it from me to do this. The one who was found to have my goblet, he shall be my servant; but you go back to your father in peace.

¹⁸Then Judah approached him and said: Please, my lord, let your servant have a word in my lord's ear, and let not your anger flare up against your servant, for you are as Pharaoh. ¹⁹My lord asked your servants: Have you a father or a brother? ²⁰We said to my lord: We have a father who is old and a young brother born in his old age; his brother is dead; he alone is left of his mother's children and his father loves him. ²¹You asked your servants: Bring him down to me so that I may set my eyes on him. ²²We said to my lord: The boy cannot leave his father; if he leaves him, his father will die. ²³But you said to your servants: Unless your youngest brother comes down with you, you shall not come into my presence again. ²⁴When we returned to your servant my father, we told him what my lord had said. ²⁵When our father said: Go back and buy us some grain, ²⁶we said: We cannot go down unless our youngest brother is with us. If we go down, we cannot see the man's face if our youngest brother is not with us. ²⁷Then your servant, my father, said to us: You know that my wife bore me two sons. ²⁸One went from me, and I said: He has been torn to pieces; I have not seen him again. ²⁹And you take this one from me as well. If something happens to him you will bring down my grey hairs in sorrow to the realm of the dead. ³⁰Now, if I go to your servant my father and the boy, whose life is bound with his, is not with us, ³¹then, when he saw that the boy was not there, he would die and your servants would bring down the grey hairs of your servant, our father, in grief to the realm of the dead. ³²Your servant has gone surety for the boy before my father. I said: If I do not bring him back to you, I shall be guilty before my father all my life. ³³Now let your servant remain as a servant to my lord in place of the boy, and let the boy go up with his brothers. ³⁴For I could not go back to my father if the boy were not with me; I could not look on the sorrow that would fall upon my father.

45:1 Joseph was unable to control himself in the presence of all his attendants and cried out: Everyone leave my presence. And so there was no one with him when he made himself known to his brothers. ²He wept so loudly that the Egyptians and the house of Pharaoh heard him. ³Joseph said to his brothers: I am Joseph. Is my father still alive? But his brothers were unable to answer him, so dumbfounded were they as they faced him. ⁴Then Joseph said to his brothers: Come closer to me! And they did. He said: I am Joseph your brother whom you sold down to Egypt. ⁵Now do not be distressed or reproach yourselves because you sold me, because God sent me ahead of you to save lives. ⁶There has been a famine in the land now for two years and there are five years more in which there will be neither ploughing nor harvest. ⁷But God sent me ahead of you to preserve you (as) a remnant in the land and to keep you alive, a great host of survivors. ⁸So it was not you who sent me down here but God, and he appointed me as a father to Pharaoh and lord over his household and ruler in the whole of the land of Egypt. ⁹Hurry, go up to my father and tell him: Joseph, your son, says: God has appointed me lord over all Egypt. Come down to me, do not delay. ¹⁰You are to dwell in the land of Goshen and be near me, you and your sons and your grandsons, your sheep and your cattle and all that you have. ¹¹I will take care of you there for there are still five years of famine to come, so that you and your household and all yours are not reduced to poverty. ¹²You yourselves and your brother Benjamin can see that it is I, my very self, who am speaking to you. ¹³Tell my father of the dignity that is mine in Egypt and of all that you have seen; hurry, bring my father down here. ¹⁴Then he threw his arms around the neck of Benjamin his brother and kissed him and wept on his neck. ¹⁵Then he kissed all his brothers and wept over them. Only then did his brothers speak to him.

¹⁶The news spread to Pharaoh's house that Joseph's brothers had arrived. Pharaoh and his courtiers were pleased. ¹⁷Pharaoh told Joseph to say to his brothers. Do this: load your animals and go to the land of Canaan. ¹⁸Take your father and your household and come to me. I will give you the produce of the land of Egypt and you shall eat of the fat of the land. ¹⁹Now you are to instruct them—do this: take wagons from Egypt for your little ones and wives and bring your father and come. ²⁰Let your eye not look with regret upon your possessions because the produce of the whole of Egypt will be yours. ²¹The sons of Israel did so. And in accordance with Pharaoh's instructions Joseph gave them wagons and provisions for the journey. ²²To each of them he gave a change of clothes, but to Benjamin he gave three hundred silver pieces and five changes of clothes. ²³To his father moreover he sent ten asses carrying the produce of Egypt, and ten she-asses carrying grain, bread, and provisions for his journey. ²⁴He sent his brothers on their way and as they went he said to them: Don't quarrel on the way. ²⁵They went up from Egypt and went to the land of Canaan, to Jacob their father. ²⁶They told him: Joseph is still alive and it is he who is ruler in the land of Egypt. He was stunned; he did not believe them. ²⁷But when they told him what Joseph had said to them, and when he saw the wagons that Joseph had sent to take him, the spirit of Jacob their father came to life. ²⁸Israel said: Enough. Joseph my son is still alive; I will go down and see him before I die.

Comment

The land of Canaan is taken up into the famine which is plaguing the ancient Near East (41:54, 57; 42:5). Jacob and his sons enter the scene after an absence of twenty-two years (Joseph was seventeen in 37:2 and he entered Pharaoh's service at thirty in 41:46; the seven years of plenty were at an end [41:43], and the famine had already lasted two years, there being five years still to run [45:11]). These four chapters are to be read together. The last words that we had heard from Jacob were: "My son's tunic: a wild animal has eaten him . . . I will go down to the realm of the dead mourning my son" (37:33, 35). At the end of chapter 45 he says: "Enough. Joseph my son is still alive; I will go down and see him before I die" (45:28). The broad narrative arc has reached its goal.

Jacob takes the initiative for both journeys down to Egypt (42:1-2; 43:2). Those who go down to Egypt are Joseph's brothers (42:3), the sons of Israel (42:5), part of the great throng of people of the ancient Near East devastated by famine (41:56-57). Ten brothers make the journey; Benjamin must stay at home (42:3-4). The storyteller is in charge throughout. He immediately introduces the ironic touch. The brothers, all unknowing, bow down before their brother (42:6; cf. 37:7, 9, 10). With the brothers, whom he recognizes at once (42:7, 9), prostrate before him, Joseph remembers his dreams (42:10). Joseph speaks harshly to them (42:7b). Why? Very probably to control his emotions. He weeps on six occasions (42:24; 43:30; 45:1-2, 14-15; 46:29-30; 50:17). The accusation that the brothers are spies echoes through chapter 42 (vv. 9b, 12, 13, 16b, 30, 34), as does the defense that they are honest, non-warlike men (vv. 11, 19, 31, 33, 34). Joseph tests them, but he knows that they will pass the test (v. 14). Joseph takes up the brothers' reference to the youngest brother (vv. 13b, 14b) who now becomes the focal point of the test (vv. 16, 20, 32, 34). This extends into chapter 43 where the discussion between Jacob and Judah about a second journey to Egypt again centers around Benjamin (43:1-14). Joseph directs his attention to Benjamin when the brothers arrive (43:16, 29, 34b). Then the episode of the silver goblet (44:1-17) is concerned entirely with Benjamin. Joseph wants to make sure that his father will come down to Egypt. His concern for his father comes more to the fore as the story moves to its climax (43:7; 43:27; 45:3, 9, 13, 23).

Part of the irony of the situation is that first, Joseph hears that he is thought to be dead, "one is no more" (42:13 [42:32]), "his brother is dead" (44:19b), "he has been torn to pieces" (44:28), and second, he learns only now, twenty-two years later, what went on in the household after he had been sold (42:21-24). And through all this the brothers "did not know that Joseph understood because he used an interpreter" (42:23). The writer is too good a storyteller to mention specifically that there was no interpreter present at the reconciliation scene (45:1-15): "Only then did his brothers speak to him."

Joseph's concern for the brothers and the household is in evidence from their first meeting: "But you, you go and bring grain to your hungry household" (42:19; cf. 42:33). Joseph has their sacks filled with grain, their silver returned, and provides for their journey home (42:25), even though he holds Simeon as hostage (42:19, 24b). He knows that they will have to return as the famine is to last another five years (45:11). But in the midst of it all, Joseph almost breaks down (42:24). When the brothers come back a second time with Benjamin, their fears are allayed by the steward (43:19-23) who tells them that "All is well" (*šālôm,* 43:23). The formalities of hospitality are carried out (43:24) and the brothers are entertained (43:32b-34). But again, Joseph almost breaks down in their presence (43:30). There is almost a resolution of the tension here, but more is to come. The storyteller is managing the scenes all the time. He includes Canaan in the famine and so brings Jacob's household to Egypt, but withholds Benjamin; he knows that the brothers will have to return to Egypt, and so Simeon is safe. He has Benjamin brought down to Egypt and the silver goblet put into his sack so as, by means of Judah's speech, to bring Joseph to breaking point, to have him make himself known to them, and ultimately to bring Jacob down to Egypt (45:9, 13, 28). The whole, from 37:35, through 42:1-2 and 43:2, moves slowly but inexorably to Jacob in Egypt.

The storyteller is at his best in the speech of Judah (44:18-34) and the recognition scene (45:1-15). Judah's speech of seventeen verses to Joseph is long by biblical standards. He uses several conventional forms of address: my lord (vv. 18, 19, 20, 22, 24, 33), your servant (Judah himself, vv. 18, [22], 33), your servants (the brothers, vv. 19, 21, 23, 31), your servant (the father, vv. 24, 27, 30, 31). He plays on the relationship between "the youngest brother," "the boy," and the father: "if the boy were not there" (vv. 20, 22, 29, 30, 31, 34), and the relationship (vv. 20, 22, 25-29, 30-31, 34). He underscores that it was Joseph who made the demand that Benjamin come (vv. 21, 22, 24, 26). He lets Joseph hear Jacob's lament for him (Joseph): "His brother is dead" (v. 20), "One went from me . . . he has been torn to pieces" (vv. 20, 28), and lets Joseph know of Jacob's grief (vv. 22, 29b, 31, 34). "My father," "his father," "our father," "your servant my father"—all this is central (vv. 20, 22, 24, 25, 27, 30, 31, 33, 34 [two times]). The rhetoric can be pushed no further. It is the relationship between the father and the youngest brother and the grief that would befall the father were this relationship damaged, that brings Joseph to breaking point. What happens now can only be what is described in 45:1-4. The tension is broken. The brothers are reassured. They have been taken up into a great saving action of God (see introduction to Joseph story Nn. 3, 4). Joseph's emotions overflow again (45:14-15). The reconciliation is complete. "Only then did his brothers speak to him" (45:15b), the same brothers who twenty-two years before "could not so much as greet him in peace" (37:4). Joseph, in his office as viceroy to Pharaoh (45:8-9, 13), invites the brothers and their father to come down and settle in Egypt. Pharaoh adds his authority to the invitation (45:17-20). Joseph assures the brothers a third time "that it is I, my very self, who am speaking to you" (45:12). The brothers return to their father with Joseph's admonition: "Don't quarrel on the way" (45:24b). Jacob is stunned at the news (45:26b) just as the brothers had been dumbfounded (45:3b). He recovers, and Israel is on his (its) definitive journey down to Egypt (45:28).

A number of repetitions in the narrative of chapters 42-45 has led some scholars to understand them as "doublets" and hence signs of more or less continuous "sources." There are two journeys to and from Egypt before the third and final journey when Israel, the father and the people, settle in Egypt. But the second journey in the present text is unintelligible without the first, and there is no sign of a journey to Egypt which knew nothing of Benjamin (Gunkel). Benjamin, as we have seen, is a central figure of discussion or action in chapters 42-43, and the one around whom the action and the speech in chapter 44 revolves (vv. 1-17, 18-34). He is mentioned again in 45:12, 14. The repetition to Jacob by the brothers (42:29-35) of their dialogue with Joseph (42:9b-20) is ordinary narrative technique (see *Comment* on ch. 24 with parallels from Homer). The father of the brothers is Israel on eleven occasions (37:3, 13; 43:6, 8, 11; 45:28; 46:1, 2, 30; 48:8, 21) and Jacob elsewhere. But one could scarcely separate 45:25-27, "they went . . . to Jacob their father . . . he was stunned; he did not believe them . . . the spirit of Jacob their father came to life . . . Israel said" (v. 28), or "God spoke to Israel in a vision by night. He said: Jacob, Jacob" (46:2). An article on the President of the United States of America, or on the Prime Minister of my own country, Australia, might speak of the President or Mr. Bush, the Prime Minister or Mr. Hawke, alternately throughout without being assembled from sources (I am writing in 1989). Jacob has also been Israel since Genesis 32:29 (28); 35:10. "The sons of Israel" (42:5; 45:21; 46:5, 8a; 50:25) is a fixed formula. When Joseph makes himself known to his brothers, he repeats in successive verses: "I am Joseph. Is my father still alive?" and "I am your brother Joseph, whom you sold down to Egypt" (45:3-4). In such an emotional scene, repetition is most natural, especially after a separation of twenty-two years. Joseph even introduces himself a third time (45:12). One brother finds his silver in his sack (42:27-28) on the first night of the homeward journey. The others find their silver when they arrive home (42:35). This is very likely narrative technique, instead of a routine "then the others opened their sacks and also found their silver" after 42:27-28.

Notes

42:5. THE SONS OF ISRAEL. *běnê yiśrā'ēl,* becomes a standard expression for the descendants of the patriarchs, Genesis 49:2; 50:25; Exodus 1:1.

18. I AM ONE WHO FEARS GOD. The storyteller has Joseph acknowledge a higher power and its due order.

19. ONE OF YOUR BROTHERS. Simeon, cf. verses 24b, 36; 43:14, 23b; regarded by some scholars as "insertions."

25. SILVER. Cf. 37:28b.

43:14. EL ŠADDAY. Cf. 17:1. This designation for God occurs as a formula of introduction in Genesis 17:1 and 35:11, and in 48:3 when Jacob recalls the episode at Luz (Bethel, 35:11); Isaac (28:3) and Jacob (43:14) call on *El šadday* to bless their son(s) at the beginning of a journey.

23. ŠĀLÔM. The steward assures the brothers that all is well; in verses 27-28 Joseph asks if all is well (*šālôm*) with the father. The brothers had not been able to speak to Joseph in peace (37:4); Jacob had sent Joseph to inquire after the well-being (*šālôm,* 37:14) of the brothers and the sheep. The peace of the family is certainly broken; but the word *šālôm* is not as dominant as one might expect.

32. SERVED HIM SEPARATELY. The Hebrew writer notes an unusual and striking custom. He may be saying either of two things, or both: (1) the Egyptians of my time do not eat with people from the land of Canaan; (2) separate tables is an old Egyptian custom.

44:5. DIVINATION. The Hebrew word to divine is *nāḥaš*, the same three consonants as in the word for a serpent. Divination was later forbidden in Israel (Lev 19:26; Deut 18:10). Joseph had been many years in Egypt from the age of seventeen. The storyteller rides easily and without comment over the pagan practice of one of the fathers of Israel.

45:7. A REMNANT IN THE LAND . . . A GREAT HOST OF SURVIVORS. It has been noted that this is the only occurrence of "remnant" (*šĕ-'ērît*) in the Pentateuch. "Remnant" and "survivors" are in parallelism in Isaiah 37:32 = 2 Kings 19:31; the words reflect later prophetic usage (Westermann 1986:143–44).

8. A FATHER TO PHARAOH. Ptahhotep, the viceroy of king Izezi of the fifth dynasty (c. 2450), speaks of himself as "God's (i.e., the king's) father. . . . " (ANET 412).

10. GOSHEN. An area on the eastern edge of the delta near the desert.

5. Jacob-Israel Goes Down to Egypt and Settles There
(46:1-30, 31-34; 47:1-12)

¹So Israel set out with all he had. When he came to Beersheba he offered sacrifice to the God of his father Isaac. ²Then God spoke to Israel in a vision by night. He said: Jacob, Jacob. He said: Here I am. ³He said: I am *hā 'ēl*, God of your father. Do not be afraid to go down to Egypt because I will make you a great nation there. ⁴I will go down with you into Egypt and I will bring you up again and Joseph shall put his hand over your eyes. ⁵Then Jacob set out from Beersheba. So the sons of Israel carried Jacob their father and their little ones and their wives on the wagons that Pharaoh had sent to bring them. ⁶And they took their cattle and their possessions which they had acquired in the land of Canaan and went down to Egypt, Jacob and all his descendants with him, ⁷his sons and his grandsons, his daughters and his granddaughters; he brought all his descendants down to Egypt with him.

In chapters 46–50 two narrative threads, the end of the Joseph story and the end of the Jacob (and patriarchal) story, P, are woven together. A series of additions or expansions is inserted into these.

Prescinding from the two expansions, 50:15-21 in the Joseph story, 46:8-27 in the Jacob story, as well as from the blessings of Jacob, there are *four* groups of additions, all attesting *genres* characteristic of the patriarchal story.

1. 46:1-5a basis is an itinerary with stations and a promise

    48:7   Rachel's death and burial (35:16, 19) in itinerary context; etiology of Abel-Mizraim (50:10b-11)

2. Etiological additions or expansion:

    (a) related to tribal history:
        48:13-20   Jacob gives Ephraim precedence over Manasseh
        48:3-6   Jacob adopts Ephraim and Manasseh
        50:23b   Joseph adopts sons of Machir
        48:22   place etiology?

    (b) 50:10b-11 place etiology, Abel-Mizraim

    (c) 47:13-26 famine and Joseph's economic measures

3. Blessings and promises:

    (a) 46:2-4 revelation and promises to Jacob
    (b) 48:15-16; 48:20a blessings
    (c) 46:4; 48:21; 50:24-25 Exodus promise

4. 50:22-26 Genealogy; Joseph's last years and death
              (Redactional expansion)

These expansions have grown out of the patriarchal story, and each out of its own context in tradition. They cannot belong to a literary source.

Figure 5

⁸These are the names of the sons of Israel who came to Egypt, Jacob and his sons. Reuben was Jacob's firstborn.
⁹The sons of Reuben: Henoch, Pallu, Hezron, Carmi.
¹⁰The sons of Simeon: Jemuel, Jamin, Ohad, Jachin, Zohar, Shaul, the son of a Canaanite woman.
¹¹The sons of Levi: Gershon, Kohath, Merari.
¹²The sons of Judah: Er, Onan, Shelah, Perez, Zerah; Er and Onan died in the land of Canaan; the sons of Perez were Hezron and Hamul.
¹³The sons of Issachar: Tola, Puvah, Iob [Yashub], Shimron.
¹⁴The sons of Zebulon: Sered, Elon, Yahleel.
¹⁵These are the sons of Leah, whom she bore to Jacob in Paddan-aram, with his daughter Dinah. His sons and daughters numbered thirty-three in all.
¹⁶The sons of Gad: Ziphion, Haggi, Shuni, Ezbon, Eri, Arodi, Areli.
¹⁷The sons of Asher: Imnah, Ishvah, Ishvi, Beriah, Serah their sister. And the sons of Beriah were Heber and Malchiel.
¹⁸These are the sons of Zilpah whom Laban gave to Leah his daughter, and these she bore to Jacob, sixteen in all.
¹⁹The sons of Rachel, Jacob's wife: Joseph and Benjamin.
²⁰Manasseh and Ephraim were born to Joseph in the land of Egypt from Asenath, the daughter of Potiphera, priest of On.
²¹The sons of Benjamin: Bela, Becher, Ashbel, Gera, Naaman, Ehi, Rosh, Muppim, Huppim, Ard.
²²These are the sons of Rachel whom she bore to Jacob, fourteen in all.
²³The sons of Dan: Hushim.
²⁴The sons of Naphtali: Jahzeel, Guni, Jezer, Shillem.
²⁵These are the sons of Bilhah, whom Laban gave to Rachel his daughter, and these she bore to Jacob, seven in all.
²⁶All the persons belonging to Jacob who went down to Egypt, direct descendants, not counting the wives of Jacob's sons, were sixty-six in all.
²⁷The sons of Joseph born to him in Egypt were two. Thus the house of Jacob when it came down to Egypt numbered seventy. ²⁸Now he sent Judah before him to Joseph to point the way before him to Goshen; so they came to the land of Goshen. ²⁹Joseph made his chariot ready and went up to meet Israel his father in Goshen. When he saw him he threw his arms around his neck and wept and embraced him for a long time. ³⁰Israel said to Joseph: Now let me die; I have seen your face again and you are alive.

³¹Then Joseph said to his brothers and his brothers' household: I will go and tell Pharaoh and will say to him: My brothers and my father's household who were in the land of Canaan have come to me. ³²The men were shepherds, yes and cattlemen, and they brought their own flocks and herds and possessions. ³³When Pharaoh summons you

and asks: What is your occupation? ³⁴You say: Your servants have been cattlemen from our youth and still are, we and our fathers; and so you will be able to remain in the land of Goshen, because all shepherds are an abomination in Egypt.

47:1 So Joseph went and told Pharaoh. He said: My father and my brothers with their flocks and their herds and all that they possess have come from the land of Canaan and are now in the land of Goshen. ²He took five of his brothers and presented them before Pharaoh. ³When Pharaoh asked his brothers: What is your occupation? They said: Your servants are shepherds, we and our fathers. ⁴And they said further to Pharaoh: We have come to sojourn in the land; your servants have no pasture for the sheep because the famine is severe in the land of Canaan. Let your servants settle in the land of Goshen. ⁵Pharaoh said to Joseph: So your fathers and your brothers have come to you. ⁶The land of Egypt lies before you. Settle your father and your brothers in the best part of the land. Settle them in the land of Goshen. And if you know that there are capable men among them, appoint them as supervisors over my cattle. ⁷Then Joseph brought Jacob his father in and presented him to Pharaoh, and Jacob blessed Pharaoh. ⁸Pharaoh said to Jacob: How many are the years of your life? ⁹Jacob said to Pharaoh: The years of my sojourning are one hundred and thirty. Few and hard have been the years of my life and they have not reached the years of the life of my fathers in the days of their sojourning. ¹⁰Jacob blessed Pharaoh, and left Pharaoh's presence. ¹¹Then Joseph settled his father and his brothers and gave them land in Egypt, in the best part of the country, in the area of Rameses, as Pharaoh had ordered. ¹²And Joseph provided his father and his brothers and the whole of his father's household with food according to the number of little ones.

Comment

The Joseph story proper ends with chapter 45. Only the epilogue remains. The conclusion of the Joseph story is woven together with the conclusion of the Jacob story in chapters 46–50 in which additional material is included, namely the list of all the descendants of Jacob who went down into Egypt (46:8-27), the tribal sayings (49:3-27) which lie outside both stories, some tribal history (48:13-20), some place etiologies (48:22 [?]; 50:10b-11), and blessings (48:15-16, 20a).

The passage 46:1b-5a is certainly not a part of the Joseph story. It is clearly a part of the patriarchal tradition. The Joseph story knows nothing of sacrifice (v. 1b) or of an appearance of God or of a direct communication by God (vv. 2-4). The movement of the whole passage is much more like that of Genesis 12:6-9. In Genesis 26:2-5, YHWH had appeared to Isaac and told him not to go down into Egypt; now God tells Jacob not to be afraid to go down (the promise material in 26:3-5 is very different from that in 46:3-4). God introduces himself as *hā 'ēl,* God of your father, i.e., as God himself (see Excursus on the religion of the patriarchs). Verse 4 has a double function; it anticipates Jacob's death and burial (47:29-31; 48:29b-33; 50:1-14), and links the patriarchs with the exodus (48:21b; 50:24-25). Westermann (1986:153–54) understands the sequence from the end of chapter 45 through chapter 46 as follows: 45:25-28 + 46:5b–46:6-7 (itinerary) + 46:28-30, expanded by the list of names (46:8-27) and set around a concluding part of the Jacob story (46:1-5a). Two statements by Jacob form an important literary arc here: "Enough. Joseph my son is still alive; I will go down and see him before I die" (45:28) and "Now let me die; I have seen your face again and you are alive" (46:30), the latter being taken up again as Jacob bequeaths his legacy: "I had not expected to see your face; but God has allowed me to see your descendants as well" (48:11). The list of those who went down to Egypt with Jacob (46:8-27), filling out the elaboration in verses 6-7, gives special importance to the four mothers of the twelve, Leah (v. 15), Zilpah (v. 18), Rachel (vv. 19,22), Bilhah (v. 25). The mention of ten sons of Benjamin (v. 21), the "youngest" about whom there was so much talk in chapters 42-44, is an anachronism in the present chronology. Westermann (1986:160–61) provides a detailed discussion of the types of names in the passage.

Following the emotion of the meeting of the father and son after twenty-two years, Jacob and his sons are to be settled definitively in Egypt (vv. 31-34). Joseph, the statesman, instructs them how to reply to Pharaoh. The text which reports how the brothers are to reply to Pharaoh is not at all clear. Joseph tells his brothers to say that they are shepherds (*ro'ê ṣo'n*) and, apparently in apposition with shepherds, "cattle men" (*'anšê miqĕneh,* vv. 32, 34a). But then "all shepherds are an abomination in Egypt" (v. 34b). When the brothers reply to Pharaoh (47:3-4), they say that they are shepherds like their fathers, looking for pasture. Whatever the confusion, it seems that Joseph wants to assure Pharaoh that his brothers are reliable, settled, sedentary people and not mobile predatories who, on the eastern border, "are an abomination in Egypt." The brothers settle in Egypt, remain as they are, and gain no advantage or advancement from Joseph's position (47:11-12).

Joseph now presents his father to Pharaoh (47:7-10) and the patriarch blesses the potentate (47:7b, 10a). Jacob speaks of himself as one who has lived a hard life (130 years already + 17 to come in Egypt [47:28]), but who has not reached the age of his ancestors, Abraham 175 (25:8) and Isaac 180 (35:28). The writer or editor resumes the settlement of Israel (47:27a) and Jacob (47:28a) in Egypt and notes that Israel was "fruitful and multiplied greatly" (47:27b), in anticipation of Exodus 1:7.

6. *Joseph's Economic Measures in Egypt. Israel Grows (47:13-26; 47:27-28)*

[13]There was no bread throughout the country and the lands of Egypt and Canaan languished because of the famine. [14]So Joseph collected all the silver in the lands of Egypt and Canaan in return for grain which the people bought and put it in Pharaoh's treasury. [15]When the silver from the lands of Egypt and Canaan had been used up, all the Egyptians came to Joseph and said: Give us bread or we shall die in front of you; the silver is spent. [16]Joseph said: Give your herds and I will give you bread for your herds if the silver is spent. [17]So they brought their herds to Joseph and Joseph gave them bread for their flocks of sheep and herds of cattle and their asses. He supported them with bread that year in exchange for their herds. [18]The year ended. They came to him in the second year and said: We cannot conceal from my lord, the silver is used up, the herds and cattle belong to my lord; nothing is left but our bodies and our land. [19]Why should we die before your eyes, we and our land as well? Acquire us and our land for bread and we and our land will be in bondage to Pharaoh. Give us seed so that we may live and not die and our land not become a desert. [20]So Joseph acquired all the land of Egypt for Pharaoh because each of the Egyptians sold his field; the famine was severe; and the land became Pharaoh's. [21]As for the people, he put them into servitude from one border of Egypt to the other. [22]Only the land of the priests he did not acquire; they had a fixed income from Pharaoh and lived from this; and so because of Pharaoh's ordinance for them, they did not sell their land. [23]Joseph said to the people: Listen, I have acquired you and your land for Pharaoh; here is seed for you; so go and sow your land. [24]But of the produce, you are to give a fifth to Pharaoh; four-fifths shall be yours to sow your fields and to provide food for you and those in your household and your little ones.

²⁵They said: You have saved our lives; we have found favor in the eyes of my lord and so we shall be slaves to Pharaoh. ²⁶So Joseph made it a statute over the land of Egypt which holds until today that a fifth belongs to Pharaoh; the land of the priests alone did not become Pharaoh's.

²⁷So Israel settled in the land of Egypt, in the land of Goshen and they possessed land there, and they were fruitful and multiplied greatly. ²⁸Jacob lived another seventeen years in the land of Egypt, so that his life-span covered a hundred and forty-seven years.

Comment

47:13-26 certainly breaks the unity of the account of the settlement of Jacob and his sons in Egypt and of his last will and testimony. Very many exegetes consider it an "insertion" or an "appendage" to explain a system of taxation in Egypt; it is to be explained as an etiology from its conclusion that Joseph instituted "a statute over the land of Egypt which holds until today that a fifth belongs to Pharaoh; the land of the priests alone did not become Pharaoh's" (47:26). Some think that it is very likely a story, based on a general knowledge of taxation in Egypt, and constructed to justify taxation in Israel in the early monarchy by grounding the practice in the patriarchal period. It is the opinion of H. Seebass (1978) that Joseph, the next in the realm of Egypt after Pharaoh, does not appear to exercise this function in the presence of his father. This is the last place for him to do so. Hence the importance of the passage which is neither secondary nor an insertion. But this interpretation is very strained. Jacob is well aware of Joseph's position from the reports of the brothers, the transport wagons, and the gifts; he has witnessed Joseph's ready access to Pharaoh and how Pharaoh in fact confirms the settlement in the land already arranged by Joseph. Some sort of etiological explanation is most likely.

Egypt and Canaan languish under famine, so Joseph gives out grain in return for silver which was stored in Pharaoh's treasury (vv. 13-15). Canaan disappears from the report after verse 15a. The silver is spent (v. 15b). Joseph gives out bread in exchange for the herds and flocks. So ends the first year (vv. 16-18ai). But everything is now used up. Hence the people and their land become Pharaoh's; the people are in servitude to Pharaoh (vv. 18aii-21); priests and their possessions are exempt (vv. 22, 26b). But a new element has entered: the people want seed to sow the land (v. 19b), and Joseph gives it

to them (v. 23b). But one-fifth of the produce of the seed is to be
Pharaoh's (v. 24a). Because Joseph has saved their lives, the people
are ready to submit to bondage under Pharaoh (v. 25). Hence
Joseph's statute which is still in effect when the author is writing
(v. 26a). The difficulty with the story is that from the first dynasty
of Egypt (3200–2700 B.C.E.) to the period of the Ptolemies (323–30
B.C.E.), the king was the owner of all land in Egypt. Herodotus, who
toured Egypt about 450 B.C.E., mentions this in Book 2.

Notes

46:28. NOW HE SENT JUDAH. The Hebrew reads: *wĕ 'et yĕhûdāh
šālaḥ*. Some authors consider this verse to be a direct continuation
of 46:5a; grammatically, it does not follow immediately; it is possible that something may have dropped out.

34. ABOMINATION. The Egyptologists assure us that this is not
demonstrable from Egyptian texts.

7. Jacob's Legacy
(47:29-31; 48:1-22)

²⁹When the time drew near for Israel to die he summoned his son
Joseph and said to him: If I have found favor in your eyes put your
hand under my thigh and show loyalty and fidelity to me. Do not
bury me in Egypt. ³⁰When I lie with my fathers, bring me out of Egypt
and bury me in their grave. He answered: I will do as you have said.
³¹And he said: Swear to me. And he swore to him. Then Israel bowed
down toward the head of the bed.

48:1 Now after these events Joseph was told: Your father is ill. So
he took his two sons with him, Manasseh and Ephraim. ²And Jacob
was told: Your son Joseph is coming to you. Then Israel summoned
up his strength and sat up on the bed. ³Jacob said to Joseph: *El šadday* appeared to me at Luz in the land of Canaan and blessed me.
⁴And he said to me: See, I will make you fruitful and multiply you
and make you into an assembly of peoples and I will give this land
to you and your descendants after you as an everlasting possession.
⁵Now your two sons born to you in the land of Egypt before I came
down to Egypt to you, Ephraim and Manasseh, are mine just as Reuben and Simeon are mine. ⁶Children born to you after them are yours;
they shall be called after the name of their brothers when it comes
to their inheritance. ⁷But I, while I was coming from Paddan, lost

Rachel—she died on the way in the land of Canaan when there was still some distance to go to Ephrath; and I buried her there on the way to Ephrath, that is, Bethlehem. ⁸When Israel saw Joseph's two sons he said: Who are these? ⁹Joseph saw to his father: these are my sons whom God has given me here. And he said: Bring them to me that I may bless them. ¹⁰Now Israel's eyes were dim and he was unable to see. But when he brought them to him he kissed them and embraced them. ¹¹Then Israel said to Joseph: I had not expected to see your face; but God has allowed me to see your descendants as well. ¹²Then Joseph took them from his knees and bowed down to the ground. ¹³Then Joseph took the two of them and put Ephraim on his right, Israel's left, and Manasseh on his left, Israel's right, and brought them to him. ¹⁴Then Israel stretched out his right hand and laid it on the head of Ephraim, he was the younger, and his left hand on the head of Manasseh, crossing his hands, for Manasseh was the firstborn. ¹⁵Then he blessed Joseph and said:

The God before whom my fathers Abraham and Isaac walked,
the God, shepherding me ever unto this day,
¹⁶the messenger, ransoming me from all ill,
may he bless the boys; they shall be called by my name,
and by the name of my fathers Abraham and Isaac;
may they spawn to be many in the land.

¹⁷When Joseph saw that his father had his right hand on the head of Ephraim, he was displeased, and he took hold of his father's hand to take it from Ephraim's head and put it on Manasseh's. ¹⁸Joseph said to his father: No, my father; this is the firstborn, put your right hand on his head. ¹⁹But his father refused and said: I know, my son, I know well; he too shall become a people, he too shall be great. Nevertheless his younger brother shall be greater than he, and his descendants shall become a multitude of nations. ²⁰That day he blessed them saying:

In you shall Israel bless itself saying:
May God make you like Ephraim and Manasseh.

And so he put Ephraim before Manasseh. ²¹Israel said to Joseph: I am about to die; but God will be with you and bring you back to the land of your fathers. ²²And I, I give you one ridge of land over your brothers which I took from the Amorites with my own sword and bow.

Comment

Israel/Jacob is the active party throughout this section as he leaves his legacy to Joseph and his sons, Ephraim and Manasseh. The whole is a collection of disparate parts which were originally unconnected:

47:29-31   Israel, near to death, has Joseph swear a promise which is ful-
           filled in 50:1-14.

48:1-2   "Now after these events. . . .," a new episode.

48:3-7   (a) vv. 3-4   Jacob recalls appearance of *El šadday* and
                          promises.
           (b) vv. 5-6   Jacob adopts Ephraim and Manasseh.
           (c) v. 7   Jacob recalls Rachel's death.

48:8-12   Jacob legitimates Ephraim and Manasseh.

48:13-20   Jacob gives precedence to Ephraim over Manasseh.
           (a) vv. 13-14   precedence conferred.
           (b) vv. 15-16   the blessing.
                           (15b, 16bii—spoken in prose.
                           15c, 16a —liturgical additions).
           (c) vv. 17-20   precedence confirmed, further blessing.

48:21   Exodus link, a "theological clamp" (46:4; 48:21; 50:24-25).

48:22   An isolated tradition of conferring of land.

The last of the patriarchs wants to be buried in the grave of the
patriarchs, "their grave" (47:30). When Joseph approaches Pharaoh for permission to go up to Canaan to bury his father he repeats
Jacob's wish: "in the grave which I cut for myself (bought for myself, NEB) in the land of Canaan, there bury me" (50:5). This should
cause no problem: (1) repetition in story is not always word for word
exact, but substantially so, a mingling of exact and varied sentences
and phrases; (2) the grave at Machpelah is Abraham's, Isaac's, and
Jacob's. Abraham exacted an oath from his faithful servant in the
same manner in 24:1-9. We do not know the meaning of 47:31b:
"Then Israel bowed down toward the head of the bed." It may be
some act of reverence on the part of the patriarch.

The function of the words "Now after these events" (48:1; cf.
15:1; 22:1; 22:20; 39:7; 40:1) "is to insert an individual event into
a broader context" (Westermann 1986:184).

Jacob's address in 48:3-7 consists of three parts. First, he recalls
the events at Luz (35:9-12). *El šadday* appeared to him there (for
the name *El šadday,* see *Notes* on 17:1). "And he said to me:

See, I will make you *fruitful* and *multiply* you and make you into
   an *assembly of peoples*
and I will give this land to you and your descendants after you as
   an everlasting possession (48:4).

The divine address at Luz ran:

> *Be fruitful and multiply.* A nation, yes *an assembly of nations* shall come from you, and *kings shall come* forth from your body (35:11).

Twice a patriarch invokes the favor of *El šadday.* Jacob prays:

> May *El šadday* be merciful to you in the man's presence. . . . (43:14).

Isaac sends Jacob on his way to Paddan-aram:

> May *El šadday* bless you and *make you fruitful* and *multiply you,* and may you become *an assembly of peoples* (28:3).

The same language and phrases which occur in 48:4; 35:11-12; 28:3, are found in the first of the *El šadday* passages, chapter 17, which begins with the formula of introduction, "I am *El šadday*" (17:1) like the Luz passage (35:11):

17:6   I will make you *very fruitful* and I will make nations of you and *kings shall come from you.*

17:8   I give you and your descendants after you the land where you sojourn all the land of Canaan as *an everlasting possession.*

17:16 I will bless her (Sarah) and she shall issue into nations; *kings of peoples shall come from her.*

17:20 I will bless him (Ishmael) and *make him fruitful and multiply* him very greatly; and he shall beget twelve princes and I will make him a great nation.

One concludes, with good reason, that these *El šadday* passages belong to the same layer of reworking. Genesis 48:3-4 is not an original part of the Joseph "short-story." (See *Comment* on 35:11-12 and table there).

Second, in verses 5-6, Jacob legitimates Ephraim and Manasseh as tribes of Israel. Though sons of his own son Joseph, they are also sons of a pagan mother. Jacob makes them his own, and so their position as tribal ancestors in Israel is traced back to the will of the dying patriarch. Third, Jacob recalls the death of his wife, Rachel, taking up very literally some of the phrases and sentences of 35:16-20:

35:16 They journeyed then from Bethel
          and when there was still some distance to go to Ephrath,
          Rachel was in labor and her birth pains were severe.

35:19 Rachel died and was buried on the way to Ephrath, that is Bethlehem.

48:7   But I, while I was coming from Paddan,
        lost Rachel—she died on the way in the land of Canaan
        when there was still some distance to go to Ephrath;
        and I buried her there on the way to Ephrath, that is Bethlehem.

This points again to the same layer of reworking.

Jacob has been told that Joseph is coming to visit him with his two sons, Manasseh and Ephraim. Jacob struggles to a sitting position (48:1-2). He asks Joseph who the boys are. Several scholars raise questions about contradictions here. If Jacob has been seventeen years in Egypt (47:28) he would know who the boys are, and more, they are no longer boys but young men about twenty. Were there two traditions then about Jacob's death, one that he died soon after coming to Egypt, when he gave precedence to Ephraim over Manasseh, and another that he lived on another seventeen years? And what of verse 10a: "Now Israel's eyes were dim and he was unable to see"? There is really no contradiction between verses 8 and 10a. An old man with failing eyesight can see and not see clearly. Israel asks that the boys come near so that he can bless them (v. 9b). He kisses and embraces them (v. 10b), but no blessing is given in verses 8-12. Both Joseph (v. 9a) and Jacob (v. 11b) mention the great action of God into which they have been taken up. It is unlikely that Ephraim and Manasseh were sitting on Jacob's knees (v. 12a); they were probably at his knees. Joseph bows in respect (*šḥh*) before his father, the last of the patriarchs (v. 12b). It seems that various traditions have been brought together in verses 1(-2), 8-12 without any thought of harmonizing them. Joseph seems to be about to withdraw in verse 12. But now, without any introduction, the precedence scene begins (vv. 13-20) which includes the blessing (vv. 15-16, 20) not given in verses 8-12 where Jacob intended to bless (v. 9b). This part is concerned exclusively with precedence (cf. v. 20). The tradition gives the patriarch the right not only to adopt the children of a pagan mother and make them tribal ancestors, but also the right to assign precedence. Westermann (1986:190–91) makes the point that verse 17 follows directly on verse 14, and that verses 15-16 are a later insertion. There would be no point in Joseph's protest (verses 17-18) if the blessing has preceded; a blessing once given remains a blessing once given and cannot be altered (cf. 27:31-38). But surely the editor was aware of this and let it sit easily.

The blessing itself is complex. Verses 15b and 16ai form a prose unit: "The God before whom my fathers Abraham and Isaac walked, may he bless the boys.'' Abraham and Isaac lived in God's presence ("walk before": 17:1 [Abraham]; 5:22 [Henoch]; 6:9 [Noah]; 24:40 [Abraham]). The lives of the three patriarchs had been paths before God. In verses 15c and 16a active participles of descriptive praise are attached to the name "God" and "messenger" (i.e., God who appears in some way and rescues). The active participle describing God at work is characteristic of the Psalms (e.g., Ps 103:5-9, six active participles; Ps 147:1-6 [six], 7-11 [five], 12-20 [five]). As Westermann (1986:189) notes, this is an important passage in the Old Testament which links the patriarchal tradition with the liturgical life of Israel for the period for which the editor was writing. But this period need not be late—exilic or post-exilic. Jacob blesses Joseph (v. 15a) and asks God to bless the boys (v. 16ai). The later precedence of Ephraim over Manasseh is anchored in the patriarchal period (v. 20d).

The first appendage (v. 21) is a theological clamp which, with 46:4 and 50:24-25, binds the story of the exodus with the story of the patriarchs. The final verse (v. 22) is an isolated tradition of which we know no more and which makes sense only if spoken in Canaan. The word "ridge" is the Hebrew *shechem,* the name of the city in north central Canaan. The verse has nothing to do with the peaceful acquisition of land by Jacob from "the sons of Hamor, the father of Shechem" (33:18-20), nor with the violence of chapter 34, which Jacob condemned (34:30-31). Jacob acquired the ridge of land "with my own sword and bow," i.e., with all his weapons. But we know no more of this.

The whole passage (47:29-31 + 48:1-22) is an amalgam of various traditions, which there has been no attempt to harmonize, together with some editorial reworking (especially in the blessing, vv. 15-16). Though one tradition has Jacob live seventeen years in Egypt (47:28) another, it seems, has him die soon after his arrival (48:1-2). Hence there is uncertainty about the ages of Manasseh and Ephraim at the time of the blessing—three-year-olds or twenty-year-olds. But this does not bother the editor/re-worker. He presents Jacob's blessing of the boys/young men, his reminiscences, and his conferring of precedence as one. That is his story. We should leave his story as his story and not try to fit it into the more precise chronology of nineteenth and twentieth century "annalistic" history.

Notes

47:31. TOWARD THE HEAD OF THE BED. The word *šḥh* is used. Though the meaning remains obscure, there is no evidence for the ancient view of Holzinger, supported by Gressmann (1923:6), that Jacob inclines toward the Teraphim which stands at the head of the bed.

48:4. EVERLASTING POSSESSION. *'aḥuzzat 'ôlām,* the phrase occurs only here and in 17:8.

16. MESSENGER. *mal'āk.* Cf. *Notes* on 16:7; God, in the way in which the divinity appears and communicates on earth.

SPAWN. The verb is *dāgāh,* found only here; it may be related to the noun *dāg,* fish, and refer to the spawning of fish.

22. RIDGE. The word *šĕhem* (shechem) means "shoulder;" hence it is reasonable to render it by "ridge" with the NEB.

8. Jacob's Pronouncements on the Tribes (49:1-28a)

¹Then Jacob summoned his sons and said:
Gather round and I will tell you what will happen to you in the days to come.
²Come together and listen, sons of Jacob, listen to Israel your father.
³Reuben, my firstborn are you, my strength and the first fruit of my vigor,

exceeding in pride and exceeding in might;
⁴ turbulent as the waters, you shall not exceed,
for you went up to your father's couch,
then you defiled my bed against me.

⁵Simeon and Levi, brothers, tools of violence their (circumcision-) blades;

⁶ in their council my soul shall not go,
in their assembly my heart shall not join;
for they murdered men in their anger,
they hamstrung oxen in their whim.
⁷ Cursed be their anger, it was fierce,
and their wrath, it was ruthless.

⁸Judah are you, your brothers laud you, your hand on the neck of your enemies; your father's sons shall bow before you.
⁹Judah,   a lion's whelp, you come up, my son, from the kill;

crouching, stretching like a lion,
like a lioness, who shall rouse him?
10 The scepter shall not pass from Judah,
nor the staff from between his feet
as long as tribute comes to him
and the obedience of the peoples is his.
11 He tethers his ass to the vine,
to the red vine his ass's colt;
he washes his cloak in wine,
his garment in the blood of grapes.
12 Darker than wine his eyes,
and whiter than milk his teeth.

13Zebulun   dwells by the shore of the sea,
a shore for ships is he,
his frontier rests on Sidon.

14Issachar,   a raw-boned ass,
crouching among the cattle-pens;
15 when he saw the resting-place good
and the land pleasant,
he set his shoulder to the burden,
and became a serving serf.

16Dan   is a judge of his people as one of the tribes of Israel;
17 let Dan be a snake on the road,
a viper on the way,
who bites the horse's fetlock
so that its rider falls backward.
18 For your rescuing action I hope, YHWH.

19Gad,   raiders raid him,
but he raids on their heels.

20Asher,   who deals out his bread,
it is he who provides delicacies for kings.

21Naphtali,   a hind let loose, bearer of comely fawns.

22Joseph,   a young bull, a young bull by a spring,
a wild ass by a wall,
23 The archers were savage against him, pressed him
hard,
plotted against him.
24 But their bow was mightily smashed,
and the sinews of their hand were loosed
by the hands of the Strong One of Jacob,
by the name of the Shepherd of (the stone of)
Israel.
25 From El, your father—may he help you,
from *šadday*—may he bless you,

with the blessings of heaven above,
with the blessings of the deep that lurks below,
with the blessings of breasts and womb.

26   The blessings of your father are stronger than
the blessings of the everlasting mountains,
the splendor of the eternal hills.
May they be upon the head of Joseph,
  upon the crown of the prince among his brothers.

27Benjamin,   a ravening wolf, in the morning he devours the prey,
  in the evening he divides the spoil.

28aThese are the whole twelve tribes of Israel, and this is what their
father said to them.

Comment and Notes

Chapter 49 is a collection of tribal sayings known generally as the
"blessings of Jacob." The sayings derive in essence from the period
of the judges (twelfth–eleventh century) and as a collection bring
the tribes together so as to give a complete picture of them at that
time. Some of the sayings have been re-edited and re-worked. They
are back-dated to the last of the patriarchs so as to give them status.
This collection is one of three. The earliest (Judg 5:14-18) was occa-
sioned by the battle between the Israelites and Jabin, king of Canaan,
where the tribes are praised or blamed according to their response
to the call to battle. The latest (Deut 33) is heavily theologized. A
complete discussion would require that these two lists of sayings be
considered. But the attention here will be primarily on the Genesis
text with an occasional reference to these lists.

The sayings do not follow any fixed pattern. Reuben, Simeon, and
Levi are censured; Judah, Dan, Gad, Naphtali, Joseph, and Benjamin are praised; Zebulun, Issachar, and Asher are blessed in varying degrees. There are word-plays on the names of Judah, Zebulun,
Issachar, Gad, Asher, and Joseph. There are animal metaphors attached to the names of Judah, Issachar, Dan, Naphtali, and Benjamin; and in the very difficult saying about Joseph there is, in the
more common interpretation, a tree or plant metaphor. Each saying may have had its own independent history, and the sayings as
single units and as collections may have originated at tribal gather-
ings (Josh 24; Judg 20:1-2). The tribe of Judah and the house of
Joseph (Ephraim and Manasseh) are given prominence, which points
to a period when these played an important part in national life,

namely during the reign of David. But many elements in the sayings would be anterior to this time.

The collection interrupts the movement of the narrative which closes the story of the patriarchs (47:9-31; 48:1-22; 49:1a, 28b-33). Verses 1a and 28b are in sequence: "Then Jacob summoned his sons (v. 1a) and blessed them, each of them, a special blessing for each (v. 28b)." Verse 1b gives the sayings a prophetic direction; Jacob is to tell the tribes "what will happen to you in the days to come" (cf. Isa 2:2; Micah 4:1). Verse 2 is editorial and reads rhythmically. Though the sayings belong originally neither to the Joseph story nor to the end of the Jacob (patriarchal) story, they should be read in the place where they stand in the Hebrew Bible because it is there that the editor wants to give them their legitimation.

The vocabulary is often obscure, the syntax is at times very complicated and unclear, and the text is not well preserved. Hence translations and interpretations differ greatly. The bibliography on chapter 49 is vast (Westermann 1986:215-18).

3-4. REUBEN. The tribe of Reuben settled east of the Jordan along the northeastern strip of the Dead Sea. It is prominent enough, though divided, in Judges 5:15, but disappearing in Deuteronomy 33:6. We know little of the tribe. Reuben is disinherited because of his misconduct recorded in 35:22. The last part of verse 4, "my bed against me," has also been rendered "the bed of the doe" with reference to Proverbs 5:18-19 (Dahood 1964:282).

5-7. SIMEON AND LEVI. Simeon inhabited an area on the edge of the desert around Beersheba and quickly disappeared, being absorbed into the tribe of Judah. Nothing is known of the early history of the tribe of Levi which became a priestly tribe without territorial inheritance (Deut 33:8-11). The misdeed of Simeon and Levi is described in 34:25-31. The word rendered "(circumcision-) blades" (*měkěrotêtem*, v. 5) is difficult. "Weapons of violence are their swords" (NAB); "their spades became weapons of violence" (NEB). The consonants of the word *krt*, to cut, are clear; in Exodus 4:25, *krt* is used "to circumcise"; with the prefix ma/mi we have *makrēt*, plural *makretîm*, "blades of circumcision" (Dahood 1961:55-56). The horror that the brothers perpetrated was in the context of circumcision. There is no report that they hamstrung oxen, though hamstringing is noted in other contexts (e.g., Josh 11:6,9; 2 Sam 8:4). Jacob has no part in their plans (v. 6, cf. 34:30). He curses their anger and wrath, but not the tribes themselves.

8-12. JUDAH. The territory of Judah covered the mountain ridge and its slopes from about ten kilometers north of Jerusalem, southward to Beersheba. There is an immediate word-play on the name Judah, *yěhûdāh;* the word *yādāh,* in the causative (*hip'il*), forms *yodû-kā,* and means "praise you." The first part of the saying praises Judah (v. 8), and the praise is continued in verse 10. A separate tribal saying (v. 9) describes the strength of Judah under the triple lion image (cf. Num 23:24; 24:9). This is the powerful Judah. The following verse (v. 10) has given rise to much discussion which has not yet issued into a consensus. The translation given follows W. L. Moran (1958) and the NEB. It reads the Hebrew *šîloh* (v. 10b) as two words, *šay,* "tribute" (Isa 18:7; Pss 68:30; 76:12, "gifts offered as homage"), *loh,* "to him." The reference is to David and the *pax Davidica;* "the conception of tribute arriving in Judah cannot have arisen before David, and at least some of his military successes in Edom, Moab, Ammon and among the Arameans to the north" (Moran 1958:415-16). Verse 11 describes the fertility of the land of Judah in highly imaginative parallelism, and verse 12 intensifies this. These three verses (vv. 10-12) are not tribal sayings but vivid descriptions of the blessings that are Judah's.

13. ZEBULUN. The territory was just north of the plain of Esdraelon, in southern Galilee, extending from somewhere westward of the southwest shore of the lake across to the environs of modern Haifa (Josh 19:10-16). Zebulun appears to have been originally landlocked; its aspirations to the sea are noted in its northern border which aims at seafaring Sidon, and in the last part of Deuteronomy 33:19. *Zbl,* prince, is a regular title of Yam (sea) in the Ugaritic texts where Yam and *ṣdn* (Sidon) are often linked.

14-15. ISSACHAR. Just south of the lake and west of the Jordan, a strong tribe (Judg 5:15) in the east of the plain of Esdraelon. The name Issachar is a word play, *'iš śākār* = wage earner. The subject of the sentences in verse 15 are both the ass and the man. He (it) found a pleasant situation, but had to pay the price for it. The words *mas 'obēd* mean "a forced laborer"; they are used in this sense in Joshua 16:10.

16-17. DAN. Dan was a southern tribe which migrated to the north (Josh 19:40-48) and settled around the sources of the Jordan facing the Hermon range. The verb *dîn* means "to judge." He judges "as one of the tribes of Israel," which indicates the settlement of Israel as a whole. Dan is small, but dangerous, like the snake or the dangerous horned viper (*šĕpîpon*).

18. A typical exclamation in the Psalms: cf. Psalms 38:16; 39:8.

19. GAD. The tribe settled east of the Dead Sea and along the edge of the desert, and so would be exposed to raiding nomads. The saying is a series of word-plays on *gad*, "to raid" (cf. the elaboration, Deut 33:20-21).

20. ASHER. Its territory lies in Galilee stretching northward from Carmel along the coast. The Hebrew letter *mem* at the beginning of the verse belongs to the end of verse 19 as a mem-enclitic. S. Gervitz (1987) has explained the saying: "Asher, though poor to the point where the tribe finds it necessary to 'apportion' or 'ration its bread,' i.e., presumably, has difficulty in feeding itself, nevertheless provides the royal establishment, '(the) king,' with delicacies" (p.161). Is this a reproach because Asher provides for the Canaanite court? (Judg 1:32).

21. NAPHTALI. The land is in eastern Galilee extending from the lower southern shore of the lake northward. The word rendered "hind," *'ayyālāh*, can, without alteration of the Hebrew consonantal text, also be rendered "terebinth," *'ēlāh;* in the second part of the verse, "fawns" may be pointed several ways, the consonants remaining intact: *'imrê* = words; *'āmirê* = crowns; *'immārê* = fawns, each in the construct state ("genitive," of) with the Hebrew word for beauty. The RSV and the NAB render the verse as in the translation above; the NEB gives: "a spreading terebinth, putting forth lovely boughs." In Judges 5:18 and Deuteronomy 33:23, Naphtali is heaped with blessings.

22-26. JOSEPH. Joseph is represented territorially by Ephraim and Manasseh which cover the area of Samaria, from south of Bethel to the plain of Esdraelon. The verses about Joseph are a collection of sayings and are very difficult in their vocabulary, syntax, arrangement, and imagery. There is no broad consensus about their translation or meaning.

Verse 22 is virtually unintelligible as it stands. Literally it reads: "The son of a fruit-tree (?) Joseph, the son of a fruit-tree (?) by a spring; the daughters (pl.) walk (or climb, sing.) upon the wall." The Hebrew *porāt*, "fruit-tree," is a feminine participle form, literally, "productive," from *pārāh*, "to bear fruit"; *ben*, "son of," means one of a class. "Walk" or "climb" renders the Hebrew *ṣā'ăd-āh* (sing.), with the word *bānôt*, "daughters," preceding it. The NEB renders the verse: "Joseph is a fruitful tree by a spring with branches climbing over the wall." It has been noted that the Hebrew word *pere'* means a wild ass (Gen 16:12); *prt* is a feminine form. In Deuteronomy 33:17, Joseph is described as *bĕkôr šôr*, "a first-born ox" and "his horns like those of a wild ox." Speiser (1964:368) has noted the Arabic *banat ṣa'dat* = wild asses, in which *ṣa'ădah* is a component term. Hence the translation given above. But so much more could be said, and so many emendations proposed, without advancing any further. Westermann (1986:237) is convinced that another saying begins in verse 24; enemies attack Joseph, but he stands firm with his bow and flexible in arms and hands. The version given above understands the archers of verse 23 as shattered by the Strong One of Jacob and the Shepherd of Israel (v. 24). The word "stone" has crept into the last part of verse 24 in some way. Perhaps it is a component part of a divine title. The syntax of verse 25a is unsatisfactory. Be that as it may, Joseph is now the object of blessings. Verse 25b, "with the blessings of heaven above, with the blessings of the deep that lurks below" is a merism, i.e., a device which embraces all by means of the two extremes; may all blessings be his. Virtually the same words are used of the blessing on the land of Joseph in Deuteronomy 33:13. Breasts and womb as symbols of fertility (v. 25c) are found in Ugaritic (breasts of Asherah) and in other parts of the Old Testament (e.g., Isa 60:16; 66:11). The blessings of the everlasting mountains and the eternal hills are found in similar, though not identical, parallelism in Deuteronomy 33:15, and verse 26c, "upon the head of Joseph, upon the crown of the prince among his brothers" occurs word for word in Deuteronomy 33:16b.

There is an accumulation of names for God in these verses (vv. 24b–25a): the Strong One (*'ăbîr*) of Jacob, the Shepherd (*ro'eh*) of Israel, El, your Father, and *šadday*. *'ăbîr* means a bull or a steer. In Canaan the bull image is a symbol of fertility, but not, of course in Israel. The shepherd image, as noted earlier, is widespread in the ancient Near East (and in Homer's *Iliad,* where Agamemnon is described regularly as "shepherd of the peoples"), and is used in Israel for God primarily as shepherd of the people (e.g., Ps 80) and then as shepherd of the individual (Ps 23). *El šadday* has already been commented on in 17:1 and 48:3. The divine appellative *El 'ăbîkā*, "god, your father" (v. 25) is used often in Ugaritic for the head of the pantheon. In Psalm 68:6, God is "the father of orphans," in Psalm 89:27, God is addressed, "you are my father." There is a general Canaanite background to these divine names.

The translation and interpretation of these very difficult sayings about Joseph which have been proposed may be paraphrased: Joseph is described under the image of a young bull (v. 22); he is attacked by archers (v. 23); the archers are repulsed by the Strong One, the Shepherd of Israel (v. 24); God, your father, *šadday* heaps all sorts of blessings upon Joseph (v. 25). These blessings of God (your father, again in v. 26a) are stronger than any blessings from elsewhere (the gods of Ugarit are gods of the mountains; Baal dwells on Saphon in the north; cf. Isa 14:13; Ps 48:3 [2]). They are to be upon Joseph, prince (*nāzîr*) among his brothers (v. 26). Much of this may be contested, as may much of anything written on the blessings of Jacob.

27. BENJAMIN. His territory begins a few kilometers north and northeast of Jerusalem and covers Jericho and Gilgal on to the Jordan. "In the morning . . . in the evening"; the prepositions *bĕ* and *lĕ* may be understood as "from morning . . . till evening."

28A. The verse sums up and, with verses 1b and 2, forms a frame for the blessings.

9. Jacob's Death and Burial.
The End of the Patriarchal Story (and of the Jacob Story) (49:1a, 28b-33; 50:1-14)

49:1a Jacob summoned his sons.
[28b]Then he blessed them, each one of them, a special blessing for each. [29]He gave them his orders and said to them: I am being gathered to my people; bury me by my fathers at the cave which is in the field of Ephron the Hittite, [30]in the cave which is in the field of Machpelah, east of Mamre in the land of Canaan, the field which Abraham acquired from Ephron the Hittite as a burial plot. [31]There they buried Abraham and his wife Sarah; there they buried Isaac and his wife Rebekah; there I buried Leah—[32]the piece of land and the cave on it (were bought) from the Hittites. [33]When Jacob had finished giving his charge to his sons, he drew his feet up on to the bed, breathed his last, and was gathered to his people.

50:1 Then Joseph threw himself on his father's face and wept over him and kissed him. [2]Joseph ordered the physicians in his service to embalm his father. And the physicians embalmed Israel. ³They took forty days, as is usual, to complete the embalmment, and the Egyptians mourned him for seventy days. ⁴When the period of mourning was over, Joseph spoke to Pharaoh's court: If I have found favor in your eyes, please speak personally to Pharaoh and say: ⁵My father made me swear: I am dying; in the grave which I cut for myself in the land of Canaan, there bury me. And now I would go up and bury my father; then I shall return. ⁶Pharaoh said: Go up and bury your father as he made you swear to do. ⁷Joseph went up to bury his father and all Pharaoh's courtiers and the elders of his household and all the elders of the land of Egypt went up with him, ⁸together with all of Joseph's household, his brothers and his father's household. Only their little ones and their flocks and herds remained in the land of Goshen. ⁹Chariots and horsemen went up with him; it was a very distinguished company. ¹⁰When they came to the threshing field of Atad which is on the far side of the Jordan, they raised a loud and very sad lament; and he mourned his father for seven days. ¹¹When the inhabitants of the land, the Canaanites, saw the lamentation at the threshing floor of Atad, they said: How sadly the Egyptians are mourning. And so the place is called Abel-mizraim; it is on the far side of the Jordan. ¹²So his sons did as he had ordered them. ¹³His sons brought him to the land of Canaan and buried him in the cave of the field of Machpelah, the field which Abraham acquired as a burial plot from Ephron the Hittite east of Mamre. ¹⁴Then Joseph returned to Egypt after they had buried his father together with his brothers and all who had gone up with him to bury his father.

Comment

As we have seen, verse 28b follows on 49:1a. Here and on to 50:14 the conclusions of the Jacob and Joseph stories are woven together. Jacob has already commissioned Joseph under oath to bury him in Canaan (47:29-31). He now commissions his sons to bury him there (49:29-32). He insists with solemn repetition on the place of burial. The patriarchs are to lie together at the end of an era. Jacob dies (49:33). The sons carry out their commission, and the writer underscores that they buried him in the proper place (50:12-13), just as Isaac and Ishmael (25:9-10), Jacob and Esau (35:29), had buried Abraham and Isaac in the proper place. The patriarchal era has ended.

The closing section of the Joseph story (50:1-11, 14) is here woven together inseparably with the end of the Jacob story. The storyteller allows us to share Joseph's emotion again (50:1) following the solemn account of Jacob's death. The forty days for the embalmment are most likely included in the seventy days of mourning (50:2-3). Moses and Aaron were mourned for thirty days (Deut 34:8; Num 20:29) and Saul for seven (1 Sam 31:13). Joseph requests permission to go up to Canaan through the court (50:4), probably because his unkempt appearance due to the mourning rites would not allow him to appear personally before Pharaoh. "My father made me swear. . . . " (v. 5a); and Pharaoh grants the request taking up Joseph's words: "Go up and bury your father as he made you swear to do" (v. 6). The words "in the grave which I cut for myself" need mean no more than "my own grave" (see above, introduction to section 7). A distinguished procession, including the military, accompanies the mortal remains of the father of the viceroy (vv. 7-9). The caravan from Egypt would usually follow the coastal road and then move east to Beersheba. The Jacob procession seems to have made a detour across the northern Sinai to the east of the Jordan. The threshing floor of Atad (the floor of [surrounded by] brambles, v. 10) is east of the Jordan. There is an incongruity here as the Canaanites who saw the procession and heard the lamentation lived west of the Jordan (v. 11). But "Canaanites" may be used in a very general sense here. The place "on the far side of the Jordan" is known as "the mourning of the Egyptians." It is not mentioned elsewhere. Joseph then returns to continue his work and end his life in Egypt (v. 14).

10. The Reconciliation Confirmed
(50:15-21)

[15]When Joseph's brothers realized that their father was dead, they said: What if Joseph should bear a grudge against us for all the evil we have dealt him. [16]So they sent off to Joseph saying: Your father spoke to us before his death: [17]Speak to Joseph thus: I beg you, forgive the crime of your brothers, their sin, the evil they dealt you. So now, forgive the crime of the servants of the God of your father. And Joseph wept at their words to him. [18]Then the brothers themselves went in and fell down before him and said: See, we are your servants. [19]Then Joseph said to them: Do not be afraid. Am I in the place of God? [20]You planned evil against me; God planned good so as to preserve the lives of many people, as we see today. [21]Now do not be afraid; I will provide for you and your little ones. So he comforted them and reassured them.

Comment

These verses have no function in the narrative of Joseph as such. Reconciliation has been effected. But they give the writer an opportunity to underscore again the all-embracing action of God. Nothing in the story but their own guilty consciences could give the brothers cause to fear. Perhaps they did concoct the instruction that they say comes from Jacob. It is a full acknowledgment of their crime and a plea for forgiveness, the first mention of forgiveness in the story. They are again, and finally, prostrate before Joseph, this time knowing who he is. They describe themselves as "the servants of the God of your father" (v. 17b) and as "your servants" (v. 18b). Joseph's emotion wells up again (v. 17c). He is not God so as to make servants for himself of God's servants (v. 19). Once again, as in 45:5a, Joseph notes their crime but does not dwell on it. It is not a matter of "Man proposes and God disposes," or of the actualization of the sayings in Proverbs 16:9; 19:21; 20:24; 21:30. Rather it is a great action of God which effects forgiveness (Joseph's action in 45:14-15 is an act of forgiveness and reconciliation, and benefits all, Egypt, the famine-stricken nations in the ancient Near East, and, with them, the family of Jacob [45:5a, 5b, 7a, 8a; 50:20b]). The brothers are told twice: "Do not be afraid" (50:19a, 21a). Reconciliation is confirmed.

Epilogue
11. Joseph's Old Age and Death
(50:22-26)

[22]Joseph remained in Egypt, he and his father's household. Joseph lived a hundred and ten years. [23]Joseph saw Ephraim's sons to the third generation. And the sons of Machir, the sons of Manasseh, were recognized as Joseph's sons. [24]Then Joseph said to his brothers: I am about to die; but God will certainly visit you and will bring you up from this land to the land which he swore to Abraham, to Isaac, and to Jacob. [25]Then Joseph made the sons of Israel swear, saying: When God does indeed visit you, you are to bring up my bones from here. [26]Joseph died at the age of a hundred and ten. They embalmed him and put him in a coffin in Egypt.

Comment

Joseph dies at the good age of a hundred and ten. He sees his descendants to the third generation. Though the second youngest of twelve brothers, he is the first to die (vv. 24a, 25a). The link with the exodus is made in vv. 24-25 (cf. 46:4; 48:21). God will visit, *pāqad,* his people (cf. Exod 3:16; 4:31). The theme of the oath to the fathers is taken up (22:16; 24:7; 26:3), a typical deuteronomic theme where it is found twenty-two times (Rendtorff 1977:75-79). Joseph's last words are addressed to the "sons of Israel" (v. 25), that is to the descendants whom God is to "lead out" from Egypt. They fulfill his request (Exod 13:19; Josh 24:32). The Book of Genesis ends in anticipation of God's action in the exodus.

Bibliography

Abel, E. L.
1973   "The Nature of the Patriarchal God 'El Shadday.'" *Numen* 20:48-59
Abou-Assaf, Ali, Bordreuil, P., and Millard, A.R.
1982   "La statue de Tell Fekherye et son inscription bilingue assyro-araméene." *Etudes Assyriologiques.* Paris: Editions Recherche sur les civilisations, A.D.P.F.
Aejmelaeus, A.
1986   "Function and Interpretation of *ki* in Biblical Hebrew." *JBL* 105:193-209.
Albright, W. F.
1939   "The Babylonian Matter in the Pre-deuteronomic Primeval History (JE) in Genesis 1-11, Part 2." *JBL* 58:102f., n. 25, 91-103.
1954   *The Archaeology of Palestine.* 2nd ed., London: Penguin Books.
1957   *From the Stone Age to Christianity.* Anchor Paperback Books. 2nd ed. Garden City, N.Y.: Doubleday.
1964   *History, Archaeology and Christian Humanism.* N.Y.: McGraw-Hill.
1968   *Yahweh and the Gods of Canaan.* University of London: Athlone Press.
1973   "From the Patriarchs to Moses: 1. From Abraham to Joseph." *BA* 36:5-33.
Alonso Schökel, L.
1985   "Donde està tu hermano? Textos de fraternidad en el libro del Génesis." *Institución san Jerónimo 19.* Valencia: Institución San Jerónimo.
Alt, A.
1966   "The God of the Fathers." *Essays on Old Testament History and Religion,* 3-77. Trans. R. A. Wilson from German, 1929. Oxford: Basil Blackwell.

Anderson, B. W.
1977   "A Stylistic Study of the Priestly Creation Story." *Canon and Authority,* 148–62. Eds. G. W. Coats and B. O. Long. Philadelphia: Fortress.
1978   "From Analysis to Synthesis: The Interpretation of Genesis 1–11." *JBL* 997:23–39.
Armstrong, J. F.
1960   "A Critical Note on Genesis 6:16a." *VT* 10:328–34.
Auerbach, Erich
1953   *Mimesis. The Representation of Reality in Western Literature.* Trans. W. R. Trask from German, 1946. Princeton, N.J.: Princeton University.
Augustine
1972   *City of God,* 636–42. Trans. H. Bettenson from Latin. Ed. D. Knowles. London: Penguin (Pelican Classics).
Avigad, N.
1984   *Discovering Jerusalem.* Trans. R. Grafman from Hebrew, 1980. Oxford: Basil Blackwell.
Avi-Yonah, M. and Stern, E.
1975–   *Encyclopedia of Archeological Excavations in the Holy Land.*
1978   4 vols. Englewood Cliffs, N.J: Prentice-Hall.

Bailey, J. A.
1970   "Initiation and the Primal Woman in Gilgamesh and Genesis 2–3." *JBL* 89:137–50.
Bailey, L. R.
1977   *Where is Noah's Ark?* N.J.: Abingdon.
Barr, J.
1977   "Some Semantic Notes on the Covenant." *Beiträge zur Alttestamentlichen Theologie für Walther Zimmerli zum 70 Geburtstag,* 23–28. Eds. H. Donner, R. Hanhart, R. Smend. Göttingen: Vandenhoeck & Ruprecht.
Barthes, R.
1974   "The Struggle with the Angel. Textual Analysis of Genesis 32:23-33." *Structural Analysis and Biblical Exegesis,* 21–33. Trans. A. M. Johnson from French, 1971. Pittsburgh, Pa.: Pickwick.
Batto, B. F.
1987   "The Covenant of Peace: A Neglected Ancient Near Eastern Motif." *CBQ* 49:187–211.
Baumann, H.
1936   *Schöpfung und Urzeit des Menschen im Mythus der Afrikanischen Völker.* Berlin: Dietrich Reimer.
Beek, M.
1962   *Atlas of Mesopotamia.* Trans. D. R. Welsh from Dutch. Ed. H. H. Rowley. London: Nelson.

Begg, C. T.
1988 "Rereadings of the 'Animal Rite' of Genesis 15 in Early Jewish Narratives." *CBQ* 50:36–46.
Biale, D.
1981/82 "The God of the Breasts: El Shaddai in the Bible." *HR* 21:240–56.
Black, M.
1985 "The Book of Enoch or 1 Enoch." *Studia in Veteris Testamenti Epigrapha 7.* Leiden: E. J. Brill.
Blenkinsopp, J.
1982 "Abraham and the Righteous of Sodom." *JJS* 32–33:119–32.
Booij, T.
1980 "Hagar's Words in Genesis xvi 13b." *VT* 30:1–7.
Bright, J.
1982³ *A History of Israel.* London: SCM.
Bultmann, R.
1961 "Adam, wo bist du?" *Glauben und Verstehen 11,* 101–16. Tübingen: J.C.B. Mohr.

CAH
1975 *Cambridge Ancient History.* 3rd ed., vol. 2, part 2. Cambridge: University Press.
Cassuto, U.
1964 *A Commentary on the Book of Genesis. Parts I & II.* Trans. Israel Abrahams from Hebrew. Jerusalem: Magnes.
Cazelles, H.
1966 "Patriarches." Cols. 81–156 in vol. 7 of *DBSup.* Paris: Letouzey & Ané.
1973 "The Hebrews." *Peoples of Old Testament Times,* 1–28. Ed. D. J. Wiseman. Oxford: Clarendon Press.
1978 "Review of Abraham in History and Tradition by J. Van Seters." *VT* 28:241–55.
1981 "Religion d'Israel." Cols. 240–77 in vol. 10 of *DBSup.* Paris: Letouzey & Ané.
Chaine, J.
1949 *Le Livre de Genèse.* Paris: Les Editions de Cerf.
Clark, W. M.
1971 "The Flood and the Structure of the Pre-patriarchal History." *ZAW* 83:184–211.
Clutton-Brock, J.
1981 *Domesticated Animals from Early Times.* British Museum (Natural History). Austin: University of Texas.
Coats, G. W.
1968 "Despoiling the Egyptians." *VT* 18:450–57.
1973 "Abraham's Sacrifice of Faith. A Form-Critical Study of Genesis 22." *Inter* 27:389–400.

1976   *From Canaan to Egypt. Structural and Theological Context for the Joseph Story.* CBQ Monograph Series 4. Washington: Catholic Biblical Association of America.

1983   *Genesis, with an Introduction to Narrative Literature.* The Forms of Old Testament Literature, vol. 1. Eds. R. Knierim and G. W. Tucker. Grand Rapids, Mich.: W. B. Eerdmans.

Coats, G. W., ed.

1985   *Saga, Legend, Tale, Novella, Fable: Narrative Forms in Old Testament Literature. JSOT* Supp. Series 35. Sheffield: Sheffield Academic.

Conrad, E. W.

1985   *Fear Not Warrior. A Study of 'al tîra' Pericopes in the Hebrew Scriptures.* Brown Judaic Studies 75. Chico, Calif.: Scholars Press.

Cooke, G.

1964   "The Sons of (the) God(s)." *ZAW* 76:22-47.

Cross, F. M.

1973   *Canaanite Myth and Hebrew Epic.* Cambridge, Mass.: Harvard University.

Crüsemann, F.

1981   "Die Eigenständigkeit der Urgeschichte. Ein Beitrag zur Discussion um den 'Jahwisten.' " *Die Botschaft und die Boten. Fests. für Hans Walter Wolff zum 70. Geburtstag,* 11-29. Eds. J. Jeremias und L. Perlitt. Neukirchen-Vluyn: Neukirchener.

Dahood, M.

1961   "MKRTYHM in Genesis 49,5." *CBQ* 23:55-56.

1964(a)   Rev. of *The Torah. The Five Books of Moses. A new translation of the Holy Scriptures according to the Masoretic text.* Philadelphia: Jewish Publication Society of America. *Bib* 45:281-83.

1964(b)   "Ugaritic Lexicography." *Mélanges Eugène Tisserant, Studi e Testi 231,* 81-104. Ed. Città del Vaticano. Bibliotheca Apostolica Vaticana.

1966–   *Psalms,* 3 vols. Anchor Bible 16, 16a, 16b. Garden City, N.Y.:
1970   Doubleday.

1968   "The Name *yismā' 'ēl* in Genesis 16,11." *Bib* 49:87-88.

1977   "Hebrew *tamrûrîm* and *tîmārôt.*" *Or* n.s. 46:385.

1978   "Ebla, Ugarit and the Old Testament." *The Month* (August) 271-76.

1980(a)   "Eblaite *ha-ri* and Genesis 40,16 *hōrî.*" *BibNot* 13:14-16.

1980(b)   "Nomen-Omen in Genesis 16,11." *Bib* 61:89.

1980(c)   "Abraham's Reply in Genesis 20,11." *Bib* 61:90-91.

1981(a)   "Eblaite *i-du* and Hebrew *'ēd,* 'Rain Cloud.' " *CBQ* 43:534-38.

1981(b)   Rev. of Harold R. (Chaim) Cohen. *Biblical Hapax Legomena in the Light of Akkadian and Ugaritic.* SBL Diss. Series 37. Missoula: Scholars Press, 1978. *Bib* 62:272-74.

Day, John
1985   *God's conflict with the dragon and the sea. Echoes of a Canaanite myth in the Old Testament.* University of Cambridge Oriental Publications 35. Cambridge: University Press.

Delitzsch, F.
1853   *Genesis.* Leipzig: Dörffling u. Franke.

Dexinger, F.
1966   *Sturz der Göttersöhne oder Engel vor der Sintflut.* Wiener Beiträge zur Theologie 13. Vienna: Herder.

Dhorme, E.
1956   *La Bible. Ancien Testament 1.* Bibliothèque de la Pléiade. Paris: Gallimard.

Dillmann, A.
1897   *Genesis Critically and Exegetically Expounded.* Trans. B. Stevenson from German, 1892⁶. Edinburgh: T. & T. Clark.

Dommershausen, W.
1975   "Der Wein im Urteil und Bild des Alten Testaments." *Trierer Theologischer Zeitschrift 84,* 253-59.

Drewniak, L.
1934   *Die mariologische Deutung von Genesis 3:15 in der Väterzeit.* Breslau (Kath-theol. Diss.): Nischkowsky.

Driver, G. R.
1954   "Problems and Solutions." *VT* 4:225-45.

Eissfeldt, O.
1923   "Stammesage und Novelle in den Geschichten von Jakob und
(1962)   seinen Söhnen." *Eucharisterion. Studien zur Religion und Literatur des Alten und Neuen Testaments Hermann Gunkel zum 60. Geburtstage.* FRLANT 36:56-57 = *Kleine Schriften I,* 84-104.

1962   *Genesis.* Cols. 366-80 in vol. 2 of *IDB.* Trans. from German, 1958. Nashville: Abingdon Press.

1965   *The Old Testament. An Introduction.* Trans. P. R. Ackroyd from German, 1956, 1964. Oxford: Basil Blackwell.

Elliger, K.
1951   "Der Jakobskampf am Jabbok. Genesis 32, 23ff. als hermeneutisches Problem." *ZThK* 48:1-31.

Else, G. F.
1965   *The Origin and Early Form of Greek Tragedy.* Martin Classical Lectures 20. Cambridge, Mass.: Harvard University.

Emerton, J. A.
1971(a)   "Some False Clues in the Study of Genesis xiv." *VT* 21:24–47.
1971(b)   "The Riddle of Genesis xiv." *VT* 21:403–39.
Engel, H.
1986   "Review of O. Loretz, 1984." *Bib* 67:287–91.

Finkelstein, J. J.
1968   "An Old Babylonian Herding Contract and Genesis 31:38f."
       JAOS 88:30–36.
Fishbane, M.
1975   "Composition and Structure in the Jacob Cycle (Gen 25:19–
       35:22)." *JJS* 26:15–38.
Fisher, E.
1970   "Gilgamesh and Genesis: The Flood Story in Context." *CBQ*
       32:392–403.
Fohrer, G.
1968   *Introduction to the Old Testament*. Trans. D. E. Green from
       German, 1965 (1969). Nashville: Abingdon Press.
Fokkelman, J.-P.
1975   *Narrative Art in Genesis*. Studia Semitica Neerlandica 17.
       Assen-Amsterdam: Van Gorcum.
Frankfort, H. A.
1948,   *Kingship and the Gods. A Study of Ancient Near Eastern Re-*
1965   *ligion as the Integration of Society and Nature*. 5th. imp.
       Chicago-London: University of Chicago.
Freedman, D. N.
1976   "Divine Names and Titles in Early Hebrew Poetry." *Magna-
       lia Dei. The Mighty Acts of God: Fests. G. E. Wright*, 55–107.
       Ed. F. M. Cross, et al. Garden City, N.Y.: Doubleday.
Freedman, R. David
1983   "Woman, A Power Equal to Man." *BARev* 9:56–58.
Frenz, A.
1969   "Vedic Parallels to Tower of Babel." *VT* 19:183–95.
Friedman, T.
1980   *"Wĕrûaḥ 'ĕlōhîm mĕraḥepet 'al pĕnê hammayîm* (Gen 1:2)."
       Beth Mikra 25, 309–12.
Fritz, V.
1982   " 'So lange die Erde steht'—Vom Sinn der Jahwistischen
       Fluterzählung in Genesis 6–8." *ZAW* 94:599–614.
Frymer-Kensky, T.
1978   "What the Babylonian Flood Stories Can and Cannot Teach
       Us about the Genesis Flood." *BARev* 4:32–41.

Gaston, L.
1980   "Abraham and the Righteousness of God." *HBTh* 2:39–68.

Gauthier-Pilters, H. and Dagg, A. I.
1981   *The Camel: Its Evolution, Ecology, Behavior, and Relation-ship to Man.* Chicago-London: University of Chicago.

Gelb, I.
1955   "The Name of Babylon." *Journal of the Institute of Asian Studies* 1:1-4.

Gevirtz, S.
1987   "Asher in the Blessings of Jacob." *VT* 37:154-63.

Gordon, C. H.
1958   "Abraham and the Merchants of Ura." *JNES* 17:28-31.

Gottwald, N. K.
1978   "Were the Early Israelites Pastoral Nomads?" *BARev* 4:2-7.
1979   *The Tribes of Yahweh,* 435-73, 765-66, 899-94, 914-15, n. 14. Maryknoll, N.Y.: Orbis.

Gressmann, H.
1928   *The Tower of Babel.* Ed. Julian Obermann. Hilda Stich Strook Lectures. New York: Jewish Institute of Religion.

Grollenberg, L.
1957   *Atlas of the Bible.* Trans. J.M.H. Reid and H. H. Rowley from Dutch, 1956. London-Edinburgh: Nelson.

Guide Bleu
1974   *Iran-Afghanistan.* Paris: Hachette.

Gunkel, H.
1910³   *Genesis.* Vandenhoeck & Ruprecht.
1964⁶   (unaltered ed.).

Gurney, O. R.
1966   *The Hittites.* London: Pelican (rev. ed.).

Hasel, G. F.
1981   "The Meaning of the Animal Rite in Genesis 15." *JSOT* 19:61-78.

Heidel, A.
1963   *The Gilgamesh Epic and Old Testament Parallels.* Phoenix Books. Chicago: University of Chicago.

Hendel, R. S.
1987   *The Epic of the Patriarch. The Jacob Cycle and the Narra-tive Traditions of Canaan and Israel.* HSM 42. Atlanta: Schol-ars Press.

1987   "Of Demigods and the Deluge: Toward an Interpretation of Genesis 6:1-4." *JBL* 106:13-26.

Hentschel, G.
1977   "Jakob's Kampf am Jabbok (Gen 32,23-33)—eine genuine israelitische Tradition?" *Dienst und Vermittlung. Fests. 25 jähr Bestehen des philos.-theol. Studiums im Priester Semi-*

nar Erfurt, 13–37. Eds. W. Ernst, et al. ErThSt 37. Leipzig: St. Benno.

Hoberman, G.
1983   "George Smith (1840–1876): Pioneer Assyriologist." *BA* 46:41–42.

Hoffner, H. A.
1968   "Hittite *tarpiš* and Hebrew *teraphim." JNES* 27:61–68.
1969   "Some Contributions of Hittitology to Old Testament Study." *TynB* 20:27–55.
1973   "The Hittites and the Hurrians." *Peoples of Old Testament Times,* 197–228. Ed. D. J. Wiseman. Oxford: Clarendon Press.

Humphreys, H. L.
1976   "Joseph Story." Cols. 491–93 in *IDB* Supp. Nashville: Abingdon Press.
1988   *Joseph and His Family. A Literary Study.* Colombia, S.C.: University of South Carolina.

Isaac, E.
1983   "1 (Ethiopic Apocalypse of) ENOCH." *The Old Testament Pseudepigrapha,* vol. 1, 5–89. Ed. J. H. Charlesworth. Garden City, N.Y.: Doubleday.

Jacobsen, Thorkild
1976   *The Treasures of Darkness: History of Mesopotamian Religion.* New Haven-London: Yale University.

James, E. O.
1966   *The Tree of Life.* Supplements to *Numen* 11. Leiden: E. J. Brill.

Jeremias, A.
1904   *Das Alte Testament im Lichte des Alten Orients.* Leipzig:
1930⁴   Hinrichs.

Johnson, M. D.
1969   *The Purpose of the Biblical Genealogies with Special Reference to the Setting of the Genealogies of Jesus.* New Testament Studies Monograph Series 8. Cambridge: University Press.

JSOT
1979   *Journal for the Study of the Old Testament.* 13:33–73.

Kikawada, J. M. and Quinn, A.
1985   *Before Abraham Was.* Nashville: Abingdon Press.

Kilian, R.
1970   *Isaaks Opferung.* Stuttgarter Bibel Studien 44. Stuttgart: Katholisches Bibelwerk.

Kircher, K.
1910   *Die sakrale Bedeutung des Weines im Altertum.* Berlin: de Gruyter (repr. 1970).

Kitchen, K. A.
1966   *Ancient Orient and Old Testament.* Chicago: Intervarsity.

Kittel, R.
1888   *Geschichte der Hebräer. Quellenkunde und Geschichte bis zum babylonischen Exil.* Gotha: Perthes.

Klostermann, A.
1896   *Geschichte des Volkes Israels.* München: Oskar Beck.

Knauf, E. A.
1983   "Midianites and Ishmaelites." *Midian, Moab and Edom. JSOT* Supp. Series 24 (147-62). Eds. J.F.A. Sawyer and D.J.A. Clines. Sheffield: JSOT.
1985(a) "El Shaddai—der Gott Abrahams?" *BZ* 29:97-103.
1985(b) "Alter und Herkunft der edomitischen Königsliste, Genesis 36,31-39." *ZAW* 97:245-53.
1987   "Camels in Late Bronze and Iron Age Jordan: The Archaeological Evidence." *BN* 40:20-23.

Knibb, M.
1978   *The Ethiopic Book of Enoch: A New Edition in the Light of the Aramaic Dead Sea Fragments,* 2 vols. Oxford: Clarendon Press.

Koch, K.
1969   *The Growth of the Biblical Tradition.* Trans. S. M. Cupitt from German, 1967 (3rd ed., 1974). London: A. & C. Black.

Köckert, M.
1988   *Vätergott und Väterverheissung. Eine Auseinandersetzung mit Albrecht Alt und seinen Erben.* FRLANT 142. Göttingen: Vandenhoeck & Ruprecht.

Koehler, L. and Baumgartner, W.
1967,   *Hebräisches und Aramäisches Lexikon zum Alten Testament.*
1974,   Leiden: E. J. Brill.
1983

Kraeling, E. G.
1920   "The Tower of Babel." *JAOS* 40:276-81.

Kramer, S. N.
1963   *The Sumerians: Their History, Culture, and Character.* Chicago & London: University of Chicago.
1972   *Sumerian Mythology.* Philadelphia: University of Pennsylvania. Harper & Row (repr. of 1961 ed.).
1986   *In the World of Sumer: An Autobiography.* Detroit: Wayne State University.

Lack, R.
1962   "Les origines de *'Elyôn,* le Très-Haut, dans la tradition cul-
          tuelle d'Israel.'' *CBQ* 24:44-64.
Lambert, W. G.
1965   "A New Look at the Babylonian Background of Genesis.''
          JThS n.s. 16:297-300.
Lambert, W. G. and Millard, A. R.
1969   *Atrahasis, the Babylonian Story of the Flood.* Oxford: Uni-
          versity Press.
Lang, B.
1985   "New Semitic Deluge Stories and the Book of Genesis.'' *An-
          thropos* 80:605-16.
Leakey, R. E.
1981   *The Making of Mankind.* London: Michael Joseph.
Lehmann, J.
1977   *The Hittites.* Trans. J. Maxwell Brownjohn from German,
          1975. London: Collins.
Lehmann, M. R.
1953   "Abraham's Purchase of Machpelah and Hittite Law.''
          BASOR 129:15-18.
Lewis, J. P.
1984   "Noah and the Flood in Jewish, Christian and Muslim Tra-
          dition.'' *BA* 47:224-39.
Loewenstamm, S. E.
1980   "The Flood.'' *Comparative Studies in Biblical and Oriental
          Literatures.* *AOAT* 204:93-117.
1984   "Die Wasser des biblischen Sintflut: Ihr Hineinbrechen und
          ihr Verschwinden.'' *VT* 34:179-94.
Lohfink, N.
1967   *Die Landverheissung als Eid.* Stuttgarter Bibel-Studien 28.
          Stuttgart: Katholisches Bibelwerk.
Lord, A. B.
1978   "The Gospels as Oral Traditional Literature.'' *The Relation-
          ships Among the Gospels: An Interdisciplinary Dialogue,*
          33-91. Ed. W. O. Walker, Jr. San Antonio: Trinity University.
Loretz, O.
1980   "Der kanaanäische Ursprung des biblischen Gottesnamens EL
          SADDAJ.'' *UF* 12:420-21.
1984   *Habiru-Hebräer. Eine socio-linguistische Studie über die Her-
          kunft des Gentiliziums 'ibrî vom Appellativum* ḫabiru. BZAW
          160. Berlin-New York: de Gruyter.
Luyster, R.
1981   "Wind and Water: Cosmogonic Symbolism in the Old Testa-
          ment.'' *ZAW* 93:1-10.

Matthews, V. H.
1981   "Pastoralists and Patriarchs." *BA* 44:215-18.
McCarthy, D. J.
1964   "Three Covenants in Genesis." *CBQ* 26:179-89.
1972(a) *"Bĕrît* and Covenant in the Deuteronomistic History." *VT*
        Supp. 23:65-85.
1972(b) *Old Testament Covenant. A Survey of Current Opinions.* Ox-
        ford: Basil Blackwell.
1981   *Treaty and Covenant.* Analecta Biblica 21A. Rome: Biblical
        Institute.
McKenzie, J. L.
1965   *Dictionary of the Bible.* Milwaukee: Bruce.
Metzler, J. B.
1984(a) *Deutsche Literaturgeschichte. Vom den Anfängen bis zur
        Gegenwart.* Eds. W. Beutin, K. Ehlert, et al. 2nd ed. Stutt-
        gart: J. B. Metzlersche Verlagsbuchhandlung.
1984(b) *Metzler Literatur Lexikon. Stichwörter zur Weltliteratur.* Eds.
        G. and I. Schweikle. Stuttgart: J. B. Metzlersche Verlagsbuch-
        handlung.
Meyer, E.
1920   *Geschichte des Altertums I–II.* Stuttgart-Berlin-Darmstadt:
1931²   Colta.
Meyer, R.
1969   *Hebräische Grammatik II.* Sammlung Göschen. 3rd ed. Ber-
        lin: de Gruyter.
Milik, J.T.
1976   *The Books of Enoch. Aramaic Fragments of Qumran Cave
        4.* Oxford: Clarendon Press.
Millard, A. R.
1967   "A New Babylonian 'Genesis' Story." *TynB* 18:3-18.
1984   "The Etymology of Eden." *VT* 34:103-06.
Millard, A. R. and Bordreuil, P.
1982   "A Statue from Syria with Assyrian and Aramaic Inscrip-
        tions." *BA* 45:135-41.
Miller, P. D., Jr.
1978   *Genesis 1–11. Studies in Structure and Theme. JSOT* Supp.
        8. Sheffield: JSOT.
1980(a) "El, the Creator of the Earth." *BASOR* 239:42-46.
1980(b) "Studies in Hebrew Word Patterns." *HThR* 73:79-85.
1984   "Syntax and Theology in Genesis XII 3a." *VT* 34:472-76.
Miller, W. T.
1984   *Mysterious Encounters at Mamre and Jabbok.* Brown Judaic
        Studies 50. Chico, Calif.: Scholars Press.

Mitchell, C. W.
1987   *The Meaning of brk "to Bless" in the Old Testament.* SBL
        Diss. Series 95. Atlanta: Scholars Press.
Moran, W. L.
1958   "Genesis, 49,10 and its Use in Ezekiel 21,32." *Bib* 39:409–25.
1959   "The Scandal of the 'Great Sin' at Ugarit." *JNES* 18:280–81.
1971   "Atrahasis: The Babylonian Story of the Flood." *Bib*
        52:51–61.
Morgenstern, J.
1962   "Sabbath." *Interpreter's Dictionary of the Bible,* vol. 4,
        135–41. Eds. G. A. Buttrick, et al. Nashville: Abingdon Press.
Mullen, E. Theodore
1980   *The Assembly of the Gods.* Harvard Semitic Monographs 24.
        Chico, Calif.: Scholars Press.
Müller, H.-P.
1985   "Das Motiv für die Sintflut. Die hermeneutische Funktion
        des Mythos und seiner Analyse." *ZAW* 97:295–316.
Mullo Weir, C. J.
1967   "Nuzi." *Archaeology and Old Testament Study,* 73–83. Ed.
        D. Winton Thomas. Oxford: University Press.
Murphy-O'Connor, J.
1986   *The Holy Land. An Archaeological Guide from Earliest Times
        to 1700.* Oxford-New York: Oxford University Press.

Nicholson, E. W.
1986   *God and His People.* Oxford: Clarendon Press.
Niditch, S.
1985   *Chaos to Cosmos. Studies in Biblical Patterns of Creation.*
        Studies in Humanities 6. Chico, Calif.: Scholars Press, 1985.
North, R.
1967   "Separated Spiritual Substances in the Old Testament." *CBQ*
        29:419–49.
Noth, M.
1981   *A History of Pentateuchal Traditions.* Trans. B. W. Ander-
        son from German, 1948. Chico, Calif.: Scholars Press.

Oden, R. A., Jr.
1987   *The Bible without Theology.* San Francisco: Harper & Row.
Oeming, M.
1983   "Ist Genesis 15:6 ein Beleg für die Anrechnung des Glaubens
        zur Gerechtigkeit?" *ZAW* 95:183–97.
Olrik, A.
1965   "Epic Laws of Folk Narrative." *The Study of Folklore,*
        129–41. Trans. J. P. Steager and A. Dundes from German,
        1909. Ed. A. Dundes. Englewood Cliffs, N.J.: Prentice-Hall.

Orlinsky, H. M.
1983   "The Plain Meaning of Genesis 1:1-3." *BA* 46:207-09.

Petersen, D. L.
1976   "The Yahwist on the Flood." *VT* 26:438-46.
1979   "Genesis 6:1-4 and the Organization of the Cosmos." *JSOT* 13:47-64.
Pettazzoni, R.
1954   *Essays on the History of Religion.* Supplements to *Numen* 1. Trans. H. J. Rose from Italian and French, 1953. Leiden: E. J. Brill.
Pettinato, G.
1971   *Das altorientalische Menschenbild und die sumerischen und akkadischen Schöpfungsmythen.* Heidelberg: Carl Winter, Universitätsverlag.
Pope, M. H.
1955   *El in the Ugaritic Texts. VT* Supp. 2. Leiden: E. J. Brill.
1965   *Job.* Anchor Bible No. 15. Garden City, N.Y.: Doubleday.
Pury, A., de,
1978   Review of *The Historicity of the Patriarchal Narratives* by T. L. Thompson and *Abraham in History and Tradition* by J. Van Seters, *RB* 95:589-618.

Rad, G., von,
1962   *Old Testament Theology,* vol. 1. Trans. D.M.G. Stalker from German, 1957. Edinburgh-London: Oliver & Boyd.
1966(a) "The Form-Critical Problem of the Hexateuch." *The Problem of the Hexateuch and Other Essays,* 1-78. Trans. E.W.T. Dicken from German, 1938. Edinburgh-London: Oliver & Boyd.
1966(b) "Faith Reckoned as Righteousness." *The Problem of the Hexateuch and Other Essays,* 125-30. Trans. E.W.T. Dicken from German, 1951. London-Edinburgh: Oliver & Boyd.
1972   *Genesis.* Trans. J. Bowden from German, 1972. 9th ed. London: SCM.
Redford, D. B.
1970   *A Study of the Biblical Story of Joseph (Genesis 37-50). VT* Supp. 20. Leiden: E. J. Brill.
Rendsburg, G. A.
1986   *The Redaction of Genesis.* Winona Lake, Ind.: Eisenbrauns.
Rendtorff, R.
1977(a) *Das überlieferungsgeschichtliche Problem des Pentateuchs.* BZAW 147. Berlin-New York: de Gruyter.
1977(b) "The Dilemma of Pentateuchal Criticism." *JSOT* 3:2-10 (responses: R. N. Whybray, J. Van Seters, N. E. Wagner, G. E. Coats, H. H. Schmid. Reply by Rendtorff).

Robert, A., Tournay, R., and Feuillet, A.
1963   *Le Cantique des Cantiques.* Etudes Bibliques. Paris: Gabalda.
Rordorf, W.
1968   *Sunday: The History of the Day of Rest in the Earliest Centuries of the Christian Church.* Trans. A.A.K. Graham from German, 1962. London: SCM.
Rosenburg, R. A.
1965   "The God Ṣedeq." *HUCA* 36:161-77.
Rowton, M. R.
1973(a)   "Urban Autonomy in a Nomadic Environment." *JNES* 32:201-15.
1973(b)   "Autonomy and Nomadism in Western Asia." *Or* 42:247-58.
1974   "Enclosed Nomadism." *Journal of (the) Economic and Social History of the Orient,* 17:1-30.
1976   "Dimorphic Structure and the Problem of the *'apiru-'ibrim.*" *JNES* 35:13-20.
1977   "Dimorphic Structure and the Parasocial Element." *JNES* 36:181-88.
1978   "Pastoralism and the Periphery in Evolutionary Perspective." *L'archéologie de l'Iraq du début de l'époque néolithique à 333 avant notre ère,* 291-303. Colloques Internationax du CNRS, 580. Paris: CNRS.
1981   "Economic and Political Factors in Ancient Nomadism." *Nomad and Sedentary Peoples, 30th International Congress of Human Sciences in Asia and North Africa,* 25-36. Ed. Jorge Silva Castillo. Mexico City: El Colegio de Mexico.
Rowton, M. T.
1982   "Sumer's Strategic Periphery in Topological Perspective." *Zikir Šumim. Assyriological Studies Presented to F. R. Kraus on the Occasion of His 70th Birthday,* 318-25. Leiden: E. J. Brill.
Ruppert, L.
1965   *Die Josephserzählung der Genesis.* SANT XI. München: Kösel.
1985   "Die Aporie der gegenwärtigen Pentateuchdiskussion und die Josephserzählung der Genesis." *BZ N.F.* 29:31-48.

Saggs, H.W.F.
1960   "Ur of the Chaldeas: A Problem of Identification." *Iraq* 22:200-09.
Sandars, N. K.
1960   *The Epic of Gilgamesh.* Penguin Books (many repr.).
Sasson, J. M.
1966   "Circumcision in the Ancient Near East." *JBL* 85:473-76.

Scharbert, J.
1983,   *Genesis 1-11. Genesis 12-50.* Die Neue Echter Bibel. Würz-
1986   burg: Echter.
Schmidt, L.
1986   *Literarische Studien zur Josephsgeschichte.* BZAW 167. Ber-
         lin: de Gruyter.
Schmidt, W. H.
1964   *Die Schöpfungsgeschichte der Priesterschrift.* WMANT 17.
Schmitt, H.-C.
1980   *Die nichtpriestliche Josephsgeschichte.* BZAW 154. Berlin: de
         Gruyter.
Scullion, J. J.
1984   "Märchen, Sage, Legende: Towards a Clarification of Some
         Literary Terms Used by Old Testament Scholars." *VT*
         34:321-36.
Selman, M. J.,
1980   "Comparative Customs and the Patriarchal Age." *Essays on
         the Patriarchal Narratives,* 93-98. Eds. A. R. Millard and D. J.
         Wiseman. Leicester: Intervarsity.
Seybold, K.
1976   "terafim." Cols. 1057-60 in *Theologisches Handwörterbuch
         zum Alten Testament.* Eds. E. Jenni and C. Westermann.
         München-Zürich: Kaiser-Theologischer Verlag.
Shanks, H.
1985   "Elie Borowski Seeks a House for His Collection." *BARev*
         11:18-25.
Simoons-Vermeer, R.
1974   "The Mesopotamian Flood Stories: A Comparison and In-
         terpretation." *Numen* 21:17-34.
Speiser, E. A.
1964   *Genesis.* Anchor Bible No. 1. Garden City, N.Y.: Doubleday.
Stade, B.
1881   "Lea und Rachel." *ZAW* 1:112-16.
Stager, L. E. and Wolff, S. R.
1984   "Child Sacrifice at Carthage. Rite or Population Control?"
         BARev 10:30-51.
Steck, O. H.
1977   "Der Wein unter den Schöpfungsgaben." *TThZ* 87:173-91.
1981   *Der Schöpfungsbericht der Priesterschrift Studien. Zur liter-
         arkritischen und überlieferungsgeschichtlichen Problematik von
         Genesis 1,1-2:4a.* FRLANT 115. Göttingen: Vandenhoeck &
         Ruprecht.

Teeple, H. M.
1978   *The Noah's Ark Nonsense.* Evanston, Ill.: Religious and
         Ethics Institute.

364   *Bibliography*

THAT
1971   *Theologisches Handwörterbuch zum Alten Testament.* Eds.
            E. Jenni and C. Westermann. München-Zürich: Kaiser-
            Theologischer Verlag.
Thesiger, W.
1964   *The Marsh Arabs.* London: Longmans, Green.
Thompson, T. L.
1974   *The Historicity of the Patriarchal Narratives. The Quest for
            the Historical Abraham.* BZAW 133. Berlin-New York: de
            Gruyter.
1987   *The Origin Tradition of Ancient Israel. 1. The Literary For-
            mation of Genesis and Exodus 1-23. JSOT* Supp. Series 55.
            Sheffield: Sheffield Academic.
ThWAT
1970   *Theologisches Wörterbuch zum Alten Testament.* Eds. G. J.
            Botterweck and H. Ringgren. Stuttgart-Berlin-Köln-Mainz:
            W. Kohlhammer.
Tigay, J. H.
1982   *The Evolution of the Gilgamesh Epic.* Philadelphia: Univer-
            sity of Pennsylvania.
Tournay, R. J.
1960   *Nouzi.* Cols. 646-74 in vol. 6 of *DBSup.* Eds. H. Cazelles and
            A. Feuillet. Paris: Letouzey & Ané, 1960.
Tromp, N. J.
1969   *Primitive Conceptions of Death and the Nether World in the
            Old Testament.* Biblica et Orientalia 21. Rome: Pontifical Bib-
            lical Institute.
Tucker, G. M.
1977   "Prophetic Superscriptions." *Canon and Authority,* 56-70.
            Eds. G. W. Coats and B. O. Long. Philadelphia: Fortress.

Van Seters, J.
1975   *Abraham in History and Tradition.* New Haven-London: Yale
            University.
1980   "The Religion of the Patriarchs in Genesis." *Bib* 61:220-33.
1983   *In Search of History. Historiography in the Ancient World
            and the Origins of Biblical History.* New Haven-London: Yale
            University.
Vaux, R., de
1948   "Les Patriarches Hébreux et les Découvertes Modernes." *RB*
            55:321-47 (esp. 327-36).
1961   *Ancient Israel. Its Life and Institutions.* Trans. J. McHugh
            from French, 1959. London: Darton, Longman & Todd.
1964   *Studies in Old Testament Sacrifice.* Cardiff: University of
            Wales.

1978 *The Early History of Israel*. 2 vols. Trans. D. Smith from French, 1971. London: Darton, Longman & Todd.

Vawter, B.
1977 *Genesis: A New Reading*. Garden City, N.Y.: Doubleday.

Vermes, G.
1975 "The Impact of the Dead Sea Scrolls on Jewish Studies during the last Twenty-five Years." *JJS* 26:1–14.

Wallace, H. N.
1985 *The Eden Narrative*. Harvard Semitic Monographs 32. Atlanta: Scholars Press.

Weidmann, H.
1968 *Die Patriarchen und ihre Religion im Licht der Forschung seit Julius Wellhausen*. FRLANT 94. Göttingen: Vandenhoeck & Ruprecht.

Weinfeld, M.
1972 "The Worship of Molech and of the Queen of Heaven and its Background." *UF* 4:133–54.

Weippert, M.
1976 "Shaddaj (Gottesname)." Cols. 873–81 in vol. 2 of *Theologisches Handwörterbuch zum Alten Testament*. Eds. E. Jenni and C. Westermann. München-Zürich: Kaiser-Theologishes Verlag.

Wiese, B., von
1982[8] *Novelle*. Sammlung Metzler. Stuttgart: J. B. Metzler.

Wellhausen, J.
1957 *Prolegomena to the History of Israel*. Trans. Menzies and Black from German, 1878. New York: Meridian Books.

Wenham, G. J.
1978 "The Coherence of the Flood Narrative." *VT* 28:336–48.

Westermann, C.
1978 *Blessing in the Bible and the Life of the Church*. Trans. K. Crimm from German, 1968. Philadelphia: Fortress.

1980 *The Promises to the Fathers*. Trans. D. E. Green from German, 1976. Philadelphia: Fortress.

1984, *Genesis 1–11, Genesis 12–36, Genesis 37–50*. Trans. J. J. Scul-
1985, lion from German, 1974, 1981, 1982. Minneapolis: Augsburg.
1986

Whybray, R. N.
1987 *The Making of the Pentateuch. A Methodological Study*. JSOT Supp. Series 53. Sheffield: Sheffield Academic.

Wilson, R. R.
1975 "The Old Testament Genealogies in Recent Research." *JBL* 94:169–89.

1977   *Genealogy and History in the Biblical World.* Yale Near Eastern Researches 7. New Haven-London: Yale University.

Winckler, H.
1903   *Abraham als Babylonier, Joseph als Ägypter. Hintergrund der biblischen Vätergeschichten auf Grund der Keilschriften dargestellt.* Leipzig: Hinrichs.

Wolff, H. W.
1966   "The Kerygma of the Yahwist." Trans. W. A. Benware from German, 1964. *Inter* 20:131–58.
1972   "The Day of Rest in the Old Testament." *CThM* 43:498–506.

Wöller, U.
1982   "Zur Übersetzung von *kî* in Genesis 8,21 and 9,6." *ZAW* 94:637–38.

Wright, G. E.
1962²   *Biblical Archaeology.* Philadelphia: Westminster.

Yadin, Y.
1975   *Jerusalem Revealed.* Jerusalem: Israel Exploration Society.

Young, G.
1977   *Return to the Marshes.* London: Collins.

Zarins, J.
1982   Review: *Domesticated Animals from Early Times* by Juliet Clutton-Brock. *BA* 45:251–53.